Current Topics in Early Childhood Education

Volume II

Current Topics in Early Childhood Education

Volume II

Editor
LILIAN G. KATZ

Associate Editors
Mary Z. Glockner, Charlotte Watkins,
and Mima J. Spencer

ERIC Clearinghouse on Early Childhood Education
University of Illinois

 ABLEX PUBLISHING CORPORATION
Norwood, New Jersey

The material in this publication was prepared pursuant to a contract with the
National Institute of Education, U.S. Department of Health, Education, and Welfare.
Contractors undertaking such projects under government sponsorship are encouraged
to express freely their judgment in professional and technical matters. Points of view
or opinions do not necessarily represent the official view or opinions of the National
Institute of Education.

ISBN 0-89391-015-5   ISSN 0363-8332

ABLEX Publishing Corporation
355 Chestnut Street
Norwood, New Jersey 07648

Contents

Preface ix

1 **Issues Raised by the Follow Through Evaluation**
Ernest R. House and Elizabeth J. Hutchins. 1

Background of the Evaluation *1*
Issues Raised by the Evaluation *6*
References *10*

2 **Mainstreaming in the Preschool**
Merle B. Karnes and Richard C. Lee 13

Introduction *13*
Mainstreaming and Related Terms *14*
Mainstreaming in the Preschool: A Review of Research *21*
Integrated Preschool Programs *31*
References *38*

3 **What Head Start Means to Families**
Ruth Ann O'Keefe 43

Three Special Head Start Programs *47*
Summary and Conclusion *64*
References *65*

4 **Infant-Toddler Group Day Care:**
A Review of Research
Sally Kilmer **69**

Introduction *69*
Effects of Day Care on Mother-Children Relationships *70*
Effects of Day Care on Other Social Interactions *86*
Effects of Day Care on Cognitive Development *92*
Effects of Day Care Attendance on Children's Health *98*
Discussion *103*
References *112*

5 **Does the Changing View of Early Experience**
Imply a Changing View of Early Development?
Dale Goldhaber **117**

The Strong Early Experience Position *117*
The Strong Life Span Position *119*
The New Zeitgeist *125*
Implications For Early Childhood Development *130*
References *136*

6 **Evaluation of Early Childhood Programs:**
Toward a Developmental Perspective
Ruby Takanishi. **141**

The Nature of Developmental Change *150*
Preliminaries to a Developmental Perspective to Evaluation *155*
What Are the Purposes of an Early Childhood Evaluation? *155*
Whom Shall the Evaluation Serve? *159*
Constraints on a Developmental Perspective *161*
Acknowledgments *162*
Appendix 1: Conclusion *162*
References *165*

7 **An Inquiry into Inquiry:**
Question Asking as an Instructional Model
Irving E. Sigel and Ruth Saunders. **169**

What Is a Question: A Structural/Functional Description *170*
The Conceptual Basis for Question Asking *174*
Basic Classroom Strategies *184*
The Distancing Model: Its Tie to Other Conceptual Frameworks *189*
Some Empirical Support for Inquiry *191*
References *192*

8 **Play and Acquisition of Symbols**
Greta G. Fein **195**

The Changing Structures of Pretend Play *197*
Theoretical Perspectives *209*
Themes for Early Education *220*
References *221*

9 **Can Education Be Made "Intrinsically Interesting"
to Children?**
John Condry and Barbara Koslowski. **227**

A Look at the Literature *228*
An Analysis of Issues Raised in Recent Research *232*
The Child's Capacities for Learning *243*
Summary *255*
References *255*

10 **How Children Understand Stories:
A Developmental Analysis**
Nancy L. Stein **261**

Introduction *261*
The Development of Story Grammars *263*
Research on Story Comprehension *268*
Conclusions *282*
Implications for Education *286*
References *288*

Preface

This series, *Current Topics in Early Childhood Education,* was initiated in 1977 in order to make available integrative reviews, analyses and syntheses of research and development of current concern in the field of early childhood education. The appearance of this second volume in the series reflects a steady level of investigation and scholarship, not only in early education but in its relevant "supply" discipline as well.

Of the ten papers presented in this volume, four represent investigations and reports of primarily programmatic or educational activities. House and Hutchins take a critical analytical look at Abt Associates' controversial national evaluation of Project Follow Through. Karnes and Lee review the data at hand that bear upon mainstreaming, a development of increasing importance in early childhood education. O'Keefe synthesizes what have heretofore been widely scattered reports of the effects of Head Start on thousands of American families. Kilmer's chapter summarizes more than thirty studies of the effects of group care on very young children, making a very timely contribution to the animated discussions of the subject frequently heard these days. While the programs and activities examined are varied, it is hoped that presenting them in one collection enhances the usefulness of each of them.

The six papers representing the major "supply" discipline of early childhood education, namely developmental psychology, also address a range of topics reflecting current issues and concerns in the field. Goldhaber calls into question some of our very basic assumptions about the relationships between early experience and mature functioning. Takanishi shows how theories and assumptions about the nature of development might more fruitfully be brought to bear on the design of evaluations of early childhood programs.

The remaining four papers bring to our attention recent findings and insights which can inform our efforts at programmatic and pedagogical innovation. Fein addresses the topic of play and gives greater definition to its value in intellectual development. Sigel's analyses and descriptions of the value of question-asking behavior in the education of young children are rich in implications for practice. Condry and Koslowski's review of research related to children's capacity for interest and related motivational variables seems to give strength to the long standing hunches practicing early childhood educators have had about the appropriate uses of external reinforcement in stimulating intellectual development. Finally, Stein's summary of her research findings on children's understanding of stories and developmental progression should enable us to use story-telling more effectively.

We look forward to hearing from readers with their reactions to the current volume and their suggestions for future topics.

Lilian G. Katz, Ph.D
*Director, ERIC Clearinghouse on Early
Childhood Education*

Current Topics in
Early Childhood Education

Volume II

1

Issues Raised by the Follow Through Evaluation

Ernest R. House

Elizabeth J. Hutchins

University of Illinois

In April, 1977, Abt Associates, Inc. (AAI) released the long-awaited evaluation of the U.S. Office of Education's Follow Through program, *Education as Experimentation: A Planned Variation Model*, Vol. 4, A-D. The AAI evaluation compared thirteen models of early childhood education, ranging from highly structured to open education approaches, as implemented in 80 sites throughout the United States. Models were grouped under the labels "basic skills," "cognitive," or "affective," according to their developmental emphasis, and comparisons were made of the test performance of children taught under each model. The news media seized upon the findings as evidence that models emphasizing "basic skills" were most successful, although this was an oversimplification of AAI's report. The evaluation itself has been strongly criticized by a panel of evaluation experts (House, Glass, McLean, & Walker, 1978) on the basis of its measurement difficulties. The evaluation is a porcupine of issues, some of which are discussed in this chapter.

BACKGROUND OF THE EVALUATION

Follow Through began in 1967 as a social service program for disadvantaged children in kindergarten through third grade. It was intended to continue the type of education provided in Project Head Start and to address change within institutions involving communities and families as well as schools.

In Follow Through's planning year, however, its budget was cut from an expected $120 million to $15 million. To sustain the program on its reduced

1

budget, officials decided to convert Follow Through into a "planned variation" experiment. That is, the government would support several types of early childhood models at a limited number of sites and eventually evaluate them to see which worked best. The focus became less that of changing social institutions and more one of finding effective techniques to educate poor children in the existing school institution. Thus, the question to be answered by the evaluation was "What worked best?" or "What worked most efficiently?" as opposed to questions such as "How does it work?" or "How can we make it work better?" Both the nature of the planned variation program and the narrowness of the evaluation deemphasized the social service aspect of the original conception of the program.[1]

The choice of planned variation as a program design was consistent with the social milieu of the period in which Follow Through was begun. At that time in the sixties most educational reformers subscribed to the "big bang" theory of reform. They believed it was possible to discover a technique or a program that would "solve a problem," such as poor students' failure to achieve in school. Not only could such a technique be found but with some effort it could be disseminated all over the country, thus solving the social problem. Hence, the solution would be relatively cheap as well as effective.

Given such a belief, it became the mission of the federal government to discover effective educational techniques and to disseminate them. This strategy was clearly enunciated in the White House Conference on Education in 1967 (Elmore, 1976). The reformers ran into difficulties, however. Early evaluation results from Head Start and Title I, ESEA, indicated that the new reform programs were unsuccessful in raising the standardized test scores of the children involved. Federal officials interpreted this failure as inadequate variation and control over the programs. They concluded that efforts should be devoted to developing different programs and then systematically evaluating them. Hence "planned variation," rather than "natural variation," became a reform strategy. Follow Through was the first attempt at "planned variation."

Program sponsors (those institutions developing the new models of early childhood education) and sites (school districts implementing the new models) were chosen by the Office of Education. Both sponsors and sites received funding from the federal government. At a meeting in Kansas City in 1968, sponsors and sites were matched to one another. Development and implementation of the models began immediately.

Evaluation was viewed as a critical part of the Follow Through plan by federal officials, particularly those within the Office of the Assistant Secretary

[1]The history of the evaluation can be traced in excellent works by Haney (1977) and Elmore (1976). The policy which produced the evaluation has been analyzed by McLaughlin (1975) and House (1978).

for Planning and Evaluation inside the Department of Health, Education, and Welfare, who had been instrumental in the planned variation conversion. Evaluation would tell which model worked best and at what cost (Rivlin, 1971). Also, the federal planners had a particular idea of what evaluation should be—a massive, controlled experiment. This was a popular view of evaluation at that time, though not one universally shared within the evaluation community.

Consequently, the evaluation was set up as a large-scale experiment, with comparison groups assigned for each of the Follow Through classes. Comparisons would be made between Follow Through and non-Follow Through classes. A multimillion dollar contract was let to the Stanford Research Institute (SRI) to conduct the evaluation, and SRI promised to evaluate all aspects of the program, including community involvement and institutional change.

When the evaluation began, however, SRI collected primarily standardized children's test scores. This upset many of the sponsors, and they protested vociferously. SRI assured them that the less tangible goals of their models would be assessed in addition to the more traditional outcomes measured by standardized achievement tests. In fact, SRI began a serious effort to develop special measures appropriate to the expressed goals of the sponsors' models.

Meanwhile, intense political pressure in Washington urged the expansion of the number of sponsors and sites. Special interest groups like blacks and bilinguals wanted their own sponsors. Political groups such as large cities wanted to become sites. The new groups were accommodated. Sponsors and sites were added in an opportunistic fashion, measurably increasing the political constituency and strength of the program in Congress. The Follow Through budget began to grow.

This caused problems elsewhere, however. Exact comparison groups were difficult to find. Often, control groups were established that were unlike the Follow Through classes. The program administrators were aware of these deviations from the evaluation plan, but they felt that the new models would be so much more effective than other public school programs, and the gains in test scores would be so dramatic, that it would not matter whether or not the comparison classes were matched to the Follow Through classes.

Follow Through grew larger and larger. At its zenith there were more than 20 sponsors operating in over 180 sites. Hundreds of thousands of children were involved. SRI tried to collect data on most of them but the logistics of data collection as well as the costs bounded out of control. Furthermore, SRI was unable to develop the new instruments it had promised. Amid an investigation by the General Accounting Office, HEW, and Nader's Raiders, the evaluation became a scandal. SRI had spent $12 million on the evaluation in the program's first four years. Finally, in 1972 the Follow Through administrators in the Office of Education resigned and the evaluation was reshaped.

THE FINAL STUDY

Under the direction of the Office of Education, the evaluation was pared down to 17 sponsors working with 80 sites. The analytic sample contained only 20,000 children. More importantly, the number of instruments to collect data was narrowed to only four standardized measures. SRI continued to collect the data but the data analysis was contracted to Abt Associates. In all, the broad scope of the evaluation was drastically narrowed in what Haney (1977) called a "funneling" effect. The determination of which childhood model was "best" would now be based on only a few standardized tests.

Throughout the course of the evaluation, the sponsors, parents of the children, and site personnel were by no means silent in their objections to events. Most continued to complain, often bitterly, about the evaluation, fearing their models and their children would not be assessed according to appropriate criteria. Many never accepted the conversion of the entire Follow Through program to an experiment; they saw Follow Through as a program providing social services to children and their families. Sponsors saw it primarily as a development program.

Faced with the problem of analyzing the test data from nonequivalent (and often mismatched) Follow Through and comparison classes, the Abt Associates analysts resorted to a complex statistical analysis. The technique chosen (analysis of covariance) adjusts the final test scores of children in such a way that their test scores are made more equivalent. Adjustments are based upon the previous achievement test scores of the students, the income level of the parents, and other variables recorded at the beginning of school. Presumably, after the statistical adjustment the scores of the two classes would be more like the scores of two properly matched classes.

Unfortunately, this statistical technique has proved to be much more unreliable in practice than it was believed to be in the late sixties and early seventies (Campbell & Erlebacher, 1975; Cronbach, 1977). The actual test score adjustments are such that the error in the procedure is quite large. The technique has now become controversial among statisticians. Yet, the entire AAI evaluation of Follow Through is based upon it.

Another controversial aspect of the evaluation is whether individual student scores or class averages should have been used in the data analysis. This is known as the "units of analysis" problem. The AAI analysis uses only individual student scores. It has been demonstrated with the Follow Through data that one can obtain dramatically different results using class rather than student scores (House et al., 1978). Many leading authorities say AAI should have used the class scores instead.

In spite of these and other difficulties, Abt Associates published its results in April, 1977. Based on their controversial techniques, they drew two types of conclusions. One conclusion was that the differences in results from site to site were very great. In other words, even within the same model (e.g., Direct Instruction) many of the sites did better in test results than the comparison classes, but in at least two or three Direct Instruction sites the results were much worse than in the comparison classes. This great intersite variation held for all models. The results varied dramatically from site to site for every model.

In fact, the intersite variation among models was so great that the AAI analysts refused to say that any particular model was best. In other words, differences among the sites *within* a given model were nearly as great as the differences *among* the models. This was an embarrassing result for a study predicated on the idea of identifying the "best" model. In fact, the Office of Education insisted that AAI continue with the comparisons of models in spite of AAI's strong reservation about doing so. In one reanalysis of the data, the finding of great intersite variation within models seemed to remain valid, despite the many flaws of the evaluation (House et al., 1978).

The second set of AAI findings revolved around the classification of the early childhood models on the basis of the model's goals. AAI classified models into three types: basic skills, cognitive/conceptual, and affective/cognitive. AAI also classified the outcome measures as basic skills, cognitive, or affective. This dual classification seemed to be arbitrary and perhaps mistaken.

The AAI analysts then matched each type of model with the corresponding outcome measure. In other words, they reasoned that the so-called "basic skills" models could best be evaluated on the basic skills measures, and so on. This gave a semblance of fairness to the evaluation, and disguised the fact that the evaluation consisted primarily of standardized achievement tests, the traditional measures on which one might expect the best performance from the "basic skills" models which emphasized rote learning skills found on such tests.

The AAI analysts found that children in the "basic skills" models did better on both basic skills outcomes and affective measures. Children in the "cognitive" and "affective" models, as a group, did better on none of the measures. All this, of course, was within a context of powerful intersite variation, which is to say that any given site from a particular "affective" model might have done extremely well on all the measures. For example, although AAI ranked the Bank Street model in the middle in terms of overall effects, one of its sites was among the best. The Bank Street sites varied substantially in measured effects.

In the milieu of the times, the AAI finding that "basic skills" models were better was seized upon by the mass media and the finding of intersite variation was virtually ignored. Articles were carried in the *New York Times, Wall Street Journal, Washington Post, Newsweek*, and most of the major newspapers in the country. The newspapers were not careful in their coverage of the findings, simplifying the results considerably. Even the AAI analysts were moved to protest the distorted coverage in the Boston newspapers.

Perhaps the most widely circulated report was that of the conservative syndicated columnist, James J. Kilpatrick. In a column that can only be labeled a parody of the AAI report, Kilpatrick wondered why it had taken the educators so much time and money to discover the obvious about schooling. His view of the "basic skills" models was no closer to reality than his description of the "affective" models. His column was widely circulated across the country under various headlines supplied by local newspapers, including "Basics Beats Funsies in School," "A Nation of Illiterates," and "Basic Education Offers Alternative to Numbskulls."

In response to protests about the evaluation by sponsors and others, the Ford Foundation funded a third-party critique of the evaluation by a panel of evaluation experts. The panel found the intersite variation finding substantially correct. However, the findings comparing the models were invalid. The critique asserted that the evaluation contained a series of errors and inadequacies.

For example, the narrowness of the scope of measurement and its bias towards certain models precluded statements about which models were best. Some of the instruments had questionable reliability, and the classification of both the models and the measures was misleading. Furthermore, the evaluation contained two substantial flaws. When these flaws were corrected, no models or model types proved to be better than any other type, even given the traditional measures used to obtain outcome data. Only the finding of intersite variation held up under reanalysis. (For the full version of the critique, see House et al., 1978).

ISSUES RAISED BY THE EVALUATION

A number of major issues were raised by the Follow Through evaluation:

The big bang theory. The idea that one can invent a model program that will "solve" the problems of disadvantaged children across the country was a strong element in the Follow Through program. That belief now seems to be dissipating slowly but steadily. The originators of the program, and possibly the sponsors, thought they could invent educational treatments that would be far superior to the schooling traditionally offered by the public schools. Such dramatic gains were not forthcoming.

It may be that any gains were severely masked by the narrowness of the traditional tests used to measure outcomes of the early childhood models. As a whole, though, the data did not show dramatic results. In the AAI evaluation, the Follow Through models as a whole did no better than did the public school classes to which they were compared. It should be noted, however, that the comparison classes themselves were often classes enriched by Title I and other compensatory programs.

Faith in testing. The faith in testing was strong. Government planners never wavered from the view that gains in scores on standardized achievement tests were the improvements they wanted, whatever else they got. To them the gains in test scores were proxies for improved chances later in life. They insisted that test scores be the focus of any evaluation.

When the sponsors protested that traditional tests were too narrow to measure their program outcomes, SRI expressed confidence that it could develop new measures to cover these new outcomes. SRI researchers tried, but failed to produce any acceptable alternative measures. At the end they questioned their faith in their own ability to develop such measures and cautioned other test developers.

Most of the sponsors felt that the tests were invalid for their models and vociferously protested their exclusive use. Yet, faith in their models led the sponsors to persist in the program; they hoped against hope that, in spite of poor tests, their own models would show up well.

Teaching to the test. A familiar issue raised by the evaluation was that of teaching to the test. It is clear that teaching the exact items on a test is an illegitimate activity—unless the items taught comprise the universe of things to be learned. Most tests, such as standardized achievement tests, only sample the domain of learning that is being assessed. Teaching the items invalidates the inference that the student knows the domain of knowledge the test is sampling.

Other than teaching the items, however, there are a number of things one might do to prepare for the test. It is about the legitimacy of those activities that people disagree. At the beginning of Follow Through, it was certain that an achievement test would be an important component of the evaluation. Reportedly, one sponsor said, "We don't care what the test is. Just tell us what it is and we'll teach it" (Egbert, 1977). Other sponsors thought this was unethical.

No matter what various sponsors did once they knew the test was the Metropolitan Achievement Test (MAT), a test readily available for inspection, it was true that sponsors did best when their curriculum materials came closest to the specific subtests. For example, the strongest performance on any subtest was turned in by Direct Instruction children on the language subtest of the MAT. The language subtest consists of two sections: one in which the students discriminate between incomplete sentences and "telling" and "asking" sentences, and one which calls for identifying errors in capitalization, punctuation, and usage.

It was on this subtest that Direct Instruction turned in by far the strongest performance of any sponsor on any test. In fact, this high score accounts for much of Direct Instruction's effectiveness on basic skills, since the language subtest was included in basic skills measures. A comparison of the subtest of the MAT with the third grade lessons in *Distar*, the commercial version of Direct Instruction, shows a close similarity between the two. The format and instructions, though not specific items, were the same. *Distar* children are repeatedly drilled on content similar to the test. Is this teaching to the test? Different people give different answers. Other sponsors may have geared some of their materials towards the test, too. We point out only one example.

Measurement problems. The evaluators were unable to come up with anything resembling a satisfactory instrument to measure the less tangible outcomes of the models. The two affective instruments had serious deficiencies. Other studies were attempted (such as assessing the impact of the models on the communities in which they were implemented), but these were often dismissed for lack of sufficient reliability. The interviews with parents and questionnaires to teachers were not fully treated in the final evaluation report. Information was ultimately limited to students filling out pencil and paper tests. The focus of the evaluation was exceptionally narrow.

Intersite variation. Even on the traditional tests employed, there was enormous variation in outcomes among sites within the same models. This was the one constant finding of the study. Even where the early childhood models had their greatest effect on test achievement, their influence was very modest, accounting for less than 10% of the overall variation in test scores. Local conditions—parents, teachers, peers, school environment, home environment—had a far stronger impact. This finding raises questions about both the efficacy and the type of federal intervention in local districts. According to this study, government programs are very limited in their power to affect traditional outcomes like test scores.

Implementation. Uncertainty has always existed as to how fully the early childhood models were implemented in the school sites. If any situation is advantageous for model implementation, certainly Follow Through should have been. The sites volunteered to work with the sponsors. Both sites and sponsors were paid a substantial sum of money to implement the models. Sponsors worked with a limited number of sites, usually fewer than ten, over a long period of time, most for many years. Several cohorts of children went through each model.

Nonetheless, there is evidence that the implementation was not perfect. Early observation studies found differences in implementation across classrooms within models (Stallings, 1975). Furthermore, some sponsors no doubt implemented their models more successfully than did other sponsors.

Statistical problems. The evaluation raised highly technical but important issues about the statistical analysis employed. The study demonstrates the limits of analysis of covariance techniques, used in this case beyond their capabilities. The implications are that certain types of studies—such as those with nonequivalent control groups—should not be conducted, since the statistical corrections cannot be made reliably. A great number of studies are of this type.

Second, the evaluation demonstrates without a doubt that the unit of analysis employed—the individual student, the class, or the school district—has a dramatic effect on the results. The selection of the unit becomes a major problem in the design of most studies. In most cases the classroom is probably the appropriate unit of analysis.

Large-scale experiments. This evaluation throws into question the utility of all large-scale experiments. The costs were exorbitant: the evaluation alone cost nearly $50 million. The information gained was not worth the cost. The idea that one can definitively determine the answer to major questions, such as "Which is the best model of early childhood education" is dubious. A series of small studies that contribute to developing knowledge over a period of time is more informative than a single massive study. The expectation that such a large experiment will resolve major problems is unrealistic.

Fairness. The sponsors were promised early in the evaluation that the less tangible outcomes of their models would be measured. The evaluation was unable to deliver on this promise. By the time the true nature of the evaluation became clear, the sponsors were heavily invested and entrenched in sites. Thus, the evaluation agreement was unfair to the sponsors. Much of the sponsors' sensitivity about the evaluation can be attributed to a feeling of being treated unfairly. Evaluators should not make promises they cannot keep. At the very least they should renegotiate the understanding between themselves and those being evaluated.

Press coverage. The interpretation of the Follow Through evaluation was significantly affected, even distorted, by the mass media. In fact, the perceptions of most people, even professionals, were shaped by the press coverage rather than the actual study. This is a serious issue. What the press seems to do is to feed stereotypes they think the public already has. This is the line of easiest and most succinct communication for them. Unfortunately, it also distorts the messages conveyed.

In this case, the press seized upon the "basic skills" label and read their own meaning into it. Since the public was concerned about "back to basics," the Follow Through evaluation was fodder for that particular movement. In the AAI study, reading was not included as a "basic skills" measure. Few parents would want "basic skills" that exclude reading. Yet the press seized only the label itself, a label supplied by the AAI analysts.

The damage done by such a misinterpretation is almost impossible to reverse. The mass media are not interested in corrections of yesterday's headlines. The fault is not entirely the media's since only a few people could understand the AAI report as it was written—2,000 pages of statistics, technical jargon, and tables. The media may seize on the simple and the familiar, and ignore the complex in self-defense. But the potential for misinformation in the interaction between expertise and the mass media is formidable. In the case of Follow Through it materialized.

Government policy. Finally, one must question the government policy that shaped the Follow Through evaluation. Policy based on the "big bang" theory assumed there could be an invention or discovery of a model program that would solve the problem of educating disadvantaged children in the early years of school. Further, it assumed that models could be successfully implemented and uniformly effective under any number of differing local conditions. These assumptions seem considerably more dubious today than when Follow Through began.

That is not to say that the federal government should not develop new programs. But one might expect the new programs to have differential effects in different settings. The same program may be desirable in one place and not in another, desirable even for one group in the same place and not for another. It does mean that the government should not propagate one "best" model to the exclusion of all others, since the effects may differ, if in fact they are even ascertainable.

A second reform is warranted in the federal government's evaluation policy. Federal evaluation policy for the last decade has been built on certain assumptions manifested in the Follow Through evaluation. It has assumed that there is agreement on program goals and on the outcome measures, almost always test scores, on which the programs are to be assessed. It also assumes simple cause and effect relationships.

There are places where such assumptions are valid, where such approaches to evaluation will work, but the United States as a whole is not one of them (House, 1978). In a society as pluralistic as the United States, people often disagree on goals for schooling. They certainly disagree on outcome measures by which to assess programs. And the cause and effect relationships in the social sciences are exceedingly complex. Perhaps the final judgment is that the Follow Through evaluation was inappropriate for the context in which it was employed.

REFERENCES

Abt Associates, Inc. *Education as experimentation: A planned variation model, Vol. IV A-D.* Cambridge, Mass.: Abt Associates, 1977. ERIC Document No. 148-490–148 492.

Campbell, D. & Erlebacher, A. "How regression artifacts in quasiexperimental evaluations in compensatory education tend to underestimate effects." In C. A. Bennett & A. A. Lumsdaine (Eds.), *Evaluation and experiment.* New York: Academic Press, 1975. Pp. 195-285.

Cronbach, L. J., Rogosa, D. R., Floden, R. E., & Price, G. G. "Analysis of covariance in nonrandomized experiments: Parameters affecting bias." Occasional paper of Stanford Evaluation Consortium, Stanford University, 1977.

Egbert, R. Interview conducted at the Center for Instructional Research and Curriculum Evaluation, Urbana, Il. April 28, 1977.

Elmore, R. F. Follow Through: Decisionmaking in a large-scale social experiment. Unpublished doctoral dissertation, Harvard University, 1976.

Haney, W. *A technical history of the national Follow Through evaluation.* Cambridge, Mass.: Huron Institute, August, 1977.

House, E. R., Glass, G. V., McLean, L. D., & Walker, D. F. "No simple answer: Critique of the Follow Through evaluation." *Harvard Educational Review*, 1978, *48*, 128-160.

House, E. R. "The objectivity, fairness, and justice of federal evaluation policy as reflected in the Follow Through evaluation." Mimeo, Center for Instructional Research and Curriculum Evaluation, Urbana, Il. 1978.

McLaughlin, M. W. *Evaluation and reform: The Elementary and Secondary Education Act of 1965/Title I.* Cambridge, Mass.: Ballinger, 1976.

Rivlin, A. *Systematic thinking for social action.* Washington, D.C.: Brookings Institution, 1971. ERIC Document 057-140.

Stallings, J. *Implementation and child effects of teaching practices in Follow Through classrooms.* SRCD Monograph, 1975, *40*, 7-8.

2

Mainstreaming in the Preschool

Merle B. Karnes

Richard C. Lee

University of Illinois, Urbana-Champaign

INTRODUCTION

During the 1960s an imposing body of theoretical and empirical evidence was offered in support of the assumption that educational intervention has maximum impact with children under 5 years of age. Scholars and scientists representing a variety of disciplines and educational philosophies generally agreed that developmental processes and behavioral responses undergo rapid change and are most maleable during the early years (Bijou & Baer, 1961, 1965; Hunt, 1961; Kirk, 1958; Piaget, 1952).

Recognizing the importance of early stimulation to later development, several investigators initiated experimental programs designed to accelerate the development of young children who appeared educationally handicapped because of experiental deprivation (Deutsch, 1964; Edwards & Stern, 1970, Karnes, 1970). Other researchers studied the effects of early intervention on mentally (Kirk, 1958), emotionally (Burke, 1972), sensorially, (Tait, 1972), and physically (Connors, 1974) handicapped young children. Although the results of these studies are equivocal, they largely reinforced the belief that developmental anomalies could be positively altered during the early years. By 1970, a network of programs serving young handicapped children was operating. These projects, funded by the Bureau of Education for the Handicapped, became known as First Chance programs.

As First Chance programs developed, a variety of factors operating within special education produced a trend away from educating handicapped learners in special classes and toward mainstreaming—the integration of handicapped learners into regular classes for the major portion of the school day. Prominent among these factors were: (1) litigation focusing on the social inequality of segregated services for the handicapped (Cohen & DeYoung, 1973), (2) a reassessment of the impact on handicapped children of special education programs in segregated classes, since the record of achievement of children in these programs was mediocre (Cjelka & Tyler, 1970); and (3) a growing commitment among special educators to the principle of normalization (Wolfensberger, 1972). As a result, these factors have increased financial incentives from federal and state governments in support of integrated services and national legislation (P.L. 94-142) which mandates the return of handicapped children to regular classrooms whenever possible. As mainstreaming gained acceptance among special educators in elementary and secondary settings, educators interested in younger children began to advocate integrated programs for preschool children as well (e.g., Karnes, 1970). Soon, programs enrolling integrated groups of handicapped and nonhandicapped preschool children began to emerge (Bricker & Bricker, 1972, 1973; Karnes, 1970). By 1972 mainstreaming had been mandated as part of Project Head Start.

Today, the integration of handicapped and nonhandicapped children is a prominent feature of many preschool programs, namely, daycare, Head Start and First Chance. With the implementation of P.L. 94-142, integrated services for preschoolers will grow even more rapidly. Despite the growing popularity of integrated preschools and the impending federal mandate, however, few attempts to examine the preschool mainstream literature have been made (Wynne, Ulfelder & Dakof, 1975). Unfortunately, previous reviews neither evaluate the literature in a systematic fashion nor identify issues that are unique to mainstreaming in the preschool.

In this discussion, a number of fundamental issues and empirical findings concerning classroom-based integrated programs for preschool children are explored. The intent is to familiarize students and early childhood educators with these issues, to review recent research, and to examine program development in this area. First, mainstreaming and related terms are defined. Next, we consider the rationale for mainstreaming, focusing primarily on the justification for beginning the process early. In the third section, recent research on several important areas in preschool mainstreaming is reviewed. The fourth section presents a brief review of preschool projects that employ integrated approaches. Finally, the paper concludes with a discussion of the issues raised by the attempts to integrate handicapped and nonhandicapped preschool children.

MAINSTREAMING AND RELATED TERMS

Terms associated with mainstreaming have proliferated in the literature of special education. To the novice, these terms can be intimidating. In this section, therefore, the meaning of four terms commonly used in the mainstreaming literature will be considered: (1) mainstreaming; (2) normalization; (3) P.L. 94-142; and (4) IEP.

Mainstreaming is defined in various ways by educators. Daily (1974), for example, notes a wide variety of definitions, one of which is merely to strip the label from the handicapped child and return him to the classroom. Other definitions stress the temporal aspect of mainstreaming; that is, the amount of time the handicapped child spends in the regular classroom. But these definitions are of limited value because they ignore the comprehensive nature of mainstreaming by failing to emphasize instructional delivery, assessment, and other vital elements of programming.

More useful definitions of mainstreaming recognize it as a comprehensive process; Birch (1974), for example, incorporates 14 factors in his definition of mainstreaming:

1. Mainstreaming refers to the assignment of handicapped pupils to regular classes and the provision of special education for them.
2. In mainstreaming, regular classroom teachers broaden and adapt instructional procedures and content so all children are incorporated into regular programs at levels manageable for each child and teacher.
3. Mainstreaming may be accomplished at any level, preschool through secondary school.
4. In mainstreaming, the handicapped pupil reports to the regular classroom teacher.
5. In conventionally organized schools or open space schools, handicapped pupils which are mainstreamed spend at least half of the day in regular classes.
6. In conventionally organized schools the special education teacher has a center to which handicapped pupils can report for periods of time from the mainstream rooms to which they have been assigned.
7. In open space schools, the special education teacher may be a member of the team serving in the open space setting or may have a separate room as headquarters.
8. Mainstreamed handicapped pupils leave the main group only for essential small group or individual instruction and educational assessment or to pick up and deliver assignments prepared by the special education teacher.
9. Regular and special education teachers agree upon individual schedules and assignments for mainstreamed children.
10. Regular teachers are responsible for grades and report cards for mainstreamed handicapped pupils, but they may consult with special education teachers.
11. Special education teachers help regular teachers by providing educational assessments and instructional consultation for regular class pupils who may not be eligible for special education in the usual sense.
12. Mainstreaming implies that handicapped pupils usually begin their education in regular kindergarten or first grade groups with special education support, and are removed to special classes or schools only

when necessary, and only for the period required to prepare them to return to regular classes.

13. Criteria for selecting handicapped pupils for mainstreaming are set in terms of matching the educational needs of children with the capability of the mainstream program to meet those needs, rather than in terms of the severity of the pupil's physical, mental, emotional or other handicap.

14. Mainstreaming has a place in the spectrum of plans for organizing instruction, space, and facilities to accommodate the educational needs of handicapped pupils.

A highly useful and often quoted definition of mainstreaming is provided by Kaufman, Gottlieb, Agard, and Kukic (1975):

> Mainstreaming refers to the temporal, instructional and social integration of eligible exceptional children with normal peers based on an ongoing individually determined educational planning and programming process and requires clarification of responsibility among regular and special education administrative, instructional and supportive personnel. (pp. 40-42)

As this definition suggests, mainstreaming is more than an administrative procedure or a temporal integration of handicapped children with normally functioning children. Rather, mainstreaming includes instructional and social integration, individualized educational planning, and the clarification of responsibility on the part of all professionals involved.

MacMillan, Jones, and Meyers (1976) add an important qualification to the definition. Categorical labels, such as mentally retarded or emotionally disturbed, should be removed from mainstreamed children.

Still another component frequently mentioned in definitions of mainstreaming is the need to provide a continuum of educational services. That is, mainstreaming applies not merely to the integration of the handicapped child into regular classrooms but to integration into the most normal or least restrictive environment.

As stipulated here, the terms *mainstreaming* and *least restrictive environment* become synonomous—that is, to place the handicapped individual in the most normal or least restrictive environment is to place him in the most appropriate mainstream setting.

Finally, Hobbs (1975) argues that the mainstreaming principle does not imply a hodge-podge or melting pot in which children's special needs tend to lose their identity; instead it is predicated upon meaningful, integrated programs that require numerous arrangements, each geared to unique individual and group needs. Hobbs writes:

> In schools that are most responsive to individual differences in abilities, interests and learning styles of children, the mainstream is actually many streams, sometimes as many streams as there are individual children, sometimes several streams as groups are formed for special purposes, sometimes one stream only as concerns of all converge. We see no advantage in dumping

exceptional children into an undifferentiated mainstream; but we see great advantages to all children, exceptional children included, in an educational program modulated to the needs of individual children, singly, in a small group, or all together. Such a flexible arrangement may well result in functional separations of exceptional children from time to time, but the governing principle would apply to all children; school programs should be responsive to the learning requirements of individual children and groups should serve this end (p. 297).

In summarizing the diverse definitions of mainstreaming the following points should be reiterated:

1. Definitions of mainstreaming vary widely from simplistic definitions which merely require that the child be delabeled and returned to the regular classroom to complex definitions which reflect the comprehensive nature of the mainstream process.
2. No consensus definition of mainstreaming is found among educators.
3. In our view mainstreaming, integration, and least restrictive alternative are essentially synonymous terms.
4. Useful definitions of mainstreaming stress the following elements: (a) the temporal integration of handicapped children with their normal peers; (b) individually determined instruction; (c) the social integration of handicapped and nonhandicapped children; (d) the clarification of professional roles; and (e) the delabeling of the child.

Normalization refers to a principle originally developed in Scandinavia (Wolfensberger, 1972), which advocates life conditions for handicapped persons which approximate "normal" as closely as possible, considering the individual's limitation. Normalization is a more comprehensive term than mainstreaming in that it applies to multiple life situations, not just education. When applied to education, normalization means to place handicapped learners into regular classrooms unless the individual's limitations are such that a more restrictive placement is essential. Normalization, when applied to education, is equivalent to least restrictive environment and therefore to mainstreaming.

P.L. 94-142 refers to the Education for All Handicapped Children Act, passed by Congress and signed into law by President Ford in 1975. This landmark document for the handicapped child contains a number of significant elements. First, by fiscal year 1978, all handicapped children between the ages of 5 and 18 are to have access to public education. By fiscal year 1980, all handicapped children from 3 to 5 are to have access to public education in states mandating services to this age group. Second, handicapped children will receive educational services in the regular classroom with nonhandicapped children whenever possible, and will always be placed in the least restrictive, yet appropriate, environment. Third, every handicapped child must have a written individualized educational plan (IEP) developed in cooperation with the school, parents, and child, when possible. IEPs are designed to ensure that every child has the opportunity to receive an appropriate education. Fourth, methods used to evaluate children must take into account the child's cultural background, primary language, and past history. Fifth, parents must be notified by the school before educational decisions (e.g., placement, curriculum changes) are made about their child, and have the opportunity to institute a formal review of placement decisions which are in their judgment, inappropriate. Sixth, procedures will be developed to ensure that procedural due process has been established. Seventh, a priority of 94-142 is the establishment of a mechanism to locate all eligible children not receiving services and to develop appropriate public education programs for these children. Eighth, the legislation provides special training funds for teachers and professional staff to become conversant with new education practice and materials. A ninth and final element in this legislation is the directive to public schools to reduce architectural barriers that limit the access of the handicapped child. For the reader interested in further details, a well-written synopsis of the law is presented by Goodman (1976) and Weintraub, Abeson, Ballard, and Lavor (1976).

An *IEP,* or Individualized Education Plan, is a written statement which describes both the content of a handicapped child's educational program and the manner in which special education and related services will be provided. An IEP is developed jointly at a multidisciplinary staff conference by the regular class teacher, the child's parent or guardian, the special services teacher, and ancillary personnel (e.g., psychologists, speech or motor therapists, social workers) who work with the child. According to the federal rules and regulations (Section 121A.225) which guide the implementation of P.L. 94-142, an IEP must contain:

1. Statement of the child's present level of educational performance in areas in which he or she receives instruction;
2. Statement of annual goals which specify the educational performance to be achieved by the child by the end of a school year;
3. Statement of short-term instructional objectives for each annual goal which represent measurable intermediate steps between the child's present level of performance and the desired level as stated in an annual goal;
4. Statement of special education and related services which will be provided, including the type of physical education program in which the child will participate, and special media and materials required to implement the child's IEP;
5. Initiation date and anticipated duration of special education and related services;
6. Description of the extent to which the child will participate in regular education programs;
7. Justification for the child's educational placement; and
8. Objective criteria, evaluation procedures, and schedules for determining on at least an annual basis whether short-term instructional objectives have been achieved. (Blankenship, 1977). (See References)

Though the law requires IEPs for handicapped children only, it is usually a good idea for teachers to develop Individualized Educational Plans for all children—handicapped and nonhandicapped alike.

RATIONALE FOR MAINSTREAMING

Because mainstreaming is a complex educational procedure, it is unlikely that educators will ever agree on a single best solution for its implementation. But while educators may not agree on how to implement mainstreaming, they do agree on why integration of handicapped and nonhandicapped of all ages is a sound and humane educational policy. The arguments which comprise a rationale for mainstreaming may be somewhat arbitrarily grouped into two areas: (1) legal-legislative arguments, and (2) benefits to children, handicapped and non-handicapped alike.

Legal-Legislative Argument

Recent legal and legislative decisions form the basis for a compelling set of arguments in support of mainstreaming. Legal mandates, which evolved from these court decisions and legislative acts, and have had the most influence on educational practice are: (1) the right of all handicapped children to a free public education; (2) the right of handicapped children to educational placement in the least restrictive environment; and (3) a guarantee of due process for parents concerning their right to review educational decisions relevant to their child.

With respect to court decisions, two cases—PARC (1971) and Mills (1974) —are of particular importance in establishing precedents for the rights of handicapped children. In *The Pennsylvania Association for Retarded Children (PARC) vs. The Commonwealth of Pennsylvania,* the right of a previously excluded group of retarded children to a free public education was ensured. The State also acknowledged the right of handicapped children to education in the least restrictive environment:

> It is the commonwealth's obligation to place each mentally retarded child in a free public program of education and training appropriate to the child's capacity, within the context of a presumption that, among the alternative programs of education and training required by statute to be available, placement in a regular public school class is preferable to placement in a special public school class, and placement in a special public school class is preferable to placement in any other type of program of education and training.

Although the PARC case is a landmark with tremendous impact on the future of special education, it covers the rights of mentally handicapped citizens only. Legal experts, however, recognized that it was only a matter of time before a similar ruling covering all handicapped children would be handed down. This ruling came in *Mills vs. The Washington, D.C. Board of Education* (1973). The Mills decision closely parallels PARC with two important exceptions: (1) rights of treatment, placement, and due process are extended to *all* handicapped children, and (2) lack of funds is not an acceptable excuse for excluding handicapped children from public schools.

At the time of the PARC and Mills litigation, a number of states (e.g.,

Tennessee, 1972, and Wisconsin, 1973) were enacting legislation intended to promote the inclusion of school-age handicapped children, regardless of degree of impairment, into the most appropriate placement in the domain of public education. Most of these state statutes reflected the basic rights of handicapped children and guaranteed due process procedures for their parents. With the weight of legal precedent and the pressure from states, the federal government finally entered the scene with the Education for All Handicapped Children Act (Public Law 94-142).

Of the many reasons presented in support of mainstreaming, the most powerful is clearly the legal and legislative mandate to educate children in the most normal environment. The message of the mandates from both legal and legislative sources is that the integration of handicapped children into programs with nonhandicapped children is no longer the exception but the rule.

Benefits to Children

The potential developmental opportunities for both handicapped and nonhandicapped children that exist in integrated environments comprise the second argument in support of mainstreaming. The weight of this argument rests on a number of factors which suggest that integrated environments best serve as educational and therapeutic environments for all children.

A first factor involves the potential benefits to handicapped children from observing more advanced peers. It seems clear from the imitation literature that children acquire new responses from observing and modeling the behavior of others (Bandura, Grusec, & Menlove, 1967; Parton, 1976). There are also indications that children selectively model those who perform responses more effectively (Strichart, 1974). These findings argue for the exposure of handicapped children to competent models in integrated environments, rather than for their restriction in segregated environments where exposure is limited to other developmentally deficient models.

Similarly, opportunities to interact with nonhandicapped children provide potential benefits to the handicapped. For example, in the area of play, Bricker and Bricker (1971) indicate that nondelayed children may provide better models of appropriate play skills than do adults. Similarly, Rubenstein and Howes (1976), in a study with toddlers, observed that the presence of peers enhances various aspects of play, including its frequency, maturity, and the creative use of objects. Moreover, a number of studies (reviewed in a later section) suggest that nonhandicapped children can serve as valuable resources by applying adaptive consequences, or modeling appropriate social and language behaviors for their handicapped peers. Once again, these findings argue for integrated environments in which handicapped children benefit by the presence of their nonhandicapped peers.

Nonhandicapped children may also benefit from integrated environments. They can develop increased understanding of, and sensitivity to, individual differences. It is likely that important attitudinal processes are positively affected by their exposure to handicapped peers. Moreover, there is considerable evidence that nonhandicapped children benefit from integrated programs to at least the same degree as would be expected had they attended nonintegrated preschools (Bricker & Bricker, 1971).

A final argument in favor of integrated programs concerns the benefit to teachers that arises from opportunities to observe a mixed group of children. Especially at the preschool level, integrated classrooms provide teachers with a ready framework for gauging child behaviors within a developmentally appropriate context.

One last word: merely placing children together in a classroom will not yield these desired outcomes. Rather, teachers must work hard to systematically arrange events and other specialized procedures which encourage and support integration.

MAINSTREAMING IN THE PRESCHOOL:
A REVIEW OF RESEARCH

In the past two or three years a small but fascinating research literature examining issues unique to mainstreaming in preprimary settings has emerged. These studies are scattered throughout a number of research periodicals and, as yet, have not been collected in any single review. In this section, we group these very recent experimental findings into three major areas: (1) social interaction in integrated preschool settings; (2) procedures to facilitate social interactions in integrated settings; and (3) the role of nonhandicapped peers as educational agents. This section closes with recommendations to researchers and educators for future research and practice.

Social Interaction in Integrated Preschool Settings

Several studies have examined the extent to which handicapped children in integrated school environments are accepted by and interact with their nonhandicapped peers (Levitt & Cohen, 1976, review this research). Almost all of this research has been conducted with children of primary and elementary school age or with adolescents. Some of these studies have produced equivocal results, but the general trend suggests that, on the basis of sociometric and observational data, school-aged handicapped children are not readily accepted by their nonhandicapped peers regardless of whether the setting is a nongraded elementary school (Goodman, Gottlieb, & Harrison, 1972), a regular classroom with supportive services (Iano, Ayers, Heller, McGettigan, & Walker, 1974), or an open space secondary school (Gottlieb & Budoff, 1973). On the positive side, however, a few writers (e.g., Kennedy and Bruininks, 1974) have found that younger, primary-aged children have less negative attitudes toward the handicapped than do older children.

Unfortunately, only a few studies examine the social and play behavior of handicapped and nonhandicapped children in integrated preschool settings. In fact, a review of the child development literature uncovered only four such studies. Since this small body of research constitutes an early source of data on an important question, these studies are summarized here in some detail.

Porter, Ramsey, Tremblay, Iaceobo, and Crawley (1978) observed the social behavior of retarded and normally functioning children during free play in an integrated preschool. Twenty-seven children ranging in age from 18 to 64 months were assigned to six groups of four children each; a seventh group contained three children. Each group had at least one child from each of the two subpopulations. During 30-minute observation sessions, each group was removed from the classroom and placed in a 12 x 16 ft. playroom. The floor of the playroom was marked off with tape to form a grid indicating distances; the room was also equipped with a one-way mirror, a roving videotape camera, and microphones suspended from the ceiling. Each day one child was selected and followed for the 30-minute play session. Over the course of the study each child was followed at least once.

Porter et al. examined two general classes of behavior: (1) the interpersonal distance between retarded and nonretarded children, and (2) the social preference of and interaction between the two subpopulations. Normally developing children maintained a closer mean proximity to other normally developing children than they did to their retarded peers. Further, they engaged in several categories of social behavior with other normal children significantly more often than they did with retarded children. Retarded children, on the other hand, displayed no consistent preferences for retarded versus normal peers. Thus, the data in this study revealed a consistent preference by nonhandicapped children for other nonhandicapped children.

In a second study, Devoney, Guralnick, and Rubin (1974) evaluated the effects of integrating handicapped and nonhandicapped preschool children on social play skills. Handicapped children in a nonintegrated situation were rated on a time-sampling basis for both positive peer interactions and social play level using a social play scale that ranged from autisticlike and isolate play to cooperative play. After a variety of unsuccessful attempts to increase substantially the quality of the handicapped children's play, a group of nonhandic pped children were introduced into the play situation. Although the introduction of these children improved the social play of handicapped children to some extent, the change was not substantial. Moreover, the authors noted few spontaneous social interactions between handicapped and nonhandicapped children. Not until the teacher systematically structured the situation, using nonhandicapped children to promote various interactions, did marked increases in social interactions and quality of play occur.

A third study examined how heterogeneous or homogeneous grouping influenced social interaction among "disadvantaged" and "privileged" preschoolers in Israel (Feitelson, Weintraub, & Michaeli, 1972). Children from both groups were identified primarily by the occupation and educational level of their parents, though a number of children among the disadvantaged group manifested mild and moderate handicaps. Parents of "privileged" children had completed at least a secondary education and held white-collar positions; parents of the "disadvantaged" had completed elementary school only and were employed in semi-skilled or unskilled occupations. Ninety-six 3-year-olds, half "privileged" and half "disadvantaged," were randomly assigned to one homogeneous "disadvantaged" group, or to one of three heterogeneous groups in which the ratio was eight "disadvantaged" to 16 "privileged." Records of social behavior were collected during 1-hour, free-play observations and analyzed at the beginning and end of the two-year project. Data showed that "disadvantaged" children in a *homogenous* environment exhibited a greater number of positive peer interactions than did their counterparts in a heterogeneous setting interacted less frequently with peers and then almost exclusively with children from their own social group (e.g., other "disadvantaged" children). There were no significant differences between "privileged" children in the settings in the number of positive interactions, and "privileged" children in both groups interacted mainly within their own social group.

Whereas the first three studies showed little interaction between handicapped and nonhandicapped children, Hawkins and Peterson (1977) found substantial peer interactions between handicapped and nonhandicapped children. Their study, which was conducted at an integrated preschool at the University of Kansas, involved frequent structured observations of social and play interactions between ten handicapped and five nonhandicapped children during free play. Several independent observers were used, and each child was followed 20 minutes daily for 18 days, using a 30-second individual recording procedure. Although a number of variables were examined and the results are complex, the data generally indicate relatively little discrimination by nonhandicapped children toward their handicapped peers.

Taken as a whole, these four studies suggest that spontaneous interactions between handicapped and nonhandicapped children are not likely to occur. Of course, before definitive claims can be made regarding social interaction in integrated preschool settings, more normative data are needed on the interaction patterns of children in such settings. Nevertheless, the available evidence suggests that teachers cannot assume that positive peer interactions will occur in integrated settings and that specialized procedures to encourage and support such interactions are needed. This is the subject of our next discussion.

Procedures to Facilitate Social Interactions in Integrated Settings

In recent years, several studies have attempted to program social interactions among preschool children in integrated settings. We shall consider first those suggestions which are teacher-oriented, and then review those which rely on the child as the agent of change.

Teacher Reinforcement. Teacher praise, contingent upon the child's positive interactive behavior, increases social integration among preschool children. Strain and Timm (1974), for example, applied contingent teacher attention to reinforce an isolate preschool child and her peers for attempts at social interaction. These writers measured interactive behavior under two conditions of contingent teacher attention. In the first condition, verbal praise and physical contact were directed to a target subject's peers for appropriate interaction with the target subject. In the second condition, verbal praise and physical contact were directed to the target subject for appropriate interaction with peers. Results indicated that the application of contingent teacher attention to peers rapidly increased appropriate social behaviors by the peers and also by the target subject. Similarly, contingent teacher attention applied to the target subject resulted in a similar increase in appropriate social behaviors for both the target subject and peers. Additionally, it was noted that the recipients of contingent adult attention initiated more appropriate social contacts than did the peers.

But teacher reinforcement can also interfere with ongoing social interaction between children. Recent research suggests that teachers should be sensitive to social interaction that occurs naturally between children. Shores, Hester, and Strain (1976) found that structuring dramatic play or role playing activities was more successful in producing social interaction between handicapped and nonhandicapped preschool children than was continued adult attention. Similarly, Strain and Wiegernick (1976) found that sociodramatic activities (for example, having handicapped and nonhandicapped children act out favorite stories) were far more effective in promoting social interaction than teacher attention alone.

These studies suggest that while teacher attention is a powerful device in promoting and maintaining social interaction, teachers should be no more obtrusive than necessary in promoting positive social interactions between handicapped and nonhandicapped children.

Arranging Physical and Spatial Events in the Classroom. Child development research suggests that certain physical and spatial features of preschool environments inhibit social interactions among children while others promote such interactions. Several studies (Green, 1933; Jersild & Markey, 1935; Murphy, 1937) in the early peer interaction literature relate space allotments to aggressive interactions among peers in preschool settings. Generally, these studies show that aggressive interactions occur more frequently when space is restricted.

Other studies (Markey, 1935; Murphy, 1937; Quillitch & Risley, 1973; Updegraff & Herbst, 1933) have examined the influence of play materials and equipment on the social behavior of young children. In several cases it was shown that certain toys and materials such as sand, clay, tricycles, wagons, and blocks elicited more cooperative play than other toys commonly found in nursery school environments. Additionally, in a number of studies (Buell,

Stoddard, Harris, & Baer, 1968; Cooper, Lee, Bierlein, Wolf, & Baer, 1966; Johnson, 1935) outdoor climbing equipment was found to produce increases in cooperative peer interactions.

Prescott, Jones, and Kritchevsky (1967) examined day care programs in the Los Angeles area. Their systematic observations of these centers showed that the availability and placement of equipment and materials were among the most powerful predictors of program quality. In addition, they found that as the quality of outdoor play areas decreased, the amount of teacher restriction and control increased, resulting in negative changes in the teacher's manner, less interest among the children, and more conflicts between children.

A powerful example of the influence that toys have on child behavior is demonstrated in a study of Quillitch and Risley (1973). These writers found that young children would play alone or together depending upon the toys available. They systematically varied the presence and absence of six "social" toys and six "isolate" toys, and found that children played with one another 78% of the time when social toys such as checkers or playing cards were present, but only 16% of the time when isolate toys such as puzzles, tinker toys, or play dough were present.

The above studies suggest that social interactions are influenced by the physical and spatial characteristics of early education settings and that teachers might find it useful to experiment with various arrangements of materials and space. Since all children in the play setting may not have the necessary skills to utilize the available materials they may have to be taught these skills. Some observers report that children must first learn to use play materials before peer interaction will occur. Allen, Turner, and Everett (1970), for example, found it necessary to teach nine severely handicapped preschoolers how to play with ordinary play materials before these materials could be used to promote social interaction with nonhandicapped peers. Teachers should provide sufficient materials to permit interactive participation by all children. Duplicate toys and materials permit, and may encourage, imitative behavior by handicapped children who observe a nonhandicapped child enjoying a toy.

Peers as Educational Agents.   Integrated preschool programs provide a number of potential and perhaps unique opportunities for nonhandicapped children to serve as valuable resources in fostering the development of their handicapped peers. The role of nonhandicapped children in promoting the behavioral development of handicapped peers has been the subject of some recent and fascinating research; specifically, these studies have examined strategies whereby normal children can aid in the development of social, language, and imitative behaviors among their less advanced peers.

A number of recent studies point to the potential of using nonhandicapped peers to promote the social development of handicapped children. In his first study, Guralnick (1976a) attempted to increase the appropriate social interactions of a child who displayed many severe isolate behaviors. Specifically, during certain activities, the teacher requested that nonhandicapped preschool children tag along with the withdrawn child, despite the fact that the withdrawn child exhibited a complex repertoire of bizarre, self-directed, and peer avoidance behaviors. Nonhandicapped peers were instructed to reinforce all positive behaviors of the withdrawn peer. Analysis of the data revealed that the close physical presence of the nonhandicapped children and their response to and reinforcement of the positive behavior of the withdrawn child substantially increased the positive social interactions of the withdrawn child. Maintenance data collected two weeks after intervention showed the target child's interaction levels to be stable at approximately the level attained during intervention.

In a second study, Guralnick (1976b) analyzed the effects of nonhandicapped peers in modifying the social play behavior of less advanced peers. A setting was arranged in which two nonhandicapped peers focused on promoting the social play of a designated handicapped child. Through role playing and direct training, nonhandicapped children were instructed to model and encourage interactive and constructive play with a particular toy and to reinforce only the appropriate social play behaviors of the handicapped child. The handicapped child's social play behavior was observed using Parten's (1932) categories: isolate, associate, and cooperative. Results showed that peer modeling and selective reinforcement procedures were effective in increasing the percentage of observation intervals in which the handicapped child engaged in associate and cooperative play.

Wahler (1967) examined the effect of peer attention on several social behaviors emitted by handicapped children. This study, which was conducted in an integrated nursery school, involved three nonhandicapped children who produced social behaviors that received high rates of peer attention and two handicapped children who produced behaviors not frequently attended to by peers. To determine the effect of peer attention on social behavior, nonhandicapped children were instructed to play with handicapped peers except when they produced designated inappropriate social behavior. As expected, social behaviors that were ignored by nonhandicapped peers decreased substantially during intervention while those that peers attended to increased. Using a single subject reversal design, these behavior changes were subsequently reversed and then recovered documenting the effects of contingent peer attention. With this demonstration, Wahler provided evidence that contingent attention applied by nonhandicapped peers can alter the inappropriate social behavior of handicapped preschool children.

Nordquist (1978) reports a case study in which an autistic boy was placed in a regular early childhood education program. In the first phase of the study the subject was taught to imitate a group of targeted nonverbal behaviors. Following imitation training, Phase 2 was initiated in which two nonhandicapped children were trained to model and reinforce the same behaviors. Each time the subject was asked to perform an activity or indicated a desire for a certain activity the teacher signaled the nearest trained peer to intercept the autistic child, model a targeted behavior and reinforce him. During both phases of the study generalization data were collected during free play when neither adults nor peers specifically modeled or reinforced the nonverbal behaviors. The results showed a very clear difference in the effects of adult versus peer reinforcement. During adult training and reinforcement very little spontaneous imitation of nontrained peers was observed. During peer reinforcement, in contrast, the percentage of spontaneous imitations of nontrained peers rose dramatically. On the basis of these results Nordquist speculates that peers may be better generalization-facilitation agents than adults.

A final study demonstrating the use of nonhandicapped preschool children to promote the social development of their handicapped peers is reported by Lee (1977). In this study, contingent teacher attention was used to increase social interactions between two children—one a socially skilled model, and the other a handicapped, socially isolated peer in each of four classrooms. Training was conducted in free-play settings in four classrooms with generalization probes made during snack and free play. In addition, four socially isolated children, one in each class, served as controls. The results indicated that contingent teacher attention was effective in increasing social interactions between the model and handicapped child in each classroom. Additionally, social interactions of the isolate subjects increased dramatically in both the free play and snack settings during intervention, and were maintained during a probe conducted four weeks later. Control children in all four settings failed to improve, and the social interactions of nonhandicapped children remained stable across all phases of the study.

Recent evidence suggests that nonhandicapped children can also serve as valuable agents in promoting the language development of their handicapped peers. In two recent studies, Guralnick (1976a, 1977) demonstrated that nonhandicapped children successfully modified the inappropriate verbalizations of handicapped peers in an integrated setting. In the first study, two nonhandicapped preschoolers were trained to attend selectively to the appropriate verbalizations of a handicapped peer. Results showed a decrease in inappropriate verbalizations and an increase in appropriate verbalizations. In the second experiment, the inappropriate language behaviors of a handicapped preschool child were modified by having the subject child observe a trained nonhandicapped peer use appropriate language forms. When the peer model was reinforced by the experimenter for appropriate form usage in the presence of the handicapped child, the latter soon began producing the same appropriate forms. Thus, by simply reinforcing language responses in a more advanced peer, the adult produced an increase in the use of those same responses by the handicapped child.

Another factor to consider when nonhandicapped children serve as agents to promote language in handicapped peers is whether the nonhandicapped children adjust their communications as a function of the listener's developmental level. Some adjustments are obviously necessary to achieve effective communication and, given that these modifications occur, it is important to determine whether these adjusted forms of linguistic input are likely to benefit the handicapped child. (Guralnick & Paul-Brown, 1977).

In an effort to assess whether nonhandicapped children adjust language as a function of the listener, Guralnick and Paul-Brown (1977) analyzed the speech of nonhandicapped children in an instructional setting as they addressed children at different developmental levels. Children included in the study were classified as mildly, moderately, or severely handicapped (or nonhandicapped according to a classification scheme developed by the American Association of Mental Deficiency). The speech of a group of designated nonhandicapped children was recorded in a setting in which the speaker was asked to provide instruction on drawing tasks to children in each of the four listening levels on an individual basis. The language was then analyzed in terms of 41 linguistic parameters.

Results clearly showed that the nonhandicapped children adjusted their language according to the developmental level of the listener. In general, their speech was more complex and diversified when addressing more advanced children. Similar results were observed when a nonhandicapped subject's speech was recorded in an experimental task during free play. Guralnick and Paul-Brown also observed that while nonhandicapped children adjusted their language, they still produced a language corpus structurally more sophisticated than the productive level of their peers. This corpus was simply adjusted to a degree appropriate to the child's developmental level. The results of this study suggest that nonhandicapped peers adjust their language to the level of the listener, and this adjustment appears to have developmental significance for the language handicapped child.

Little doubt exists that young children learn to produce new behaviors by observing and imitating the actions of others. Such a process is called *learning by imitation,* and its effects have been clearly documented (Parton, 1976). Observations of a model have produced behavioral changes across a widely disparate range from reducing overt fear responses (Bandura, Grusec, & Menlove, 1967) to increasing appropriate behaviors (Guess, Sailor, Rutherford, & Baer, 1968). Additionally, the studies cited earlier in the areas of social and language development are examples of learning by imitation; indeed, most learning in integrated settings *is* by imitating others.

But many young handicapped children do not know how to imitate and thus are deprived of learning opportunities unique to integrated settings. Recent research in Sonoma, California employs a direct conditioning procedure for training developmentally delayed toddlers and preschoolers to imitate nonhandicapped classmates. The intervention procedure, termed peer imitation training, consists of verbally and physically prompting a child to imitate the behavior of a classmate and then replacing the prompting with adult praise for imitative behavior. Two studies employing peer imitation training have been reported.

One study (Apolloni, Cooke, & Cooke, 1977) investigates the feasibility of training delayed toddlers to imitate motor responses, material use, and verbal responses of nondelayed peers. Three developmentally delayed subjects and two non-delayed peers, all under 3 years of age, were used in the study. Results indicated that under highly structured conditions, delayed subjects could be trained to imitate their nondelayed age mates. A probe for generalization in a nontraining, free-play setting without adult presence found, however, that increased levels of imitative behavior, especially verbal imitations, were not maintained.

Thus, a second study (Peck, Apolloni, Cooke, & Cooke, 1976) was directed toward developing peer imitative behavior that would be maintained under nontraining free-play conditions in the absence of an adult experimenter. The authors reasoned that since previous research had substantiated that generalization is likely to be obtained when there is a high degree of similarity between the training and generalization settings, peer imitation training should be carried out in free-play settings. Two experiments followed. In the first, an adult experimenter prompted and praised developmentally delayed subjects for imitating the ongoing free-play behavior of nondelayed children. Peer imitation was defined as "a response similar in topography to one emitted five seconds or less previously by another child and which was observed by the subject" (Peck et al., 1976, p. 61). During generalization sessions the adult experimenter left the play area. Results from this experiment demonstrated that peer imitation training could teach developmentally delayed preschoolers to imitate the free-play behavior of nondelayed classmates. Additionally, consistent increases in the imitative responses of delayed subjects under nontraining conditions were noted. Finally, the researchers also recorded reciprocal increases in social interaction between delayed subjects and nondelayed subjects under training and nontraining conditions.

The second experiment replicated the procedure of the earlier study with 2-year-old subjects, with the addition of a bidirectional training procedure; that is, both delayed and nondelayed participants were trained to imitate one another in a variety of material and motor activities. Once again, the experimenter left the play area following the training session. The results of the second experiment replicated those of the first with one notable exception; nondelayed children imitated delayed children under training conditions but not under nontraining conditions.

In summary, the two studies provide tentative evidence to support the feasibility of training young delayed children to imitate the behavior of non-delayed classmates under highly structured conditions. Further, generalized peer imitation across stimulus conditions and to responses never directly trained were observed. Finally, generalized increases in social interaction between handicapped and nonhandicapped children accompanied training.

So far, the studies reviewed support the feasibility of using nonhandicapped children to assist in the development of their handicapped peers. But what about the effects of integration on nonhandicapped children? Certainly, integrated programs must meet the individual needs of all children, including those who are nonhandicapped.

Data to answer this question are limited; however, evidence collected in integrated preschool settings, as measured by standardized tests, systematic observations, informal anecdotal evidence, and later school success, suggests that nonhandicapped children benefit from integrated programs at least to the same degree as would be expected if they had attended nonintegrated preschools.

Bricker and Bricker (1971, 1972), for example, used standardized intelligence tests and parental evaluation to assess the effects of the presence of handicapped children on the development of normal children. The development of normal children, as measured by standardized pre-and post-tests, progressed as expected with no regression effects noted. In terms of parental evaluations, the Brickers (1972) noted:

> The parents of all nine non-delayed children in the first year of the project and ten out of twelve of the non-delayed children in the second year were willing to re-enter their children in the program. None of the parents in the first year felt their non-delayed child had suffered any negative effect from interacting with less capable children, while two out of twelve during the second year said perhaps their children had picked up some undesired responses from non-delayed children. (pp. 6-7)

Similarly, Guralnick (1977) reports on preliminary data from a study in the experimental preschool at the National Children's Center in Washington, D.C. This program integrates handicapped and nonhandicapped children. Evidence from this study revealed no decrease in the constructiveness or appropriateness of the play of nonhandicapped children when playing with either handicapped or other nonhandicapped children. Some reduction in the frequency of associative play did occur, however, in the heterogeneous setting, but associative play seems to be increasing over time as interaction patterns become more firmly established.

Although the findings to date are reassuring, they are tentative, and additional explorations of the effects of integration on nonhandicapped children are needed.

Recommendations to Researchers and Educators. A need for continued research exists. Replications of many of the studies reported here are needed to determine if similar results will be obtained with different populations. Additionally, further research is needed to examine:

1. Normative patterns of social and play behavior between handicapped and nonhandicapped children in integrated preschool settings. Judgments cannot be made regarding the necessity for behavior change

strategies in integrated settings until we know more about the social behavior in such settings.

2. The extent to which young children with pronounced physical disabilities are accepted by and interact with their nonhandicapped peers. It may be that young nonhandicapped children will react more negatively to obvious physical disabilities than to more subtle handicaps like speech, language, and mental deficits.

3. The effect on social interaction of grouping children in structured activities. Are there optimal arrangements for grouping children according to developmental levels? Or according to interpersonal compatibility?

4. The effects on social interaction of furniture arrangements. Do open spaces facilitate interaction more readily than closed areas? Can different patterns of furniture arrangement be identified and their effects on social interaction assessed?

5. The effectiveness of nonhandicapped children in teaching academic and language concepts in structured instructional settings to their handicapped peers. Can teachers in small group settings train children as tutors or models while they focus attention on another, perhaps more disabled child?

6. The effects of placing children at different developmental levels in integrated settings. It seems plausible that developmentally delayed children would respond differently to peers of varying developmental levels. Researchers should begin to investigate the optimal developmental skill blend for integrated programs. Such research would, in turn, provide the educator with data on how best to match handicapped and nonhandicapped children by developmental skill levels.

7. The optimal ratio of handicapped to normal children in integrated settings. Do various ratios have a differential effect on the social and verbal behaviors of handicapped children? Of nonhandicapped children?

INTEGRATED PRESCHOOL PROGRAMS

Scattered throughout the early education literature are descriptions of preschool programs that have successfully integrated handicapped and nonhandicapped children. Several of the more prominent approaches to mainstreaming young children are briefly described in this section.

1. Kennedy, Northcott, McCauley, and Williams (1976) have reported on a program that integrates selected hearing-impaired children into a regular preschool setting with their normally hearing peers. This project, jointly sponsored by the University of Minnesota, the Minnesota State Department of Education, and the Minneapolis Public Schools, serves hearing-impaired children from birth through 6 years of age. Among its distinguishing features are: (1) an emphasis on

early detection and intervention, (2) the inclusion of parents in the educational process, and (3) integration into regular nursery school programs whenever possible. The project developers conduct a careful follow-up of their subjects and report that a high percentage of these children are later integrated into regular classes in the elementary and secondary grades. Kennedy et al. also investigated the social acceptance of a selected sample of hearing-impaired children by their normally hearing peers and found that their social acceptance was not significantly different, in general, than that of their hearing peers.

2. The Program at the Liberty County Preschool in Bristol, Florida, is another example of a center-based integration program. Here, handicapped and economically disadvantaged children ages 3 to 5 are grouped with their nonhandicapped peers. A special feature of this preschool program is a resource classroom which handicapped children attend for part of the day to receive intensive, individualized instructional services.

3. Another integrated preschool approach is the Handicapped Early Childhood Assistance Program sponsored by the Child Care and Development Services of Los Angeles, California. This program has as a primary goal the identification of emotionally handicapped children (ages 2 to 6) from low income homes and their integration with nonhandicapped children in a day care setting. Parents and paraprofessional aides study the basic concepts of child development and master techniques for educating young children. The development of techniques that parents and aides can use to enhance social interaction between handicapped and nonhandicapped children are emphasized in this program.

4. The Demonstration Diagnostic Intervention Model for Early Childhood at Houston, Texas, serves handicapped children in integrated settings that vary from Head Start to kindergarten programs. Initially, children are screened in hearing, distant vision, fine and gross motor coordination, language, learning skills, and social interaction. Children receive diagnostic services through individualized programs provided at model Kindergarten Learning Centers (KLCs). A highly skilled diagnostic team operates the KLCs within regular kindergarten classes and offers parent training programs.

5. Project PEECH (Precise Early Education of Children with Handicaps) is located on the Urbana-Champaign campuses of the University of Illinois. PEECH serves children who are mildly to moderately handicapped as well as children who exhibit multiple handicaps. Children attend one of seven integrated classrooms, each of which serves approximately ten handicapped and five normal children. Each classroom has a certified teacher and one or two paraprofessionals. In addition, each handicapped child is served by an ancillary staff consisting of a psychologist, a language therapist, and an occupational therapist,

all of whom aid the classroom teacher in writing individualized educational programs for each child and provide specialized instructional services for the handicapped child, both in therapy rooms and within the classroom itself during free play and small group activities.

The core of the PEECH approach is the individualization of educational objectives for both handicapped and nonhandicapped children. Instructional objectives are developed for each child in six areas of functioning: language, social, self-help, math, gross-motor, and fine motor. Programming toward each child's strengths and weaknesses is stressed. An initial assessment of each child is made through systematic observation of the child's functioning using a classroom assessment instrument entitled SCOAP (Systematic Classroom Observation Assessment and Programming) that was developed at the University of Illinois and is currently undergoing field testing at the PEECH replication sites.

The content and sequence of curriculum components used in PEECH are based on developmental guidelines. In this way, programming for handicapped and nonhandicapped children on the same set of normalizing objectives is possible.

In addition to instructional activities, numerous less structured activities, including various play, music, art, and other events, form additional key components of the PEECH program and constitute the majority of the day's activities. Children from all developmental levels are integrated. The extensive involvement of children at different developmental levels during play and other social and cultural activities reflects both the relative ease with which integration can occur in these more dynamic and free-flowing activities as well as the potential benefits of these interactions for the less advanced children.

PEECH, a nationally validated project being replicated throughout the country, is currently responding to the needs of staff members at these replication sites by further investigating methods for promoting social integration. Among the methods currently under study are peer modeling, peer reinforcement, peer imitation in the classroom, and the structuring of learning centers to promote social integration.

6. In Saginaw, Michigan, Project PAR prepares mentally handicapped 4- and 5-year-old children for placement in regular classes in the public school. PAR, which is coordinated with the Saginaw public school system, provides a high quality day care program to help preschoolers develop the skills and behaviors which ensure success in public school kindergartens.

7. Another project designed to help handicapped preschool children enter regular classrooms in the public schools is GOOD START, located within the Washington, D.C. Public School System. Eligible children are those who have never attended school or who have attended school in the primary grades but now need additional help for part of the school day before full placement in a

regular program can be achieved. The program serves children from 5 to 7 years of age for a half-day, five days a week.

8. The Behavioral Sciences Institute, Carmel, California, has developed an Accountable Re-entry Model (ARM) for handicapped children ages 4 to 8. The major objective of this project is to demonstrate that handicapped children, with systematic and programmed assistance, can reenter the mainstream. Children attend both a special class and a regular class until they demonstrate the academic, social, and motor skills needed to sustain them in the regular class. Parents and aides work directly with children in the special classroom.

9. The Diagnostic Resource Unit of the Martin Luther King, Jr. Child Development Center in Atlanta, Georgia, is working to integrate handicapped children into regular programs. The initial plan integrates three handicapped children into each of six local preschool programs. Center staff members offer diagnostic and resource assistance to the local programs.

10. Project Maine Stream, located in Cumberland Center, Maine, also serves as a consultant center for local nursery school teachers who have handicapped children integrated into their classrooms. A similar consulting function is provided by teachers, students, and faculty members at the integration model associated with Framingham State College, Framingham, Massachusetts.

11. A prominent example of an integrated open classroom for preschool children is the Eliot-Pearson Children's School, the laboratory school of the Department of Child Study, Tufts University, Boston. Approximately 100 children ranging in ages from 2½ to 6 years, attend Eliot-Pearson. Approximately 20% of these children have handicaps which range in severity from mild to moderate and include cerebral palsy, developmental delay, speech impairment, orthopedic handicaps, hearing impairment, emotional disturbance, epilepsy, learning disability, and Down's Syndrome. Students and faculty at Eliot-Pearson are currently investigating the unique problems associated with integrating handicapped and nonhandicapped children in open education environments.

12. In the learning center of Federal City College, Washington, D.C., handicapped children ages 2 to 6 are integrated into an open education environment with nonhandicapped peers. Weekly training sessions for the staff are open to parents, and concentrate on helping teachers meet the special needs of educating handicapped children in open environments.

13. Project RAPYHT (Retrieval and Acceleration of Promising Young Handicapped and Talented) at the University of Illinois is another example of a preschool program which integrates handicapped and nonhandicapped children in an open classroom. RAPYHT, however, also offers a structured program based on the Guilford model of intelligence. A unique feature of RAPYHT is its attempt to identify and serve gifted children who are also handicapped, and to integrate gifted handicapped children with nonhandicapped children.

14. Bricker and Bricker (1971, 1972, 1973, 1976) have developed an early intervention project at the Mailman Center in Florida that integrates developmentally retarded toddlers with normally developing nonhandicapped children. Their investigations focus on the effects of integration on the nonhandicapped child. As mentioned earlier, the Brickers conclude, on the basis of data collected through standardized tests, structured behavioral observations, and anecdotal information, that the development of the nonhandicapped child is not adversely affected by integration. In addition, the responses of parents of the nonhandicapped children have been positive and generally supportive of the program.

15. Researchers at the Teaching Research Infant and Child Care Center, Monmouth, Oregon, are currently investigating the feasibility of integrating severely handicapped preschool children into a normal program with nonhandicapped peers. Preliminary results suggest that, given a highly trained staff capable of delivering highly specialized services, severely handicapped preschool children can be mainstreamed and will benefit from systematic exposure to normally functioning peers. The results also suggest, however, that mainstreaming the severely handicapped into normal preschool settings is probably not feasible on a widespread basis, and should be restricted to settings with highly trained personnel and a very low student-teacher ratio (e.g., 2 to 1).

16. The Sonoma County Office of Education, in collaboration with Santa Rosa Junior College and California State College, currently directs three projects that provide integrated educational experiences to handicapped and normally developing youngsters from 6 months to 6 years of age. The functional level of the handicapped children ranges from severely/multiply impaired (IQ of 25) to mildly delayed (IQ: 65-85). A major goal of the Sonoma project is to generate educationally effective strategies for promoting social interaction between handicapped and nonhandicapped children that can be replicated. The current area of research interest at the Sonoma project is peer imitation training.

17. Michael Guralnick (1976a) reports on research conducted at an integrated preschool in the National Children's Center in Washington, D.C. The development of replicable strategies for using nonhandicapped preschoolers as intervention agents in the development of their handicapped peers is an important area of research here. In general, Guralnick's studies suggest that the presence of nonhandicapped children has an independent positive effect on their handicapped peers.

The list of integrated preschool projects reviewed here is extensive but by no means exhaustive. Numerous other integrated approaches are reported in the preschool literature. These include Head Start programs (Klein & Randolph, 1975) and programs integrating hearing-impaired (Luterman & Luterman, 1974; Pollack & Ernst, 1973) and blind (Tait, 1974) preschoolers with their normally functioning peers.

Preschool integration offers exciting challenges and raises a number of issues. In part, these issues are common to all early childhood intervention programs but become more complex with heterogeneous populations. In this final section, seven basic issues pertaining to the integration of handicapped and nonhandicapped preschool children are identified: (1) preservice training, (2) inservice training, (3) training for university faculty, (4) preschool models for integrating handicapped and nonhandicapped children, (5) the integration of handicapped children into different model approaches, (6) criteria for least restrictive placement, and (7) the evaluation of integrated preschool programs.

Preservice Training

Successful mainstreaming in preschool settings will necessitate substantial modifications in the preservice training of all *future* preschool teachers. The crucial issue involved here is, who will teach in integrated preschool settings? Presently, training programs prepare teachers to work exclusively with either handicapped or normal preschool children. Course work for these two groups differs, and programs for teachers of the handicapped emphasize assessment, evaluation, and behavior management. The critical questions seem to be: (1) Should we prepare teachers of normal young children to teach the mildly and moderately handicapped? (2) Should teachers of the handicapped be trained to work with normal young children as well? (3) Should resource specialists be trained to work with young children with a variety of handicaps?

Inservice Training

An intensive program of ongoing inservice training for all staff personnel is an important component of any integrated program for at least two reasons. First, problems associated with any preschool program become more complex when that program integrates handicapped and nonhandicapped children. Teachers in such preschools must stay abreast of current developments in research and practice. Secondly, many teachers and ancillary personnel active in preschool programs have never worked with handicapped children but soon will be required to do so. It is of critical importance to disseminate basic knowledge about handicapped children to such personnel and to monitor their attitudes toward handicapped children.

What competencies should be included in inservice training? These may vary with the site, but the following competencies are essential: (1) mastering identification and screening procedures, (2) conducting diagnostic evaluations, (3) promoting language development, (4) achieving strong parent involvement, (5) ensuring the total development of the child, (6) implementing a comprehensive and efficient data collection, (7) securing and maintaining administrative support, and (8) individualizing instruction.

Training University Faculty

Mainstreaming training for preschool teachers will require early childhood educators as well as special education faculties to participate in joint planning and program development. If course work regarding handicapped students is merged with courses in the regular education curriculum, special education faculty members must act as resource consultants to the regular education faculty. There are other cooperative endeavors these faculties might initiate: they could aid each other in preparing reading lists and resource guides; they might team-teach courses; they could develop joint research programs; and they might work together to adapt already existing curriculum materials.

Integrated Handicapped Children into Different Model Approaches

Most effective early childhood programs, whether or not they are integrated, are conducted within an identifiable educational or developmental framework. Some early childhood programs, for example, reflect a Piagetian bias, others a behavior-analytic approach, and still others employ an open education framework. In each instance the program's theoretical base decidedly influences the implementation of various programming components (e.g., the structure of facilities, the nature of teacher-child interaction, the organization of space and time) which limits a program's ability to successfully accommodate children with differing handicapping conditions. An open classroom, for example, stresses complex and independent interactions with materials, and is therefore probably better suited to children with mildly handicapping conditions than children with moderate or severe disabilities.

Considering the widespread use of model approaches in early childhood, a major task for the field is to attempt to match a child to the model approach most sensitive to the varied, complex, and often subtle needs posed by his unique handicapping condition. This will require educators to identify those components of a given approach most likely to influence its success in integrating handicapped preschool children.

Criteria for Least Restrictive Environment

Young handicapped children with varying degrees of disabilities currently receive educational services in one of the following settings: (1) self-contained schools on the grounds of residential facilities; (2) self-contained private schools; (3) self-contained public schools; (4) self-contained classes within regular schools; or (5) regular classes within regular schools.

These placements represent a continuum from the most to the least restrictive environment. According to P.L. 94-142, the placement of children in each of these environments must be justified. Yet, in preschool education, no criteria exist. While we offer no criteria here, the following considerations should be useful in establishing criteria:

1. The development of standardized checklists of behaviors, based on developmental guidelines, for functioning levels in each environment.
2. The ratio of handicapped to nonhandicapped students.
3. The extent to which environments will need to be reinforced to support handicapped children.
4. The extent to which the organization of the school day and the content of curriculum resembles a regular class environment.
5. The extent to which children require specialized ancillary services.

Evaluation of Integrated Preschool Programs

A final issue to be discussed concerns the most appropriate dimensions on which to evaluate integrated preschool programs. In the past, integrated programs for older children have depended upon pre-post standardized intelligence measures. But, as has been noted many times (e.g., Evans, 1974, Evans, E. Measurement practices in early childhood education. In R. Colvin (ed)., Preschool Education: theory and practice. New York: Springer, 1974.), such measures are often unreliable with young children, especially the handicapped.

Instead, success in integrated programs can be evaluated in a number of ways. First, and most significantly, an integrated program can be assessed for its ability to meet the developmental needs of children. Second, benefits received by handicapped children that are directly linked to involvement with nonhandicapped children must be examined. For example, does the observation by handicapped children of their nonhandicapped peers facilitate learning? Third, the extent to which a program promotes positive social contacts between handicapped and nonhandicapped peers may be evaluated. Fourth, the satisfaction of parents of handicapped and nonhandicapped children should be assessed, as well as the attitudes of the parents of normal children toward the handicapped children. Fifth, later school adjustment of handicapped and nonhandicapped childred who attended integrated preschools will need to be examined. Each of these assessments will require the adaptation of existing instruments and the development of new instruments for appropriate and sensitive evaluation.

REFERENCES

Allen, K. E., Benning, P. M., & Drummond, W. T. Integration of normal and handicapped children in a behavior modification preschool: A case study. In G. Semb (Ed.), *Behavior Analysis and Education.* Lawrence, Kansas: University of Kansas Support and Development Center, 1972.

Allen, K. E., Turner, K. I., & Everett, P. M. A behavior modification classroom for Head Start children with problem behaviors. *Exceptional Children,* 1970, *37,* 119-127.

Apolloni, T., Cooke, S. A., & Cooke, T. P. Establishing a normal peer as a behavioral model for delayed toddlers. *Perceptual and Motor Skills,* 1977, *44,* 231-241.

Bandura, A., Grusec, J., & Menlove, F. Vicarious extinction of avoidance behavior. *Journal of Personality and Social Psychology,* 1967, *5,* 16-23.

Bijou, S. W., & Baer, D. M. *Child development: Universal stage of infancy,* Vol. 2. Englewood Cliffs, N.J.: Prentice-Hall, 1965.

Bijou, S. W., & Baer, D. M. *Child development: A systematic and empirical theory,* Vol. 1. Englewood Cliffs, N.J.: Prentice-Hall, 1961.

Birch, J. W. *Mainstreaming: E.M.R. children in regular classes.* Reston, Virginia: Council for Exceptional Children, 1974.

Blankenshop, C. S. Illinois Interim Resource Manual for Preparing Individualized Education programs. Springfield, Il., Illinois Office of Education, 1977.

Body, M. K. Patterns of aggression in nursery school. *Child Development,* 1955, *26,* 3-11.

Bricker, W. A., & Bricker, D. D. The infant, toddler and preschool research and intervention project. In T. D. Tjossem (Ed.), *Intervention strategies for high risk infants and young children.* Baltimore, Md.: Univ. Park Press, 1976.

Bricker, D. D., & Bricker, W. A. Infant, toddler and preschool research and intervention project report: Year III. IMRID Behavioral Science Monograph 23, Institute on Mental Retardation and Intellectual Development. Nashville, Tennessee: George Peabody College, 1973.

Bricker, D. D., & Bricker, W. A. Toddler research and intervention project report: Year II. IMRID Behavioral Science Monograph 21, Institute in Mental Retardation and Intellectual Development. Nashville, Tennessee: George Peabody College, 1972.

Bricker, D. D., & Bricker, W. A. Toddler research and intervention project report: Year I. IMRID Behavioral Science Monograph 20, Institute on Mental Retardation and Intellectual Development. Nashville, Tennessee: George Peabody College, 1971.

Buell, J., Stoddard, P., Harris, F. R., & Baer, D. M. Collateral social development accompanying reinforcement of outdoor play in a preschool child. *Journal of Applied Behavior Analysis,* 1968, *1,* 167-174.

Burke, J. Children with visual disabilities. In R. Reger (Ed.), *Preschool programming of children with disabilities.* Springfield, Ill.: Charles C. Thomas, 1970, Pp. 94-103.

Cegelka, W. J., & Tyler, J. L. The efficacy of special class placement for the mentally retarded in proper perspective. *Training School Bulletin,* 1970, *67,* 33-68.

Cohen, J. S., & DeYoung, H. The role of litigation in the improvement of programming for the handicapped. In L. Mann & D. A. Sabatino (Eds.), *The first review of special education,* (Vol. 2), New York: Grune & Stratton, 1973.

Cooper, M. L., Lee, C. J., Bierlein, M. W., Wolf, M. M., & Baer, D. M. The development of motor skill and consequent social interaction in a withdrawn nuersey school child by social reinforcement procedures. Unpublished manuscript, University of Kansas, 1966.

Dailey, R. Dimensions and issues in "74": Tapping into the special education grapevine. *Exceptional Children,* 1974, *40,* 503-507.

Devoney, C., Guralnick, M. J., & Rubin, R. V. Integrating handicapped and nonhandicapped preschool children: Effects on social play. *Childhood Education,* 1974, *50,* 360-364.

Deutsch, M. Facilitating development in the preschool child: Social and psychological perspectives. *Merrill-Palmer Quarterly,* 1964, *10,* 249-263.

Edwards, T., & Stern, C. A comparison of three intervention programs with disadvantaged preschool children. *Journal of Special Education,* 1970, *4,* 205-214.

Feitelson, D., Weintraub, S., & Michaeli, O. Social interaction in heterogeneous preschools. *Child Development,* 1972, *43,* 1249-1259.

Fredericks, H. D., Jordan, V., Gage, M. A., Levak, L., Alrick, G., & Wadlow, R. *A Data-based classroom for the moderately and severely handicapped.* Monmouth, Oregon: Instructional Development Corp., 1975.

Goodman, L. V. A bill of rights for the handicapped. In *American Education.* Washington, D.C.: U.S. Department of Health, Education and Welfare, U.S. Govt. Printing Office, 1976.

Goodman, H., Gottlieb, J., & Harrison, R. H. Social acceptance of E.M.R.'s integrated into a nongraded elementary school. *American Journal of Mental Deficiency, 1972, 76,* 412-417.

Gottlieb, J., & Budoff, M. Social acceptability of retarded children in nongraded schools differing in architecture. *American Journal of Mental Deficiency, 1973, 78,* 15-19.

Green, E. H. Friendship and quarrels among preschool children. *Child Development, 1933, 4,* 237-252.

Guess, D., Sailor, W., Rutherford, G., & Baer, D. M. An experimental analysis of linguistic development: The productive use of the plural morpheme. *Journal of Applied Behavior Analysis, 1968, 1,* 297-306.

Guralnick, M. J. A planning process for developmental programming for handicapped preschool children: Language development as a model. Paper presented at the annual meeting of the Council for Exceptional Children, Atlanta, Georgia, 1977.

Guralnick, M. J. The value of integrating handicapped and nonhandicapped preschool children. *American Journal of Orthopsychiatry, 1976,* (a) *46,* 236-245.

Guralnick, M. J. Early childhood intervention: The use of nonhandicapped peers as edutional and therapeutic resources. Paper presented at the International Congress of the International Association for the Scientific Study of Mental Deficiency, Washington, D.C., 1976. (b)

Guralnick, M. J., & Paul-Brown, D. The nature of verbal interactions among handicapped and nonhandicapped preschool children. *Child Development, 1977, 48,* 254-260.

Hobbs, N. *The Futures of Children.* San Francisco, Calif.: Jossey-Bass, 1975.

Hunt, J. McV. *Intelligence and Experience.* New York: Ronald Press, 1961.

Iano, R. P., Ayers, D., Heller, H. B., McGettigan, J. F., & Walker, V. S. Sociometric status of retarded children in an integrative program. *Exceptional Children, 1974, 40,* 267-271.

Jersild, A. T., & Markey, F. V. Conflicts between preschool children. *Monographs of the Society for Research in Child Development, 1935, 21.*

Johnson, M. W. The effect on behavior of variation in amount of play equipment. *Child Development, 1935, 6,* 56-68.

Karnes, M. B., & Teska, J. A. Children's responst to intervention programs. In J. J. Gallagher (Ed.), *The application of child development research to exceptional children.* Reston, Virginia: Council for Exceptional Children, 1975. Pp. 196-243.

Karnes, M. B. A meliorative preschool program. *Horizons, 1970, 3,* 1-2.

Kaufman, M., Gottlieb, J., Agard, J., & Kukic, M. Mainstreaming: Toward an explication of the construct. In E. L. Mayer, L. A. Vergason, & R. J. Whelan (Eds.), *Alternatives for teaching exceptional children.* Denver, Colo.: Love, 1975, 35-54.

Kennedy, P., Northcott, W., McCauley, R., & Williams, S. Longitudinal sociometric and cross-sectional data on mainstreaming hearing impaired children: Implications for preschool programming. *The Volta Review, 1976, 78,* 71-81.

Kennedy, P., & Bruininks, R. H. Social status of hearing impaired children in regular classrooms. *Exceptional Children, 1974, 40,* 336-342.

Kirk, S. A. *Early education of the mentally retarded.* Urbana, Ill.: Univ. of Illinois Press, 1958.

Klein, J. W., & Randolph, L. A. Placing handicapped children in Head Start Programs. *Children Today, 1974, 3,* (6), 7-10.

Lee, R. C. The use of contingent teacher attention to increase the frequency of positive social interactions between a socially isolated preschool child and a socially outgoing peer. Unpublished manuscript, University of Illinois at Champaign-Urbana, 1977.

Levitt, E., & Cohen, S. Attitudes of children toward their handicapped peers. *Childhood Education,* 1976, *52,* (3).

MacMillan, D. L., Jones, R. L., & Meyers, C. E. Mainstreaming the mildly retarded: Some questions, cautions and guidelines. *Mental Retardation,* 1976, *14,* (17), 3-10.

Markey, F. V. Imaginative behavior of preschool children. *Monographs of the Society for Research in Child Development,* 1957, *28,* 149-159.

Mills v. Board of Education of the District of Columbia, Civil Action No. 1939-71 (D.D. C. 1973).

Murphy, L. B. *Social behavior and child personality.* New York: Columbia Univ. Press, 1937.

Parton, D. A. Learning to imitate in infancy. *Child Development,* 1976, *47,* 14-31.

Peck, C. A., Apolloni, T., Cooke, T. P., & Cooke, S. R. Teaching developmentally delayed toddlers and preschoolers to imitate the free-play behavior of nonretarded classmates: Trained and generalized effects. Unpublished manuscript, 1976.

Peterson, N. L., & Haralick, J. G. Integration of handicapped and nonhandicapped preschoolers: An analysis of play behavior and social interaction. *Education and Training of the Mentally Retarded,* 1977, *12,* (3).

Piaget, J. *The origins of intelligence in children.* New York: International Universities, 1952.

Pollack, D., & Ernest, M. Learning to listen in an integrated preschool. *Volta Review,* 1973, *75,* 359-367.

Porter, R. H., Ramsey, B., Tremblay, A., Iaccobo, M., & Crawley, S. Social interactions in heterogeneous groups of retarded and normally developing children: An observational study. In G. P. Sackett (Ed.), *Observing behavior. Vol. 1: Theory and applications in mental retardation.* Baltimore, Md.: Univ. Park Press, 1978.

Prescott, E., Jones, E., & Kritchevsky, S. Group day care as a child rearing environment: An observational study of day care programs. Pasadena, Calif.: Pacific Oaks College, 1967. ERIC No. ED 024-453.

Quilitch, H. R., & Risley, T. R. The effects of play materials on social play. *Journal of Applied Behavior Analysis,* 1973, *6,* 573-578.

Rubenstein, J., & Howes, C. The effects of peers on toddler interaction with mother and toys. *Child Development,* 1976, *47,* 597-605.

Shores, R. E., Huster, P., & Strain, P. S. Effects of teacher presence and structured play on child-child interaction among handicapped preschool children. *Psychology in the Schools,* 1976, *13,* 171-175.

Smith, J. O., & Arkans, J. R. Now more than ever: A case for the special class. *Exceptional Children,* 1974, *40,* 497-502.

Strain, P. S., & Wiegernik, R. The effects of sociodramatic activities on social interaction among behaviorally disordered preschool children. *Journal of Special Education,* 1976, *10,* 71-75.

Strain, P. S., & Timm, M. S. An experimental analysis of social interaction between a behaviorally disordered preschool child and her classroom peers. *Journal of Applied Behavior Analysis,* 1974, *7,* 583-590.

Strichart, S. S. Effects of competence and nurturance on imitation of nonretarded peers by retarded adolescents. *American Journal of Mental Deficiency,* 1974, *78,* 665-674.

Tait, P. E. Believing without seeing: Teaching the blind child in a regular kindergarten. *Childhood Education,* 1974, *50*(5), 285-291.

The Pennsylvania Association for Retarded Children (PARC) v. The Commonwealth of Pennsylvania, Civil Action No. 71-42 (E.D.Pa. 1971).

Updegraff, R., & Herbst, E. K. An experimental study of the social behavior stimulated in young children by certain play materials. *Journal of Genetic Psychology*, 1933, *42*, 372-391.

Wahler, R. G. Child-child interactions in free field settings: Some experimental analyses. *Journal of Experimental Child Psychology*, 1967, *5*, 278-293.

Weintraub, F., Abeson, A., Ballard, J., & Lavor, J. L. *Public policy and the education of exceptional children*. Reston, Virginia: Council for Exceptional Children, 1976.

Wolfensberger, W. *The principle of normalization in human services*. Toronto, Canada: National Institute on Mental Retardation. 1972.

Wynne, S., Ulfelder, L. S., & Dakof, G. *Mainstreaming and early childhood education for handicapped children: Review and implications of research*. Final Report, Contact OEC–74–9056. Washington,D.C.: Bureau of Education for the Handicapped, 1975.

3

What Head Start Means to Families

Ruth Ann O'Keefe

*Family Services Planning Director,
Department of the Navy;
Washington, D.C.*

Head Start was conceived and implemented from its earlier moments as a broad, comprehensive program which was to provide educational, health, and social services to low-income children with a family context. The purpose of this discussion is to highlight and describe some of the specific ways and areas in which Head Start is charged with involving and serving parents and families, and to present available evidence bearing on the extent to which Head Start is in fact doing what it has been charged to do. Attention will also be given to three efforts within Head Start which are especially family-focused: the Parent-Child Centers, Home Start, and the Child and Family Resource Program.

The information is drawn from both written and oral sources, all of which are detailed in the references. Specifically cited written sources include 18 original Head Start studies/evaluations and 6 major reviews/analyses of Head Start (and other) studies. In addition, other written documents (such as handbooks, guides, Performance Standards, letters) are cited, while numerous others, although not cited specifically, served to provide a backdrop and to validate the general context and findings presented in the paper. In addition, about fifteen individuals with extensive Head Start knowledge and experience contributed suggestions, opinions, and facts that helped shape the paper.

[1] Dr. Ruth Ann O'Keefe served as the National Director of the Home Start and the Child and Family Resource Programs of the Head Start Bureau, Administration for Children, Youth, and Families, HEW, 1971 to 1978.

The assumption underlying parent involvement has been that benefits to parents which resulted from opportunities for their development and participation would both directly and indirectly be passed on to the children in the family. Considerable evidence to support this assumption has emerged over the years from the work of a number of researchers. For example, Susan Gray (Gray & Ruttle, 1978)—who originally coined the term "vertical diffusion" to describe the benefits to all children within a family when parents are the focus of the child development program—has found sustained gains in children over a 2-year period, when parents were an important focus of a program. Phyllis Levenstein (1978) found that the parenting behavior of parents of 4-year-old children correlated well with various aspects of the children's competence when observed two years later, at age 6, in the child's classroom. And Irving Lazar (1977) found that the persistence of program effects for children in child development programs was particularly strong when parental involvement and participation were high.

The Cooke memo (1965) which outlined the philosophical foundation for Head Start, laid the groundwork for parent participation as we know it today by recommending that parents assist in planning the program, participate in parent education programs, participate in their children's classrooms, serve as a link between children, staff and neighborhood, and fill appropriate job roles in the program (Cooke, 1965, p. 4).

Accordingly, the evaluation study which looked at the very first Head Start effort during the summer of 1965 included descriptions of, and effects on parents, families, and communities, as well as the children themselves (Cort, H. R., Jr., Commins, W. D., Deavers, K. L., O'Keefe, R. A., and Ragan, J. F., Jr., 1966). While the actual impact of the 1965 summer program could barely be assessed at the time of the evaluation study, the evaluation was able to document parent participation and the considerable opportunities provided by these earliest programs for the parents' own development. Thus, even though in the summer of 1965 many Head Start programs construed Head Start goals fairly narrowly as school readiness (Cort et al., 1966, Sec. III, p. 29), 74% of the teachers felt responsible for helping families solve problems, 42% felt responsibility for helping parents learn about their children, and hundreds of programs— even in the crunch of that first brief summer program—offered programs to parents in childrearing, and homemaker and consumer education (Cort et al., 1966, Sec. III, p. 35).

Of course, the early Head Start programs were considerably different in quality from recent ones, and our primary interest here is in how Head Start relates to and supports parents, families, and communities today. Still, it is worth remembering that many of the Head Start ideas and experiences taken for granted today were revolutionary in the early days of the program. For example, a study of 25 parents whose children were enrolled in the Dane County Wisconsin

Head Start program (Adams, 1976) at various times during the 1966-1972 period revealed that for nearly all these parents (96%), preschool for their children was a totally new idea. And for all of them, a preschool experience of any kind for their child would have been impossible without Head Start. None of these parents had ever been visited in their home by a "school" person before, and the idea and experience of "volunteering" was totally new (Adams, 1976, pp. 6-7). Thus, the ideas and experiences that form the very foundation of Head Start—and which can easily be taken for granted today—were startingly new to many parents when Head Start began. Little precedent existed for the idea that low-income parents could not only be valued contributors and participators in programs but could have important decision-making roles.

In 1972 a giant step was taken with the issuance of the Head Start Program Performance Standards (U.S. Department of Health, Education and Welfare, July, 1975). Revised in 1975, these standards are the programmatic heart of the program. Although it is well-known that the Parent Involvement Performance Standards spell out Head Start's responsibilities to parents, it is not as well-known that, in fact, all program component areas (education, health, and social services, as well as parent involvement) address the role of Head Start parents. Three of the 5 program objectives in the Education component are aimed directly at parents, as are 3 of the 5 Social Service, and 6 of the 14 Health objectives. All the Parent Involvement Performance Standards clearly place parents at the core of the Head Start program, and both require and provide extensive opportunities for parents to be served by the Head Start program as well as to serve (participate in) the program.

It is clear that parent participation and involvement are intended to permeate Head Start and that Head Start is intended to affect, build, and strengthen parents (and through them, entire families), as well as children. If Head Start has done this and is continuing to do so, its effect must be widespread, for since 1965 Head Start has involved not only 6,500,000 children in the more than 10,000 Project Head Start Child Development Centers, but also 7 million parents, and 15 million brothers and sisters (as well as 500,000 adult staff and volunteers) (Datta, in press).

Let us look now at specific aspects of Head Start as it relates to parents, families, and communities, to see what such aspects really mean and how well Head Start is fulfilling its charge.

Decisionmaking

Parents as decision makers in the Head Start program and parents as childrearers are the two "fundamental roots" of parents' relationships to Head Start.[2] A

[2] An important offshoot of the decision-making "root" which was especially notable in the early days of Head Start was the kind of political action exemplified by parents involved in the Child Development Group of Mississippi (CDGM). For a complete account of the CDGM experience, see Greenberg (1969).

1978 study by Associate Control, Research and Analysis, Inc. (ACRA) which looked at opportunities for parent involvement in a nationally representative sample of 38 Head Start programs, found that 89% of the members of the policy-making councils/committees were in fact parents or former parents (Stubbs, Godky, & Alexander, 1978, p. 19). All programs had parents on their SAVI (program self-assessment) teams and in 91% of the programs parents helped in developing the plans to correct whatever weaknesses were identified in the SAVI process (Stubbs et al., 1978, p. 25). Parents' ideas and suggestions were reflected in the program work plans of 87% of the programs, 58% of the programs involved parents in conducting a community needs assessment, and 80% involved parents in hiring of staff (Stubbs et al., 1978, pp. 21, 23). Parents were also involved in making decisions about program operations at the center and classroom levels; 88% of the programs indicated that parents helped in such functions as determining parent volunteer activities, deciding on how parent activity funds would be used, and selecting sites for field trips (Stubbs et al., 1978, p. 22). Ninety-two percent of the programs indicated they had a specific process (such as survey, written communication, or meeting) to solicit parents' ideas about program operations (Stubbs et al., 1978, p. 20).

The ACRA study also looked at parent involvement in decision making for each program component. Most of the decision making revolved around reviewing the work plans for the various components and raising questions, suggesting changes, and working on revisions (Stubbs et al., 1978, p. 32). For most of the 38 programs, there was more parental involvement in planning the nutrition, health, and social services components than in the education component.

Parents and Their Own Children

Head Start offers almost unlimited opportunities for parents to strengthen their understandings and skills as parents. In the ACRA study 86% of the Head Start teachers sampled reported that they had provided parents with training on how to recognize opportunities and activities that could be capitalized upon as learning activities in the home. All 76 teachers in the sample held informal conferences with parents about their children's progress, and 92% held scheduled conferences (Stubbs et al., 1978, p. 42).

Teachers also sent home activities for the children to do; 66% of the Head Start teachers in the ACRA study said they regularly sent "homework" suggestions, 87% of the teachers reported that parents requested such reinforcement suggestions, and, in fact, about 21% of the requests for home activities were initiated specifically by the parents (Stubbs et al., 1978, p. 42). According to the Head Start teachers, 43% of the children showed evidence that someone was working with them at home to help reinforce experiences in the classroom (Stubbs et al., 1978, p. 43).

Recent program data show an increasing interest among parents in the Head Start home-based option (1978) in which parents are helped by Head

Start Home Visitors to fulfill Head Start goals for their own children in the home setting. Initially favored primarily by rural communities as a necessary alternative to a preferred center-based program, the home-based option is now being more widely accepted by urban families who want support from Head Start in helping them identify and meet their children's developmental needs at home. About one-third of all Head Start programs now offer a home-based option to some or all of their families, and about 7% of Head Start children are currently enrolled in such an option (Head Start, 1978). (It is worth noting that about 90% of the home-based programs do provide regular—generally weekly—group experiences for the children in addition to the Home Visit program (Coleman, 1977, p. 10).

Parents as Paid Employees and Volunteers

The ACRA study indicated that about 32% of Head Start staff were parents of children currently or formerly enrolled (Stubbs et al., 1978, p. 46). Employed parents were provided many opportunities for further training. Another recent study of HSST/CDA showed that 38% of CDA trainees were employed Head Start parents (Gilman & Signatur, 1978; Personal communication with Gilman, June 8, 1978).

Volunteering is an important part of Head Start. In the ACRA study an average of about 5 parents per program volunteered in the classroom on a weekly basis, another 10 volunteered at least once a month, and another 13 parents volunteered their time in the classroom about once every six months (Stubbs et al., 1978, p. 46). Parents also volunteered in the other program components, although opportunities were not as extensive as in the education component.

Parent volunteers in Head Start perform a wide variety of functions, including assisting with children in the classroom, helping with health screenings done in the center, planning menus (for example, 83% of the programs in the ACRA study used ideas suggested by ethnic parents), purchasing food, preparing meals (in 80% of the programs), planning holiday celebrations, recruiting families for Head Start, keeping records, helping with communications (phone calls, newsletters, etc.), and transporting children (Stubbs et al., 1978, pp. 47-50). Parents also serve on policy councils and work with their own children.

In another recent study (Abt Associates, 1978), 95% of the center directors of 32 nationally representative Head Start programs rated parent involvement as "frequent" or "occasional." Sixty-seven percent of the parents themselves said they had helped in the classroom, and 49% said they had helped at least once a month (Abt Assoc., 1978, p. 19).

These statistics as well as others, indicate clearly that Head Start is not yet reaching and actively involving all parents of enrolled children and must continue its efforts along these lines. (For example, if 49% of parents are helping out in the classroom at least once a month, then 51% of the parents are helping *less* than once a month. Indeed, for whatever percentage of parents who are involved and participating in any aspect of Head Start, there is a countervailing percentage of parents who are not.) However, it should also be noted that, although such figures certainly give an indication of the degree of some types of parent participation in Head Start, they do not give a complete picture because they do not reflect the innumerable instances of "invisible" parent participation: that is, participation and commitment of parents who, by choosing to place their children in Head Start, are investing time and effort in many ways not previously required, such as in readying the child on time each day or welcoming staff into their home. In fact, a 1976 study (by Adams) of 25 parents whose children had been in Head Start at various times between 1966 and 1972 highlighted the idea that, to many parents, the entire notion of receiving program staff into one's home or participating as volunteers or as policy-makers, or as contributors to any kind of program policy, planning or operation, was totally foreign to them prior to their Head Start experience (Adams, 1976, p. 7).

Although we do know that some parents in virtually all programs do participate in Head Start along the lines delineated in the Standards, there is little information available on what parent involvement and participation may mean to some parents who are not visibly and actively involved with the program as specified by the Standards. Indeed, for a family coping with unusual problems or a temporary crisis, having the child ready for bus pick-up may be just as meaningful as the involvement shown by another parent in contributing several hours in the classroom or actively engaging in policy council meetings. Thus, what is meant by active and meaningful parent participation really varies from family to family depending on the set of circumstances at any given time in each family's situation. The crux of the question, then, is "What constitutes active and meaningful involvement and participation for an individual parent?"

While the Performance Standards mandate and describe some areas of participation, they (rightly in our view) leave flexible how and to what extent individual parents should participate. Some parents undoubtedly play a more active role in the program per se than other parents—and it is important to encourage, document and study such participation. But if we are to arrive at a clearer and fuller understanding of parent involvement within Head Start it is just as important to document and study what parent involvement can mean and does mean to those parents to whom participation is personally significant, although less publicly evident.

Parents, Head Start, and the Community

The first Head Start study to document extensively the relationship between Head Start programs and the communities in which they are located was done by Kirschner Associates (1970). A representative national sample of 58 communities with full-year Head Start programs was studied from July, 1968 to January, 1970 to determine whether community health and educational institutions had changed in specific ways relevant to Head Start. Field interviews were done in 42 of the 58 communities, and 7 additional communities in which there was no Head Start were used for comparison purposes.

The study identified 1,496 changes in the Head Start communities, 80% of which were education-related and 20% of which were related to health institutions. By contrast, almost no changes were observed in the comparison communities. The Kirschner study was—and is—considered strong evidence of Head Start's positive influence in bringing about four categories of community change: (1) increased emphasis on the educational needs of the poor and minorities; (2) modification of health services and practices to serve the poor better and more sensitively; (3) increased involvement of the poor with community institutions, especially with respect to decision making; and (4) increased employment of local people in paraprofessional jobs (Kirschner Assoc., 1970, p. 6).

Positive changes were seen in all communities in the study. Considering that at the time this study began (Fall, 1968) most full-year programs had been in operation scarcely a year, these findings seem especially significant. And they seem to hold up over time. The recent ACRA study in April, 1978 identified five types of Head Start program community involvement as shown in the table below (Stubbs et al., 1978, p. 39).

The ACRA (Stubbs et al., 1978, p. 37) study also indicated that 97% of the programs had a list of available community resources for parents, that almost all programs (92%) distributed the lists to individual parents, and that in 82% of the programs parents received training in how to use the lists. (Parents themselves were involved in developing the resource lists in 71% of the programs.)

Types of Involvement	Percentage of Programs Involved
Head Start staff has joined community organizations to increase community's awareness of family needs	63.2%
HS staff has helped form community organizations	28.9%
Staff encourages parents to join organizations	76.3%
Training is given to parents on how they can participate in organizations	60.5%
Parents are encouraged to discuss the proceedings of public meetings with other parents and staff	71.1%

Head Start is also bringing families directly into contact with a number of social service agencies in communities. For example, the recent Abt study (March, 1978) indicated that when mental health, guidance, family planning clinics, or recreation facilities are available, they are used by 86%-90% of the programs (Abt Assoc., 1978, p. 17).

Some Head Start efforts are focused on making local communities more responsive to Head Start-related needs; other efforts are more broadly targeted. The Kirschner report cites (1970 pp. 6-12) many examples of Head Start's community involvement bringing about a change beneficial to the broader community, such as:

1. changing a regulation that required students in a school to purchase lunch (rather than having the option to bring a bag lunch) even though many students could not afford to buy a lunch.
2. getting a midwestern school system to employ indigenous teacher aides in low-income neighborhoods to tutor children after school.
3. desegregating a mental health facility in the South so that it actively reached out to black families.
4. establishing a visiting nurse program in Appalachia to provide routine nursing care to the sick, in an area with scarce medical services.

More recently, the California State Parent Association, comprised primarily of former Head Start parents, studied and took a stand on social issues such as housing, Proposition 13, and television commercials. And a 1976 study of 25 parents who were involved in Head Start at various times between 1966 and 1972 found that nearly half (44%) now serve on other community and agency boards and are involved actively and broadly in their communities (Adams, 1976, p. 12).

Some parents use their Head Start experience as a foundation on which to build strength in other Head Start programs and in the broader community. For example, a group of experienced Head Start parents in Washington, D.C. has organized as a consulting firm to train others in such areas as how to get and keep parent involvement, understanding group dynamics, conducting a business meeting, and organizing/using standing and special committees.

Countless parents have used their Head Start experience to equip themselves for jobs which exert a positive influence on the community. According to several long-time experts in Head Start parent programs, an impressive number of parents has gone on to become Community Action Program (CAP) directors, Head Start directors, consultants, teachers, officials in local and state governments, family day care providers, and business people.

Parents, Handicapped Children, and Head Start

In 1977, more than 18,000 parents of handicapped children (a significant increase over the previous year) received special services such as counseling, information and materials, referrals to other agencies, and transportation assistance (U.S. Dept. of Health, Education, and Welfare, 1978, p. 28). Handicapped parents who also had handicapped children often received instructional and other supportive services (Applied Management Sciences, 1978, p. 27).

Head Start has often played a powerful advocacy role on behalf of many handicapped children and their parents (e.g., with regard to legal rights, transition into public schools, and identification and mobilization of resources). For example, a recent account (from a New York State Head Start) details a seven-month struggle on the part of a Head Start "Child Services Specialist" to obtain legally allowable transportation for a handicapped child (Addition, 1978). The author of the case history—and there are many such case histories—concludes, "Looking back at the 7-½ months of red tape, I wonder how any parent can be expected to do all this, unless they have the supportive services of an involved agency."

The recent (April, 1978) evaluation study by Applied Management Sciences on the mainstreaming effort in Head Start indicated that parents of 27% of the children were very active in program activities, and another 29% were moderately active. The degree of parent activity was minor for 31% and nil for only 13% of the parents (Applied Management Sciences, 1978, p. 11.2). The major ways in which parents were involved with the Head Start program for their handicapped children were: keeping informed of the child's progress (81%), teaching the child at home (71%), approving the child's individual plan (53%), assisting in the evaluation of their child's progress (48%), and participating in classroom activities (38%) (Applied Management Sciences, 1978, p. 11.9).

According to available Head Start/Home Start program statistical data, about 18% of children in home-based programs are handicapped (as contrasted with 13% in overall Head Start). There are indications that parents are often working actively with Home Visitors to enable these children to participate in a regular "mainstreamed" Head Start program, in addition to receiving home-based services.

Increased Social Contacts

In a recent Abt study (March, 1978, pp. 6-10) 94% of the parents reported that Head Start provided welcome opportunities to get together with other parents. Countless parents have reported feeling that some of the isolation imposed by their environment and circumstance has been alleviated.

Family Needs Assessment

Recent contact with dozens of Head Start programs indicates that many programs are routinely conducting an assessment of family needs, strengths, and goals. Thus, upon enrollment of the child, information is obtained in such areas as the family's status and needs regarding housing, employment, education, vocational training goals, health, and transportation, as well as their eligibility for services such as EPSDT, food stamps, or public housing. The program staff then works with the family to help the family achieve its own goals and effectively link up with appropriate community services and resources.

Exploring Parenting

The Exploring Parenting program, a new curriculum aimed at increasing parents' effectiveness as the primary educators and developers of their own children, has been enthusiastically received by parents who have worked through the sessions. It will soon be available to all Head Start parents.

An adaption of Exploring Childhood (developed by Education Development Corporation, Massachusetts under an HEW contract), the program has five goals for parents: to get to know oneself better; to learn more about children; to examine various approaches to childrearing; to recognize and improve one's own parenting skills; and to examine how society influences family and children (Roy Littlejohn Assoc., 1977, pp. 66-67).

Three of the original 13 content sessions are focused on parents, families and the community, examining family relationships, ways in which such stress affects the family, and the expectations other groups outside the family have of the family and its members (Roy Littlejohn Assoc., 1978, p. 28). All parents who have evaluated Exploring Parenting have expressed a desire to see it continued and offered to other parents (Roy Littlejohn Assoc., 1978, p. 61), and, upon the strong recommendation of the parents in the pilot program, the number of sessions in this course has been increased from 13 to 20.

Post-Head Start Parent Involvement

Reference has already been made to ways parents use their Head Start experience as a springboard for future activity. However, the fact that many parents continue their community activism is important enough to merit another look at Head Start as it relates to parents after they leave Head Start.

The recent (March, 1978) Abt study of Head Start "graduates" tells us that most (82%) of Head Start graduates' parents have gone to their child's elementary school to meet and talk with the teacher (Abt Assoc., 1978, pp. 6-53). In addition, the large majority of parents felt that Head Start had helped them with regard to elementary school (Abt Assoc., 1978, p. 20): (See table on p. 53).

In addition to school-related post-Head Start parent activities, many parents have assumed responsible positions within and outside Head Start and in the community (as board members, etc.); and many have formed organizations through which to promote Head Start-related goals in the community. Thousands of parents have responded to educational and training opportunities by completing high school (G.E.D.), enrolling in and/or completing other educational courses, and generally improving their own skills and abilities.

Parents' Activities and Knowledge of the Current School Year	Percentage of Head Start Parents Agreeing
Head Start gave me a better under-standing of what children do in school	89%
HS helped me get acquainted with my child's teacher	62%
HS helped me to help my child with current schoolwork	80%
HS helped me to understand how children learn	91%
HS helped me to plan my child's current school program	79%

Impact on Parents and Families

This section recounts study findings—some of which have been mentioned earlier—which shed light specifically on the impact of Head Start on parents and, via parents, on families and communities.

Before 1969. Evidence of Head Start's impact on parents, families, and communities prior to 1969 is sketchy at best. The study of the Summer 1965 Head Start program reported on interviews with 1,742 parents, most of whom considered their contacts with Head Start teachers, parent meetings and other Head Start-related activities to have been worthwhile (Cort et al., 1966, Sec. IV, p. 128). The vast majority (88%) said they had a more hopeful outlook for their child's future as a result of Head Start, and 80% felt a new awareness in the community of concern about their problems (Cort et al., 1966, Sec. IV, p. 128). However, only a small percentage of parents felt that they themselves had directly received help, improved their job status, or planned to continue their education as a result of Head Start.

With regard to communities, some agencies were very supportive of, and involved with, Head Start during that first summer, and some were not. Public health, welfare agencies and schools were generally very supportive. In general, the people interviewed for the study (agencies in more than 1,000 communities which had a Head Start in Summer, 1965) considered the project to be worthwhile and believed it should be continued (Cort et al., 1966, Sec. IV, pp. 2, 9, 20). (The report also included summaries of a number of independent studies done during that first summer program. These studies, mostly funded by the Office of Economic Opportunity, focused on the effects of the program on the children.)

The evaluation of the 1966 full-year program did not focus on parents at all, but rather on the effects on children, with length of time in Head Start as the main independent variable and children's test scores as the main dependent variable (Cort, Commins, Henderson, Mattis, O'Keefe and Orem, 1967, p. 8).

The well-known "Westinghouse Report" studied children who had moved from Head Start into first, second, or third grade during the June, 1968-May, 1969 period. Although the study focused almost entirely on the impact of Head Start on children, parents of children in the study were interviewed and "voiced strong approval of the program and its influence on their children" (Westinghouse Learning Corp., 1969, p. 8). They also reported on their participation in the activities of the centers (Westinghouse Learning Corp., 1969, pp. 112-113).

1969-1976. An extensive and careful review (Mann, Harrell and Hurt, 1977) of Head Start research between 1969 and 1975 specifically examined findings concerning Head Start's impact on parents, families and communities. The reviewers identified 17 studies (9 of which were dissertations) done between 1969 and 1975 which addressed the question of impacts on (a) attitudes of parents towards their children, (b) behavioral changes in parents, and (c) parent participation as a factor in producing gains for children and their families. In addition, the reviewers identified 3 studies (two done in 1970 and one in 1972) which addressed the question of Head Start's role in influencing changes in the community. The findings are recounted below:

1. *Impact on attitudes.* The majority of studies reported an improvement in parenting abilities as well as satisfaction with the educational gains of their children. Indeed, parental reaction to Head Start was termed "overwhelmingly positive" (Mann et al., 1977, pp. 13, 40).
2. *Impact on behavior.* The studies which looked at changes in parents' behavior reported an increase in positive interactions between mothers and their children, as well as an increase in parent participation in later school programs. (The Home Start evaluation was specifically cited as showing that Home Start mothers, in comparison with mothers of control children, allowed their children to help more with household tasks, did more teaching of reading and writing skills, provided more books and playthings, and read to their children more often.) (Mann et al., 1977, pp. 13, 41)
3. *Impact on gains for children and families.* The reviewers concluded that parent participation is associated with positive gains for children and their families, but that the research to date had not identified what kinds of parent involvement result in most gain (Mann et al., 1977, p. 13). However, the reviewers commented, ". . . it is clear that high parental involvement is associated with gains both on the part of the child and the parent (p. 43). The 1972 MIDCO study, which was, of course, cited by the reviewers but is referred to now as a primary source, even suggested that "the mere identification with Head Start may be an asset to parents" (MIDCO Educ. Assoc., 1972, p. 45).

4. *Impact in and on the community.* The reviewers concluded that Head Start plays a role in bringing about community change (Mann et al., 1977, pp. 13, 44-45). Two of the studies were on Head Start (Kirschner, 1970, and MIDCO, 1972) and one on the Parent-Child Center (1970). The 1972 MIDCO study found that the greatest number of community changes—as well as the most significant changes—were reported in centers in which parent participation in both decision-making and learner-activities was rated high (MIDCO Educ. Assoc., 1972, p. 48).

1976-August, 1978. Phase II of the previously mentioned ACRA study will focus on the impact of various aspects of Head Start on parents and families—as well as children (Stubbs et al., 1978, p. 39). Until that study is completed, probably the richest source of current research data on the impact of Head Start on parents (and families) is the survey of Head Start "graduates" done by Abt Associates (1978, pp. 6-53).

In this study, 33% of the Head Start parents reported that Head Start had been either of some help, or a great deal of help, in dealing with family or personal problems. Only 16% of parents who had had children in other types of preschool programs responded in a similar manner. In addition, 82% of the Head Start parents reported that the program provided them with an opportunity to get together with other parents at least once a month, while only 48% of the other preschool parents reported this. The Abt report notes: "Meager as these data are, they suggest that a closer study of social services in Head Start would reveal that the program is successfully responding to a number of personal and family needs " (p. 18). Parents reported receiving medical and dental services, and felt they had greater knowledge of how to provide better nutritional and personal hygiene practices for their families (Abt Assoc., 1978, pp. 1-3). They reported that Head Start helped give them a better understanding of how children learn, what children do in school, how to help with the child's homework, and how to plan the child's school program. And 95% of the parents endorsed Head Start as being helpful to them personally (Abt Assoc., 1978, pp. 6-13, 15, 20). However, only 8% of the 647 parents responding in this study reported that Head Start had helped them find jobs, and only 9% that Head Start had helped them acquire further education (Abt Assoc., 1978, pp. 6-9).

In addition to the Abt study, there are other sources of information about the impacts of Head Start on parents and families:

The Region III study (Personal Communication with Dr. Paul Vicinanza, June 6, 1978). The Children, Youth, and Families Unit in Region III (Philadelphia) is currently completing a study in which more than 800 statements were obtained from parents in 13 programs in Region III during the 1976-77 program year concerning their views of Head Start's impact on them. It was found that the bulk of the family support services were provided in the health area through the health component. The nurse or health aide often served as a "medical social worker," making referrals, counseling, etc. The study also found that parents in

programs that had more personalized contact (for example, via home visits) between staff and parents tended to see themselves as having a more important
role in their own child's development than parents who had less personal contact
with the program.

The Dane County, Wisconsin study (Adams, 1976, p. 12). This study of 25
Head Start parents has been cited several times in this review. The study identified eight levels of parent involvement and related the parents' involvement to
the program's impact (or perceived impact) on the parents. The results described
and documented the eight levels of parent involvement and indicated that all
parents in the study felt that their participation had had favorable effects on
them regardless of their level of involvement. Most respondents reported changes
at several levels of involvement. The study notes that "the more intensely involved respondents seem to have more pronounced changes in themselves, and
give evidence of equally vast changes in economic status. Of the 13 highest on
the intensity index, 11 have moved from being "On Welfare to being Off Welfare" (pp. 13-14). Other types of effects or impacts reported included: increased
communication skills (84%), overwhelmingly favorable attitude towards Head
Start as a good entry into the job market, improved understanding of children,
widened horizons on the world of childrearing, increased acceptance by own
peer group, ability to apply new practical information to own lives, increased
education, increased employment opportunities, and increased commitment to
and participation in the broader community.

The Hertz impact study (1977). This review of federally funded early childhood
programs and how they affect children, parents, families and communities
serves to reinforce the trend of the cumulative findings of other studies: "The
bulk of the findings concerning impact on the family relate to changes in parental
attitude" (p. 27).

"The Parents Speak" study (1978) (Robinson & Choper, in press). This report
contains anecdotal evidence of the influence Head Start has had not only on the
children enrolled but on parents and families as well. Approximately 90 parents
in several programs across the country were interviewed, and were virtually
unanimous about the positive effects of Head Start, reporting:

1. Increased ability to deal with "the system";
2. More knowledge about children and child development;
3. Greater sense of control over own life;
4. More ability to feel at ease in social situations;
5. Increased appreciation of idea that they, as parents, are the key to
   their child's development—and increased ability to follow through on
   this idea;
6. Increased skills related to employment and employability;

7. Increased desire and opportunity to help others; and
8. Increased ability to continue involvement into the public school, as well as into the broader community.

Other aspects of the impact of Head Start on parents which have not been documented in writing but have been consistently mentioned by parents to ACYF specialists include:

1. Improved ability to identify and attain realistic goals;
2. Improved ability to deal with older siblings;
3. Strengthened cultural identity and self-concepts; and
4. Reduction in frequency of perceived family crises. (Personal Communications with Johnson, Davis, James, & Clark)

THREE SPECIAL HEAD START PROGRAMS

Virtually all the data and discussion in the preceding sections have been in reference to the regular Head Start program which enrolls preschool children between the ages of 3 and 5 and is governed by the Head Start Program Performance Standards. Three other programs, outside the regular Head Start program but funded as part of the overall Head Start effort, merit special attention because of their extensive commitment to support parents and families. These three programs are the Parent-Child Centers, Home Start, and the Child and Family Resource Program. A brief discussion of each follows.

Parent-Child Centers

First funded during 1968, the 36[3] Parent-Child Centers (PCCs) were a direct outgrowth of a 1966-1967 White House Task Force on Early Childhood which was convened by President Johnson (Costello, 1970, pp. 1-2). The program concept grew out of the increasing recognition at the time "that it is essential to assist children as early as possible in their lives, even before they are born" (Johnson, 1974, p. 4). The PCC strategy was to provide an array of services to low-income families who had at least one child under age 3.

Of the eight criteria that all PCC programs were required to meet, four were related specifically to parents and families, providing for: (1) health education for parents and siblings, family planning services and prenatal care; (2) parent activities designed to strengthen their understanding of child development; competence as family managers; skills essential to making a living, including maximum opportunities for PCC employment; self-confidence and self-image as parents; family relationships; and role of father within family; (3) social services

---

[3] In 1970 three of the 36 were renamed Parent-Child Development Centers and began concentrating on research and the development of specific program models.

for entire family[4] ; and (4) programs to increase family participation in the neighborhood and community (Costello, 1970, pp. 2-3).

Like Head Start, PCCs have provided employment to PCC parents; in 1974, 35% of all PCC staff were PCC participants (Johnson, 1974, p. 6).

Evaluations of PCC were undertaken in 1969 (Kirschner Assoc., 1969) and in 1972 (Center for Community Research, 1972).

The 1969 study. Some of the findings from the Kirschner (1969, pp. 140, 141, 155, 157-158, 163) report were:

1. Parents who had a genuine opportunity to select the kinds of programs they wanted tend to choose services for themselves, such as job training and employment, rather than direct services for the child.
2. Many PCCs saw themselves as "junior-sized Community Action Agencies" which would coordinate all possible services to families (p. 141).
3. The benefits to mothers in the areas of relaxation, socializing, and reducing loneliness were very important.
4. Parent participation was most active when the program was relevant to the parents.
5. PCC was perceived by most of the center directors as a service and education program focused on infants and their families.
6. Mothers reported improved health for themselves and, to some extent, for other family members (Costello, 1970, p. 36).
7. Most centers reported favorable effects on family life (Costello, 1970, p. 36).
8. PCCs were very effective in bringing together a variety of agencies serving children and families (Costello, 1970, p. 37).

Parents in PCCs were involved in all aspects of the program from the beginning. Among the types and examples of parent participation documented in the 1969 Kirschner study (p. 153), were: observing and assisting with children in the nursery; attending social functions such as "family nights" and outings; working with PCC staff to develop and plan activities not only for children, but for other family members as well; taking responsibility for implementing particular program activities; attending lectures and demonstrations; and initiating suggestions to make the program as relevant as possible.

The 1972 study. The 1972 PCC evaluation, conducted by the Center for Community Research in New York, provided a more complete picture of the PCCs.

---

[4]Between 1972 and 1974, 7 PCCs were funded with special "advocacy" components to expand their scope of activities. This effort was designed to identify and address, through a process of advocacy, the unmet needs of families with children from the prenatal stage through age 5 in a given target area served by the program. Such families included those being served by the PCC, as well as other families outside the PCC program but living in the area.

The evaluators visited 32 of the 33[5] PCCs between October, 1971, and January, 1972, and interviewed 385 parents and 327 PCC staff members. There were at that time about 100 children in each PCC, with an average age of 26 months.

The study documented a wide variety of health, education, and social service benefits to parents. About 95% of the parents reported positive impacts in areas such as their education, self-confidence, home-making and parenting (e.g., decrease in use of corporal punishment, increase in ability to recognize and meet children's needs and to enjoy their children) (Center for Community Research, 1972, pp. iv-v).

Although at that time there were few teen-age mothers in the PCCs, there was a huge increase in involvement from fathers, from almost none at the time of the 1969 study to more than 500 at the time of the 1972 study (Center for Community Research, 1972, pp. 23, 111).

There was ample evidence in the 1972 study that the PCCs offered a multitude of direct services to the families enrolled (e.g., 18 programs had the equivalent of their own social services *department,* 19 had a fund earmarked for family emergencies, and virtually all offered their own home management education). Most PCCs served also as a key coordinating mechanism for linking families to other existing medical, educational, legal, community and public agencies, departments and organizations (Center for Community Research 1972, pp. 31-32, 35, 36).

PCCs today. PCCs continue to garner enthusiastic support from participating parents, and, for the most part, are developing as strong family-focused programs. The Head Start Program Performance Standards are currently being revised to include Standards for PCCs, and additional technical assistance will soon be made available to the PCCs.

Home Start

The 16 Home Start demonstration programs were funded for a 3-½ year period (March, 1972 to June, 1975) to evaluate the feasibility of providing comprehensive Head Start services through a delivery system considerably different from that used in most Head Start programs. In Home Start, Head Start home visitors were trained and employed to work with parents in their own homes, helping them provide for their children the same kinds of activities, experiences, and services available in center-based programs. Three of the four major Home Start objectives addressed parents directly: to involve parents directly in the educational development of their children; to help strengthen in parents their capacity for facilitating the general development of their own children; and to demonstrate methods of delivering comprehensive Head Start-type services to children and parents (or substitute parents) for whom a center-based program is not feasible (O'Keefe, 1971, p. 2).

[5] The PCC in Alaska was not visited.

Each of the 16 Home Start demonstration programs received approximately $100,000 with which to serve about 80 families for each 12-month period. At any given time there were about 1,100 families participating in the 16 programs. They came from a wide variety of locales and represented many different ethnic, cultural and language backgrounds, including white, black, urban, rural, Appalachian, Eskimo, Native American, migrant, Spanish-speaking, and Oriental.

An evaluation of Home Start revealed that Home Visitors on the average undertook about eight different activities during a typical 60- to 90-minute home visit. Examples of various types of activities include (O'Keefe, 1973):

1. Nutrition:
Read and evaluate newspaper food ads with mother.*
Help mother develop shopping list.
Prepare snack or part of meal with mother and child as a means for increasing knowledge of nutrition.
Show mother how involving the child in meal preparation can be a learning experience for the child (e.g., noting colors, shapes and textures of food; counting eggs, spoons and other items; and language-expanding conversation).
Help family obtain food stamps of other food supplements for which family is eligible.
Arrange for local home economists to demonstrate preparation of nourishing but inexpensive food to small groups of mothers.

2. Health:
Help parents accompany child on visits to doctor or dentist.
Arrange first aid and home safety courses for parents.
Help parents assess and correct home hazards.
Give parents health information.
Show mother how to keep home health records.
Show mother how to assist child with oral hygiene.

3. Social Services:
Help parents obtain the referrals their family needs.
Acquaint parents with community and its resources, as necessary.
Help families arrange transportation.
Help arrange social activities to provide much needed social and recreational outlets.

4. Education:
Help parents recognize "everyday living experiences" that can be capitalized upon to become effective learning experiences.
Accompany parent and child to library.
Read story to child with mother.
Hold group meetings on child development.
Help parents learn ways of enhancing their children's language development.

*The mother was usually the adult at home; when the father was available, he was included in as many ways as possible.

Although the Home Start guidelines implicitly involved families, the program's operation made it inevitable:

> Each week brought Home Visitors into living rooms where children and parents played and lived; into kitchens where there often wasn't any food for the evening meal; and into complicated family affairs where husbands or wives were ill, in-laws needed help or older children were plagued by emotional or physical problems. (Hewett, Grogan, Rubin, Nauta, Stein and Jerome 1978, p. 106)

Siblings in the home were almost always (85% of the time) included in the home visit activities (Love, Nauta, Coelen, Hewett, Ruopp, 1976, p. 36).

More complete descriptions of these activities and of actual processes of Home Start (program operations, activities, parent involvement, staff training, etc.) can be found in the evaluation mentioned and in two other major Home Start publications, *A Guide for Planning and Operating Home-Based Child Development Programs* (Kirschner Assoc., 1974) and Hewett's *Partners with Parents* (Hewett et al., 1978).

The evaluation provided clear evidence that mothers working at home to promote the education and development of their own children could, with the support and assistance of a Head Start Home Visitor, elicit outcomes comparable to those attained by children attending regular Head Start centers (Love et al., 1976, p. 16). Home Start mothers did, in fact, encourage their children to help with household tasks, teach prereading and prewriting skills to their children, and provide books and playthings for their children (Love et al., 1976, pp. 14-16).

The Hertz (1977, p. 29) analysis of the impact of selected federal programs concluded, after analyzing the Home Start evaluation, that in Home Start, impact on parent attitudes and behavior followed the same lines as in Head Start, but appeared to be more positive and comprehensive.

The findings of the Home Start demonstration program have encouraged a number of Head Start programs to capitalize even more on the strengths of the parents vis-a-vis their own children. At present, approximately 400 Head Start programs (about one-third of all programs) are serving a total of about 20,000 children through a home-based option.[6] (As in the Home Start demonstration, the home-based options usually provide a regular group experience—usually weekly—for the children, in addition to the home visit.) An even larger number of Head Start programs are using information gained from the Home Start experience to expand and strengthen their parents' roles in the program. For example, there are indications that many programs which consider themselves a

---

[6] In 1975 some of the original 16 Home Start demonstration programs were converted into Home Start Training Centers (HSTCs) to provide training and technical assistance to the entire home-based effort within Head Start. There are currently 6 HSTCs: West Virginia, Tennessee, Wisconsin, Arkansas, Utah, and Nevada.

"variation in center attendance program," in which children attend the center fewer than five days per week, are also increasing the number of home visits aimed at involving parents in Home Start-type ways.

As indicated earlier, strong evidence has been gathered from many sources (e.g., Bronfenbrenner, 1974; Lazar et al., 1977), in recent years concerning the benefits of involving parents in a true program-parent partnership; but the Home Start demonstration and the current home-based options provide perhaps the clearest evidence of the general feasibility of such intensive parent-participatory programs within the Head Start context.

The Child and Family Resource Program

The Child and Family Resource Program (CFRP) was launched in 11 locations throughout the country in 1973 as the most family-focused demonstration program ever undertaken within the Head Start context. The unit of enrollment in CFRP is the family rather than the child, and the CFRP is, in effect, a family support program, with emphasis on promoting the healthy development of the young children in the family from the prenatal stage through third grade. All four major objectives of CFRP directly involve parents (ACYF, 1978 revised, p. 4):

1. to individualize and tailor programs and services to meet the child development-related needs of different children and their families;
2. to link resources in the community so that families may choose from a variety of programs and services while relating primarily to a single resource center (i.e., the CFRP) for all young children in the same family;
3. to provide continuity of resources available to parents, that will help each family to guide the development of its children from the prenatal period through their early school years; and
4. to enhance and build upon the strengths of the individual family as a childrearing system, with distinct values, culture, and aspirations. The CFRP will attempt to reinforce these strengths, treating each individual as a whole and the family as a unit.

To fulfill these objectives, each CFRP uses a Head Start program as a base to develop a community-wide system linking a variety of programs and services to families who have children from the prenatal stage through age 8. And, as in Head Start, each CFRP encompasses a comprehensive approach to child development and provides for education, health services (including physical and dental health, mental health, and nutrition), social services, and extensive parent involvement and participation.

One of the key elements of the CFRP is the family assessment, in which the needs, strengths and goals of the family as a whole (as well as each family member) are identified by the family and CFRP staff working together. The assessment results in a Family Action Plan, which addresses a comprehensive array of potential family needs (such as health, social services, educational and vocational training, child care, etc.). The plan also includes steps that can be taken by the family itself and/or the CFRP and/or other agencies to help meet the family's current specific needs as well as to sustain and promote the family and its strengths.

The backbone of the CFRP staff is the family advocate who, working closely with families throughout all phases and aspects of the program, makes sure that appropriate services, linkages, referrals, supports, and resources are provided to families on a continuing basis as new needs emerge. Each CFRP receives a yearly grant of about $135,000 as a supplement to its basic Head Start grant, and serves at least 80 families. (In the spring of 1977, 1,058 families were enrolled in CFRP; these families had 2,333 children from the prenatal stage through age 8.)

Program impact. One of the areas of impact on which some reliable data are available is the relationship of CFRP to other community resource/service agencies. Almost all (85%) of the 80 agencies interviewed for that study reported that CFRP helped them do their jobs better in the community (Development Assoc., 1978, App.D, p.D 19). In addition, about a quarter of these agencies reported that CFRP was responsible for sparking changes in their service delivery (changes such as an agency's increasing its interaction with families by going beyond the immediate problem to look at the total family situation in an effort to build family strength, or an agency's changing its style of providing services) (Dev. Assoc., 1978, App.D, p. D 9-10).

Another area of impact for which some data are available concerns improvement in overall family functioning with regard to home environment, safety, health care, and housing. The source of information on these changes is a 15-month field study conducted from February, 1977 to May, 1978 by the General Accounting Office. The study reviewed and analyzed a number of early childhood and family development programs and included an in-depth look at services provided to a total of 82 families in four of the eleven CFRPs, as well as an estimate of change in overall family functioning. On a 4-point scale describing home environment factors (with 0 = critical, and 4 = excellent), findings indicated the reviewers gave families an average rating of 1.99 on the scale at the time of entry into CFRP, 2.51 after 1 year in CFRP, and 2.92 after 2-4 years in the program.

In addition, interviews were conducted with 64 families and with a number of community agency officials, all of whom were consistently positive with regard to their perceptions of CFRP's value and impact.

Although there are few other reliable program impact data available so far, the feasibility of such a family-focused approach within the Head Start context is being amply demonstrated. All eleven sites have been able to implement the program guidelines and are successfully conducting (and taking action on) family needs assessments, implementing programs for parents of infants and toddlers, individualizing services, linking effectively with other community resources, and earning a favorable reputation for themselves among the enrolled families and the community at large. CFRP, then, is serving as a valuable "laboratory" within Head Start to develop, refine, and demonstrate a variety of models and ways by which Head Start programs can move further in the direction of becoming family-oriented child development programs. Certainly the CFRP experience has already demonstrated that many parents and families do welcome active participation in such a program, community agencies do cooperate and even see their cooperation as beneficial to their own operation, services can be and are being individualized in accordance with assessed needs, and program staff have been and are able to learn to broaden their own skills to accommodate the comprehensive approach engendered in CFRP.

CFRP's foundation is not only its philosophical concept, which places the family at the heart of the program, but also the actual experience of the many Head Start, PCC, PCDC, Home Start, and myriad other child development programs that have laid the groundwork for a program which Dr. Edward Zigler (1977) recently predicted would become Head Start's "wave of the future."

SUMMARY AND CONCLUSION

From the beginning, Head Start was intended to be a parent and family program in which all services to children would be viewed in a family context. As the years passed, the actual program operations have moved more and more toward these intentions. All studies and evaluations which have looked at the relationship between Head Start, parents, and families have documented a number of program activities and services which involve and support parents and families, and considerable data have accumulated over the years testifying to the favorable effects of the program on parents' attitudes and behaviors as well as on Head Start communities.

Although there is still a need to increase the number of Head Start parents who take advantage of the opportunities for parental involvement and participation, and although there is still a need for further study and documentation of program effects on families (e.g., on family structure, family functioning, siblings, economic status, etc.), there seems to be ample evidence at present to support the view that Head Start is indeed "building families."

REFERENCES

Abt Associates. National survey of Head Start graduates and their peers. Cambridge, Mass.: Abt Assoc., 55 Wheeler St., March 1978.

Adams, D. Parent involvement: Parent development. Oakland, Cal. Ctr for the Study of Parent Involvement, 5240 Boyd St., January, 1976.

Addition, K. Obtaining transportation services for preschool children through family court proceedings in New York State: A case history. Otsego, NY: County Head Start, April, 1978.

Administration for Children, Youth & Families, U.S. Dept. of Health, Education, & Welfare. The child and family resource program: An overview. Washington, D.C. ACYF, P. O. Box 1182, 1978 (Revised).

Administration for Children, Youth & Families, U.S. Department HEW, Head Start Program Performance Standards, July, 1975.

Applied Management Sciences. Evaluation of the process of mainstreaming handicapped children into Project Head Start. Silver Spring, MD AMS, 962 Wayne Ave., April, 1978.

Bronfenbrenner, U. *A report on Longitudinal evaluation of preschool programs,* Vol. II: *Is early intervention effective?* Washington, D.C. ACYF Children's Bureau, 1974.

Center for Community Research. Report on preliminary impact data: A national survey of the Parent-Child Program. New York. Center for Community Research, 33 West 60th Street, New York, NY, 10023, January, 1972.

Clark, E. Personal communication with Region IX ACYF Specialist in Parent Involvement and Social Services, June, 1978.

Coleman, F. Status of the home-based option within Head Start. Washington, D.C. Children First, 525 School St., S.W., 1977.

Cooke, R. (chrmn.) Recommendations for a Head Start program. U.S. Department of Health, Education and Welfare, February, 19, 1965.

Cort, H. R., Commins, W. D., Deavers, K. L., O'Keefe, R. A. and Ragan, J. F., Jr. Results of the Summer 1965 Project Head Start. Washington, D.C./McLean, VA: Planning Research Corp., May 9, 1966.

Cort, H. R., Commins, W. D., Henderson, N. H., Mattis, M. A., O'Keefe, R. A., & Orem, R. C. A study of the full-year 1966 Head Start program. Washington,D.C./McLean, VA: Planning Research Corp., July 31, 1967.

Costello, J. Review and summary of a national survey of the Parent-Child Center program. New Haven, Conn. Yale Univ, Child Study Center, August, 1970.

Datta, L.-E. What has the impact of Head Start been: Some findings from national evaluations of Head Start. In E. Zigler & J. Valentine (eds.), *Project Head Start: A legacy of the war on poverty.* New York: Free Press, in press.

Davis, G. Personal communication with Region X ACYF Specialist in Parent Involvement and Social Services, June, 1978.

Development Assoc. Final report on a project to conduct an evaluation of the implementation, effects and costs of the Child and Family Resource Program during the Third and Fourth years of the program operations. Arlington, Va.: Dev. Assoc., October, 21, 1977.

Gilman, A. Personal communication, June 6, 1978.

Gilman, A. & Signatur, D. Draft report on a national survey of HSST/CDA Competency-based training programs. Chicago, Ill. Kirschner Assoc., May 22, 1978.

Gray, S. & Ruttle, K. The family-oriented Home Visiting program: A longitudinal study. Nashville, Tenn. DARCEE, George Peabody College, 1978.

Greenberg, P. *The devil has slippery shoes: A biased biography of the Child Development Group of Mississippi.* New York. MacMillan, 1969.

Head Start. Home-based option program data, 1978. (in-house statistical data, Administration for children, Youth and Families, HEW)

Hertz, T. The impact of federal early childhood programs on children. Washington, D.C. Office of the Asst. Secy. for Planning and Evaluation, U.S. Dept. of Health, Education, and Welfare, July, 1977.

Hewett, K., Grogan, M., Rubin, A., Nauta, M., Stein, M. and Jerome, E. Abt Assoc., & High/Scope Educational Research Foundation. *Partners with parents: The Home Start Experience with preschoolers and their families.* Washington, D.C. Home Start, ACYF, P. O. Box 1182, 1978.

James, L. Personal communication with Region III ACYF Specialist in Parent Involvement and Social Services, June, 1978.

Johnson, R. Personal Communication with ACYF Washington, D.C. Specialist in Parent Involvement and Social Services, June, 1978.

Johnson, R. "Parent and child centers: What have we learned from five years of operation?" Paper presented at CWLA Learning Regional Cong., Cleveland, Ohio, April 4, 1974.

Kirschner Assoc. Parent and child center national evaluation. Progress report, No. 13, May 1, 1969.

Kirschner Assoc. A national survey of the impact of Head Start Centers on community institutions. Chicago, Ill. Kirschner, May, 1970.

Kirschner Assoc. A guide for planning and operating home-based child development programs. Chicago, Ill. Kirschner, June, 1974. (Available from Home Start, ACYF, P. O. Box 1182, Washington, D.C. 20013.)

Lazar, I. Hubbell, V. R., Murray, H., Roshce, M. and Royce, J. The persistence of preschool effects: A long-term follow-up of fourteen infant and preschool experiments. Summary of Final Report for Grant No. 18-76-07843, October, 1977. Available from Research Division, ACYF, P. O. Box 1182, Washington, D.C. 20013.

Levenstein, P. The parent-child network: The verbal interaction component. Paper presented at the International Conference of Parents and Young Children, Central Institute for the Deaf, Washington University, St. Louis, Mo., June 20, 1978. (Available from Dr. Levenstein, Verbal Interaction Project, 5 Bway, Freeport, N.Y. 11520.)

Love, J., Nauta, M., Coelen, C., Hewett, K. and Ruopp, R. National Home Start evaluation: Final report, March, 1976. High/Scope and Abt Assoc. (Available from Home Start, ACYF, P. O. Box 1182, Washington, D.C. 20013.)

Mann, A. J., Harrell, A., Hurt, M. A review of Head Start research since 1969 and an annotated bibliography. Social Research Group, George Washington University, May, 1977.

MIDCO Educational Assoc. Investigation of the effects of Parent Participation in Head Start. Denver, Colo. MIDCO, 10403 West Colfax Ave., October, 1972.

O'Keefe, A. The Home Start Program: Guidelines, December, 1971. (Available from Home Start, ACYF, P. O. Box 1182, Washington, D.C. 20013.)

O'Keefe, R. A. Home Start: Partnership with parents. Children Today, January-February, 1973, pp. 12-16.

Robinson, J. & Choper, E. The parents speak: Another perspective on the Head Start program.: In E. Zigler, & J. Valentine (eds.), *Project Head Start: A legacy of the war on poverty.* New York: Free Press, in press.

Roy Littlejohn Assoc., Inc., Exploring parenting: Final report. Washington, D.C. Littlejohn Assoc., 1328 New York Ave., N.W., October, 1977.

Stubbs, J., Godley, C., & Alexander, L. National Head Start parent involvement study, Part I: Opportunities for parent involvement. Washington, D.C. ACRA, 1000 Vermont Ave., N.W., April 15, 1978.

U.S. Dept. of Health, Education, & Welfare. The status of handicapped children in Head Start programs: Fifth annual report to the Congress of the U.S. on services provided to handicapped children in Project Head Start. Washington, D.C. HEW, February, 1978.

Vicinanza, P., Personal communication with Region III Child Development Specialist, June 6, 1978.

Westinghouse Learning Corp./Ohio State University *The impact of Head Start: An evaluation of the effects of Head Start on children's cognitive and Affective development,* Vol. 1., New York, June 12, 1969.

Zigler, E. Speech at the National Head Start Conference, El Paso, Texas, May 23-25, 1977.

4

Infant-Toddler Group Day Care: A Review of Research[1]

Sally Kilmer

University of Illinois

INTRODUCTION

The effects of day care on infants and toddlers is a topic of continuing debate among professionals, policy makers, and the general public. Advocates of day care view it as a child-centered service which meets the "needs of children for experiences which will foster their development as human beings" *(Day Care 1,* 1971, 1), while opponents warn of irreparable damage to children, their families, and society (Boyd, 1976; *Congressional Record,* 1975a, 1975b). These arguments summarize the concerns about the impacts of care for a substantial part of the day by someone other than the mother: While some see day care as supporting and enhancing a child's development, others equate group day care with institutionalization and permanent separation from the mother.

Although day care began in the United States nearly a century and a quarter ago, until recent years there was little interest in studying the effects of such experiences on children. In the 1960s, interest was stimulated by both political and sociological events, primarily the increasing number of mothers of young children entering the labor force and the introduction of a federal welfare reform proposal which included a work requirement. Both of these developments involved the care of young children for a large part of the day by someone other than the child's own parent, thereby challenging the traditional concept of mothering. While attendance in half-day nursery schools and Head Start programs is now considered not only acceptable but desirable for many 3- to 5-year-

[1] This paper was prepared for ERIC Early Childhood Clearinghouse, December, 1977.

olds, the possibility of longer daily separation from mothers, especially for younger children, has aroused grave concerns and has stimulated considerable research in the last decade.

The theoretical basis for most day care research has been the assumption that early experiences have an important effect on later development. However, unlike research on half-day programs, in which the emphasis (since 1965, at least) has been on the potential for educational and other benefits, much of the day care research has focused on predicted harmful effects, especially on social— emotional development. Another area of concern has been the potential effects of day care on infants' physical health and well-being, and to a lesser extent, possible intellectual retardation of day care children.

While a variety of studies have addressed these issues, the growing literature has not been integrated and evaluated for policy implications, and for directins of future research. The purpose here is to review such research conducted in the United States and Canada for impacts of infant and/or toddler day care attendance on children. For this discussion, day care is defined as the care, education, and supervision provided for children on a regular basis, for twenty or more hours per week, which augments that given by parent(s) or others with legal responsibility for the children. This review is limited to studies of group care outside the family setting and includes no children who were diagnosed as handicapped.

The review begins with summaries of day care research related to the area of greatest concern, the mother—child relationship, and continues with effects on other social relationships, as well as on cognitive and physical development. The discussion includes consideration of the practical implications of day care research, theoretical issues, and needs for further study.

EFFECTS OF DAY CARE
ON MOTHER—CHILD RELATIONSHIPS

Much of the concern about the care of very young children outside the home has centered around its potentially harmful effects on the mother—child relationship, especially on the development of attachment. The theoretical basis for such investigation has been almost exclusively Bowlby's (1951, 1969, 1973) ethological model in which attachment is considered a special affective, reciprocal relationship between infant and mother (or other attachment figure) based on proximity and responsiveness. According to Bowlby, young children want to be near their mothers, generally reacting positively to their presence and with distress to their departure. Infants may be attached to more than one person and the principal attachment figure can be someone other than the biological mother, provided that this person treats the child in a "mothering" way, primarily by engaging in lively social interactions with the child and by responding readily to his advances (Bowlby, 1969, p. 306). However, for brevity, the term mother is used in this discussion to signify the attachment object, either the biological mother or another figure.

Although the ability to form an attachment is seen as instinctive, Bowlby considers its development to be dependent on the mother's responsiveness to the infant. Initially, the mother must assume total responsibility for reducing the distance between the infant and herself; but as the child learns to signal the mother and develops the physical mobility to establish or maintain proximity, the responsibility becomes more shared. Chronologically, infants begin orienting and directing signals toward a discriminated figure around 4 months of age, and usually show clear differentiation in orientation by 6 to 7 months. From about 6 months to 2½ to 3 years of age, young children are active in initiating and maintaining contact with an attachment figure. Tolerance for greater distances between the object of attachment and child increases with the child's growing curiosity and mobility, and by age 3 most children readily spend some time away from their mothers.

However, when an attachment relationship is not established or is interrupted during the formative period, severe developmental consequences (such as the acute anxiety, excessive need for love, and powerful feelings of revenge, guilt, and depression found in institutionalized children) can result (Bowlby, 1951). Effects vary with the degree of disruption, but even when children under age 3, who had good attachment relationships with their mothers, were hospitalized for a few days, their behavior was altered both during the absence and after their reunion with their mothers. Bowlby felt that the distressing effects of separation in such settings can be reduced by familiarity with the environment, presence of siblings, and care by single mother substitutes.

Since day care involves both daily separation from the mother (the presumed attachment figure) and care by other persons, one of the major research questions has concerned the effects of such care on the development and maintenance of attachment relationships. Based on Bowlby's conceptualization, it was expected that infant and/or toddler day care would have detrimental effects on attachment relationships. Furthermore, it was thought that such effects would be directly related to a child's age at time of entry into group care. More serious outcomes were expected for children entering day care between 6 and 24 months of age.

A number of university-based projects have been undertaken to investigate the effects of day care on children and to demonstrate model infant–toddler care. These studies usually included measures of several developmental areas, and nearly all included some assessment of attachment. The attachment measure was generally some version of the "strange situation" developed by Ainsworth and her colleagues (Ainsworth & Bell, 1970) in which the child's behavior is observed in a standard sequence of episodes during which the child's mother and/or a stranger was present, departed, and returned. Dependent variables were changes in proximity, posture, facial expression, protest, crying, and other signs of distress from baseline behavior when only mother and child were present. (Summary data from studies with measures of attachment of infants and toddlers in day care are shown in Table 1.)

One of the earliest infant care research programs was the Demonstration Project for Group Care of infants at the University of North Carolina (Keister, 1970a, 1970b). The Center was modeled after good home care. Children were cared for in small groups with one adult for each 5 to 6 children. Staff goals were to provide consistent, affectionate, and individualized care within an age-appropriate, challenging play environment.

Over a period of 21 months, matched pairs of middle-class day care and home-reared children were assessed periodically with the Bayley Infant Development Scales and/or Stanford–Binet; Vineland Social Maturity Scale and Pre-School Attainment Record (PAR) (an unstandardized extension of the Vineland covering children from birth to 84 months); and two experimental situations designed to measure self-assertion and readiness to separate from mother. In a comparison of the initial and final assessments, the only significant difference on social–emotional measures between the two groups was a higher slope on the unstandardized PAR indicating a faster rate of development for day care children. (Results of intellectual measures are discussed in the following section of this review.) Unfortunately, no data were reported on the length of the day care experience for the research sample although infants could enter the program at 3 months of age, and there was an indication that some children had attended for nearly 3 years.

A second large research and demonstration program was undertaken at Syracuse University. The Children's Center was designed to serve children from 6 months to 3 years in an environment which would "offset any development detriment associated with maternal separation and possibly add a degree of environmental enrichment frequently not available in families of limited social, economic, and cultural resources" (Caldwell & Richmond, 1968, p. 327). The program provided an "atmosphere in which people and objects give proper levels and quantities of stimulation in a context of emotional warmth, trust, and enjoyment" (Caldwell, Wright, Honing, and Tannenbaum, 1970, p. 402).

Several reports have been published on children from this program. Caldwell, et al. (1970) compared primarily lower-class Caucasian and Black 30-month-olds who had been enrolled in day care 6 to 9 hours daily for an average of 18.8 months with home-reared children of the same age. Measures of mother-child attachment, home stimulation, and children's intellectual development were used. Seven different behaviors considered part of attachment were rated by observers for mothers and children during semistructured interviews with a social worker at the Center. Judgements of both mothers and children were made for good affiliation, nurturance, hostility, permissiveness, dependency, happiness, and emotionality. Home visits were used to complete a 72-item

Table 1 Summary of Research Attachment Behavior of Infants and Toddlers in Group Day Care

Author/ Date	Children	Day Care Experience	Measures of Major Dependent Variables	Summary of Major Results
Keister, 1970a, 1970b	14 Day Care (DC) matched with 14 Home-Reared (HR) for sex, race, age, education, of parents and birth order when possible. Most middle class.	6-9 hr./da. total; length of attendance not reported; could be enrolled at 3 mo.; some children in DC for 21 mo. Demonstration project for group care of infants. Adult-child ratio: 1:4/5. Enrollment: 31 3 mo.-3 yr. Staff: All have children; minimum high school education; 20-55 yr. old. Program: Modeled on good M.C. home care; small group; age-appropriate, challenging play; individual attention; continuity & consistency.	Repeated measures at 3, 6, 9, 12, 18, 24, 30, 36, 42, & 48 mo. of age. Preschool Attainment Record (PAR). Vineland Social Maturity Scale. Readiness to separate from mother. Assertiveness.	(Analysis for differences between initial and final measures only.) DC steeper slope of development for PAR only significant difference on social-emotional measures.
Caldwell et al., 1970	18 DC; 23 HR. All 30 mo. old. Caucasian & Black. Mostly LSES (groups not matched.)	6-9 hr./da. $\bar{X}$ attendance = 18.8 mo. Range = 5-24 mo.; most enrolled prior to 12 mo. Syracuse Demonstration Center. Adult-child ratio: 1:4 under 3 yr. Enrollment: 65-70 6 mo.-5 yr.	Ratings of attachment behaviors (affiliation, nurturance, hostility, permissiveness, dependency, happiness, emotionality) for both child and mother based on observations of semi-structured interview with mother and child.	DC children more dependent. DC mothers less permissive. No difference in other attachment ratings.

Table 1 cont'd

Author/ Date	Children	Day Care Experience	Measures of Major Dependent Variables	Summary of Major Results
		Program: "...atmosphere in which people & objects give proper levels of stimulation in context of emotional warmth, trust & enjoyment" (p. 402). 20 min. individual attention to each child daily.		
Kearsley et al., 1975	24 DC 3½-20 mo.; 28 HR 3½-20 mo. Raised exclusively at home; matched for age, sex, ordinal position, family background. All 1st or 2nd born; full-term preg. & delivery; free of physical abnormalities. Predominantly working class. 94% stable nuclear families. Approx. 50% Chinese; 50% Caucasian.	Began DC at 3½ mo.; min. 4 hr./da./5 da./wk. Adult-child ratio: 1:3 infants; 1:5 toddlers; children assigned to specific caregivers. Capacity: 15 infants; 20 toddlers. Staff: Mature women from community, all mothers; stable during study. Program: Emphasized importance of individualized social interaction.	Observation of separation behavior at 3½, 5½, 7½, 9½, 11½, 13½, and 20 mo. Separation situation: child playing contentedly with toys; mother says "Bye-bye," leaves. Observed 2 min. or terminated after 15 seconds crying or fretting.	Age only significant result. Marked increases in protest at 9½ and 11½ mo.; levels off at 20. Protest representative of total group, not a few extreme cases.

Table 1 cont'd

Author/ Date	Children	Day Care Experience	Measures of Major Dependent Variables	Summary of Major Results
Kagan et al., 1977	33 DC 3½-30 mo.; 63 HR 3½-30 mo. Approx. 50% both groups Chinese, 50% Caucasian; 50% working class, 50% middle class. (Some children same as those reported by Kearsley et al., 1975).	Same as Kearsley et al. 1975. Program: Middle-class bias in curriculum; encouraged cognitive development; 1-1 affective interactions between child and caregiver; maximized opportunity for successful mastery experiences.	Assessment batteries at 3½, 5½, 7½, 9½, 11½, 13½, 20, 29 mo. of age. 20 mo. social-emotional measures, Solo free play[a]; peer play[a]; attachment; & separation (same as Kearsley et al., 1975). 29 mo. social-emotional measures: Same as 20 mo.[a] & visit to unfamiliar center.	Results reported only for 20 and 29 mo. assessments. Little difference between HR & DC. DC less vigilant & less inhibited in behavior with unfamiliar peers. Working class DC Chinese less apprehensive in unfamiliar situation.
Ricciuti, 1974 (Study B)	12-13 mo. old; 5 full day; 4 half day; matched with HR. No background data reported.	Entered DC 2-6 mo. old; 7-10 mo. In DC. Adult-child ration: 1:3 Staff: Same 2 female caregivers throughout year. Program: Individualized, warm, affectionate care with staff continuity. Balance of consistency & variety in both caregiving practices and physical environment. Responsivle environment so baby can exercise some control & learn that learning is pleasurable.	"Strange situation" paradigm with child with mother and/ or with stranger. Ratings of response to different approaches of stranger (slow, quick) at different points in testing session. Independent ratings by 2 observers every 10-12 seconds of visual & manipulative-postural directionality and affectivity.	No difference between DC & HR in response to stranger with mother present; reactions to stranger more negative in mother's absence.

Table 1   cont'd

Author/ Date	Children	Day Care Experience	Measures of Major Dependent Variables	Summary of Major Results
Ricciuti, 1974 (Study D)	Same as above & 1973 study children; matched HR controls. Range = 12-19 mo. old. $\bar{X}$ = 16 mo. 1974 children range = 12-13 mo.; $\bar{X}$ = 12.5 mos.	Entered DC 2-6 mo. old; 7-10 mo. in DC. No information re day care experience after 13 mos. of age. Adult-child ratio: Ratio and program same as above.	Variation of "strange situation" paradigm; ratings of child's responses to entering large playroom with mother where teacher & 3-4 children are seated at table. Variables were distance from & physical contact with mother; maintenance of distance during mother's absence; visual orientation to mother & children; & general affective state.	DC farther from mother and closer to children; less sustained physical contact and less active looking at mother; more time looking at children.
Blehar, 1974	20 DC; 20 HR. Age younger group $\bar{X}$ = 30.2 mo.; older $\bar{X}$ = 39.6 mo. at time of study. All M.C.; 2-parent families; all but 1 Caucasian; 80% DC, 60% HR were first-born. 3-HR = 40 mo. attended nursery school 2-3 mornings/wk.	10 entered DC at $\bar{X}$ = 25.7 mo.; 10 entered at $\bar{X}$ = 34.8 mo. $\bar{X}$ DC attendance = 4.6 mo. (4 DC children had been cared for by babysitter 4 mo. before group care.) Children enrolled in 4 different private centers. Adult-child ratio: 1:6; 1:8. Program: "Traditional nursery school regimes with little emphasis on structural academic programs" (p. 685). Children segregated into age groups.	Home visit with mother & child immediately after which visitor rated on Caldwell inventory of Home Stimulation & Q-sort for mother's empathy/social sensitivity. Ainsworth & Bell "Strange Situation" procedure with continuous description of child's behavior recorded. Measures were 15 second frequency counts of exploratory manipulation, oral behavior, & distance interaction with mother. Rating of social interaction scores for seeking,	No difference between DC & HR on Home Stimulation or empathy. DC cried more; engaged in more oral behavior in absence of mother with stranger present; resisted & avoided mother more. HR interacted more with mother across distance & maintained closer proximity to stranger. Age X group interaction with oldest DC lowest in exploration & doing most searching for mother during her absence.

Table 1 cont'd

Author/ Date	Children	Day Care Experience	Measures of Major Dependent Variables	Summary of Major Results
			avoiding & proximity & contact & social interaction	Age × group × episode interaction showed older DC engaged in more proximity seeking after first separation from mother & youngest HR most proximity seeking after second separation from mother.
Ragozin, 1975, n.d.	14 DC: 5 = 17-29 mo. 9 = 30-38 mo. old. DC matched with HR. All from intact, 2-parent families; mother well-educated. $\bar{X}$ = 17 yr. education. 75% mothers were full-time students.	At least 4 mo. in DC. 2 centers: both high quality; 1 private non-profit, low-budget; 1 model University center. Adult-child ratio: 1:4. Program: No information reported.	"Strange situation" procedure similar to Ainsworth. 2 observers recorded different aspects of children's behavior at 6 second intervals. Variables: child-initiated distance (more than 3 ft.) between members of dyad; child-initiated proximity; touching; giving/taking objects; communicating; resisting proximity; play; locomotion; crying; and proximity seeking during mother's absence.	No differences for play & locomotion; calling for & passively maintaining proximity to absent mother; touching; communicating with & total distance from mother when she was present. DC created & maintained distance from mother at significantly higher rates; no difference in total distance. Younger DC initiated more proximity. DC engaged in less give/take of objects with stranger.
Doyle, 1974, 1975	12 Canadian DC matched with HR for age; sex; parental education, occupation & age; no. siblings.	$\bar{X}$ = 7 mo. attendance; newly established center. Adult-child ratio: 1:4. Enrollment: 45 total; 20 under 2½ yrs.	Attachment; Ainsworth & Bell "strange situation" procedure.	HR looked more at stranger when she first entered room. No evidence of weakened or insecure attachment.

Table 1 cont'd

Author/ Date	Children	Day Care Experience	Measures of Major Dependent Variables	Summary of Major Results
	Age $\bar{X}$ = 18.5 mo.; range = 5-30 mo. 10 male; 14 female. Most middle class. All Caucasian, Anglophile.	Program: Balance free play and structured group activities. Each child assigned to a primary caretaker who spent at least 15 min./da. in 1:1 play.	Monthly assessment completed on 2 separate days, once with caregiving 1st and once with stranger 1st.	Up to 7 mo., same responses (generally positive) to both caregiver & stranger; beginning at 8 mo., positive responsive to caregiver cont'd., responses to stranger, less positive.
Ricciuti, 1974 (Study A) Ricciuti & Poresky, 1973	12-13 mo. old; 8 male, 2 female. No background data reported.	Entered DC 2-3½ mo. old; remained approx. 10 mo., 4 hr./da./5 da./wk. Adult-child ratio: 1:3. Staff: Same 2 female caregivers throughout year. Program: Individualized, warm, affectionate care with staff continuity. Balance of consistency & variety in both care-giving practices & physical environment. Responsive environment so baby can exercise some control & learn that learning is pleasurable.	"Strange situation" paradigm with child & mother alone & with caregiver or stranger; child alone with caregiver, stranger. Independent ratings by 2 observers every 10-12 seconds of visual & manipulative-postural directionality & affectivity.	Absence of general negative response to strangers; with mother present but did become less positive after 7 mo.; considerable variability among children. More negative affective responses to stronger in mother's absence; approach of caregiver increased positive affect before 7 mo. & reduced distress after 7 mo. Beginning at 6-7 mo., similar distress at being left with stranger by either mother or familiar caregiver. Being left alone with caregiver produced little or no distress until 12 mo. Distress then less than being left with stranger.
Farran & Ramey, 1977	23 9-31 mo. LSES.	Began DC 6-12 wk. of age. 7 hr./da./5 da./wk. No information reported regarding care.	Child observed in laboratory with mother, teacher, male stranger; child given task which requires help.	17 of 23 children moved to mother's side when placed in experimental room.

Table 1 cont'd

Author/Date	Children	Day Care Experience	Measures of Major Dependent Variables	Summary of Major Results
			Variables: time spent in various areas; use of toys; physical contact; behavior with item requiring assistance. Home observation for measurement of the environment completed for all at 6 mo. of age.	Children spent more time in mother's side of room, engaged in more interactive behavior with mother, & sought help only from mother. No difference in interactions with teacher & stranger; great variability in behavior among children; not related to age, sex, or IQ. Maternal Involvement Scale of HOME positively related to frequency of child's visits to teacher's side of the room & negatively related to contacts & time spent with mother. Mothers rated as punitive at 6 mo. were less apt to have toys extended to them.
Ragozin, 1975	20 DC; Sample divided into 2 groups. $\overline{X}$ = 17-24 mo. Range = 17-29 mo. $\overline{X}$ = 34 mo. Range = 30-38 mo. Exact numbers not reported. 2-parent families; mother well-educated, all but 1 had some college. $\overline{X}$ = 17 yr. education.	At least 4 mo. in DC; enrolled full-time; 2 high-quality centers; 1 private nonprofit, low-budget 1 model university center. Adult-child ratio: 1:4. Program: No information reported.	Observed arrival, separation, mother's absence, & reunion. Variables: proximity, exploratory behavior, distress; & peer-directed behavior.	No age effects; wide individual differences. Increased proximity to mother; child-initiated proximity, touch & communication with mother during reunions. When both mother & teacher were present, children stayed closer to mothers, touched, followed & communicated more with them.

Table 1 cont'd

Author/ Date	Children	Day Care Experience	Measures of Major Dependent Variables	Summary of Major Results
	75% mothers were full-time students.			Comparisons with strange situation results revealed little intraindividual consistency.
Willis & Ricciuti, 1974	10 DC (7 male, 3 female). M.C. working parents or students.	Began DC 2-6 mo. old; 6 attended 8 hr./da./5 da./wk. 4 attended 4 hr./da./5 da./wk. Adult-child ratio: 1:4. Staff: 3 different caregivers with 2 present at all times.	Observations of daily arrival & departure twice per week for 7 mo. Begun after all babies had been in program at least 2 mo. Standardized procedure for arrivals; parent removes coats outside of classroom; care-giver opens door; greets parents & child; caregiver moves closer, talks, holds out arms, & takes baby; parent touches baby or arms or hands, say goodbye, & leaves. Each segment rated on 9 pt. scale for pleasure-displeasure; & approach-withdrawal, both visual & postural-locomotion.	No statistical analyses. Children less positive about parent's departure. 4 hr. most positive affective response to caretaker's greeting. Older 8 hr. consistently least positive to both caretaker's greeting & parent leaving. All clearly positive affective responses to parent's arrival at end of day; developmental change at 12-13 mo. with children less apt to want to leave center.
Dittmann, 1967	5 infants in each; own home, day home, group care. Matched for age, sex & socio-economic status of caretaker; education	Group care provided commercially by private individuals. Adult-child ratio: Varied in all settings.	4 morning hr. of time sample observation of 10 variables for each child: Infant's location, state, posture, activity; caretaker's proximity, verbal behavior; routine and	General patterning of infants' activities, motor behavior, & routine care was similar for all. DC babies more apt to be confined to crib or play pen.

Table 1 cont'd

Author/Date	Children	Day Care Experience	Measures of Major Dependent Variables	Summary of Major Results
	of caretaker; education of caretaker primarily high school or less, All Caucasian infants. $\bar{X}$ age = 9 mo.; range = 6-11 mo.	"Probably, all three of the settings . . . were frankly custodial in nature" (p. 109).	affectional activities; number of different caregivers; number of adults and number of children within 6 ft.	Group DC cared for by more different people, more rarely isolated from other children & more frequently within 6 ft. of 2 other children. Little difference between group and family day care. Mothers more "affectional," both positive & negative interactions.
Rubenstein & Howes, 1976	15 DC full term, normal, healthy. Caucasian. Age = 17-20 mo. Matched with HR for sex, age, ordinal position, parents' education & religion.	$\bar{X}$ = 4.7 mo.; 5 different centers. Adult-child ratio: 1:4. Program: Mostly "free play." No other information reported.	2-2½ hr. observations of each infant during normal activities of discrete behaviors & sequences occurring in time unit.	No difference in amount of time (50%) spent in positive interaction with adult or number of interactions initiated by child or adults; total amount of adult verbal interaction; nonrestrictive adult speech; or frequency of child-initiated exchanges. DC more adult-infant play; goal play; sharing of objects with adults; positive response of adult to sharing; reciprocal s smiling; & adult noncaretaking touching. HR cried more & responded more to mothers' talking. Adults at home were 4 times mo more restrictive.

Inventory of Home Stimulation and either the Stanford—Binet or the Cattell Infant Intelligence Scale was used to measure cognitive development at 12 and at 30 months.

Using a conservative level of significance (*p*-values of less than .10) in order to avoid Type II errors on the attachment measures, Caldwell et al. found day care children to be more dependent than home-reared children, and mothers of day care children to be less permissive than mothers of home-reared children. There would have been no differences, however, if *p*-values of .05 had been used.

At Cornell University Ricciuti (Johnson & Ricciuti, 1974, Ricciuti, 1974; Ricciuti & Poresky, 1973) and his colleagues conducted a series of studies on the effects of extended day care on infants' responses to familiar and strange adults.

The children were enrolled in a small experimental nursery which was part of a research and demonstration program concerned with the development of guidelines for quality infant group care (Willis & Ricciuti, 1975). No background data were reported for any of the subjects.

In a study conducted in 1972–73, a small sample of children in day care four or eight hours daily and a matched home-reared group were observed monthly in an experimental strange situation, from 2–3¾ to 12–13 months of age (Ricciuti, 1974, Study B). There were no significant differences between the two groups although day care children exhibited more distress than did the home-reared sample when left by the mother with a stranger.

Later observations were made of the approach to a new social situation by these same children and those in an earlier study who had attended day care only four hours each day duing their first year (Ricciuti, 1974, Study D). At the time of the follow-up, all the children were between 12–19 months of age, although no information about day care experiences beyond the first year were included. The research setting was a large playroom with a teacher and three or four 3-year-old children seated around a table. In a standardized sequence the mother entered the room with the child, encouraged him/her to play with the children, and moved out of sight. Variables were contact, proximity, and visual orientation to the mother and movement toward the children. Children who had attended day care during their first year moved farther from their mothers and spent less time looking at them or in direct physical contact than did the home-reared group. Day care children also spent more time closer to and looking at the other children than did the home-bound.

The most recent longitudinal investigation of day care infants included both working- and middle-class children from predominantly intact families in the Boston area (Kagan, Kearsley, and Zelazo, 1977; Kearsley, Zelazo, and Kagan, 1975). About half of the children were Chinese and half Caucasian. Participation in the program was limited to children who were first- or second-born, normal full-term pregnancy and delivery, and free from physical abnormalities. Home-reared children were matched for sex, ordinal position, and family background. All were assessed every two months from 3½ to 13½ months of age and then again at 20 and 29 months. The day care children entered the center at approximately 3½ months of age and attended for over two years. The program emphasized individualized social interactions and cognitive stimulation.

Kearsley et al. (1975), reported reactions of these children in a laboratory setting in which the mother left the child contentedly playing with toys. Data from repeated observations of day care and home-reared children from predominantly working-class families indicated that the only significant effect was age. Day care and home-reared children were similar in marked increases in protest at 9½ and 13½ months, which leveled off some at 20 months. The protest was representative of the total group, and not just a few extreme cases.

Later data for a larger group of children in the same day care program revealed a drop in separation protest at 29 months (Kagan et al., 1977). Using several different measures of social—emotional development as a part of a larger study, Kagan and colleagues found little difference for 20 and 29 month assessments between home-bound and children who attended the center for over two years. Differences which were observed favored the day care population. In situations with strange peers, day care children were less inhibited and less vigilant. The only cultural and class difference found for the social—emotional measures was that working-class Chinese day care children were less apprehensive during a visit to an unfamiliar center than were peers who were home-reared.

In addition to the longitudinal investigations of a range of infant day care questions, several short-term studies of attachment have also been undertaken. The only report of any significant negative effects of day care was that of Blehar (1974), which has received considerable attention. In that study, 30- and 40-month-old middle-class children who had attended day care approximately 4½ months compared unfavorably with home-reared children of the same ages. Data from the Ainsworth and Bell "strange situation" showed that the day care children cried more; engaged in more oral behavior in the presence of strangers when their mothers were absent: and resisted and avoided theirs mothers more. Home-reared children, on the other hand, engaged in more distal interaction with their mothers and maintained closer proximity to strangers. Age by group interactions revealed that the oldest day care children engaged in the least exploration and the most searching for their mothers during their absence. Age by group by episode interactions showed the older day care children doing more proximity-seeking after their first separation from their mothers and the youngest home-bound group engaged in the most proximity-seeking after the second separation. These results have been interpreted by Blehar as revealing anxious ambivalent attachment in the older day care children and avoidant behavior in the younger day care population, similar to the effects found for major separations.

However, a later study using the same experimental setting and approximately the same age children revealed few differences between home-reared and day care samples (Ragozin, 1975; n.d.). The one result similar to Blehar's was that day care children engaged in less give and take of objects with a stranger. Ragozin also found that day care children created and maintained distance from their mothers at significantly higher rates than did home-reared, but there were no significant differences in total distance between mothers and children in the two groups.

Differences in methodology and data reduction techniques may account for some of the discrepant results of the two studies. Blehar coded from transcripts using 15-second intervals for frequency measures and ratings for the social interaction variables, while Ragozin used two observers to simultaneously code different aspects of the children's behavior at 6-second intervals. Ragozin also excluded from analysis all dependent measures which were not exhibited by 30% of the sample and occurring at a rate of 4% in one of the episodes in analysis; thereby eliminating three of the variables Blehar found significant—resisting proximity to mother, crying, and actively seeking mother in her absence. Ragozin also had fewer younger children.

A third investigation using the same methodology but with much younger children yielded results similar to Ragozin's. Doyle (1974, 1975) also found day care children attending less to the stranger than a carefully matched group of home-reared children, but found no evidence of weakened or insecure attachment.

A second source of data about the effects of day care on mother—child attachment comes from the child's relationship with his/her caregiver. Are caregivers mother-replacements, mothers-substitutes with whom children also develop close relationships, or disinterested, unresponsive persons? Several investigators have examined these questions, both in laboratory and naturalistic settings, with consistent results. There was no evidence of preference for caregivers by day care children when both mothers and caregivers were present. Relationships with caregivers were less clearcut. In some instances, familiar caregivers were generally viewed positively by the children and appeared to also be attachment figures with whom children had relationships, although not as strong as those with the mothers. In others, day care children reacted the same toward their caregivers as they did to strangers.

Ricciuti and Poresky (1973) and Farran and Ramsey (1977) observed infants' reactions to mothers and caregivers in laboratory settings. Ricciuti and Poresky conducted a longitudinal study with monthly observations of infants from the time they entered day care at 2 to 3½ months of age until they were 12 to 13 months old. The same three staff members provided consistent care for the year. A variation of the strange situation procedure was used on two different days, once with the caregiver present first and once with the stranger present first. Until 7 months, responses to both the stranger and caregiver were generally positive. Beginning with the eighth month, the infants discriminated between the two, continuing to react positively to the caregiver and becoming less positive to the stranger. Beginning around 7 months, the child displayed similar distress at being left with the stranger by either the mother or the caregiver. When the infant had been left alone with the stranger, the approach of the caregiver increased the positive affect or reduced the distress of the child. Being left alone with the caregiver produced little or no distress until 12 months; but then, the distress was less than when the infant was left alone with the stranger.

With a different task, a much wider age range, and Black children from lower socioeconomic families, Farran and Ramsey found overwhelming preferences for mothers but no differences in behavior with teachers and a stranger. No information was included about either the program or the caregivers in this particular situation. There was, however, some indication that a child's behavior with a teacher may reflect the mother–child relationship. Correlations with the Home Observation for Measurement of the Environment instrument completed when each child was six months old showed visits to the teacher's side of the room were positively related to the Maternal Involvement Scale and negatively related to contacts and time spent with the mother. Also, mothers rated as punitive when their babies were six months old were less apt to have their children extend toys to them.

Reports of child behavior during their arrival, separation, and reunion in the day care setting confirmed these laboratory results. In addition to the previously cited laboratory data, Ragozin (1975) also observed two days in the day care center. She found increased proximity and communication with the mothers at the end of the day with no difference in the behavior of 2- and 3-year-olds. When both teacher and mother were present, children stayed closer to their mothers and touched, followed, and communicated more with them. An interesting methodological note was the finding that comparisons of this data with that obtained in the laboratory strange situation revealed little intra-individual consistency.

Data from a pilot longitudinal study of children from 2 to 13 months of age suggested both some developmental trends and differences related to the age of children at the time of enrollment and daily amount of time spent in the center (Willis & Ricciuti, 1974). Although the sample was small and there were no statistical analyses, observations over a 7-month period indicated day care children had generally positive reactions to caregivers' greetings with less positive responses to their parents' departure. At the end of the session, children were clearly pleased at their parents' return although there was some decline of positive responses around 12 months of age. The authors attributed the decline to increasing autonomy rather than feelings against the parents. The least positive reactions were exhibited by children who had begun day care around 5 months of age and who were in the center eight hours a day.

Additional insight into possible day care effects may be gained from data regarding similarities and differences in the quantity or the quality of care provided by mothers and other caregivers. In a small study of infants being cared for in different settings, Dittman (1976) found the patterning of general activities, motor behavior, and routine care to be similar for infants being cared for by their own mothers and for those in family day care or in centers. The major differences were that mothers caring for their own infants displayed more "affectional" behavior, both positive and negative, than did other caregivers, and that day care babies were more apt to be confined to crib or play pen. Babies in groups were cared for by more different people and were less often isolated from other children than were infants at home.

Differences favoring day care children were found in comparisons of matched groups of toddlers in centers and home settings (Rubenstein & Howes, 1976). Although there were no differences in total amount of positive interaction with adults, there were variations in the nature of that exchange. More adult—infant play, more goal play, more sharing of objects with adults, more reciprocal smiling, and more adult noncaregiving touching were observed in the day care centers. Differences found for other adult—child interactions were that home-reared children responded more to their mothers' talking than day care children did to their teachers. However, home-bound infants also cried more and their mothers were four times as restrictive as adults in the centers.

EFFECTS OF DAY CARE ON OTHER SOCIAL INTERACTIONS

Group care is a social setting which provides experiences with both adults and children not available to home-bound children, and the data clearly indicate greater peer interaction among day care children. (Studies of other social interaction are summarized in Table 2.)

Observations of 6- to 12-month-olds in day care, showed even the youngest babies initiating contact with peers (Durfee & Lee, 1973). At all ages the contacts were very brief, with modes of initiation changing with increasing age. As the children grew older, they changed from visual regard to approach and exploration of the peer and his/her toys to more sophisticated overtures such as smiling or offering a toy.

Studying older children who had attended day care at least 4.7 months, Rubenstein and Howes found 17- to 20-month-olds spent about 25% of their time in active interaction with peers in day care. Only 1% of that time was in conflict situations. Over half of the time was engaged in play with mutual involvement in activities or mutual awareness of each other. Furthermore, the developmental quality of play with inanimate objects was enhanced when the toddlers were engaged with peers.

MacRae and Herbert-Jackson (1976) compared 2-year-olds who had been in day care a little over a year with peers who had attended one to six months. The children with more day care experience were rated by their caregivers as getting along better with their peers than did the newer children.

Table 2 Summary of Research Regarding Other Social Interactions of Children in Infant and/or Toddler Day Care

Author/ Date	Children	Day Care Experience	Measures of Major Dependent Variables	Summary of Major Results
Durfee & Lee, 1973	7 male; 2 female. Age = 6-9 mo. at beginning of study.	Enrolled in DC approximately 5 mo. at beginning of study.	Observed approximately 1 hr/da/6 mo.; recorded as many complete encounters as possible.	Encounters are complex, with developmental changes in modes of encounter & babies taking different roles in relation to contact. Infant-infant encounters incorporated both social and nonsocial components. Wide individual differences.
Rubenstein & Howes, 1976	15 DC full term, normal, healthy. Caucasion. Age = 17-20 mo. Matched with HR for sex, age, ordinal position, parents' education & religion.	$\bar{X}$ = 4.7 mo. 5 different centers. Adult-child ratio: 1:4. Program: Mostly "free-play." No other information reported.	2-2½ hr observations of each infant during normal activities of discrete behaviors & sequences occurring in time unit.	DC spent 25% of time in active interaction (talking to, smiling at, touching, imitating, exchanging or sharing objects) with other children. 1% of peer interactive time spent in conflict; 13% in mutual involvement in activities or in activities in which there was mutual awareness of or reciprocal responding to each other. Developmental level of play with inanimate objects higher when infant was interacting with peers.

Table 2 cont'd

Author/Date	Children	Day Care Experience	Measures of Major Dependent Variables	Summary of Major Results
Doyle, 1974, 1975	12 Canadian DC matched with HR in age; sex; parental education, occupation & age; no. siblings. Age $\bar{X}$ = 18.5 mo.; range = 5-30 mo. 10 male; 14 female. Most middle class. All Caucasian, Anglophile.	$\bar{X}$ = 7 mo. attendance. Newly established center. Adult-child ratio: 1:4. Enrollment: 45 total; 20 under 2½. Program: Balance free play & structured group activities. Each child assigned to a primary caretaker who spent at least 15 min./da. in 1:1 play.	Peer interaction: 10 min. video tape sample. HR-DC pairs playing in room with toys with mothers at edge of room. Scored every 10" for type, tone, & target of behavior; duration; reaction to friendly & aggressive behaviors.	DC initiated fewer social interactions, both positive & negative.
Kagan et al., 1977	33 DC 3½-30 mo.; 63 HR 3½-30 mo. Approx. 50% both groups Chinese, 50% Caucasian; 50% working-class; 50% middle-class. (Some children same as those reported by Kearsley et al.)	Same as Kearsley et al. Program: Middle-class bias in curriculum; encouraged cognitive development; 1:1 affective interactions between child & caregiver; 1-2 hr./da. of interaction; maximized opportunity for successful mastery experiences. Each child had primary caregiver, usually same ethnicity; changed after 13 mo.	Assessment batteries at 3½, 5½, 7½, 9½, 11½, 13½, 20, & 29 mo. of age. 20 mo. social-emotional measures: Solo free play[a]; peer play[a], attachment; & separation (same as Kearsley et al.). 29 mo. social-emotional measures: Solo free play[a]; peer play[a]; separation[a]; visit to unfamiliar day care center.	(Results reported only for 20 & 29 mo. assessments.) Little difference between HR & DC. DC less vigilant & less inhibited in behavior with unfamiliar peers. Working class DC Chinese less apprehensive in unfamiliar situation.

Table 2   cont'd

Author/ Date	Children	Day Care Experience	Measures of Major Dependent Variables	Summary of Major Results
MacRae & Herbert-Jackson, 1976	8 pairs of 2-yr.-olds matched on age & sex. Parental occupations ranged from manual laborer to college professor with student the most frequent occupation.	½ attended DC at least 13 mo.; ½ attended DC 1-6 mo. No other information reported.	Caregivers rated children on 7-point scales for tolerance for frustration; cooperation with adults; compatibility with peers; spontaneity; physical & verbal aggression; motor activity; problem-solving; playfulness; ability to abstract.	"Old" DC rated better on ability to get along with peers, problem-solving, ability to abstract and planfulness.
Schwarz et al., 1973	16 DC matched for age, sex, race, parental occupation & education with 16 children with no previous group day care. (Some had been cared for by others at home, babysitters.) DC $\bar{X}$ = 3 yr. 10 mo. HR $\bar{X}$ = 3 yr. 6 mo.	Attended Syracuse Children's Center. 6-8 hr./da./5 da./ wk. $\bar{X}$ = 36 mo.; range = 24-47 mo.	All children observed and rated on 1st day attendance in new DC program for: 1) Affect 2) Tension 3) Social interaction Follow-up rating 5 wk. later.	DC rated more positive affect upon arrival; no difference later in 1st day or at 5 weeks. No difference in tension. DC engaged in more social interaction initially & showed greater increase over time.

Table 2 cont'd

Author/ Date	Children	Day Care Experience	Measures of Major Dependent Variables	Summary of Major Results
Lay & Meyer, 1971	19 matched pairs; 1 unmatched pair. Most children same as Schwarz et al., 1971. $\bar{X}$ age = 3.95 yr. both groups at beginning of study.	Approx. same as Schwarz et al., 1973	Observed patterns of behavior in open environment for: 1) children's choice of play locations 2) interactions with peers 3) interactions with adults Observed over 7 mo. period; point-time sampling. Total = 8,264 min. observation.	DC played more in active area; less in expressive & task-oriented areas. DC more verbal interaction with peers; more positive verbal interaction with peers; more interaction with other DC peers. No difference in snack, invitational, outdoor play; gestural or tactile interaction or interaction with adults.
Schwarz et al., 1974	Same as Lay & Meyer, 19 matched pairs.	Approx. same as Schwarz et al., 1973	Children rated on 9 bipolar trait scales; tolerance for frustration; compatibility with peers; spontaneity; physical & verbal aggression; motor activity; problem-solving; playfulness; ability to abstract. Rated after 4 mo. by 9 teachers; rated after 8 mo. by 4 observers.	DC less cooperative with adults; more physically & verbally aggressive with peers & adults; more motor activity. No difference on other traits.

aSame as 20 mo.

With strange peers, results were mixed. Doyle found children of the same age as those studied by Rubenstein and Howes to initiate fewer interactions with strange peers during a laboratory session than did home-reared children with their mothers present. However, younger day care toddlers in the Ricciuti study (D) spent more time looking at unfamiliar children, and Kagan et al. found day care children to be less vigilant and less inhibited than the homebound with unfamiliar peers.

Children in the preceding studies appeared to be primarily middle-class. Follow-up data for lower-class children who had been enrolled in infant—toddler day care also revealed greater social interaction in comparison with newly enrolled peers, but with some possible negative overtones.

A series of follow-up studies of children who had attended the Syracuse Children's Center provides information about some longer-term social—emotional effects of infant group care. Twenty children who had attended the Children's Center an average of three years transferred to a new program in which 20 matched peers with no previous group program experience were also enrolled. (Some children in the day care sample were the same as those reported in the previous Caldwell et al. research.)

Schwarz, Kralick, & Strickland (1973) observed 16 pairs of these children on their first day in the new program and again five weeks later. The previous day care group was rated as having more positive affect at the beginning of the first day but there were no differences later that day or after five weeks in the program. The Children's Center group also was judged to be more socially interactive with greater increases across time.

Lay and Meyer (1971) investigated the patterns of behavior in an open environment program setting with all forty of the children. Based on point—time sample observations collected over seven months, the children with previous day care experience engaged in more large muscle activity, participated less in creative and dramatic play, and played less with small manipulative materials and language activities than did the more recently enrolled peers. In the area of social interaction, there were no differences between the two groups in their conduct with adults. With peers, however, children with previous day care experience had both more verbal interaction and more positive verbal interactions than did the new children. The Children's Center transfers also interacted more with those peers who had been enrolled in the infant—toddler program with them.

Data based on ratings of these same children at two different points during the school year confirm the preference for motor activity for previous day care children (Schwarz et al., 1974). However, in contrast to Lay and Meyer, Children's Center children were judged less cooperative with adults and more physically and verbally aggressive with both adults and peers than the children enrolled in group day care for the first time.

Infant and toddler day care also facilitated cognitive development. (See Table 3 for a summary of these studies.) The most dramatic differences reported between day care and control children around 2 years of age were for low-income Blacks who entered the Frank Porter Graham Child Development Center at the University of North Carolina, Chapel Hill (Robinson & Robinson, 1971). The mean Stanford—Binet and Peabody Picture Vocabulary Test scores for these day care children between 2½ and 4½ years of age were 120 and 107, respectively, compared with 86 and 78 for home-reared peers. Infants in the same day care program who entered between 4 and 6 months of age also performed better than the control group on the Bayley Scales, especially on the Mental Scale at 18 months when scores for the home-reared dropped. Day care children generally did better on verbal measures than on sensorimotor tasks.

Although only limited information was reported, the content of the program seemed to be exceptionally enriched, especially for the older children. It was a comprehensive service including medical care, with structured curricula in language, sensorimotor skills, perception, reading, scientific and numerical concepts, music, art, and French.

Data for a younger and probably slightly less disadvantaged group of Canadian children revealed significantly higher Developmental Quotations for day care children but they were in favor of children entering the center at 9 months rather than those beginning at 16 months (Fowler, 1974). The Canadian day care children scored better on nonverbal problem-solving than on verbal items. Both Fowler and Caldwell, however, found the performance of their day care groups was largely attributable to a decline in the scores of the home-reared children. The decline for Canadian children occurred between 11 and 25 months of age and between 12 and 30 months for the Syracuse population. Neither Keister nor Kagan found such drops for their samples. Kagan found little difference between day care and home-reared children although the day care group performed better on nonlanguage items. Total cognitive development was significantly facilitated only for the working-class Chinese. Conversely, Keister's middle-class day care children both scored higher on the Bayley Mental Scale and exhibited a steeper slope of development.

Some cognitive effects of longer-term day care were found for lower-class 5-year-olds who had attended the Syracuse Children's Center for an average of 43 months (Lindstrom & Tannenbaum, 1970). The day care children were significantly superior to a control group just beginning Head Start, on every measure of intellectual development.

On other variables which may be related to cognitive performance, Fowler's day care children who had attended the center 18 months improved in ratings of verbal expressiveness, inquisitiveness, attentiveness, concentration, perseverence, sensitivity to stimulation and objects, directedness, attention span

Table 3 Summary of Research Regarding Cognitive Development of Infants and Toddlers in Group Day Care

Author/ Date	Children	Day Care Experience	Measures of Major Dependent Variables	Summary of Major Results
Robinson & Robinson, 1971	31 children. 19 infants selected before birth; roughly balanced for sex and race, no gross anomalies; 12 toddlers. 24 different families; 15 Caucasian middle-class children, 16 Black, mostly low-income. 2 control groups; 1 followed from infancy; other used for preschool comparison only.	Infants entered DC between 4 wk.-6 mo. of age. Toddlers entered 23-36 mo. Attended up to 2½ yr. Program: Comprehensive & university sponsored; stimulating, included health care, structured educational program with curricula in language, sensorimotor skills, perception, reading, scientific and numerical concepts, music, art, French. Children housed in multi-age groups of up to 16 total. Children from same families housed together. Child-focused work with parents through daily conversations with staff, contacts with pediatrician and home visits by public health nurse.	Infants tested every 3 mo. to 18 mo. of age with Bayley Infant Scale. Toddlers tested every 6 mo. ages 2½-4½ with Stanford-Binet; Peabody Picture Vocabulary; Illinois Test of Psycholinguistic Abilities; Arthur Adaptation of Reiter Scale; Draw-a-Man. 1st 16 children & controls also tested at age 4 with Wechsler Primary and Preschool Inventory; Frostig Test of Visual Perception; Caldwell Preschool Inventory.	DC infants higher on Bayler Mental & Motor Scales. Difference over time only for Mental Scale, especially at 18 mo. when control group dropped. DC consistently higher scores on verbal tasks than sensorimotor. Older Black DC toddlers higher on Stanford-Binet (PPVT). No differences reported for other measures.

Table 3 cont'd

Author/ Date	Children	Day Care Experience	Measures of Major Dependent Variables	Summary of Major Results
Fowler, 1974	Urban, Canadian children attending community center; *N* varies; maximum = 24. Largely single parent, multiethnic, factory working class to skilled blue collar & clerical. Matched comparison groups on basis of age; sex; IQ; parent education, ethnicity, occupation; sibling number, spacing & parental age as feasible. Controls reared at home by parents or babysitters.	Minimum admission age = 6 mo.; all day attendance up to 21 mo. in center. Adult-child ratio: 1:2.5 infants; 1:5,6 toddlers; 1:9 preschool. Program: Community center; Curriculum designed to further child's development of cognition, language, gross & fine perceptual motor processes, motivation & socio-emotional functioning, physical health & development; learning experiences center around developmental care routines, play & guided learning. Parent guidance through demonstration of guided learning—play interaction techniques discussion of child-rearing, toy lending library, home visits & parent meetings.	Measures administered at entry and 6 mo. intervals. Griffiths Scales of Mental Development (GQ); Bayley Infant Behavior Record; Schaffer & Aaronson Infant Behavior Inventory; Caldwell Home Stimulation Inventory; Schaffer & Aaronson Infant Education Research Inventory. Assessment of maternal abilities, Wechsler Scale of Adult Intelligence.	(Results for 1st 2 yr. of project.) DC & HR GQ same at 11 mo. DC total GQ and nonverbal problem-solving subtest higher after 14 mo. in program; gains for children entering at 9 mo. greater than for those entering at 16 mo. Except for problem-solving, group differences largely a function of declines of HR. After 18 mo. in center, DC gained on ratings of verbal expressiveness, inquisitiveness, attentiveness, concentration, perseverance, sensitivity to stimulation & objects, goal directedness, attention span & endurance. (Significance level not reported. No data for HR.) DC girls decline in fine motor skills, gain more than DC boys on curiosity-exploratory, concentration, perseverance, verbal expression, lack of irritability, enthusiasm. DC better than HR on emotional and verbal responsiveness of mother & maternal involvement with child.

Table 3 cont'd

Author/ Date	Children	Day Care Experience	Measures of Major Dependent Variables	Summary of Major Results
Kagan et al., 1977	33 DC 3½–30 mo. 63 HR 3½–30 mo. Approx. ½ both groups Chinese, ½ Caucasian, ½ working-class, ½ middle-class.	Same as Kearsley et al. Program: Middle-class bias in curriculum; encouraged cognitive development; 1-1 affective interactions between child & caregiver; maximized opportunity for successful mastery experiences.	Assessment batteries at ages 3½, 5½, 7½, 9½, 11½, 13½, 20, & 29 mo. 20 mo. measures: Vocabulary recognition; age-appropriate Bayley Infant Scale items. 29 mo. measures: Concept Familiarity Index; Embedded Figures Task; Memory for Locations Task.	Results reported only for 20 & 29 mo. assessments. Little difference between HR & DC. DC higher on nonlanguage Bayley items. Facilitated cognitive development for working-class Chinese DC.
Caldwell et al., 1970	18 DC; 23 HR. All 30-mo.-old. Caucasian and Black. Mostly LSES (groups not matched).	6-9 hr./da. $\bar{X}$ attendance = 18.8 mo.; range = 5-2½ mo.; most enrolled prior to 12 mo. Syracuse Demonstration Center. Adult-child ratio: 1:4 under 3 yr. Enrollment: 65-70 6 mo.-5 yr. Program: "atmosphere in which people & objects give proper levels of stimulation in context of emotional warmth, trust & enjoyment" (p. 402). 20 min. individual attention to each child daily.	Stanford-Binet or Cattell Infant Intelligence Scale (DQ). Home visit to complete Inventory of Home Stimulation.	HR higher DQ at 12 mo.; no difference at 30 mo. due to drop in HR DQ. No difference on Home Stimulation. Positive relation between DQ & Home Stimulation for HR only.

Table 3 cont'd

Author/ Date	Children	Day Care Experience	Measures of Major Dependent Variables	Summary of Major Results
Keister, 1970a, 1970b	14 DC matched with 14 HR for sex, race, age, education of parents & birth order when possible. Most middle-class.	6-9 hr./da. total. Length of attendance not reported. Could be enrolled at 3 mo. Some children in DC for 21 mo. Demonstration project for group care of infants. Adult-child ratio: 1:4/5. Enrollment: 31 3 mo.-3 yr. Staff: All have children; minimum high school education; 20-25 yr. old. Program: Modeled on good M.C. home care; small group; age-appropriate, challenging play; individual attention; continuity and consistency.	Repeated measures at 3, 6, 9, 12, 18, 24, 30, 36, 42 and 48 mo. of age. Bayley Infant Scales or Stanford-Binet.	(Analysis for differences between initial and final measures only.) DC higher on Bayley Mental Scale. DC steeper slope of development for Bayley Mental Scale.

Table 3 cont'd

Author/ Date	Children	Day Care Experience	Measures of Major Dependent Variables	Summary of Major Results
Lindstrom & Tannenbaum, 1970	23 DC children approximately 60 mo. 23 control (19 enrolled in Head Start 3 wk. at time of testing) matched on age, race, sex, presence or absence of father, number of children in home; & parental education & occupation when possible. 17 DC & 7 control mothers worked. All low-income.	Attended Syracuse Children's Center X̄ = 43 mo.; range = 32-55 mo. Program: Emphasized cognitive and linguistic development.	Final set of measures before children left program. Stanford-Binet; Preschool Inventory (PSI); Boehm Test (PPVT); Auditory-Vocal Automatic, Motor Encoding, Auditory-Vocal Association, and Vocal Encoding subtests of Illinois Test of Psycho-linguistic Abilities (ITPA).	C 1 mo. older than DC. DC higher IQ (106 to 97); total PSI and Associative Vocabulary Subtest; PPVT; Boehm Test of Basic Concepts; total for 4 subtests of Auditory-Vocal Association Subtest & ITPA.

and endurance. MacRae and Herbert-Jackson, cited in Table 2, found caregivers rated middle-class 2-year-olds who had attended day care for more than a year better at problem-solving, ability to abstract, and planfulness than peers in day care for less than six months; but Schwarz et al. (1974), found no differences on these same items between lower-class 4-year-olds in day care for three years and age mates in their first year of center care.

EFFECTS OF DAY CARE ATTENDANCE ON
CHILDREN'S HEALTH

Another major concern of infant care has been the health of the children. Since babies are a physically vulnerable population and group care may expose them to more pathogenic sources than home care, day care infants were expected to have more illnesses. Perhaps the most graphic expression of this concern came from the pediatric consultant for one of the earliest infant care programs, who is reported to have said while inspecting the proposed facilities, "You know, I'm not at all sure this room will be adequate for Sick Bay. You realize, don't you, that there may be days when all the babies will have to be in Sick Bay?" (Keister, 1970a, p. 22). Fortunately, neither evidence from that particular center nor any other medical data collected has supported this prophecy.

The most comprehensive medical evaluation comes from children attending the Frank Porter Graham Center, previously described in relation to Robinson's work (Loda, 1971; Loda, Glezen, and Clyde, 1972). (A summary of health-related research is given in Table 4.) In that program, children ages 6 weeks to 5 years were housed in mixed-age groupings, with those under 30 months usually spending a portion of the day away from the older children. Daily records of health status for each child were maintained and ill children attended except for cases of measles and chicken pox. Sick children were seen by a nurse, epidemiologist and/or pediatrician but they were not isolated from the group. All children with respiratory illnesses had throat cultures for viruses, mycoplasm, group A streptococci and either nasopharyngeal swabs for bacteria or nasal washings for viruses and bacteria.

Analyses of data collected for 45 children from 29 different families over a three-year period showed a mean incidence rate of 8.4 respiratory illness per child—year for the total group. Rates were highest for children under 1 year (9.6 per child—year) and gradually decreased with age to 6.7 per child—year for 5-year-olds. Only one child was hospitalized for lower respiratory illness and that child was exposed at home, not at the day care center. There were no increases of nonrespiratory illnesses.

Regarding the patterns of respiratory illnesses, new viral agents were found to spread rapidly through the group and then disappear. There was little consistent seasonal variation within a year although there were slightly fewer illnesses

Table 4 Summary of Research Regarding Health of Infants and Toddlers in Group Day Care

Author/ Date	Children	Day Care Experience	Measures of Major Dependent Variables	Summary of Major Results
Loda, 1972 Loda et al., 1972	45 DC from 29 different families. Ages 6 wk.-5 yr. Approx. 50% Black; 50% Caucasian.	Average = 40 hr./wk.; in center. Children in mixed age groupings, 6 wk.-5 yr. Complete health care provided. Ill children admitted and not isolated. Data gathering covered 30 mo. Capacity: 40 children in 2 separate units; mixed ages 6 wk.-5 yr. Program: Children under 30 mo. separated from older children for part of day.	Daily record of health status for each child. Ill children seen by nurse, epidemiologist and/or pediatrician. Children with respiratory illnesses had throat cultures for viruses, mycoplasm, group A streptococci; and nasopharyngeal swabs for bacteria or nasal washings for virus & bacteria. Cultures for all children taken on scheduled basis.	$\bar{X}$ = 8.4 respiratory illnesses per child per year. Highest rate = 9.6 per child under 1 yr. Lowest rate = 6.7, 5-yr. = olds. Little seasonal variation within each year; were periods of incidence variability over the years of study (monthly range = 2-11 illnesses for every 10 children). New viral respiratory agents spread rapidly & disappeared. No increase over expected for nonrespiratory infections.
Kearsley et al., 1975	24 DC 3½-13 mo. old. 28 HR matched for age, sex, ordinal position, & SES. 94% stable nuclear families.	Enrolled at 3½ mo. of age. Minimum attendance 4 hr./ da./5 da./wk. Capacity: 15 Infants; 20 toddlers.	Impressions of physician. Attendance records.	Daily attendance fluctuated between 80-100%. Incidence of respiratory disorders appeared similar to surrounding community.

99

Table 4 cont'd

Author/ Date	Children	Day Care Experience	Measures of Major Dependent Variables	Summary of Major Results
	Urban. Predominantly working-class. All children were 1st or 2nd born; normal, full-term pregnancy, free of physical abnormal normalities. 50% Chinese; 50% Caucasian.	Adult-child ratio: 1:3 infants; 1:5 toddlers. Children with minor illnesses examined & allowed to participate.		(Analysis only for differences between initial & final measures.) DC more illnesses, primarily diaper rash, colds, & runny noses. No differences in height & weight.
Keister, 1970 a, 1970 b	14 DC matched with HR for sex, race, age, education of parents, & birth order when possible. Most middle-class.	6-9 hr./da. in center. Length of attendance not reported for total sample. Can enroll at 3 mo. Some in DC for 21 mo. Adult-child ratio: 1:5 under 20 mo.; 1:5/6 over 20-36 mo. Capacity: 31; 21 birth-36 mo.; separated into groups; birth-14 mo.; 15-20 mo.; 20-36 mo. Pediatric Consultant 2-4 hr./wk.; "Sick Bay" for minor illnesses.	Repeated measures at 3, 6, 9, 12, 18, 24, 30, 36, 42, & 48 mo. Pediatric examination. Illness reports by staff & parents during weekly telephone interviews.	

Table 4 cont'd

Author/ Date	Children	Day Care Experience	Measures of Major Dependent Variables	Summary of Major Results
Doyle, 1975	12 Canadian DC matched with HR in age, sex, parental education, occupation, & age, siblings. Age $\bar{X}$ = 18.5 mo.; range = 5-30 mo. 10 male; 14 female. Most middle-class.	$\bar{X}$ = 7 mo. attendance. Adult-child ratio: 1:4.; staff member was R.N. No information re health policies. Capacity: 45 total; 20 under 2½ yr.	Frequency of: infectious diseases, rash, fever, constipation, flu, colds, & ear infections. Assessed in 4 semi-monthly telephone calls to home.	DC greater incidence of flu.

during summers. There were, however, periods during the study in which more illnesses occurred than at other times. The highest monthly rate of incidence was 11 illnesses for 10 children and the lowest, 2 for 10.

With one exception, the authors found these results similar to those for the same age group of home-reared children in two other studies. Data gathered on the etiology of respiratory illnesses, conducted simultaneously in the same community as the day care centers showed the same viral causes of infection and seasonal variations and a similar age distribution of infection as was observed in the day care population.

In comparison with the results of a 10-year study of middle-class, home-reared children in Cleveland, Ohio, the North Carolina day care infants under 1 year of age had more respiratory illnesses, 9.6 compared with 8.3. Rates were fairly comparable for older children. The respiratory diseases of the day care children also were accompanied by fever nearly twice as often as those of the Cleveland sample. However, since the Cleveland data was based on children who were brought to the physician's office, and the day care children were regularly seen by medical personnel, it is unclear whether there was actually a greater frequency or whether the closer surveillance of the day care children resulted in the detection of more low-grade temperature elevations.

Loda (1972) has suggested that the Chapel Hill results may reflect the multi-age groupings and that the number of illnesses might be increased for infants and toddlers in homogeneous age groups. However, results from three other programs, all with children grouped according to age, correspond with the Chapel Hill data. Based on their impressions, Kearsley et al. felt the incidence of respiratory illnesses of Chinese and Caucasian infants and toddlers from predominantly working-class backgrounds, in the day care center studied was similar to that for the surrounding community.

Health data for children attending the Greensboro program were obtained through periodic pediatric examinations and from illness reports by parents and staff over a three-year period. Sick infants and toddlers were permitted to attend the center but were isolated in "sick bay." Health care was supervised by a pediatrician and the program paid "meticulous attention to staff health, hand-washing, toy washing, floor cleaning, and other environmental safeguards" (Keister, 1970a, p. 22). Again, there were no more serious diseases among center children than for the home-bound. There were also no differences in height and weight. There were, however, significantly more minor illnesses, especially diaper rash, colds, and runny noses in the center children. An interesting methodological problem also was reported which may account for the results. Initially, center health information was obtained from the nurse. However, it was found that mothers of day care children reported more illnesses than did the center nurse who examined the same children. Ironically, the nurse whose child was enrolled in the center also reported more illnesses for her child as a mother in the study than she did as the center nurse. Later center health data were based on staff observations. However, mothers continued to report more illnesses than did the staff for the same children.

Doyle (1975) collected illness data by telephone from parents for day care toddlers and a matched group of home-bound children over a two-month period. She found significantly more flu in center children. However, in view of the Chapel Hill results, these differences may be an artifact of the limited period of data collection. If the incidence of disease is no greater but merely spreads more quickly among children in group care, then it is possible that two months was not long enough to ascertain the true incidence in home-reared children.

DISCUSSION

The preponderance of available research revealed few differences between infants and toddlers attending group day care and peers who stayed at home with their mothers. With limited exceptions, most differences were in favor of the day care children. The value of the research to date is this clear consensus that a priori day care is not harmful to young children. There are, however, limitation to the existing studies in conceptualization, methodology, and generalizability.

Effects on mother—child relationships have been the greatest concern about group care of very young children. The major theoretical issues relate to the development of attachment. At its broadest level, the research question has been whether or not there were any differences in attachment between day care and home-reared children. In nine studies of attachment, only one found significant negative effects for day care children. Blehar reported more crying, more oral behavior, and more avoidance and resistance of their mothers by the day care group. The explanation for the Blehar data is unclear since two replications of the design, one with same age children and the other with younger ones, have not confirmed her results. There were, however, some methodological differences in both data gathering and analysis among the studies, and possibly some variation in the quality of group care.

Critical attachment variables suggested by Bowlby's ethological perspective involve the age of children in care, and the number and responsiveness of caregivers to the individual children. Considering first the effects of age, enrollment during the time when attachments are being formed (between 4 and 30 months) would be expected to interfere with the development of mother—child attachment. Infants and toddlers in the studies reviewed entered group care between the ages of 6 weeks and approximately 34 months. Most researchers, however, did not consider age as a dependent variable. The two who did investigate age effects involved children with average ages of two years and over. One of these reported significant negative effects for children who began day care at 26 and at 35 months of age. The other found no differences for similar aged children. A third report of a pilot study suggested an interaction between age of entry and amount of time spent each day in the center. Children who entered an infant center at 5 months and attended 8 hours a day had less positive reactions to aspects of the day care situation than children who entered at the same age but stayed only half days or other children who also attended all day but who began at a younger age. These results and those from other studies in which no differences were reported for infants beginning care before 4 months of age support the hypothesis that group care may not be disruptive to the mother—child relationship, especially if it is begun before the onset of the attachment process. The interaction between age and attendance suggests the possibility that disturbances may be related to disruption in the attachment process rather than to relationships with multiple caregivers. There may, however, be a maximum number of people with whom young children can relate.

The adult—child ratio was either 1:3 or 1:4 in all studies except those by Keister and Blehar. Keister gave no exact figure but it appeared to be 1:4/5. Blehar, the only evidence of significant negative outcomes, involved centers with the highest number of children per adult, 1:6 and 1:8. This strongly suggests a relation between the number of adults available and the effects on children; however, no day care study has experimentally tested this hypothesis.

In addition to the total number of caregivers, the number of different individuals relating to a child, the stability of the staff, and the quantity and quality of interactions may also have an influence. Such data were less frequently reported, although several programs indicated consistent staff, both in their assignment to individual children and over the duration of the projects. As is discussed later, such information is essential for relating care to outcomes for children.

While there is little data regarding the care actually provided for children in the centers studied, program descriptions imply excellent, individualized care. Limited data from two of the research programs suggest that the staff members are, indeed, responsive to individual children. Based on observations over a seven-month period in the Cornell Infant Nursery, Johnston and Ricciuti (1974) found caregivers responded within ten seconds to over 70% of infants' fussing or crying. In only 11% of the instances did it take staff longer than 30 seconds to attend a child. Somewhat more indirect evidence comes from observations in the Syracuse program. Studying information processing, Honig et al. found that 97% of the total information processing transactions for 1- and 2-year-olds came from adults, implying that staff were available for supplying and responding to information exchanges. The proportion of a child's time spent in such interactions, however, was not reported.

Regardless of tthe number of caregivers or quality of interaction, there was consistent evidence that young children did not consider staff members the same as their mothers. When a choice was available between mothers and teachers, day care children overwhelmingly preferred their mothers. There was some indication, however, that day care children, especially infants with consistent, nurturant caregivers, were capable of forming multiple attachment relationships as shown by positive greetings to caregivers, limited signs of distress at parental departure, and by the ability of the caregiver to reduce distress in the mother's absence, thus supporting previous findings of multiple attachments of home-reared children (Schaffer & Emerson, 1964).

Although these results were not completely consistent, they do suggest major revisions in Bowlby's constructs. Whatever the unique features of mother–child relationships, they clearly were maintained even though children began group care as young as 2 to 3 months of age and were away from their mothers up to 40 or more hours a week during the first three years of life. Bonding either occurs much earlier in an infant's life, requires less continuous interaction, and/or is more adaptable than Bowlby has predicted. Considering the level and quality of interaction evidently present in most of the day care settings, the results suggest a conclusion similar to Schaffer's (1963). Based on work with hospitalized infants, he concluded that the *amount* of social stimulation may be more critical than an infant's relationship with one specific figure, although such a relationship is obviously required for attachment.

The paucity of differences in attachment between home-bound and group care infants found to date does not necessarily mean there are no effects. Rather, it may reflect limitations in the conception and/or the assessment. The operational definition of attachment has been primarily the child's behavior in a strange and stressful situation and there is presently considerable controversy about the meaning of behaviors elicited by such procedures and their relation to mother–child attachment (Rheingold & Eckerman, 1973; Sroufe, 1977). Whatever this technique reveals about children's affective and/or cognitive development, it provides only limited data. It does not provide information about the interactive nature of a relationship nor about affiliations with other family members.

A whole range of other variables (which may be related to attachment as well as to other domains) also need study. Qualitative variables such as communication styles, language patterns, affect, control techniques, responsiveness, opportunities for exploration, stimulation, and learning environment all merit study in both homes and centers. There is no basic data about the amount and quality of time spent with children by either mothers or other family members. The assumption that mothers remaining at home with their children have more or better interactions with their offspring than do parents of day care children is basically undocumented.

In this reviewer's opinion, the framing of research questions primarily as prediction of negative outcomes from group care has severely limited the study of day care. Is there an optimal level of attachment or of mother–child interaction? If centers provide for one-to-one relationships and for appropriate, stimulating experiences, what are day care children gaining over home-bound?

The cross-sectional data suggested that although mothers at home were more emotionally involved with their babies, they were also much more punitive than center caregivers and their children cried more.

One area in which center children clearly have more opportunities than do home-bound children is for social interactions with nonfamily members. Day care children were consistently less interested in strange adults than were the home groups. It was unclear whether this was due to anxiety, either about strangers or their own attachment to their mothers, to learned ability to play independently, or to limitations in the number of adults with whom children could or would relate.

Behavior with caregivers was less definitive. Infants with consistent caregivers seemed to establish some attachment to them, but results from other studies ranged from no differences in the behavior of toddlers with strangers and teachers to less cooperation with, and more physical and verbal aggression expressed toward, teachers by older preschoolers who had attended group care for several years. Some of these results may be explained by developmental differences in dependence on adults.

The presence or absence of attachment to caregivers may also reflect differences in relations with them. Unfortunately, none of the studies reported data on the quality or quantity of relationships with children and only a few gave information about the stability of such relationships.

However, a follow-up study of London children who had been cared for by someone other than the mother for most of the day for at least one year during the first three years found day care boys to more active, aggressive, and less concerned with parental approval than home-bound boys. Day care girls wanted more attention than girls cared for only at home (Moore, 1964). Increased negative interactions with adults have also been related to nursery school participation for older children in previous research (Raph, Thomas, Chess, & Korn, 1968). Further study is needed to determine the cause(s) of the greater independence and self-confidence of group participants: whether it results from less interaction with parents or other adults or from inceased peer influence.

Day care children of all ages generally interacted with peers, although the nature of the encounters varied from positive to physical and verbal aggression. Babies as young as 6 months visually scrutinized other infants. One-year-olds made clear social overtures such as smiling or offering a toy, and toddlers spent 25% of their time in active interaction with other children. This interest usually extended to strange peers, but day care children clearly were more socially active with familiar classmates.

Since several of these studies of peer behavior included measures of mother—child attachment with no difference between home and day care children, it seems that peer interaction is not a substitute for poor or inadequate parental attachment, but is rather an added benefit of the group setting. These findings are, however, based primarily on ratings, especially for the older children, and to a large extent involved children from only one day care setting. These results need to be replicated and refined with more data-based designs. There are also other areas of development which merit investigation. The one finding of increased aggression of older children with peers needs to be studied further, since it was inconsistent with a previous study of some of the same children and with data from Raph et al. It does raise some intriguing questions regarding the socialization of aggression since peer groups have been found to be major contributors to its development (Hartup, 1977). Further study is needed to determine whether this outcome is valid, and if so, to ascertain whether it represents accelerated, delayed, or a different pattern of social development. As Moore (1969) has suggested, it may be that group participation and home care may lead to different personality dimensions, but that both patterns fall within the "normal" range.

In addition to offering unique opportunities for the investigation of the development of peer relations and the effects of age, composition, size, and stability on the children involved, there are other aspects of children's social and emotional development which merit study. Based on their work with day care centers, Prescott and Jones (1971) have suggested the possibility of adverse effects on self-concepts due to limited opportunities for privacy, for testing the outer limit of abilities and skills, for expression of strong emotions, and for successful management of unplanned events. They also raised intriguing questions about the knowledge day care children can gain about the adult world (activities and interaction) when children are confined to peer-oriented settings. All these issues are yet to be investigated.

Infant and toddler day care also generally facilitated cognitive development especially for most lower- and working-class children. For these children, day care enrollment beginning before 12 months of age seemed to help to maintain developmental levels while the scores for their home-reared peers dropped between the ages of 12 and 30 months. It is, however, still possible for children starting day care at a later age to make large gains on cognitive measures. One group of lower-class children who entered around age 2 experienced the greatest gains after spending 6 months to 2 years in the program. This group also appeared to be the most disadvantaged of all those studied.

The effects of the length of enrollment were less evident since all children in these studies attended an average of a least 19 months. The greatest differences between the home-reared control groups and day care children were for those who had been enrolled the longest.

There also may have been some differential effects of programs on various aspects of intellectual development. Children in some centers performed better on verbal measures while children from others did better on nonverbal items. Although the content of most programs sounded similar, there were undoubtedly differences in the implementation. Some support for this hypothesis comes from the Fowler program in which the largest proportion of teacher attention was directed toward problem-solving in visual—spatial skills, the area on which the day care children showed superior performance.

In regard to the health of children, the consensus of physicians associated with day care programs studied was that there were no serious medical consequences of day care programs studied if the center maintained adequate space, sanitation, staff, and medical supervision. Illnesses of children in day care seem to parallel those in the community in which the children lived, although infections spread more quickly in the group setting. There was, however, some indication that day care children, especially those under one year, have more minor respiratory illnesses but no more serious diseases than do home-bound infants and toddlers.

Since two programs admitted ill children with no adverse effects, serious doubt is raised about current requirements for excluding most sick children from day care attendance. Personal observations suggest more sick children presently attend day care centers than are officially acknowledged. However, it would be worthwhile to evaluate systematically the effects on a broader scale and in programs with much less health consultation than the model centers studied. Data are needed regarding the care of sick children in group settings. What kind of care do sick children receive? What effect does this have on staff time and responsibilities for well children? How are prescriptive and other medications used with children? How much supervision by medical professionals is necessary?

Some of the more interesting questions suggested by this research related to the operational definition of an adequite, safe, and healthy environment, and the interface with the provision of a stimulating program for young children. Very little information was available about the standards of health and safety actually met in the programs studied. How do health and sanitation standards affect outcomes for children? Do they influence the type and quality of play materials for infants and toddlers? Can children have experiences observing in the kitchen, preparing and serving food, setting tables, and cleaning up after themselves, and still maintain a healthy environment? Are there relations between the health of the staff and that of the children?

What about accidents? Are particular types of injuries more apt to occur in groups than at home? What are children learning about health and safety?

There are also other aspects of physical well-being of children which have yet to be studied. Although there were no reports of the effects of nutritional aspects of child care, there is some indication that centers provide both better balanced meals and greater variety than do the low-income families of children (Rosenbluth, 1977). Data are needed for both consumption patterns and developmental outcomes. What are the effects of center snacks and meals on fatigue and energy levels, concentration, or continuing food habits?

In addition to the discussions of each content area, there are several other issues which generally apply to all of the day care studies. These relate to the methodology, conceptualization, and generalizability of the current research.

First, research questions have been formulated to identify differences between children attending group day care and those remaining at home with their mothers. Future research needs to be directed toward the greater refinement and specificity of the behaviors involved and causal relations.

Second, in regard to methodology, studies of day care are not experimental. Although nonattenders were often carefully matched on several dimensions with day care children, they were not a single population randomly assigned to treatments. Consequently, it is impossible to make definitive statements about the effects of day care.

In addition, few measures are available for adequately evaluating social—emotional development and for making fine discriminations in other areas for infants and toddlers. The most standardized measures, other than the medical, were those for cognitive development. For other aspects, researchers often devised instruments. Several studies of social—emotional behavior relied on ratings. Even in instances in which different investigations used similar methodology, there were differences in technique which may explain the results. Blehar and Ragozin, for example, both used the "strange situation" procedure, but the former scored behaviors every 15 seconds and also used global ratings while the latter used 6 second intervals. Not only for the study of day care but for all research with infants and toddlers, effort must be directed toward developing valid standardized instruments and procedures for assessing all aspects of development.

Data frequently were collected only in laboratory situations. Since it is common knowledge that behavior varies with setting, future study of the effects of group care must be based on evidence collected in appropriate settings. The one study which assessed attachment in both center and laboratory situations found little intraindividual consistency in attachment behaviors.

Third, both home and group day care have been treated as single independent variables in all of the research. Virtually no information was reported about the care home-reared children received except when differences in care were the foci of the research, and only general statements were made about the centers. Yet, there are documented differences in the ways mothers and other family members interact with their infants and toddlers with diverse outcomes (Clarke-Stewart, 1973; White, Watts, Barnett, Kabar, Marmer, and Shapiro, 1973). There was also some indication that variations existed among the programs studied, although there were a number of apparent commonalities.

Day care experiences must also vary for individual children attending the same program, depending on their ages, the times of day, total number of hours in group care, and the stability of arrangement. While children studied were generally those with consistent arrangements, there is evidence that some children lack this continuity. Fowler reported a 25% drop-out rate and Saunders and Keister (n.d.), 14%. As Winett, Ruchs, Moffatt, and Nerviano (1977 p. 156) have aptly stated, research questions must be rephrased as "What kinds of children from what kinds of families, in which kinds of child care settings behave and develop in what sorts of ways?"

The final caution in the interpretation of this research is the relationship between these results and the impacts of day care programs presently available to most families. Because of the similarity of many of the findings, it is questionable whether these results are as program specific as has been suggested (MacRae and Herbert-Jackson, 1976), or whether it is the *quality* of care which is critical.

As discussed earlier in this review, little is known about the exact care provided. However, a number of dimensions appeared to the common among centers in which research children were enrolled. Many of these variables have been considered indicators of good quality day care (Caldwell, 1973; Fitzsimmons and Rowe, 1971). They were:

1. *Staff:* Personnel were carefully selected and there seemed to be little staff turnover. Programs were planned and supervised by persons with advanced degrees in child development or related fields. Although the staff caring for the children usually were paid minimum wage and had no specific training for working with infants and toddlers, they were primarily middle-class women with some college education, with previous experience with young children, and with an ability to interact warmly and responsively with individual children. Projects also provided considerable pre- or in-service training and other opportunities for staff communication. It is also probable that most staff members were motivated by being involved in an experimental program which offered stimulation well above that in typical day care centers. Regular services of pediatricians, social workers, and other auxiliary professionals were often included in the programs.

2. *Population:* Again, as was discussed in regard to attachment, the caregiver—child ratio was 1:3/4 for infants with slight increases for toddlers. The total number of children enrolled in most of the centers was 30 to 40, with stable populations of both children and staff throughout the period of the studies. Usually 15 to 20 was the maximum infant or toddler group size.

3. *Curriculum Content and Methods:* All programs emphasized responsive, individual child—caregiver relationships within a developmentally appropriate and stimulating environment. Programs usually had some articulated conceptual orientation and guidelines within which daily activities were planned and carried out. "Activities" included both a high level of adult—child verbal interactions and the availability of a range of interesting developmentally appropriate play materials.

4. *Health and Sanitation:* Children were cared for in clean, safe surroundings with continuing health surveillance. Good sanitation practices were

employed, both in relation to food handling and child care. Most centers employed nurses and/or pediatric consultants who established health policies, regularly reviewed the physical well-being of the children, and supervised the health practices of the program. Illnesses were detected early and treated appropriately. Staff maintained regular communication with parents about children's health. Also, children in most programs spent a portion of the day playing out of doors.

5. *Space and Facilities:* Although most programs indicated the need for improvements in facilities, location, or arrangement of available space, there seemed to be more than minimal play space, both indoors and outside. Centers were mostly located at ground level, usually with easy access. Surroundings were kept clean, attractive, and inviting for both children and adults. The organization of the space and the equipment available were designed to facilitate the provision of good child care.

There is no systematic data about infant—toddler programs available to the public but there is little reason to expect the quality to differ from that of existing day care for 3- to 5-year-olds. The limited information about preschool centers suggests few provide the quality of care found in the research programs.

In a 1970 survey of a national, cross-section sample of 289 centers, about one-quarter of these centers were providing custodial care *(Day Care Survey— 1970)*. Custodial care in this instance was defined as offering "food, shelter, and adult supervision, but makes no attempt to provide education, or other services such as health care or family counseling" *(Day Care Survey—1970,* p. 8). The label was not intended to convey program quality; however, the profile of custodial centers suggests limited supplies and equipment, no written schedules, large numbers of children per adult, and few trained staff.

Approximately half of the centers in the survey sample provided "some kind of educational program." The remaining 25% included both educational and other services such as health care, parent participation, counseling, etc.

The provision of custodial, education, or developmental services was closely related to program sponsorhsip. Over three-fourths of all custodial centers were proprietary, but only 17% of those categorized as developmental were. For the entire sample, proprietary programs accounted for 58% of the total number of centers and provided care for an estimated half of the children in day care centers.

In a second study of quality, the National Council of Jewish Women assessed 431 centers throughout the country (Keyserling, 1970). Members visited programs and administered a standardized interview to selected staff members. All the information collected was used in making global ratings of quality. Data included adult-child ratios, size of groups, staff training, staff salaries, educational and other services provided, hours of center operation, parent involvement, and interviewers' impressions of space, facility, and equipment, and quality of care. Poor care was found in 50% of the proprietary programs, and only fair care was being given in an additional 35%. Nonprofit programs were providing somewhat better care, with 40% rated good to superior. Still, 50% of these centers were providing only fair care.

Observations of Rubenstein and Howes in five community centers suggested infant programs of quality: yet ancedotal observations in urban and rural infant centers in a large midwestern state (Weir, 1973) revealed poor infant care. During visits to six different programs to gather data about caregiver language, child care staff were observed to be unresponsive to the children's needs and to have many directive or restrictive interactions. Staff members provided few interesting activities, often ignored children and talked with other adults, listened to radios or engaged in clean-up, housekeeping, and other maintenance tasks. Supplies and equipment were inadequate. The facilities for two of the six centers were not conductive to good programming. One center director is reported to have indicated to the observer that she hoped the program was not being observed, because "with this age group [3 months to 3 years] it's not possible to have a program" (Weir, 1973, p. 104).

In conclusion, research to date has revealed few significant differences between infants and toddlers cared for in group day care and those reared exclusively by their mothers. Although the range of developmental domains has been studied, only a limited number of issues were examined. Research questions have been global, directed primarily at the identification of differences between the two groups and the children studied were attending primarily university-affiliated programs with high adult—child ratios, selected staff, and planned, articulated philosophies and curricula. It seems time to move on to more refined hypotheses which reflect the range of children, families, programs, and developmental phenomena involved in day care settings.

REFERENCES

Ainsworth, M. Reversible and irreversible effects of maternal deprivation on intellectual development. In *Maternal deprivation*. New York: Child Welfare League of America, 1962, 42-62.

Ainsworth, M., & Bell, S. Attachment, exploration and separation: Illustrated by the behavior of one-year-olds in a strange situation. *Child Development,* 1970, *41,* 49—67.

Ainsworth, M. The development of infant—mother attachment. In B. M. Caldwell, & H. N. Ricciuti (Eds.), *Review of child development research* (Vol. 3). Chicago: Univ. of Chicago Press, 1973, 1-94.

Blehar, M. C. Anxious attachment and defensive reactions associated with day care. *Child Development,* 1974, *45,* 683-692.

Bowlby, J. *Maternal care and mental health.* Monograph Series No. 2. Geneva: World Health Organization, 1951.

Bowlby, J. *Attachment and loss.* Vol. 1: *Attachment.* New York: Basic Books, 1969.

Bowlby, J. *Attachment and loss.* Vol. 2: *Separation.* New York: Basic Books, 1973.

Boyd, M. The case against day care. *Washington Monthly,* 1976, *8,* 22-31.

Brownlee, M. A comparison of the psychological development of children with group and family infant day care experience and children reared at home for the first three years of life. Paper presented at the biennial meeting of the Society for Research in Child Development, New Orleans, March, 1977.

Caldwell, B. M. & Richmond, J. B. The children's center in Syracuse, New York, In L. L. Dittmann (Ed.) *Early child care*. New York: Atherton, 1968, 326-358.

Caldwell, B. M., Wright, C., Honing, A., & Tannenbaum, J. Infant day care and attachment. *American Journal of Orthopsychiatry*, 1970, *40*, 397-412.

Caldwell, B. M. Can young children have a quality life in day care? *Young Children*, 1973, *28*, 197-208.

Clarke-Stewart, K. A. Interactions between mothers and their young children: Characteristics and consequences. *Monographs of the Society for Research in Child Development*. Chicago: University of Chicago Press, 1973.

Congressional Record—House, December 1, 1975, H11552-11559. (a)

Congressional Record—Senate, November 19, 1975, S20397-20399. (b)

Day Care 1. A statement of principles. Washington, D.C.: U.S. Department of Health, Education, and Welfare, Office of Child Development, DHEW Publication OCD 72-10, 1971.

Day Care Survey—1970. Summary Report and Basic Analysis. Washington, D.C.: Office of Economic Opportunity, Evaluation Division, 1971.

Dittmann, L. L. A study of social interaction between infant and caretaker in two types of day care settings. Unpublished Ph.D. dissertation, University of Maryland, 1967.

Doyle, A. Infant development in day care. Paper presented at the meeting of the Canadian Psychological Association, Windsor, Ontario, June, 1974.

Doyle, A. Infant development in day care. *Developmental Psychology*, 1975, *11*, 655-656.

Durfee, J. T., & Lee, L. C. Infant—infant interactions in a day care setting. Paper presented at the annual meeting of the American Psychological Association, Montreal, Canada, August, 1973.

Farran, D. C., & Ramey, C. T. Infant day care and attachment behaviors towards mothers and teachers. Revision of a paper presented by C. Ramey at the annual meeting of the American Psychological Association, Chicago, September, 1975.

Farran, D. C., & Ramey, C. T. Infant day care and attachment behaviors toward mothers and teachers. *Child Development*, 1977, *48*, 1112-1116.

Fitzsimmons, S. J., & Rowe, M. P. *A study in child care*. Vol. 1: *Findings*. Day Care Programs Reprint Series. U.S. Department of Health, Education, and Welfare/Office of Education, National Center for Educational Communication. OE-20169, 1971.

Fowler, W. A developmental learning approach to infant care in a group setting. *Merrill-Palmer Quarterly*, 1972, *18*, 145-175.

Fowler, W. From intuitive to rational humanism: The comparative effects of group and home care on infant development. Paper presented at the annual meeting of the Canadian Psychological Association, Windsor, Ontario, June, 1974.

Fowler, W. How adult/child ratios influence infant development. *Interchange*, 1975, *6*, 17-31.

Freeman, H., Jr. *A study of families in group and family infant day care programs*. Paper presented at the biennial meeting of the Society for Research in Child Development, New Orleans, March, 1977.

Golden, M. New York City infant day care study overview. Paper presented at the biennial meeting of the Society for Research in Child Development, New Orleans, March, 1977.

Hartup, W. W. Peer interaction and the processes of socialization. In M. J. Guralnick (Ed.), *Early intervention and the integration of handicapped and nonhandicapped children*. Baltimore: Univ. Park Press, 1977.

Honing, A. S., Caldwell, B. M., & Tannenbaum, J. Patterns of information processing used by and with young children in a nursery school setting. *Child Development,* 1970, *41,* 1045-1065.

Hunt, J. McV. *Intelligence and experience.* New York: Ronald, 1961.

Johnson, J. E., & Ricciuti, H. N. Crying and the relief of distress in an infant day nursery. Technical Report, Cornell Research Program in Early Development and Education. Ithaca, N.Y.: Cornel University, January, 1974.

Kagan, J., Kearsley, R. B., & Zelazo, P. R. The effects of infant day care on psychological development. *Evaluation Quarterly,* 1977, *1,* 109-142.

Kearsley, R. B., Zelazo, P. R., Kagan, J., & Hartmann, R. Separation protest in day-care and home-reared infants. *Pediatrics,* 1975, *55,* 171-175.

Keister, M. E. *"The good life" for infants and toddlers.* Washington, D.C.: National Association for the Education of Young Children, 1970. (a)

Keister, M. E. *A review of experience-establishing-operating-evaluation-a demonstration nursery center for the daytime care of infants and toddlers, 1967-1970.* (Final Report, Grant No. D-256, Children's Bureau, U.S. Department of Health, Education, and Welfare, Child Welfare Research and Demonstration Grants Program and the University of North Carolina at Greensboro.) June 1970. (b)

Keyserling, M. D. *Windows on day care.* New York: National Council of Jewish Women, Inc., 1970, 130-165.

Lay, M. Z., & Meyer, W. J. *Effects of early day care experience on subsequent observed program behaviors.* (Final Report to the Office of Education, Subcontract 70-007). Syracuse, N.Y.: Syracuse University, 1971.

Lindstrom, D., & Tannenbuam, J. Concept and language development of a group of five year olds who attended the Syracuse University Children's Center Intervention Program. Paper presented at the annual meeting of the American Psychological Association, Miami, 1970.

Loda, F. The health of children in group day care. In R. Elardo & B. Pagan (Eds.), *Perspectives on infant day care.* Orangeburg, S.C.: Southern Association on Children Under Six, 1972.

Loda, F. A., Glezen, W. P., & Clyde, W. A., Jr. Respiratory disease in group day care. *Pediatrics,* 1972, *49,* 428-437.

Maccoby, E. E., & Feldman, S. S. Mother—infant attachment and stranger-reactions in the third year of life. *Monographs of the Society for Research in Child Development,* 1972, *37* (1, Serial No. 146).

MacRae, J. W., & Herbert-Jackson, E. Are behavioral effects of infant day care program specfic? *Developmental Psychology,* 1976, *12,* 269-270.

Moore, T. W. Children of full-time and part-time mothers. *International Journal of Social Psychiatry,* Special Congress Issue, 1964, No. 2.

Moore, T. W. Stress in normal childhood. *Human Relations,* 1969, *22,* 235-250.

New York City Infant Day Care Study. Input Section: Final Progress Report, February 1, 1972—October 31, 1974, Office of Child Development (DHEW), OCD-CB-118. New York: Medical and Health Research Association of New York City, Inc.

Peterson, F. C. A study of nutritional aspects of day care programs. Unpublished master's thesis, The Pennsylvania State University, 1973.

Policare, H. J. A comparison of the psychological experience of infants in group and family day care. Paper presented at the biennial meeting of the Society for Research in Child Development, New Orleans, March, 1977.

Prescott, E., & Jones, E. Day care for children—Assets and liabilities. *Children,* 1971, *18,* 54-58.

Ragozin, A. Attachment behavior in day care children: Field and laboratory findings. Paper presented at the biennial meeting of the Society for Research in Child Development, Denver, April, 1975.

Ragozin, A.   Attachment behavior of day care and home-reared children in laboratory settings. (ADAI Report No. 77–23.) Seattle: Univ. of Washington, n.d.

Raph, J., Thomas, A., Chess, S., & Korn, S. The influence of nursery school on social interactions. *American Journal of Orthopsychiatry*, 1968, *38*, 144-152.

Rheingold, H., & Eckerman, C. D. Fears of the stranger: A critical examination. In H. W. Reese (Ed.), *Advances in child development and behavior* (Vol. 8). New York: Academic Press, 1973, 186-223.

Ricciuti, H. N. Fear and the development of social attachments in the first year of life. In M. Lewis & L. Rosenblum (Eds.), *The origins of human behavior: Fear.* New York: Wiley, 1974.

Ricciuti, H. N., & Poresky, R. Development of attachment to caregivers during the first year of life. Paper presented at the biennial meeting of the Society for Research in Child Development. Philadelphia, March, 1973.

Robinson, H. B., & Robinson, N. M. Longitudinal development of very young children in a comprehensive day care program: The first two years. *Child Development,* 1971, *42*, 1673-1683.

Rosenbluth, L. A comparison of the nutrition provided to infants in group and family day care in their day care setting. Paper presented at the biennial meeting of the Society for Research in Child Development, New Orleans, March, 1977.

Rubenstein, J. L., & Homes, C. Caregiving and infant behavior in two natural environments. Paper presented at the Annual Convention of the American Psychological Association, Washington, D.C., September, 1976.

Saunders, M., & Keister, M. E. *Family day care: Some observations.* Washington, D.C.: Day Care and Child Development Council of America, n.d.

Schaffer, H. R. Some issues for research in the study of attachment behaviors, In B. M. Foss (Ed.), *Determinants of infant behavior,* (Vol. 2). New York: Wiley, 1963, 179-199.

Schaffer, H., & Emerson, P. The development of social attachments in infancy. *Monographs of the Society for Research in Child Development,* 1964, *29.*

Schwarz, J. C., Kralick, G., & Strickland, R. G. Effects of early day care experience on adjustment to a new environment. *American Journal of Orthopsychiatry.* 1973, *43*, 340-346.

Schwarz, J. C., Strickland, R. G., & Kralick, G. Infant day care: Behavioral effects at preschool age. *Developmental Psychology,* 1974, *10*, 502-506.

Sroufe, L. A., & Waters, E. Attachment as an organizational construc. *Child Development,* 1977, *48*, 1184-1199.

Weir, M. K. *An observational study of language behavior of caregivers toward infants enrolled in day care centers.* Unpublished doctoral dissertation, University of Illinois, 1973.

White, B. L. An experimental approach to the effects of early experience on human behavior. In J. P. Hill (Ed.), *Minnesota Symposia on Child Psychology* (Vol. 1). Minneapolis: Univ. of Minnesota Press, 1967, 201-226.

White, B. L., Watts, J. C., with Barnett, I. C., Kaban, B. T., Marmer, J. R., & Shaprio, B. B. *Experience and environment. Major influences on the development of the young child.* Englewood Cliffs, N.J.: Prentice–Hall, 1973.

Willis, A., & Ricciuti, H. Longitudinal observations of infants' daily arrivals at a day care center. Technical Report, Cornell Research Program in Early Development and Education. Ithaca, N.Y.: Cornell University, January 1974.

Willis, A., & Ricciuti, H. *A good beginning for babies.* Washington, D.C.: National Association for the Education of Young Children, 1975.

Winett, R. A., Ruchs, W. L., Moffatt, S. Q., & Nerviano, V. J. A cross-sectional study of children and their families in different child care environments: Some data and conclusions. *Journal of Community Psychology,* 1977, *5*, 149-159.

5

Does the Changing View of Early Experience Imply a Changing View of Early Development?[1]

Dale Goldhaber

University of Vermont

There is a small but growing movement occurrng in child development which is directed at the keystone of most early childhood education theory. It argues that the early childhood years (0 to 5) are not disproportionately more influential in defining the course of development. In fact, for some aspects of development, the early years may even be relatively unimportant. This paper first reviews the theoretical and empirical basis supporting both the traditional strong early experience position and the newer strong life span position. It then defines the factors responsible for the emergence of this new view of early development. Finally, the paper discussed the implications of this new view for our understanding of the role of early experience and the facilitation of early childhood development.

THE STRONG EARLY EXPERIENCE POSITION

Evans (1975) argues that a strong early experience view involves five basic assumptions:

1. Children are, by nature, malleable and their growth and development can be modified extensively in a variety of directions.
2. The earlier one can effect a plausible intervention, the better.

---

[1] Earlier versions of this paper were presented at the Society for Research in Child Development meeting, New Oreleans, 1977 and The Fifth Biennial Conference in Human Development, Atlanta, 1978.

3. The manipulation of early experience will influence subsequent psychological functioning. This influence can be salutary or hindering. In either case, cumulative development is involved.
4. The provision of qualitatively sound experience can mollify or compensate for basic lacks in the child's environments. Such lacks define the basis on which experiences can be built. Furthermore, since the school's scholastic emphasis demands certain basic learning capabilities, such capabilities must become the focus for early intervention.
5. Children who fail to reap the benefits of planned intervention are likely to develop in ways that are counter productive to extant social-educational conditions. Or, since a high level capacity for symbolic (cognitive) activity is one of man's greatest strengths, children who manifest disorders in cognitive performance are failing to achieve their human potential. Thus, resources must be marshalled to prevent or remediate such disorders. (p. 6)

Clearly, no scholars have been more responsible for the development of these assumptions than Benjamin Bloom (1964) and J. McV. Hunt (1961, 1964, 1969). Bloom's (1964) analysis of the major longitudinal studies led to a number of conclusions concerning the course of human development. Among these were that "variations in the environment have their greatest quantitative effect on a characteristic at its most rapid period of change and least effect on a characteristic during the least rapid period of change" (p. vii), and that "in terms of intelligence measured at age 17 about 50% of the development takes place between conception and age 4, about 30% between ages 4 and 8, and about 20% between ages 8 and 17" (p. 88). Bloom's conclusion about intellectual development at age 4 is of course both widely known and held by many teachers and parents of young children.

In *Intelligence and Experience,* Hunt (1961) convincingly laid to rest the outmoded views of intelligence as fixed and predetermined. In its place, he provides a learning theory-oriented interpretation of Piaget that supports a developmental epigenetic view "the concept of the match." The concept of the match implies that successful development occurs through the successive, cumulative exposure of children to increasingly complex and symbolic materials and experiences.

Although Hunt and Bloom arrived at essentially identical conclusions, they did so by way of different routes. Bloom's was statistical and psychometric. He made extensive use of Anderson's (1939) overlap hypothesis. The hypothesis states that the "correlations in longitudinal data are a direct function of the percent of the development at one age which has been obtained at an earlier age" (Bloom, 1964, p. 28). According to Bloom, this view of longitudinal data is most clearly true for characteristics which are additive. That is, what is obtained by one age is not lost and is included in the measure of the characteristic at a later age. Height is an excellent example. Correlations between measures at two points in time are assumed a function of the height present at time one plus the gain between time one and time two. As the rate of gain decreases, the degree of overlap increases and the resulting correlation increases. Since Bloom's

50% statement was based on an overlap analysis, it is reasonable to conclude that he also viewed intellectual development as an additive process.

Hunt's (1969) analysis was based on the view that "the effects of cultural deprivation are analogous to the experimentally found effects of experiential deprivation in infancy" (p. 47). These found effects were of three types. The first were studies of animals who experienced atypical or abnormal early rearing experiences. These included the work of Denenberg (1969), Harlow (1949, 1958), Levine (1957, 1961), Riesen (1958, 1961), and Scott (1968). The second were reports of children experiencing atypical abnormal early experiences. These included the work of Dennis (1938, 1940, 1941), Goldfarb (1955), John (1963), and Lewis (1961, 1966). The third were studies of planned early childhood inte-intervention experiences. These included the work of Bereiter and Englemann (1966), Karnes and Hodgins (1969), Klaus and Gray (1968), Skeels (1966), Skeels and Dye (1939), Weikart (1967) and White and Held (1966).[2]

Along with the writings of Caldwell (1967), Hebb (1949), and Fowler (1962), the works of Bloom and Hunt provided much of the theoretical and empirical justification for the legislation of federal monies over the past decade toward programs for young children and their families.

THE STRONG LIFE SPAN POSITION

Although the strong life span position sees early experience as an essential link in the developmental chain, it does not view early experience as necessarily having any long-term significance upon adult behavior (Clarke, 1968). Rather, the degree to which early experiences continue to influence subsequent development depends upon the mechanisms insuring the continuity of those early experiences (Zigler, 1977), as well as the potency of the environment in which the individual is currently functioning (Kagan & Klein, 1973).

Put more simply, the strong early experience position views early experience as both a necessary and, in many instances, a sufficient condition for future development. The strong life span position views early experience as a necessary but not sufficient condition for future development. One should not interpret this strong life span view as implying that the early years are unimportant. To say that experiences during the early years are not sufficient for future development does not make these experiences any less necessary.

The most complete reviews of the importance of early experience within a life span framework have been done by the Clarkes (Clarke, 1968; Clarke &

---

[2]This list of studies supporting a strong early experience view is not meant to be necessarily current. Since the focus of the first section of this discussion is on the origins of a strong early experience view, more contemporary studies are not included. For a more contemporary review, the reader is referred to Evans (1975), Day and Parker (1977), Morrison (1976), and Fein and Clarke-Stewart (1973).

Clarke, 1972; Clarke & Clarke, 1976; Clarke, Clarke & Reiman, 1958). Their work has examined the issues of critical periods in early development, the long term durability of early experiences, the relevance of animal research on the effects of early experience, and the reversibility of early trauma.

They believe that:

1. the notion of a critical period of development exercising a powerful influence on later characteristics does not accord with some evidence of the development of deprived children, and particularly of those who had experienced significant environmental change;
2. normally, and for most children, environmental change does not occur, so in later life one may be looking at the outcome, not merely of early experience, but of continuing experiences;
3. experimental studies of extreme deprivation in animals, while important, must for a number of reasons be regarded with caution before extrapolation of these findings to humans; and
4. important experiments on reversing the effects of early experience in animals remain to be carried out. (Clarke & Clarke, 1976, p. 12)

As the Clarkes (1976) point out, the strong early experience advocates have always used the animal literature as a source of evidence for their hypothesis. This inclination is no doubt a reflection of Hunt's (1969) comparison between cultural deprivation and atypical or abnormal early rearing experiences in animals. Historically, the works of Sluckin (1964), Harlow (1963), Levine Levine & Lewis, 1959), Thompson and Heron (1954), and Melzack (1954) have been most prominent. Data from these experiments invariably support a critical period view of early experience.

The issue is not, however, as clear-cut as the studies listed above would lead one to believe. Critical periods have been artificially extended (Salzen & Sluckin, 1959). Harlow (Harlow, Schiltz, & Harlow, 1969) has reported that isolated monkeys showed less abnormal behavior with subsequent pregnancies. And Peters and Murphy (1966) have suggested, that, at least for rats, later traumatic experiences may have a more permanent effect than earlier experiences.

In a more recent review of the effects of early experience on later behavior in rats, Erlenmeyer-Kimbling (1972) reports that "out of a total of 40 studies testing the permanence of early treatment effects there were 37 in which at least one of the tested strains failed to display a significant difference between the experimental and control condition" (p. 192). Further, early experience did not significantly influence performance on the subsequent behavioral task in 87 out of the total 162 studies reviewed. In fact, she concludes, it seems that we have a better than even chance of not finding a significant relationship between an early treatment and a subsequent measure of behavior.

Regardless of the viewpoint supported by research with animals one must still question the extent to which data can transfer across phylogenetic lines (see King, 1958). Comparative developmentalists may some day answer this question; for now it is worth remembering Hebb's (1949) observations that (1) more complex relations can be learned by higher species at maturity; (2) simple relations are learned about as promptly by lower as by higher species; and (3) the first learning is slower in higher than in lower species.

Research on the influence of early experience with humans has typically taken one of two forms—the reversibility of early developmental trauma, or the long-term stability of early personality characteristics.

Early developmental trauma has been operationalized both in terms of biomedical events surrounding the birth process (e.g., anoxia, use of medication) and inhuman rearing conditions associated with abuse and neglect and with severely substandard institutionalization.

In a recent review Sameroff (1975a) failed to find a consistent association between early short-term trauma and subsequent developmental status. He notes that the St. Louis studies on anoxia found that although anoxic infants, when compared to nonanoxic controls, did poorly on newborn measures and still showed deficits at age 3, they performed almost as well as nonanoxic controls by age 7. Sameroff also failed to find stable relationships between events related to pregnancy, prematurity, and delivery on subsequent developmental status.

Sameroff believes that the long-term significance of early experience depends upon the amount, intensity, and duration of subsequent experiences. Only when an early experience initiates a cumulative sequence would one expect long-term predictability.

Sameroff's reference to the work of Weiner, Bierman, and French is a good example. Weiner et al. followed up all 670 infants born on the island of Kauai Hawaii. Each infant was initially scored on a four-point scale for severity of prinatal complications. At 20 months and again at 10 years of age, these perinatal scores were related to assessments of physical health, psychological status, SES, family stability, and mother's IQ. At 20 months, low SES infants who had suffered severe perinatal stress were found to be four or five times more impaired than high SES infants experiencing the same initial trauma. But by the 10-year evaluation, neither SES group showed a correlation between 10-year status and nature and degree of perinatal status.

Sameroff concludes that perinatal complications are consistently related to later physical and psychological development, only when combined with, and supported by, persistently poor environmental circumstances. The data further suggest that risk factors operative during the perinatal period tend to disappear during childhood as more potent familial and social factors exert their influence.

Although initial work on the long-term consequence of early severe developmental trauma was extremely pessimistic as to outcome (e.g., Bowlby, 1951; Dennis & Najarian, 1957; Goldfarb, 1943; Trasler, 1960), follow-ups (Sayegh & Dennis, 1965), reinterpretations of data (Rutter, 1972), extensions of data gathering (Clarke, Clarke & Rieman, 1958), and newer data (Rigler & Rigler, 1975) suggest a much more optimistic prognosis. Two studies in particular are worthy of further mention. The first is Kadushin's (1970) evaluation of older child adoptive placements and the second is Kagan and Klein's (1973) study of Guatemalyan Indian children.

Children classified as "hard to place" by social services agencies are age 3 or older, and have usually lived for a period of time with their biological parents or parent. Separation from the parents results from death, abandonment, abuse, or neglect. Because these children are not readily adoptive and because the legal ties of the child to the biological parent are often not completely severed, they may live in as many as four or five foster homes before being cleared for adoption. The early lives of these children are often insecure, inconsistent, indeterminate, harsh, and abusive.

Kadushin (1970) evaluated success of placement for a group of 91 children (51% female, 49% male) between 5 and 12 years of age at the time of adoptive placement. The children's early histories are characterized by large families (52% had five or more siblings), substandard housing, low income, poorly educated parents (only 2% of the fathers completed high school), high degree of parental conflict, physical neglect, and emotional indifference.

All of the children became available for adoption through legal termination of parental rights. Given the court's traditional reluctance to terminate parental rights (see Goldstein, Freud, & Solnit, 1973), Kadushin sees the court's action as corroborating the social worker's negative characterization of the home.

The children experienced several changes of residence (average, 2.3) before adoptive placement and were in their middle teens at the time of follow-up. Success of placement was determined through separate semi-structured interviews with each adoptive parent. The focus of the interviews centered on the parents' satisfactions and dissatisfactions with the adoption, the problems they encountered, and the adaptations they made. Two measures were obtained from the interviews. The first was a satisfaction-dissatisfaction ratio derived from the transcripts of the interviews; the second, a checklist which provided an overall measure of satisfaction in the adoption experience.

Drawing conclusions from the composite of the two measures, Kadushin judged 78% of the adoptions successful, 13% unsuccessful, and 9% mixed. In an attempt to explain the findings, Kadushin examined a number of possible factors. Three factors were negatively related to success of placements: (1) age of child at placements; (2) number of previous placements; and (3) degree of manifest pathology by the child. Seven factors showed no relation to success of placements: (1) sex of child; (2) age of adoptive parents; (3) religion of adoptive parents; (4) socioeconomic status of adoptive parents; (5) extent of socioeconomic change of adoptive parents from biological home; (6) previous experience as parents; and (7) composition of the adoptive family. Acceptance of the adoptive child as a member of the family and a lack of self-consciousness on the part of the parents concerning their adoptive status were the two factors correlating positively with success of placement.

Given the very high percentage of successful placements, it is reasonable to conclude that for most children the influence of their present environment more than offset the influence of their past environment.

Perhaps the most dramatic evidence bearing on the influence of early experience are the findings of Kagan and Klein (1973). Their sample of one-year-old Guatemalyan Indian infants, raised by American standards in a severely deprived environment, showed marked developmental retardation when compared to a same age American sample. However, an 11-year-old Indian sample having an identical infancy without deliberate intervention, showed no retardation when compared to an 11-year-old American sample. They conclude that:

> These data do not indicate the importance of early environments but rather the potency of the environment in which the organism is functioning. There is no question that early experience seriously affects kittens, monkeys, and children. If the first environment does not permit the full actualization of psychological competencies, the child will function below his ability as long as he remains in that context. But if he is transferred to an environment that presents greater variety and requires more accommodations, he seems more capable of exploiting that experience and repairing the damage wrought by the first environment than some theorists have implied. (p. 960)

In explaining why similar findings have not been found with our disadvantaged populations, Kagan and Klein note that "we live in a society in which the relative retardation of a 4-year-old severely influences his future opportunities because we have made relative retardation functionally synonymous with absolute retardation" (p. 961).

The early intervention literature is another area evaluating the influence of early developmental trauma.

Notwithstanding recent papers by Palmer and Siegel (1977), and Seitz, Apfel, and Efron (n.d.), most follow-up studies (see Bronfenbrenner, 1975) have found little evidence for the long lasting effects. These negative results have, of course, been interpreted in a number of ways. Bronfenbrenner (1975) argues that permanence will only be demonstrated when the family is given a more significant role in the intervention process. Jensen (1969) believes that the deficiencies are primarily genetic in origin and therefore not sensitive to environmental manipulation. Rohwer (1971) and Elkind (1969, 1976) each believe that the prime time for intervention is not the preschool but rather the elementary school years. Finally Ginsburg (1972) finds the deficit present in the culture, not the children.

It is important to note that a strong life span view would only require significant treatment effects, measured at program completion, to justify an intervention effort. If children completing the intervention program were significantly different than initially comparable groups of children either experiencing different programs or none at all, then it is reasonable to conclude that the program works. Since from the strong life span view, events cumulatively interact with each other, conclusions from long-term follow-up evaluations would be ambiguous since it would be difficult to unravel the intervention component from postintervention components. The insistence on such inappropriate evaluation criteria as long-term follow-up has much to do with our failure to convince funding sources of the legitimacy of our intervention efforts.

I know of no research at any other point of the life span that has as consistently shown significant pre-post test differences as has the early intervention literature. Yet because of our support of an increasingly questionable view of early development, we have found ourselves making excuses for the failure of a theory, rather than advocating for the repeatedly justified success of a program.

Studies of longitudinal growth and development provide still another source of evidence concerning the stability of early developmental characteristics. As hypothesized by Clarke (1968):

> If in early life the basic characteristics of the individual are firmly laid down as a result of genetic and experiential factors in combination and interaction, then one would expect a high correlation between personality assessments of the very young child and those of the same individual when adult. (p. 1067)

Evidence from longitudinal studies does not support such a hypothesis.

The Fels (Kagan & Moss, 1962) study found virtually no correlation between adult behaviors and child behaviors during the 0 to 3 or 3 to 6 age periods. Significant predictors of adult behaviors did not appear until the 6 to 10 age period, and they were not only low in magnitude but only present if the behavior was consistent with culturally sanctioned sex role standards. For Kagan and Moss, it was the years of 6 to 10 and not the preschool and infancy years that were the critical periods.

They conclude that the first four years of contact with the school and peer environments crystallize behavioral tendencies that are maintained through young adulthood.

MacFarlane (1963, 1964), in summarizing results from the Berkeley longitudinal studies, noted that only one-third of the adult status predictions derived from early childhood indicators proved accurate. Approximately 50% turned out more stable and effective as adults than predicted, and 20% less so.

In discussing the 20% that did less well than predicted, she observed that:

> Here too the theoretical expectations were rudely jarred by the adult status of a number of our subjects who early had had easy and confidence-inducing lives. As children and adolescents they were free of severe strain, showed high abilities and talents, excelled at academic work and were the image of success. One now sees among them at age 30 a high proportion of brittle, discontented, and puzzled adults whose high potentialities have not been actualized, at least of now. (1964, p. 121)

Elder's (1974) description of his more deprived middle-class sample growing up during the depression provides a similar pattern. Individuals from the deprived middle-class sample were found more likely to be functioning well as adults than the nondeprived individuals.

THE NEW ZEITGEIST

Much of the literature bearing on the relative merits of a strong life span view of early experience is not new. Why then are we (Sameroff, 1975; Clarke, 1976; Goldhaber, 1977) now considering a reevaluation of the role of early experiences? I believe this new zeitgeist is the result of the convergence of five relatively overlapping areas of research. These areas are:

1. the continuing reinterpretation of Piaget;
2. the increasing usage of transactional developmental methodology;
3. the reemergence of stage based developmental models;
4. the reemergence of a strong life span developmental psychology; and
5. the reemergence of a "sympathetic" understanding of the child.

Continuing Reinterpretation of Piaget

In *Intelligence and Experience*, Hunt (1961) devoted a large portion of the book to the review, interpretation, and evaluation of Piagetian theory. It is clear from Hunt's treatment of Piaget that he saw the theory as supporting a strong early experience position. Others (e.g., Lavetelli, 1968; Kamii & De Vries, 1977; Weikart, 1972) have also made similar interpretations of Piagetian theory.

Strong life span proponents, however, also seem comfortable with Piagetian theory. Elkind (1969) has noted that "while children all over the world and across wide ranges of cultural and socioeconomic conditions appear to attain concrete operations at about the age of 6 or 7, the attainment and use of formal operations in adolescence, in contrast, appear to be much more subject to socioculturally determined factors such as sex roles and symbolic proficiency" (p. 333). Flavell (1971), in commenting on a paper delivered by Beilin on "Developmental Stages and Developmental Processes," says that Beilin's reinterpretation of Piaget's theory as essentially maturationist is "a reinterpretation with which I am largely in accord although I didn't realize it until last year or so" (p. 190).

For Piaget (1971) neither camp seems to offer much shelter. In the general discussion that followed Flavell's comments on Beilin's paper, Piaget made the following observation:

> My friend Daniel Berlyne wrote an article maintaining I was a neobehaviorist, and today Beilin has read a paper showing that I am a maturationist. In fact, I am neither one nor the other. I refuse to admit the necessity of a choice between these alternatives, and Beilin's paper has proven very instructive in that it has shown how difficult it is for me to make myself understood. (p. 192)

It would seem as if American developmentalists' ability to assimilate Piagetian theory is a reflection of their present level of cognitive functioning, specifically, of their concrete need to organize information into either/or type categories. As Furth (1973) well points out, Piagetian theory is concerned with species-specific developmental experiences. Such experiences do not lend themselves to factorial analysis. Rather than arguing whose side Piaget really is on, developmentalists would do better to spend their time determining how Piagetian concepts can best be used to facilitate the development of young children. I will return to this point in a later section.

Increasing Use of Transactional Developmental Methodology

If early experiences are best viewed as a necessary but not sufficient link in the developmental chain, how are these influences best documented and understood?

Traditionally, the answer to this question has been through the use of analysis of variance (ANOVA) type procedures. These procedures are compatible with the principles of parsimony and rigorous experimental control that have guided most developmental research for the past two decades.

Central to the appropriate use of ANOVA models is the assumption of additivity—specifically, that the relative influence of factors can be parceled out and separate variance estimates attributed to each. It is becoming increasingly clear, however, that this additive model is an inappropriate representation of the developmental process. It is becoming equally clear that additive models must be replaced with models that have both ecological validity (Bronfenbrenner, 1977) and a transactional perspective (Sameroff, 1975a, 1975b).

Bronfenbrenner (1977) has said that "much of American developmental psychology is the science of the strange behavior of a child in a strange situation with a strange adult" (p. 278). Although we are able to measure such behavior with great rigor, we are often left with information that has little significance outside of that strange situation. It would seem that when laboratory-oriented developmentalists adopted the methods of the physical and biological sciences, they failed to appreciate the difference between recreating the natural environment within the laboratory and merely studying an event under laboratory controlled conditions. In fact, the degree of control (or perhaps the larger sample) necessary to produce a desired effect within the laboratory may well be inversely related to that variable's influence in a more typical environment.

Transactional developmental models permit the study of interactions over time. In so doing, they make it possible to show that interrelationships between individuals within settings are not constant over time. They also make it possible to show that a continuity of experiences is necessary to maintain the influence of an early developmental event.

In concluding his review of early influences on development (a review stressing the necessity of transactional developmental models), Sameroff (1975a) notes that:

> Despite the reasonableness of the notion that one should be able to make long range predictions based on the initial characteristics of a child or his environment, the above review has found little evidence for the validity of such predictions. One view of the inadequacy of developmental predictions sees their source in the scientist's inability to locate the critical links in the causal chain leading from antecedents to consequents. A second view, propounded above, is that such linear sequences are non-existent and that development proceeds through a sequence of regular restructerings of relations within and between the organism and the environments (p. 285).

Reemergence of Stage-based Developmental Models

As previously noted, the strong early experience position reflects a quantitative, continuous, linear development model; the strong life span position, a qualitative, discontinuous, transactional developmental model. The growth of the strong life span position reflects, in part, the growing acceptance of stage based developmental models.

According to Reese and Overton (1970), developmental stages are best understood as levels of organization. Level of organization, in turn, is best defined as a unique set of structure-function relationships. "As organization changes to the extent that new system properties emerge and become operational, we speak of a new level of organization which exhibits a basic discontinuity with the previous level" (Reese & Overton, 1970, p. 143). The notion of a basic discontinuity clearly contradicts the cumulative assumption of a linear model. Hence the life span position.

Our changing view of stage theory is illustrated by the types of research that Piagetian theory has generated. Whereas initial work attempted to either disprove (e.g., Hall & Simpson, 1968) or "create" (Gagne, 1968) Piagetian stages, later work seems to have acknowledged their "realness" and has instead focused on acceleration (White, 1975) and application (Poulsen, Magay, & Luber, 1976) of stage-based development.

Reemergence of a Strong Lifespan Developmental Psychology

Closely tied to the issue of stage-based developmental models has been the re-emergence of a strong lifespan developmental psychology. (Baltes & Schaie, 1973; Datan & Ginsberg, 1975; Goulet & Baltes, 1970; Nesselroade & Reese, 1973).

As the "terminal status" (Bloom, 1964) for development is extended beyond adolescence through adulthood to the aging years, evidence of long-term stability from the early childhood years becomes increasingly difficult to find. In some instances, it is rather the accumulation of relatively discrete events that eventually produces a developmental outcome (e.g., Sameroff & Chandler, 1975). In others, it is the development during adulthood of still additional developmental stages (Riegel, 1973). And in still others, it is the emergence of developmental events that has little, if any antecedent in the preadult years (Neugarten, 1969). This broadening of perspective is clearly forcing a reevaluation of the significance of events during the early years.

The life span perspective is especially useful in helping to unravel the multiple determinants of continuity and discontinuity—specifically, in separating the influence of the historical-cultural context on development from the maturational context (Stein & Baltes, 1975). For example, the data from Fels longitudinal study (Kagan & Moss, 1962) showed that

> the degree of continuity of these response classes was intimately dependent upon its congruence with traditional standards for sex role characteristics. The differential stability of passivity, dependency, aggression, and sexuality for males and females emphasizes the importance of cultural roles in determining both behavioral change and stability. (p. 268)

If their conclusion is correct, a replication of the study with a group of children socialized toward androgyny should result in a very different pattern of correlations across time.

Reemergence of "Sympathetic" Understanding of the Child

In concluding her very insightful book *Life Among the Giants,* Young (1966) remarks that only when we come to enjoy children for what they are rather than what they might become can we truly facilitate their development. Hers is a sympathetic understanding of the child.

Although there is nothing inherently unsympathetic in the strong early experience view its' assumed direct casual link to later development gives the early years a unique focus, intensity, and concern. White's (1975) recent book serves as a good example. White warns parents that if they have not provided the proper environment for their child by age 3, they may have so handicapped their child that subsequent intervention may be virtually useless. Conversely, if they have done a good job, a few years of a mediocre school system should have little impact on the child. Bijou (1976) takes a similar view when he predicts that future educators will view "preschool as the most important educational experience in a person's life" (p. 164). It would be hard for parents simply to enjoy their children knowing the gravity of their rearing techniques.

A strong life span view sees the early years in a different light. It sees the early years as a more canalized period (Waddington, 1962) than those developmental stages that follow (although it is likely that the aged years may prove an equally canalized period).

According to Fishbein's (1976) explanation of canalization:

The genotype of an individual contains a set of instructions for the potential interactions of the developing phenotype with the environment. Owing to environmental or genetic differences, there are aspects of development which will vary across individuals of a species such as rate of growth, size, and shape of various bodily structures, specific coloration of skin or hair, and certain behavioral and physiological functions. There are other aspects of development, however, that are relatively invariant or constant across individuals despite environmental or genetic differences, e.g., two eyes and one nose, and certain behavioral and physiological functioning, e.g., the sucking reflex and temperature regulation. Both aspects of development are under the control of a number of genes, but the constancies are said to be canalized. By this we mean that the developmental pathways of the phenotype are resistant to moderate genetic and environmental stresses which might deflect development away from those phenotypes. In a sense, at each point in development, for all members of a species, and for a variety of phenotypic characteristics, a set of targets is aimed for, and despite underlying genetic variability, genetic processes operate together to ensure that the targets will be hit. This is a very active process in which genes compensate for, or collaborate with one another to ensure that phenotypic development will reach these targets, by whatever route is necessary. (pp. 34-35)

I would be the first to recognize that the concept of canalization raises more questions than it answers concerning the course of early development. Up to what age is behavior strongly canalized? Is cognitive development more canalized than social development? Is canalization more or less of a factor in highly industrialized societies? Notwithstanding these and other questions, the concept of canalization deserves serious attention as an alternative way of viewing the early years.

There are others who have reached similar conclusions. Elkind (1974) believes that the child's early development is more resilient to stress than previously thought. Sameroff (1975a) argues that "despite the great variety and range of influences on development, there are a surprisingly small number of developmental outcomes. Evolution appears to have built into the human organism regulative mechanisms to produce normal developmental outcomes under all but the most adverse of circumstances" (p. 283). Skolnick (1976) notes that before age 7 maturation plays a major role in developmental change. After age 7, learning and culture become the major forces in psychological development. And as previously noted, Flavell (1971) has come to hold such a view. He believes that cognitive changes during childhood have formal "morphogenetic" properties which must have a biological growth process as their substrate: "The major cognitive changes in neurologically intact children are largely inevitable, momentous, directional, uniform and irreversible" (p. 191). From such a view, one is again forced to share Kagan and Klein's (1973) conclusion that "we live in a society in which the relative retardation of a 4-year-old severely influences his future opportunities because we have made relative retardation functionally synonymous with absolute retardation" (p. 960).

IMPLICATIONS FOR EARLY CHILDHOOD DEVELOPMENT

Before discussing the implications of a strong life span view for early childhood development I want to state clearly what are *not* the implications. They are *not* that early developmental experiences are unimportant, unnecessary, and of no value. They are *not* that the best intervention is no intervention. They are *not* that we should return to early childhood programs consistent with the views of Gesell (1940) and Goodenough (1934). On the contrary, a strong life span view sees the early years as very important. Where the strong life span view differs from the strong early experience view concerns the nature of development during the early years and how this development can be best facilitated. Specifically, the strong life span position offers three major implications for early childhood development:

1. a greater appreciation of the distinction between species-specific and culture-specific development;
2. a greater emphasis on the importance of the continuity of educational experiences; and
3. a role for early childhood educators that emphasizes horizontal extension rather than vertical acceleration.

Distinction Between Species-specific and Culture-specific Development

Species-specific characteristics are those aspects of behavior and development that are found in all members of a species. Such characteristics are relatively unaffected by environmental circumstance, and with the exception of organically impaired individuals, develop in a similar rate and sequence. For humans, the two most obvious examples are language development and the development of sensory-motor skills.

Culture-specific behaviors are unique to a historical time and place. Since they are not common to all members of the species, they may be considered as acquired skills. Whereas the ability to use language is species-specific and therefore does not require a deliberate acquisition process, the acquisition of a particular technology does require some deliberate form of intervention. The relative importance, influence, and dominance of species-specific and culture-specific development is not constant across the life cycle. The strong life span view supports the hypothesis that the early years are more a period of species-specific development than subsequent developmental periods. Statements supportive of the hypothesis by Flavell (1971) and Skolnick (1976) have already been mentioned. Sameroff and Chandler (1975) make strong reference to the self-righting tendencies of the young child. Further, Kagan and Klein (1973) conclude from their San Marcos sample that:

> The properties of the motor or autonomic system occur because each physiological system or organ naturally exercises its primary function. The child explores the unfamiliar and attempts to match his ideas and actions to some previously acquired representation because these are basic properties of the mind. The child has no choice. (p. 961)

There is a striking parallel between the species-specific/culture-specific distinction and the cultural difference/cultural deficiency interpretations of developmental differences between priviledged and nonpriviledged racial, ethnic, and social groups. It should be clear that since a strong life span view sees the early years as a period of strong species-specific development, it would also support Cole and Bruner's (1972) argument that the differences between cultural groups are at most superficial and Ginsburg's (1972) argument that the environment of the poor child is quite adequate for promoting the basic forms of cognitive activity.

Importance of the Continuity of Education Experiences

Clearly one of the most important implications of the strong life span view is that for an environmental intervention to be significant, it must have a high degree of continuity. As Kagan and Klein (1973) note, such a view does not indicate the impotence of early environments, but rather the potency of the environment in which the organism is functioning.

For the early childhood educator, the continuity issue takes two forms: (1) insuring continuity with both subsequent education experiences (school-preschool continuity) and contemporaneous educational experiences (preschool-parent continuity); and (2) making sure that the preschool does not become the scapegoat for children's failure in the elementary school (Elkind, 1969).

Although the strong life span view is certainly not alone in advocating strong continuity within the child's early developmental experiences, the assumptions of this view change the advocacy from one of preference to one of necessity. The fact that there is a paucity of information in the literature concerning continuity is perhaps some indication of its relative importance from a strong early experience perspective.

What we do know about home/school continuity clearly supports Bronfenbrenner's (1975) conclusion that "without family involvement, intervention is likely to be unsuccessful, and what few effects are achieved are likely to disappear once the intervention is discontinued" (p. 470).

The family involvement need not be solely in terms of direct intervention. Thomas and Bowermaster (1974) believe that continuity in terms of expectations and ease of transition may be equally important. They find that children whose home experience is congruent with their school experience seem to have greater success in school. For early childhood educators, this means a renewed emphasis on explaining to parents at the beginning of the program all aspects of program functioning, staffing, evaluation, and intervention. Home/school continuity can be enhanced through the use of home visits, parent meetings, use of parent resources in the school, and the incorporation of home values into the educational program (e.g., bicultural and bilingual programs).

As difficult as these goals are to obtain in preschool programs, they become even more elusive in day care programs. Powell's (1977a, 1977b) analysis of parent-caregiver relationships in day care settings found the "highest frequency of parent-caregiver exchange occurs at the transition point when parents leave and pick up their children at the center" (1977b, p. 5). Telephone contact were the next most frequent communication made and parent conferences, always a strong component of preschool programs, last (less than 25% of the parents had a scheduled conference with center staff). When one considers the confusion at the transition time, the fact that some parents never even leave their car, the fact that at pick-up time most parents are tired and eager to get home, and that because of staggered staffing patterns a particular child's caregiver is less likely to be present than during the middle of the day, it is a miracle that any communication takes place at all. Where good parent-caregiver communicatoion exists, it was more a function of informal friendship networks than planned efforts to enhance continuity. This finding reinforces the notion that day care should function as an extended family. Powell's (1977b) conclusion is bleak:

> If these research findings are used to construct the social world of day care children, the image which emerges is one of fragmentation and discontinuity. For many children it appears the boundaries of the child care center and the family are sharply defined and narrow in intersection. Evidences of system interdependency are few. The world is a disconnected one, with the child's family, other children's families and the day care center functioning as independent, detached systems. (p. 18)

Improving preschool/school continuity is a no less necessary and no less elusive goal. Continuity can be improved through two actions—maintenance of the peer group across transition, and greater teacher-to-teacher communication patterns. Wolff and Stein (1966) have found that stability of Head Start gain is partially a function of the percentage of the kindergarten class that were Head Start participants. Specifically, they found that gains were maintained through the kindergarten year as long as a minimum of 25% of the group had participated in Head Start. Their findings reinforce those of Powell (1977a, 1977b) concerning the importance of factors maintaining the community context of the educational experience. Unfortunately, as Thomas and Bowermaster (1974) note, as long as composition of the peer group is considered more important than the continuity of the peer group, little improvement in this area is likely.

Elkind and Lyke (1975) offer a number of practical suggestions for improving teacher/teacher continuity. They believe that the growth of early childhood programs has often increased tensions between early childhood and kindergarten teachers. First, the increased emphasis on cognitive development, stemming from a strong early experience view, has resulted in many early childhood programs incorporating activities and materials into their curriculum that were once the sole province of the kindergarten. Second, the approach to education is often different.

> Despite the current emphasis upon cognitive training, most early education programs maintain their traditional child-centered and informal approach to classroom organization. At the elementary school level, however, the new emphasis on structural management systems for learning is being extended downward to the kindergarten classrooms. The result is that children from early education programs come bounding into kindergarten classrooms as autonomous creatures used to a lot of self-selected learning experience, only to be met by a classroom teacher who in many instances, must get them through a programmed learning experience. (p. 396)

To resolve these tensions, Elkind and Lyke suggest communication focusing on overlap and complement, sharing and coordination of materials and activities, and exchange visits to become more familiar with one another's classrooms, facilities, and teaching demands. Only then will we begin to approach Anderson and Shane's (1972) "seamless learning."

Recent reports on the persistence of preschool effects (Lazar, Hubbell, Murray, Rosche, & Royce, 1977; Palmer, 1977; Vopava & Royce, 1978) might lead one to question the importance of the continuity of educational experiences. Consistent with a main effects model these reports show that children having participated in one of a number of early intervention programs were less likely, during the middle grades, to be found in special education classes or to have been required to repeat a grade, than were children who had not participated in early intervention programs. How are these encouraging findings explained? The Consortium on Developmental Continuity report implies that the differences are due entirely to events that occurred before the children entered the public school. At no point in the report does there appear any discussion concerning the interaction of preschool and school experiences. In fact, not one of the report's recommendations addresses the issue of the continuity of educational experiences. I frankly find it hard to believe that there can be a direct causal link between events separated by years independent of the experiences during that time span. Zigler (1977) seems to share my skepticism:

> The evidence for these projects allows for but one conclusion: There are long-lasting effects from early intervention programs. Even minimal intervention efforts such as Palmer's where a child came to the program a couple of hours each week, show measurable differences several years later. What is mediating

those effects? I do not really believe that two hours a week can make that much difference in the life of a child. The real lever that produces these effects may turn out to be what the program stimulates the mother to do with the child. (p. 6)

A much better understanding of the long-term consequences of early developmental experiences is provided by recent reports from Shipman (1978) and Honig, Lally, and Mathieson (1978).

Shipman and her colleagues were interested in identifying the developmental sequence experienced by high and low achieving children between preschool and grade three. Of particular interest to Shipman were those children who deviated most from the preschool estimates of their later school performance. Their (1978) conclusion is clear:

> Of primary importance was the finding that a warm, supportive home atmosphere combined with a warm, supportive school setting creates an upward spiraling in a child's ability to achieve. In other words, cognitive gains are likely to be greatest when the total ecology of the child is supported at home and in school. A corollary to that observation is that the quality of either parent-child or teacher-child interaction alone is generally not sufficient for modifying the deleterious effects of poverty that act upon the developing child. Rather sustained intellectual growth depends on the quality of relationships established between parents, teachers, and child. (p. 4-5)

Honig's findings are equally significant. She found that by first grade the difference between the intervention and nonintervention children (initially in favor of the intervention children) had become nonsignificant. Follow-up observations on the children in first grade showed why the initial advantage was eroding. What she found was a significant increase in teacher-directed antisocial behavior among the intervention children. These behaviors were not found during the kindergarten follow-up. Honig believes that the abrupt change in class size and organization beginning in first grade left many intervention children with attention-getting strategies that were once (but no longer) appropriate. As a result they were forced to adopt increasingly more negative behaviors in order to maintain the level of teacher attention they had come to expect. To put it another way, the gains these children made did not fade away; they were extinguished through a lack of continuity.

A Role for Early Childhood Education
That Emphasizes Horizontal Extension

What types of educational experience should young children have? For what are these years the prime time? They are the prime time for expansion of those developmental skills which are universally found in preschool-age children.

A strong life span view argues that stage-based development through the early childhood years is virtually universal among all organically intact children. As a result, efforts to accelerate this development are unnecessary, of little lasting effect, and, in a sense, harmful, because they occupy time that could be better used in other ways. Harmful because "the data suggest the hypothesis that the longer we delay formal instruction, up to certain limits, the greater the period of plasticity and the higher the ultimate level of achievement" (Elkind, 1965, p. 332).

Piaget has noted that children are not always able to apply their cognitive structure equally well in different content areas (the sequence of conservation acquisitions being a prime example). Even though two tasks involve the same logical relations and are presented in a parallel manner, the child is often able to master one before the other. Piaget has referred to the phenomenon as horizontal decalage. Although there is clearly an ad hoc quality to the concept (Phillips, 1975), a possible explanation may lie in the tendency of our educational system (including preschool formal instruction) to emphasize instruction in limited areas, namely language and cognition. As Kohlberg (1968) argues, however, Piaget and his followers have systematically studied the development of preschool children in a wide range of activities including play, their conversations with one another, their conceptions of life, death, and reality, and their concepts of sexual identity, and of "good and evil" (pp. 1056-7). In other words, the proper goal of early education is to broaden the usage base of stage-based developmental skills. If, as Flavell (1971) suggests, development is a sort of megaphone with the small end toward birth and the large end toward maturity, efforts to broaden the circumference of the small end could produce results of geometric proportions.

There is a second proper goal for early education. It should help make learning and mastery fun.

> The guiding principle of early education (preschool and elementary) should be to provide the child with repeated experiences of gratification resulting from intellectual activity. Lest this recommendation be grossly misread, it must be emphasized that it refers to satisfying work and play, not to training in techniques of self-indulgence and mediocrity. (Rohwer, 1971, p. 338)

Both Elkind (1965) and Rohwer (1971) express concern that the extension of formal academic instruction into the early years may result in intellectually burned out children. They both believe that early formal instruction blunts the child's intrinsic motivation for learning.

The goals of horizontal extension and gratification from learning experiences are no less proper, no less urgent, and certainly of no less lasting significance than those consistent with a strong early experience view. For those who see the strong life span view as questioning the need for any form of planned early childhood educational experience, I would argue that exactly the opposite conclusion is true.

REFERENCES

Anderson, J. E. The limitations of infant and preschool tests in the measurement of intelligence. *Journal of Psychology*, 1939, *8*, 351-78.

Anderson, R. H., & Shane, H. G. Implications of early childhood education for life-long learning in I. Gordon (Ed.), *Early childhood education.* Chicago: NSSE, 1972.

Baltes, P. B., & Schaie, K. W. *Life span developmental psychology: Personality and socialization.* New York: Academic Press, 1973.

Bereiter, C., & Engelmann, S. *Teaching disadvantaged children in the preschool.* Englewood Cliffs, N.J.: Prentice-Hall, 1966.

Bijou, S. W. *Child development: The basic state of early childhood.* Englewood Cliffs, N.J.: Prentice-Hall, 1976.

Bloom, B. J. *Stability and change in human characteristics.* New York: Wiley, 1964.

Bowlby, J. *Material care and mental health.* Geneva: World Health Organization, 1951.

Bronfenbrenner, U. Is early intervention effective? In J. Hellmuth (Ed.), *Exceptional infants*, Vol. 3. New York: Bruner/Mazel, 1975.

Bronfenbrenner, U. Ecological factors in human development in retrospect and prospect. In H. McGurk (Ed.), *Ecological factors in human development.* Amsterdam, Holland: North-Holland, 1977.

Caldwell, B. M. What is the optimal learning environment for the young child? *American Journal of Orthopsychiatry*, 1967, *37*, 8-20.

Clarke, A. D. B. Learning and human development. *British Journal of Psychiatry*, 1968, *114*, 1061-1077.

Clarke, A. D. B., & Clarke, A. M. Revovery from the effects of deprivation. *Acta Psychologica*, 1959, *16*, 137-144.

Clarke, A. D. B., & Clarke, A. M. Consistency and variability in the growth of human characteristics. In W. D. Wall & V. P. Varma (Eds.), *Advances in Educational Psychology*, Vol. 1. New York: Barnes & Noble, 1972.

Clarke, A. M., & Clarke, A. D. B. *Early experience: Myth and evidence.* New York: Free Press, 1976.

Clarke, A. D. B., Clarke, A. M., & Reiman, S. Cognitive and social changes in the feebleminded—three further studies. *British Journal of Psychology*, 1958, *49*, 144-157.

Clarke-Stewart, A. K. Interactions between mothers and their young children: characteristics and consequences. *Monographs of the Society for Research in Child Development*, 1973, *38*, (6-7, Serial No. 153).

Cole, M. & Bruner, J. Preliminaries to a theory of cultural differences in I. Gordon (Ed.), *Early childhood education.* Chicago: NSSE, 1972.

Datan, N., & Ginsberg, L. H. *Life span developmental psychology: Normative life crises.* New York: Academic Press, 1975.

Day, M. C., & Parker, R. K. *The preschool in action* (2nd ed.). New York: Allyn & Bacon, 1977.

Denenberg, V. The effects of early experience. In E. S. E. Hofez (Ed.), *The behavior of domestic animals* (2nd ed.). New York: Baillieu, Tindall & Cox, 1969.

Denenberg, V., & Karas, G. G. Interactive effects of age and duration of infantile experience on adult learning. *Science*, 1960, *131*, 227-8.

Dennis, W., & Dennis, M. G. Infant development under conditions of restricted practice and minimum social stimulation: a preliminary report. *Journal of Genetic Psychology*, 1938, *53*, 151-156.

Dennis, W., & Dennis, M. G. The effect of cradling practice upon the onset of walking in Hopi Indians. *Journal of Genetic Psychology*, 1940, *56*, 77-86.

Dennis, W., & Dennis, M. G. Infant development under conditions of restricted practice and minimum social stimulation. *Genetic Psychology Monographs*, 1941, *23*, 149-155.

Dennis, W., & Najarian, P. Infant development under environmental handicap. *Psychological Monographs*, 1957, *71*, 1-13.

Elder, G. H. *Children of the great depression.* Chicago: Univ. of Chicago Press, 1974.

Elkind, D. Piagetian and psychometric conceptions of intelligence. *Harvard Educational Review*, 1969, *39*, 319-337.

Elkind, D. *A sympathetic understanding of the child: Birth to sixteen.* Boston: Allyn & Bacon, 1974.

Elkind, D. *Child development and education.* New York: Oxford Univ. Press, 1976.

Elkind, D., & Lyke, N. Early education and kindergarten: Competition or cooperation. *Young Children*, 1975, *30*, 393-401.

Erlenmeyer-Kimling, L. Gene-environment interaction and the variability of behavior. In L. Ehrman, G. S. Omenn, & E. Caspari (Eds.), *Genetics, environment and behavior.* New York: Academic Press, 1972. Pp 181-209.

Evans, E. D. *Contemporary influences in early childhood education* (2nd ed.). New York: Holt, Rinehart, & Winston, 1975.

Fein, G. C., & Clarke-Stewart, A. *Day care in context.* New York: Wiley, 1973.

Fishbein, H. D. *Evolution, development, and childrens learning.* Pacific Palisades, Calif.: Goodyear, 1976.

Flavell, J. H. Comments on Beilins paper. In D. R. Green, M. P. Ford, & G. B. Flamer (Eds.), *Measurement and Piaget.* New York: McGraw-Hill, 1971. Pp. 189-191.

Fowler, W. Cognitive learning in infancy and early childhood. *Psychological Bulletin*, 1962, *59*, 116-152.

Furth, H. G. Piaget, IQ, and the nature-nurture controversey. *Human Development,* 1973, *16*, 61-74.

Gagne, R. Contributions of learning to human development. *Psychological Review,* 1968, *75*, 177-191.

Gagne, R. M., & Paradise, N. E. Abilities and learning sets in knowledge acquisition. *Psychological Monographs*, 1961, *75*, 14 (Whole No. 518).

Gesell, A., Halverson, H. M., Thompson, H., Ilg, F. L., Castner, B. M., & Ames, L. B. *The first five years of life.* New York: Harper & Row, 1940.

Ginsburg, H. *The myth of the deprived child.* Englewood Cliffs, N.J.: Prentice-Hall, 1972.

Goldfarb, W. The effects of early institutional care on adolescent personality. *Journal of Experimental Education*, 1974, *12*, 106-29.

Goldfarb, W. Emotional and intellectual consequences of psychologic deprivation in infancy: A re-evaluation. In W. Hock, & J. Zubin, (Eds.), *Psychopathology of childhood.* New York: Grune & Stratton, 1955. Pp. 105-119.

Goldhaber, D. E. Early experience: A life-span perspective. Paper presented at the Society for Research in Child Development meeting, New Orleans, 1977.

Goldstein, J., Freud, A., & Solnit, A. J. *Beyond the best interests of the child.* New York: Free Press, 1973.

Goodenough, F. L. *Developmental Psychology.* New York: Appleton-Century, 1934.

Goulet, L. R., & Baltes, P. B. (Eds.). *Life span developmental psychology: Research and theory.* New York: Academic Press, 1970.

Hall, V. C., & Simpson, G. J. Factors influencing extinction of weight conservation. *Merrill-Palmer Quarterly,* 1968, *14*, 197-211.

Harlow, H. F. The formation of learning sets. *Psychological Review,* 1949, *56*, 51-65.

Harlow, H. F. The nature of love. *American Psychologist,* 1958, *13*, 673-85.

Harlow, H. F. The maternal affectional system. In B. M. Foss (Ed.), *Determinants of infant behavior.* London: Methuen, 1963.

Harlow, H. F., Schiltz, K. A., & Harlow, M. K. The effects of social isolation on the learning performance of rhesus monkeys. In C. R. Carpenter (Ed.), *Proceedings of the second international congress of primatology*, Vol. 6. New Orleans, La.: Krager, 1969.

Hebb, D. O. *Organization of behavior.* New York: Wiley, 1949.

Honig, A., Lally, J. R., & Mathieson, D. A. Personal-social adjustment of school children after five years in a family enrichment program. Paper presented at the Fifth Biennial Southeastern Conference on Human Development, Atlanta, 1978.

Hunt, J. McV. *Intelligence and experience.* New York: Ronald Press, 1961.

Hunt, J. McV. The psychological basis for using preschool enrichment as an antidote for cultural deprivation. *Merrill-Palmer Quarterly,* 1964, *10*, 209-248.

Hunt, J. McV. *The challenge of incompetence and poverty.* Urbana, Ill.: Univ. of Illinois Press, 1969.

Jencks, C. *Inequality.* New York: Basic Books, 1972.

Jensen, A. R. How much can we boost IQ and scholastic achievement? *Harvard Educational Review,* 1969, *39*, 1-123.

John, V. P. The intellectual development of slum children: Some preliminary findings. *American Journal of Orthopsychiatry,* 1963, *33*, 813-822.

Kadushin, A. *Adopting older children.* New York: Columbia Univ. Press, 1970.

Kagan, J. Resilience in cognitive development. *Ethos,* 1975, *3*, 231-247.

Kagan, J., & Klein, R. E. Cross-cultural perspectives on early development. *American Psychologist,* 1973, *28*, 947-962.

Kagan, J., & Moss, H. A. *Birth to maturity.* New York: Wiley, 1962.

Kamii, C., & DeVries, R. Piaget for early education. In M. C. Day & R. K. Parker (Eds.), *The preschool in action* (2nd ed.). Boston: Allyn & Bacon, 1977.

Karnes, M., & Hodgins, A. The effects of a highly structured preschool program on the measure intelligence of culturally disadvantaged four-year-old children. *Psychology in the Schools,* 1969, *6*, 89-91.

King, J. A. Parameters relevant to determining the effects of early experience upon the adult behavior of animals. *Psychological Bulletin,* 1958, *55*, 46-59.

Klaus, R. A., & Gray, S. W. The early training project for disadvantaged children: A report after five years. *Monograph of the society for research in child development,* 1968, *33*, 4 (Serial No. 120).

Kohlberg, L. Early education: A cognitive developmental view. *Child Development,* 1968, *39*, 1013-1063.

Labov, W. The logical non-standard English. In F. Williams (Ed.), *Language and poverty.* Chicago: Mark Lane Press, 1970.

Lavatelli, C. A Piaget-derived model for compensatory preschool education. In J. Frost (Ed.), *Early childhood education rediscovered.* New York: Holt, Rinehart, & Winston, 1968.

Lazar, I., Hubbell, V. R., Murray, H., Rosche, M., & Royce, J. *The persistence of preschool effects.* DHEW Publication No. (OHDS) 78-30129, 1977.

Levine, S. Infantile experience and consummatory behavior in adulthood. *Journal of Comprehensive and Psychiological Psychology,* 1957, *50*, 609-612.

Levine, S. Psychophysiological effects of early stimulation. In E. Bliss (Ed.), *Roots of behavior.* New York: Hoeber, 1961.

Levine, S., & Lewis, G. W. The relative importance of experimenter contact in an effort produced by extra-stimulation in infancy. *Journal of Comparative and Physiological Psychology,* 1959, *52*, 368-9.

Lewis, O. *The children of Sanchez.* New York: Random House, 1961.

Lewis, O. The culture of poverty. *Scientific American,* 1966, *215*, 19-25.

MacFarlane, J. W. From infancy to adulthood. *Childhood Education,* 1963, *39*, 336-342.

MacFarlane, J. W. Perspectives on personality consistency and change from the guidance study. *Vita Humana,* 1964, *7*, 115-126.

McCall, R. B. Challenges to a science of developmental psychology. *Child Development,* 1977, *48*, 333-345.

Melzack, R. The genesis of emotional behavior: An experimental study of the dog. *Journal of Comparative and Physiological Psychology,* 1954, *47*, 166-68.

McClelland, D. C. Testing for competence rather than for "intelligence." *American Psychologist*, 1973, *28*, 1-14.

Morrison, G. S. *Early childhood education today.* Columbus, Ohio: Merrill, 1976.

Nesselroade, J. R., & Reese, J. W. (Eds.). *Life span developmental psychology: Methodological issues.* New York: Academic Press, 1973.

Neugarten, B. L. Continuities and discontinuities of psychological issues into adult life. *Human Development*, 1969, *12*, 121-130.

Palmer, F. H. The effects of early childhood educational intervention on school performance. Paper prepared for the President's Commission on Mental Health, 1977.

Palmer, F. H., & Siegel, R. J. Minimal intervention at ages two and three and subsequent intellectual changes. In M. C. Day & R. K. Parker (Eds.), *The preschool in action* (2nd ed.). Boston: Allyn & Bacon, 1977.

Peters, J. E., & Murphy, O. D. Emotional trauma in rats: Age as a factor in recovery. *Conditional Reflex*, 1966, *1*, 51-56.

Phillips, J. L. *The origins of intellect: Piagets theory.* San Francisco: Freeman, 1975.

Piaget, J. General discussion comments on Beilin, H. Developmental stages and developmental stages and developmental processes. In D. R. Green, M. P. Ford, & G. B. Flamer (Eds.), *Measurement and Piaget.* New York: McGraw-Hill, 1971.

Poulsen, M. K., Magay, J. F., & Luber, G. I. (Eds.). *Piagetian theory and the helping professions.* Los Angeles: Univ. of Southern California Press, 1976.

Powell, D. R. A social-psychological study of the relationship between parents and day care programs. Paper presented at the American Educational Research Association meeting, New York, 1977   (a)

Powell, D. R. The coordination of preschool socialization: Parent-care giver relationships in day care settings. Paper presented at the Society for Research in Child Development meeting, New Orleans, 1977   (b)

Reese, H. W., & Overton, W. F. Models of development and theories of development. In L. R. Goulet & P. B. Baltes, *Life span developmental psychology: Research and theory.* New York: Academic Press, 1970, 116-150.

Riegel, K. F. Dialectic operations: The final period of cognitive development. *Human Development*, 1973, *16*, 346-370.

Riesen, A. H. Plasticity of behavior: Psychological aspects. In H. F. Harlow & C. N. Woolsey (Eds.), *Biological and biochemical bases of behavior.* Madison, Wisc.: Univ. of Wisconsin Press, 1958.

Piesen, A. H. Stimulation as a requirement for growth and function in behavioral development. In D. W. Fiske & S. R. Maddi (Eds.), *Functions of varied experience.* Homewood, Ill.: Dorsey, 1961.

Rigler, D., & Rigler, M. Persistent effects of early experience. Paper presented at the biennial meeting of the Society for Research in Child Development, Denver, 1975.

Rohwer, W. D. Prime time for education: Early childhood or adolescence. *Harvard Educational Review*, 1971, *41*, 316-342.

Rutter, M. *Maternal deprivation reassessed.* Baltimore, Md.: Penguin, 1972.

Salzen, E. A., & Sluckin, W. The incidence of the following response and the duration of responsiveness in domestic fowl. *Animal Behavior*, 1959, 7, 172-179.

Sameroff, A. Early influences on development: Fact or fancy? *Merrill-Palmer Quarterly*, 1975, *21*, 267-295.   (a)

Sameroff, A. Transactional models in early social relations. *Human Development,* 1975, *18*, 65-79.   (b)

Sameroff, A., & Chandler, M. J. Reproductive risk and the continuum of caretaking casualty. In F. D. Horowitz (Ed.), *Review of child development research*, Vol. 4. Chicago: Univ. of Chicago Press, 1975. Pp. 187-245.

Sayegh, V., & Dennis, W. The effects of supplementary experiences upon the behavioral development of infants in institutions. *Child Development*, 1965, *31*, 174-183.

Scott, J. P. *Early experience and the organization of behavior.* Belmont, Calif.: Brooks/Cole, 1968.

Seitz, V., Apfel, N. H., & Efron, C. Long term effects of intervention: A longitudinal investigation. Unpublished manuscript, n.d.

Shipman, V. Notable early characteristics of high and low achieving black low-SES children. Project Report 76-21. Princeton, N.J.: Educational Testing Service, 1978.

Skeels, H. M. Adult status of children with contrasting early life experiences: A follow-up study. *Monographs of the Society for Research in Child Development*, 1966, *31*, 3 (Serial No. 105).

Skeels, H. M., & Dye, H. B. A study of the effects of differential stimulation of mentally retarded children. *Proceedings of the American Association of Mental Deficiency*, 1939, *44*, 114-36.

Skolnick, A. *Rethinking childhood.* Boston: Little, Brown, 1976.

Sluckin, W. *Imprinting and early learning.* London: Methuen, 1964.

Sluckin, W. *Early learning in man and animals.* Cambridge, Mass.: Schenkman, 1970.

Sptiz, R. A. Hospitalism: An inquiry into the genesis of psychiatric conditions in early childhood. *The Psychoanalytic Study of the Child*, 1945, *1*, 53-74.

Stein, A. H., & Baltes, P. B. Theory and methods in life-span developmental psychology: Implications for child development. Paper presented at the Society for Research in Child Development meeting, Denver, 1975.

Thomas, S. B., & Bowermaster, J. *The continuity of educational development.* ERIC Document PS007 571, 1974.

Thompson, W. R., & Heron, W. The effects of early restriction on activity in dogs. *Journal of Comparative and Physiological Psychology*, 1954, *47*, 77-82.

Trasler, G. *In place of parents.* London: Routledge & Kegan Paul, 1960.

Vopava, J., & Royce, J. Comparisons of long-term effects of infant and preschool programs on academic performance. Paper presented at the American Educational Research Associate Meeting, Toronto, 1978.

Waddington, C. H. *New patterns in genetics and development.* New York: Columbis Univ. Press, 1962.

Waddington, C. H. *Principles of development and differentiation.* New York: Macmillian, 1966.

Weikart, D. C. (Ed.). *Preschool intervention: A preliminary report of the Perry preschool project.* Ann Arbor, Mich.: Campus Publ., 1967.

Weikart, D. C. Relationship of curriculum, teaching and learning in preschool education. In J. C. Stanley (Ed.), *Preschool programs for the disadvantaged.* Baltimore, Md.: Johns Hopkins Press, 1972.

White, B. L. *Human infants.* Englewood Cliffs, N.J.: Prentice-Hall, 1971.

White, B. L. *The first three years of life.* Englewood Cliffs, N.J.: Prentice-Hall, 1975.

White, B. L., & Held, R. Plasticity of sensorimotor development in the human infant. In J. F. Rosenblith & W. Allen Smith (Eds.), *The causes of behavior: Readings in child development and educational psychology*, (2nd ed.). Boston: Allyn & Bacon, 1966.

Wolff, M., & Stein, A. *Six months late: A comparison of children who had Head Start summer 1964 with their classmates in kindergarten.* ERIC document ED015025, 1966.

Young, L. *Life among the giants.* New York: McGraw-Hill, 1966.

Zigler, E. The effectiveness of Head Start: Another look. Paper presented at the annual meeting of the American Psychological Association, San Francisco, 1977.

6

Evaluation
of Early Childhood Programs:
Toward a Developmental Perspective[1]

Ruby Takanishi

University of California, Los Angeles

The widespread evaluation of social action and educational programs is barely a decade old (Ross & Cronbach, 1976). Much of this evaluation activity has centered on programs serving low-income and minority group children and their families. The mandate for the evaluation of these early childhood programs took the fields of developmental psychology and early childhood education by surprise. Few individuals existed in either field in the mid-sixties who were knowledgeable and trained in evaluation, which itself lacked a theory unique to its special problems (Guba, 1969). In this vacuum, evaluation became associated with the measurement of child outcomes which could be reliably assessed. One result was that certain valuative, epistemological, and conceptual assumptions related to research with young, developing children were overlooked.

For a number of reasons, the evaluation of programs serving young children and their families continues to be an important social and scientific issue. The most important reason for continued controversy is the diversity of strongly held beliefs regarding the effectiveness of these programs among diverse constituencies (Katz, 1975; Zigler, Note 10). This paper acknowledges the inherently political nature of evaluation activities (Datta, 1976; House, 1973), but focuses on presenting a developmental perspective on evaluation and suggesting how this perspective can inform future evaluation studies of early childhood programs.

[1] A version of this paper was presented at the annual meeting of the American Educational Research Association, Toronto, Canada, March 28, 1978.

141

The major points of this paper can be summarized as follows:

1. The evaluator's model of development, whether explicit or implicit, is reflected in his or her design and doing of evaluation. Models of development influence decisions about what are considered meaningful problems or questions to pose in an evaluation, what methods of data collection and analysis will be used, how the data will be interpreted, and what implications for policy are drawn. Progress in evaluating early childhood programs should not be associated only with increasingly sophisticated research designs and advanced statistical techniques. Fundamental questions about the nature of human development as well as the purposes of evaluation are also involved.

2. The evaluation of early childhood programs, like most evaluation studies, is dominated by psychometric, experimental, and behavioristic models (Eisner, 1977; Guba, 1969; House, 1976; Levine, 1974; Patton, Note 4). Program outcomes have been limited to standardized measures which can be reliably assessed, e.g., IQ and achievement, with less attention to the meaningfulness of what is being measured (Messick, 1975). Within the dominant evaluation model, change is defined quantitatively as the acquisition of more pieces of information, knowledge, and experiences without attention to the structures underlying observed changes. A child's behavior or performance is assessed to determine his position in relation to single standards, e.g., intelligence tests (Riegel, 1972).

3. Evaluation lacks a perspective which is grounded in the nature of developmental change and in which means-ends relations and their transformations are central. I will argue that there is an incongruity between current evaluation strategies and the phenomena under study. Within a developmental perspective, change is considered to be qualitative as well as quantitative: "New properties emerge, irreducible to lower levels and, therefore, qualitatively different from them" (Overton & Reese, 1973, p. 70). There are multiple influences on development which result from a complex transaction between internal and external forces. The nature of developmental change is considered to be dynamic and differentiated, with multiple outcomes as well as multiple pathways to similar behavior. A developmental perspective encourages multigenerational and multicultural standards (Riegel, 1972).

4. The evaluation of early childhood programs would benefit from a developmental perspective to guide its activites. The purposes of evaluation would then be changed to focus on program, adult, and child development. This paper represents some steps toward a developmental perspective on evaluation and is far from being complete. The developmental perspective must be considered because of the importance of evolving evaluation strategies that are uniquely suited to early childhood programs and that also share in emergent models in the general field of evaluation itself (Hamilton et al., 1977; Willis, 1978).

MODELS OF DEVELOPMENT

Katz (1975), in her discussion of early childhood programs and ideological disputes, observed that in the formal research and evaluation literature the exchange of divergent views concerning what young children need and how these needs should be satisfied is typically couched in the language of theory, methodology, and evaluation. She argued that the conflicts are not theoretical ones, but ideological ones related to strongly held conceptions of childhood, development, and the good life, which cannot be settled by appeals to evidence. Several other writers in child development have pointed out that a major problem in the evaluation of early childhood programs is the failure to relate evaluation strategies to multiple views of learning and development (Almy, 1975; Kamii & Elliott, 1971; Kohlberg & Mayer, 1972; Murphy, 1973; Sigel, 1972).[2]

For the purposes of this paper, it is argued that the evaluator's idea or model of development with its related values is reflected in his design and doing of evaluations. Models create lenses from which certain phenomena are seen and others excluded (Petrie, 1972). They determine what are considered meaningful questions for an evaluation, what methods of data collection and analysis will be used, how the data will be interpreted, and what implications for policy are drawn. Evaluators are socialized to certain values and models of development as part of their training and to a shared sense of what is acceptable to their colleagues or reference groups. Evaluation involves evaluators-as-persons involved in networks of scholarly, social, and political relationships which, in turn, affect their evaluation designs (Sjoberg, 1975).

The evaluations of Sesame Street illustrate the fact that two groups of investigators with different value perspectives asked different questions and derived different conclusions. Ball and Bogatz (1970) accepted and used the curriculum goals of the program and found that Sesame Street met the goal of stimulating the growth of children who watched the show more than comparable groups that did not. Cook and his associates (1975) interpreted the goal of Sesame Street to be a decrease in the gap between low- and middle-income children in terms of learning, and concluded that the program was not successful in narrowing the gap between the two groups.

[2]Economic and political ideologies have influenced the concept of development in American developmental psychology (Riegel, 1972). Riegel contended that quantitative models are associated with the "capitalistic" orientation of the Anglo-American countries, and represent continuous growth models in which all individuals are evaluated against single standards. The "mercentalistic-socialistic" orientation of the European continent is represented by qualitative models which focus on the organization and structure of experiences and which evaluate individuals according to multiple standards. Detailed analyses of the ideological and philosophical underpinnings of models of development have been described elsewhere (Riegel, 1972; Kvale, 1973, 1976) and will not be covered here.

In agreement with Kuhn's (1962) notion of science as ideology, a model cannot be judged true or false, but only more or less useful as a model from which to view reality:

> ... since no paradigm ever solves all the problems it defines and since no two paradigms leave all the same problems unsolved, paradigm debates always involve the question: *Which problem is it more significant to have solved?* Like the issue of competing standards, that question of values can be answered only in terms of criteria that lie outside of normal science altogether, and it is that recourse to external criteria that most obviously makes paradigm debates revolutionary. (pp. 108-109)

The argument for a developmental perspective on the evaluation of early childhood programs is based in the belief that the most significant problem for evaluation of programs for young children is how programs affect the full development of children and other participants (parents and staff) as human beings. Central to this argument is a consideration of alternative models of conceptualizing development and developmental change. In order to organize the following argument for a developmental perspective on the evaluation of early childhood programs, two models of development and their corollary assumptions as described by Reese and Overton (1970; Overton & Reese, 1973; see also Looft, 1973) will be utilized as a foundation.

Two Models

Reese and Overton (1970) identified two models of development in psychology: the organismic (active organism) and mechanistic (reactive organism) world views. Their position, shared by this author, is that these models reflect different ways of looking at phenomena and are incompatible in their implications (see above, Kuhn, 1962). This position does not mean that the use of one model precludes the use of the other. At different stages in an evaluation, one of the models may be more useful in answering the questions posed. However, the integration of the two into a common model is not possible. Both models of development have evolved over time and often are not represented in their "pure" forms. These refinements will be noted in the course of the discussion.

The mechanistic model. This model is based on the metaphor of the machine. Component parts and their relationships form the reality to which complex behavior can be reduced and expressed in quantitative and functional relationships often called laws. The meanings of behavior remain constant over time. Prediction is possible and important since the knowledge of the machine at one point in time allows for inferences about the state of the machine at another point in time, given knowledge of past and potential efficient or material causes.

Development is defined in terms of observable behavior, and theories of development are extensions of learning theories. The epistemological position is that of naive realism, in which the knower plays no role in the known and is assumed to apprehend the world in a standard way. Thus, development can be assessed by how individuals measure up to single standards. Change occurs over time and does not result from changes in the structures of the organism.

The organismic model. This model is based on the metaphor of person as actively influencing and shaping experience. The epistemological position is that of constructivism (Magoon, 1977). The knower, in this case the child, actively constructs reality (Harré, 1974; Kamii, 1975). What is known is the product of the interaction between the active organism and the environment. Knowledge is gained only as the knower constructs the world.

Development is defined as change in the organism of a structure which cannot be directly observed and must be inferred from behavior. The relationship between structure or processes and functions or purposes is central. The organismic model assumes qualitative change, in that the meaning of behaviors changes through the course of ontogenesis. Since change is the result of formal causes rather than efficient causes (although efficient causes may inhibit or facilitate change), the possibility of a strictly predictive and quantifiable world is precluded.

The organismic model of development has rarely been represented in evaluations of early childhood programs, but it is pervasive in Piagetian preschool curricula (Kamii, 1973; 1975). In the sense that this model is closely related to what have been called qualitative (Hamilton et al., 1977; Willis, 1978) and constructivist approaches to educational research and evaluation (Magoon, 1977), these approaches are not well represented in evaluation in general. Educational evaluation is dominated by a model which focuses on products (behavior and achievement) over processes, and on quantitative change rather than qualitative change (Eisner, 1977; Levine, 1974; Partlett & Hamilton, 1976; Patton, Note 4).

Corollary Model Issues

Reese and Overton (1970; Overton & Reese, 1973) identify corollary model issues which affect the analysis and understanding of development. These issues are considered to be model-like or pre-theoretical and not open to empirical test. These issues will be described with their implications for the evaluation of early childhood programs.

Elementarism versus holism. The mechanistic model holds that the whole is predictable from its parts, that physically identical elements have the same "meaning." In contrast, the organismic model considers the person as an organized totality in which the parts derive meaning from the whole. Reese and Overton (1970) state:

> Rather than assessing behavior in terms of material identity, this (holistic) assumption directs assessment in terms of the function of the behavior in the

whole or context in which it is embedded, that is, according to the function
or ends, or goals of the organism or part processes which are being investigated
(p. 137).

This statement has several implications for the evaluation of early childhood programs, particularly in the measurement realm. The idea that behaviors
that are physically identical do not have the same meaning places the organismic
model squarely in the qualitative-phenomenological (Merleau-Ponty, 1962) and
ethnographic tradition (Wilson, 1977). The phenomenological tradition asserts
that human behavior cannot be understood without understanding the subject's
interpretation of the situation, a position consistent with Piagetians (Kamii,
1975). Furthermore, there are multiple interpretations of any given situation
depending upon the participants and their perspectives and the past and current
social context of the observed behavior. The phenomenological tradition also
intersects with the psychodynamic one since both are concerned with latent and
underlying meanings in participants' experiences. (For a psychodynamic perspective on curriculum evaluation, see Tyler, 1978.)

The use of observational systems in evaluations to obtain information on
classroom processes and behavior is typically concerned with behavior as "facts"
rather than with the meaning of the observations in relation to the child, teacher,
and the social milieu of the classroom. The need to examine further how
children interpret and construct their experiences in early education classrooms
is highlighted by Karlson's (cited in Shapiro, 1973) observations that within a
Montessori preschool, each child created his own curriculum. Shapiro (1973)
also observed that children do not have the same experiences in the same
physical setting such as the classroom. Thus observational data on the "implementation" of a certain curriculum does not mean that all individuals within the
setting had the same experiences of that curriculum. The mechanistic model's
assumption that physically identical elements have similar meaning is thus
challenged. Assessment of classroom environments and curricula must be
redirected in terms of how different individuals interpret classroom environments
and curricula (Tyler, 1978; Mehan, et al., Note 3; Takanishi & Spitzer, Note 8).
Similarly, observations of teacher and child behavior must be collected and
analyzed in terms of their meaning for the participants (Magoon, 1977; Wilson,
1977).[3]

Moving from observations of classroom environments and behavior, the
holistic-elementaristic distinction also has important implications for assessing
child outcome variables in evaluations. Messick (1975), in reviewing the status of
constructs, meanings, and values in educational research and evaluation, points
out that educational measurement has been concerned mainly with predictive
and content validity, and has neglected an important form of validity, namely

---

[3]Pinar's (1978) essay on *currere*, the analysis of the individual's lived experience of
a curriculum, richly expands on the ideas expressed here.

construct validity. He emphasizes that "the meaning of the measure must be also pondered in order to evaluate responsibly the possible consequences of its proposed use" (p. 956).

Since intelligence, achievement, and other standardized tests have been heavily used in assessing child outcomes in evaluations, the focus of the discussion will be on these tests as meaningful measures. The controversies surrounding intelligence testing are well-known, focusing on genetic and environmental factors (Jensen, 1969). Attention has also centered on the testing situation as a special setting constraining the child's behavior (Cazden, 1970; Shapiro, 1973; Sigel, 1973). Others have challenged the predictive validity of intelligence and achievement tests with reference to success within and outside the educational system (Kohlberg & Mayer, 1973; McClelland, 1973; Sigel, 1972). These arguments and positions are relatively well known and will not be elaborated further.

However, critiques of the testing situation have moved to another level, namely, inquiry into the meaning of standardized assessment situations to children[4] (Cicourel et al., 1974; Mehan, 1978; Murphy, 1973; Tyler, 1978). Cicourel and his associates conducted a number of studies related to the social context of intelligence testing and children's interpretative competence in the testing situation. These workers found that answers judged to be "wrong" may result because the child does not share the test constructors' constructions of correctness (for a similar argument, see Messick, 1975). Validation of the Cicourel et al. (1974) findings can be found in studies conducted in the Piagetian tradition (Kamii, 1973; 1975). The standardized testing situation is based on the assumption all children will approach the items in the same way. However, studies on the meaning of standardized test items indicate that a child's "incorrect" answer may result from a different interpretation of the testing materials (Mehan, 1978). Students with incorrect answers were often found to be performing the very cognitive operation being tested by the questions. This finding challenges the assumption that low scores necessarily reflect lack of ability in the child, particularly when the child is a member of a minority group: "It is necessary to examine the structure of the child's accounting practices and reasoning processes in order to draw valid inferences about his competence" (Cicourel et al., 1974, p. 5).

Another significant challenge to the assumptions of standardized testing comes from Mehan's (1978) careful studies of videotaped testing situations which show that testing results are jointly produced through the child and tester's interactions. Particularly in individually administered tests, testers emphasize certain words, praise correct answers, or cut off the child's questions. The child may ask questions of the tester which require him to respond when guidelines for administration caution against engaging in interaction with the

---

[4]For an excellent and detailed discussion of this research, see Mehan (1978), pp. 49-56.

child. Test results are thus socially negotiated in the interactions between child and tester.

To summarize, the implications of the elementarism-holism distinction can be found in the issue of the meaningfulness of behavioral observations and of educational testing situations. The distinction implies that observations cannot be dealt with solely at the level of *facts*, but must be analyzed with respect to their *meaning-in-context*. Observations of classroom life must be analyzed in terms of their meaning for the participants (Magoon, 1977). Educational testing situations must be seen as constructions of the test makers which incorporate their use of language and values, and these constructions may not be shared by those being assessed (Almy, 1975; Mehan, 1978; Messick, 1978). Thus, the validity of the testing situations and information obtained therein are challenged.

The elementarism-holism distinction is also important in relation to conceptualizations of development in early childhood programs. Within the last 15 years there has been a diversification of the curriculum with concomitant expansion of conceptions of children's development. A conception of the "child-as-a-whole," however, has the longest tradition. Almy (1975) describes this concept as emphasizing both the uniqueness of the individual child and the organized whole of physical, mental and social development. The concept necessitates the consideration of the impact of programs on all aspects of the child's development.

These ideas can be found in arguments for "comprehensive," multidimensional assessment in evaluation (Frank, 1968). A major obstacle to multidimensional assessment, however, is the lack of reliable and valid instruments, in the social and emotional domains in particular. Likewise, the focus of instrument development has tended to be more developed in assessing *what* has been learned rather than *how* a person learns. As Zimiles (1977) has argued, a nomothetic, standardized approach to personality assessment required by large-scale evaluations that attempt comprehensiveness is currently not feasible, and he suggests an idiographic approach to personality assessment. Likewise, Shipman et al. (note 6) found in their intensive case study examination of low-income Black children that a given aspect of individual functioning must be evaluated in relation to other aspects and in the environmental conditions in which the child was living. Shipman, too, argued for a multidimensional assessment of individuals and their environments in future studies, since for different children, different clusters of variables appear to be differentially important at different points in time (see also Sigel, 1972).

Structure-function versus antecedent-consequent. In the mechanistic model, analyses focus on antecedent-consequent relations or causes and effects. The organismic model focuses on the relationship between the operation of structures and functions. In the former, the locus of the critical aspect of developmental dynamic is external: the organism changes in response to external forces.

In the latter, the locus is internal to the organism, as structures within the organism change (Looft, 1973).

In discussing meaning in evaluation, Messick (1975) argued: "The major point is that in evaluating the efficacy of programs it is not sufficient simply to gauge the size of effects or to appraise input-output differences relative to costs. In addition, one should seek evidence about the nature and meaning of the processes that produced the effects, for *an understanding of these instrumentalities is necessary for a full and proper judgment of the value of the outcome*" (p. 963). A critical aspect of this distinction in the organismic model is that qualitatively different structures, processes, or modes of operation may result in the *same* behavioral achievements. The conception of multiple pathways to similar observed behavior is a key feature of a qualitative growth model (Riegel, 1972).

A related value assumption is that some structures are "higher order" than others, even though each may lead to the same behavior. In his critical remarks about the evaluation of preschool interventions, Glick (1968) pointed to the importance of making distinctions between behavioral achievement and the processes or structures underlying the achievement. He argued: "It is not enough to simply demonstrate that criterion performance (that is, achievements) increase with age or are changed by intervention. What is necessary in order to make any argument which is basic to developmental questions is to show that the processes underlying the achievement have in fact been shifted to a higher developmental level" (p. 218). Glick suggested that the study of processes underlying behavioral achievement could focus on transferability of behavior and on analysis of patterns of responses in given situations.

One implication of the structure-function/antecedent-consequent distinction is a shift away from a preoccupation with criterion performance or outcomes to a concern with the processes underlying performance. This shift can also be characterized as a move from quantitative models to qualitative models of development, and a concern with the transformational characteristics of developmental change (Wohlhill, 1973).

The distinction between behavioral achievement and structures is further highlighted in examinations of the relationship between psychometric and Piagetian assessments of intelligence. DeVries and Kohlberg (1977) note that the psychometric conception of intelligence is based on the assumption that assessment can be based on the number of right answers the child gives relative to other children of the same chronological age, i.e., his or her position on the normal curve. In contrast, a Piagetian conception views intelligence in terms of an individual's place in a universal, invariant sequence of development, through which individuals pass at different rates. Assessment includes not only "right" answers, but the analysis of "wrong" answers and children's reasoning behind their answers.

Piaget (Evans, 1973, cited in DeVries & Kohlberg, 1977) has contended that intelligence tests measure performance and do not get at internal structures or operations. DeVries and Kohlberg (1977) studied the empirical relationship between psychometric and Piagetian tests of intelligence. Their results indicated that Piagetian, developmental stage tests measure something in common with and are also distinguishable from psychometric tests of primary mental abilities. DeVries (1974) found that while Piagetian, IQ, and achievement tests overlapped to some degree, they each measured qualitatively different aspects of cognitive functioning.

These studies indicate that the distinction between performance and structures on processes is a useful one for the evaluation of early childhood programs. Performance is typically measured by IQ and achievement tests, and the predictive validity of thest tests in terms of life success has been questioned (Kohlberg & Mayer, 1973; McClelland, 1973; Sigel, 1972). The failure to make a distinction between performance and structure is a critical one if the purposes of early childhood programs are *really* aimed at optimal human development, rather than increased school achievement (Kohlberg & Mayer, 1973).

THE NATURE OF DEVELOPMENTAL CHANGE

Assumptions about the nature of developmental change and the way that change occurs (Overton & Reese, 1973; Reese & Overton, 1970) can be related to the evaluation of early childhood programs. These assumptions include conceptualizations of change as behavioral versus structural, or continuous versus discontinuous. Additional assumptions concern the cause of change: whether it occurs by unidirectional causality versus reciprocal causality or linear causality versus organized complexity.

The nature of behavioral versus structural change. In the mechanistic model, it is behavior or responses that change over time. In the organismic model, inferred structures and functions change over time. In the former model, change is determined by efficient or material causes; in the latter, change occurs in the structure or organization and functions as development moves toward a goals or purpose.

Glick (1968) argued that the distinction between the performance of an act and the capability to perform that act has profound consequences for the assessment of children's development in programs. We cannot infer from changes in test performance that the underlying cognitive structure or ability has changed. Zigler and Butterfield (1968) demonstrated that the Binet scores for low-income children varied by a mean of 10 points depending upon whether the child was tested under standard testing conditions or under conditions designed to make the child comfortable and thus to obtain his optimal level of performance. Zigler and Butterfield compared standard and optimal forms of IQ testing on children prior to entering a preschool program and seven months later. They found that while tested IQ showed a rise during the year, optimal IQ scores did not. Other researchers have also pointed to the importance of the distinction between performance in the standardized testing situation and the child's capacity to perform in other situations (Cazden, 1970; Cicourel et al., 1974; McClelland, 1973; Murphy, 1973; Shapiro, 1973). Accordingly, the focus of attention moves from "gains" in scores to the underlying structures.

Continuous versus discontinuous change. Integrally related to the behavioral change-structural change dimension is the question of whether developmental change is continuous or discontinuous. Mechanistic models are characterized by notions of continuous, additive, linear change. Organismic models assume discontinuity in development. (Looft (1973) notes that continuity is part of an organismic approach in a derivative sense.) Since change in the organization of parts results in an *emergent* system, change cannot be predicted from knowledge of the parts.

Unidirectional causality versus reciprocal causality. Reese and Overton (1973) distinguish between unidirectional causality, in which the effect is dependent upon some external cause, and reciprocal causality, in which both the environ ment and the organism affect each other in an ongoing manner.

Linear causality versus organized complexity. A mechanistic model assumes that there is a linear relationship between a cause and an effect, that individual causes are additive in their effects, and that causation is unidirectional. However, a developmental perspective presumes the idea of organized complexity, that is, changes in the organization of the parts. In light of reciprocal causality and organized complexity, explanation of developmental change is not possible in terms of efficient or material causes. What may facilitate development in one person may not operate similarly for another. The idea of organized complexity also encompasses cultural, socioeconomic, and regional differences in development.

   Sigel (1972) described change as organized complexity resulting from pre- school intervention programs. The child is composed of a variety of subsystems (perceptual, cognitive, emotional, etc.) whose relationships to each other vary over time. Change in one subsystem is related to changes in others. Sigel noted that even though development is, overall, a cumulative process, "the cumulative effect may express itself in various effects at different times" (p. 369). The distinctions regarding the nature of developmental change have profound impli- cations for the evaluation of early education programs. Evaluation of early childhood programs, almost without exception, exhibits a unidirectional bias in which the program is viewed as the "treatment" which causes some change in the child. This unidirectional bias is often reflected in discussions of the "predictive validity" of a program. The complexities involved in such prediction are highlighted by Shipman et al. (Note 6), who caution that

> The prediction of a child's achievement from early indices of the home environment should not be interpreted to mean that these predictors necessarily determine the child's achievement. Families, children, and schools can do change, with corresponding change in the nature of their interactions, and such change can be facilitative or harmful (pp. 48-49; see Sigel (1972) for a similar argument).

If one takes a developmental perspective, there is much less concern with prediction of later behavior, given multiple, interacting, and conflicting influences on behavior. Based on her own longitudinal studies (Murphy, 1962) and those at the Institute of Human Development (Jones, Bayley, Macfarlane, & Honzik, 1971), Murphy (1973) stated, "To a large extent, each child's development is a mystery story whose outcome we cannot really predict" (p. 344). Jones et al. (1971), in their studies of the physical, mental, emotional, and social development of individuals, point to the difficulty in predicting in these areas, and stress the individuality and plasticity of growth patterns. In a recent publication based on the Berkeley Growth Study data, McCall, Eichorn, and Hogarty (1977) conceptualized change in mental development as reflecting periods of instability of individual differences and/or discontinuities in developmental function across age. The emphasis of their study was on locating and describing developmental change and transition, not continuity and stability.

The best, and perhaps only, example of the complexities involved in prediction from preschool intervention programs is found in the Shipman et al. (Note 6) case studies of low-income Black children who were participating in the ETS-Head Start longitudinal study. Given the dynamic interrelations among physical, affective, social, and cognitive development, Shipman and her colleagues concluded that it is extremely difficult to predict whether a child who is doing well in Head Start will continue to do so in his later elementary school years, or whether a child who is doing badly will continue to have problems in later life. The Shipman et al. conclusions are supported by those of other longitudinal studies (Murphy, 1962; Jones et al., 1971). Given the complexities involved, a developmental perspective on evaluation needs to be reoriented toward description and understanding (Strike, 1972) and toward concurrent, contemporary validity (McCall, 1977) rather than prediction. McCall's distinction between the continuity/discontinuity of developmental functions and the stability/instability of individual differences requires closer attention in longitudinal studies.

The evaluation of early childhood programs could benefit from a reciprocal causation perspective in which *both* children and their environments are viewed as changing over time (Riegel, 1972; Sameroff, 1975). S. White (Kilmer & Weinberg, 1974) argued for a conceptualization of the child as capable of making "multiple cognitive adaptations to (a variety of) contextual specific demands" (p. 61). A reciprocal causality approach is suggested by Shapiro's (1973) discussion of how children in early education programs "construct" their own curriculum within the program. Through the child's own activity and interpretation, a different "treatment" can be said to exist for different children in the program, resulting in a variety of outcomes for different children (Zimiles, 1977).

Implications for assessing program effectiveness. A developmental perspective on evaluation accepts the idea that there are serious limitations to proving the "effectiveness" of early childhood programs. Furthermore, this perspective rejects an efficient cause approach to studying program impact. There are other difficulties in proving that our programs are effective (McCall, 1977). Most of the evaluation studies are correlational and causality cannot be inferred. Even in those projects which are experimental and under more strict control and monitoring than the majority of programs, other limitations are present. There are multiple pathways to any observed outcome. Just because we are able to demonstrate that a program was effective in terms of certain outcomes, we cannot prove that the results were due to the program per se. Also, positive results based on one program cannot be generalized to other programs in other communities (Cronbach, 1974). For example, the recently published positive results of infant and preschool intervention projects (Lazar et al., 1977) may not be generalizable. The findings were based on 14 experimental programs with "deliberate cognitive curricula" (Lazar et al., 1977, p. 2). Many of the programs were university-based and small in scale, and received closer control and supervision than most early childhood programs.

Another challenge to generalizability of program effects has been raised by House and his colleagues in their critique of the Abt Associates' evaluation of Planned Variation Follow Through. House, Glass, McLean, and Walker (1978) stressed the importance of "local individuality" (p. 474), meaning that models that worked well in one community worked poorly in another. They argued that local setting variables (individual teachers, schools, neighborhoods, homes) had more effect on achievement than did the labeled program models.

These reservations will raise the wrath of some of my colleagues who will undoubtedly accuse me of joining the ranks of Jensen, Herrnstein, Eyenck, and others who do not have much faith in the results of Head Start and other early childhood programs. I will probably be accused of making statements detrimental to the future funding of early childhood programs just when we appear to have evidence of long-term effects. Hence, these comments are made with uncertainty and regret. There is, however, a hopeful side to my observations. A developmental perspective to evaluation with its dimensions of reciprocal causality and organized complexity discussed earlier suggests that the search for long-term effects of programs is illusionary. In the linear-unidirectional causation model, the preschool intervention program, often conceived of as the "treatment," is assumed to affect a child's development as a significant main effect and have persistent effects later in the child's life. Koocher and Broskowski (1977) have labeled this mode of thinking as "the single-input fallacy" (p. 584). Assessment of program impact must take into account mtuliple and competing influences on the child during the program and in the period of time after the program ends and the follow-up study begins. When the child is in the program and in the intervening years, she is exposed to multiple socializing influences, many of which we are not able to (and possibly should not) control. Concerns over "fadeout" or maintenance of "gains" are considerably diminished.

I am aware that committed advocates of early childhood programs strongly believe that they must demonstrate the long-term effectiveness of preschool intervention (often without knowing how programs function and why effects are observed) before public monies will flow again. But I would argue that as advocates for young children we have gotten ourselves into a peculiar situation. We are not in a position, from a research and an evaluation stance, to demonstrate the long-term effectiveness of any early childhood program. The presumed demands of the policy makers outstrip the state of the art in methods, instruments, and resources (Zimiles, 1977). Yet we persist in doing so, because we think that is the kind of information policy makers want.[5] Perhaps this question reflects my limited experience and naivete, but why do we try to build up expectations that we know will go unmet? Why not say we cannot at present demonstrate effectiveness, and that we should have programs for children for certain desirable social goals and values, and not because the evaluations say we should? Perhaps part of the answer lies in the tendency of American social scientists to believe that the demonstration of the effectiveness of social programs is imminently possible and that policy decisions will be made in a rational, systematic manner (Sarason, 1978).

We should take cognizance of the conclusions of a number of contributors to C. Weiss' (1977) volume, *Using Social Research in Public Policy Making*, that evaluation findings remain only one source of information for decision makers. Ethical, legal, economic, and political considerations are also important factors in decision making. Datta's (1976) detailed account of the impact of the Westinghouse/Ohio evaluation on the development of Head Start confirms the importance of these factors and their complex, often unpredictable interrelationships.

[5]A problem worthy of careful consideration is what kinds of information policy makers want about early childhood programs. The focus on child outcomes, specifically measured by intelligence and achievement tests, is itself an interesting social fact. Most of the arguments that Head Start "does not work" (which are generalized to other early intervention programs) are based solely on cognitive outcomes. However, there is considerable agreement that Head Start "works" in areas related to health screening and treatment, nutrition, and parent and community participation. Head Start serves as a potential model for the coordination of child and family services. This coordination of services was, in fact, a major thrust of its original mission (Datta, 1976).

PRELIMINARIES TO A DEVELOPMENTAL
PERSPECTIVE TO EVALUATION

Ross and Cronbach (1976) note the importance of considering "what epistemological stance, what view of the political system, or what assumptions about the purposes of evaoluation lead to each of the divergent positions taken by evaluators, researchers, and decision makers . . ." (p. 19). The epistemological stance has already been discussed in the presentations of alternative models of development. What is being proposed here is a rationale for working *toward* a developmental perspective, which represents a closer match between evaluation strategies and the phenomena under study. I am not yet ready to present this perspective in great detail at this point, but will share some of my thoughts-in-formation. In this section, views of the political system and assumptions about the purposes of evaluation enter into a rationale for a developmental perspective to evaluation of early childhood programs. In all my considerations, I have been guided by Albert Einstein's statement: "A perfection of means and confusion of aims seems to be our main problem."

WHAT ARE THE PURPOSES OF
AN EARLY CHILDHOOD EVALUATION?

The question of the purposes of an evaluation is critical because purposes shape the design, instrumentation, and interpretation of an evaluation (Messick, 1975). If, for example, the purpose of an early childhood program is to increase school achievement and IQ test scores, then an evaluation may be designed to assess them easily. However, a number of early educators have argued that increases in school achievement and in performance on IQ tests are not the purpose of early childhood programs (Kamii, 1973), particularly of programs that are not aimed toward achievement in the school sense (Kohlberg & Mayer, 1973). Hence, standardized tests are not appropriate.

From the models of development presented in the previous section, it follows that a developmental perspective to evaluation is not primarily concerned with achievement data. On the contrary, the purposes of evaluation of early childhood programs are directed toward involving the participants, including the evaluators, in understanding program development, adult (staff and parent) development, and child development. Evaluation is directed toward enabling all involved in the program to reflect critically about what is happening (Carini, 1975; Eisner, 1977; Cronbach, 1974; Partlett & Hamilton, 1976). Thus evaluation is geared toward providing feedback about the program to the staff and other audiences in terms that are comprehensible and that lead to more sound practices.[6] The most important criterion against which an evaluation is judged

---

[6]For an extended discussion of this point, see Stake (1978).

is its utility, or the extent to which the evaluation results in program improvement and child development.

A related criterion for an evaluation is the degree to which it enhances the development of all participants and their dignity as human beings (Sjoberg, 1975; Tyler, 1978). Thus, considerable attention should be focused on how evaluation is actually practiced and how it affects the participants' self-esteem (Report of the Task Force on Testing and Assessment of Children, 1976; Tyler, 1978).

A developmental perspective on the evaluation of programs is compatible with more formative modes of evaluation and with an "extended" view of evaluation described by Ross and Cronbach (1976). Evaluation is seen as a continuing part of program management and planning. This view is also consistent with Public Law (PL) 94-63 of the Community Mental Health Centers (CMHC) Amendments of 1975 (Davis, Windle, & Sharfstein, 1977; Guidelines for Program Evaluation in CMHCs, 1977) which obligates federally funded community mental health centers to conduct program evaluations on an ongoing basis to improve services and to be more responsive to clients. The evaluator is part of the program; she studies what was delivered and how people interacted during the program. The evaluator functions as a naturalistic observer whose inquiry grows out of her observations. These strategies are also compatible with a qualitative approach to evaluation (Eisner, 1977; Hamilton et al., 1977; Stake, 1967; Wilson, 1977; Willis, 1978; Wolf & Tymitz, 1977; Campbell, Note 1).

A developmental perspective on the evaluation of programs. In evaluations based on the experimental paradigm, programs are "treatments" which are assumed to be similar across sites and which can be replicated in other sites. This conceptualization of programs is based on the ideal of generalizable knowledge (Cronbach, 1975). However, large-scale evaluations of early childhood programs indicate that the assumption that programs can be treated as a set of unitary variables is questionable. House, Glass, McLean and Walker (1978) point to local setting variables as more important in determining achievement scores than the labeled program models in Project Follow Through.

An alternative conceptualization is programs-as-cultural systems (in contrast to programs-as-treatments) with histories, traditions, and values. The anthropologist Clifford Geertz (1973) has aptly expressed the distinction I am making: "The concept of culture I espouse . . . is essentially a semiotic one. Believing, with Max Weber, that man is an animal suspended in webs of significance he himself has spun, *I take culture to be those webs, and the analysis of it to be therefore not an experimental science in search of law but an interpretative one in search of meaning*" (p. 5). Of central interest in evaluations of programs would be how children and adults structure meaning out of their experiences and create the daily routine of program life (see, for example, Mehan, 1978). It is understood that in any program there will be multiple interpretations of what the program is (Hamilton et al., 1977). Methods for studying programs-as-cultures may include case studies (Hamilton et al., 1977; MacDonald & Walker, 1975; Stake, 1978), ethnographic approaches (Mehan, 1978; Mehan, et al., Note 3); documentation (Carini, 1975; Hamilton & Partlett, 1976), among others in a rich, emerging area (Willis, 1978).

A developmental perspective is also concerned with the study of programs and classroom environments in terms of their *change* over time. Guttentag (1977) articulated this idea: "Given the nature of most social programs, it is not realistic to presume that they can be kept the same over time .... When evaluators act as though the program was indeed unchanging over time, it is nearly always a fiction. Results based on such seemingly 'unchanging' programs are hard to believe, and may lead to false inferences" (p. 19).

Most studies of classroom environments assume that these environments do not change over time (e.g., during the school year). However, people who are involved with early childhood programs know that there are forces for change— both improvement and regression. Programs rarely remain static entities. For example, in Weikart's (1972) Ypsilanti Project, there was continuous opportunity for improvement and change in what teachers were doing in their classrooms. A developmental perspective is sensitive to these changes within programs and concerned with documenting and describing them in a way which can be related to the program's influence on adults and children. Evaluation is part of a dynamically evolving program.

A developmental perspective on adult development. Evaluations of early childhood programs have been almost exclusively focused on children. Understanding staff relationships and parent and staff development is important to the provision of early childhood programs and should be systematically examined in future evaluations.

Katz (1971; 1973; 1977) has outlined some problems in the sociology of early childhood education which take into account the social and political context in which early childhood educators work. The effects of mandated, often shifting, program requirements and the conditions of the work place, particularly the special problems involved in working with young children (Katz, 1971; 1977), should be examined in evaluations. Developmental stages of preschool teachers (Katz, 1972) might be applied to looking at staff development in programs. Weikart (1972) argued that teacher motivation, supervision, and resourcefulness appear to be particularly important in program operations. He argued that any project must have an effective staff model which includes high intensity of planning and supervision.

Another potential area for evaluation is the way in which early educators accept and use developmental theories and research, and curriculum and instructional materials. This kind of examination challenges the taken-for-granted assumption that research can provide suggestions for teaching by the translation of child development research into curriculum (Katz, 1973). Jackson and Kieslar (1977) have effectively challenged this linear approach to the relation between research and practice. They point out that we know very little about how theory and research actually become part of educational practice. Of particular interest is how theory and research match or fit into the "vision of reality" (Jackson & Kieslar, 1977) of the teachers. Inasmuch as the educators' view of reality is linked to possible adaptive consequences of working with young children (Katz, 1971), research into the belief and culture of early educators is important in understanding how programs develop over time, and is an important component of qualitative evaluations of educational innovations (Magoon, 1977).

A developmental perspective on evaluation would also focus seriously on understanding parental and family development in early childhood programs. Reviews of the effects of intervention programs identify the importance of the mother's teaching style and attitudes and her role in "maintaining gains" of the programs (Bronfenbrenner, 1973; Shipman et al., 1976). Sigel (1972) pointed to the importance of considering changes in the child as a result of the program in relation to changes in the behavior and attitudes of the parents. Mothers reportedly have gone back to work and school and have become involved in community life as a result of their children's participation in the program. Yet, in most evaluations, our knowledge of the relationships between early childhood programs and parental and family development is not fully utilized, often treated in anecdotal asides (see, however, Falender & Heber, 1975; Slaughter, Note 7).

Evaluations in this area should not focus solely on parental behavior via-a-vis the child, but also on parents as persons with their own needs and interests. Research on parenthood as a developmental stage (Benedek, 1959; Leifer, 1977) provides some concepts for examining the adaptations parents may make to their or their child's involvement in an early childhood program. Brown's (1975) work on family dialectics in clinical situations is also useful.

A developmental perspective on assessing children. It is striking that with all the evaluations of early childhood programs—many of which involve the same children for a number of years—we still know very little about how *individual* children develop in these programs.[7] Although staff members talk a great deal about how individual children develop in their programs, we have few descriptive, longitudinal records of assessment of change over age within individuals. There are two reasons why more attention should be placed on the child as the unit of analysis. If one of the goals of early childhood programs is to enhance the child's life chances, then the individual child is the appropriate unit of analysis. Furthermore, in longitudinal studies, the only unit that has continuity

---

[7]Existing laws (PL 94-142 and PL 93-380) require that certain programs determine their impact on individual children. According to PL 94-142, teachers must evaluate the child's progress according to the Individualized Educational Plan (IEP).

over time is the individual child (Haney, Note 2). There is a great need for individual developmental histories of children in programs, such as the histories constructed in the Berkeley Growth Studies (Jones, Bayley, Macfarlane & Honzik, 1971) and Murphy's (1962) studies of the Topeka children. Intensive case studies from the ETS-Head Start longitudinal sample augur well for the future (Shipman et al., Note 6).

The importance of longitudinal studies has been identified by many researchers (Lazar et al., 1977; Shipman, 1976; Sigel, Secrist, & Forman, 1972; Shipman et al., Note 6). However, more systematic attention should be given to fundamental problems of conceptualizing development and change in these longitudinal studies. In their case studies, for example, Shipman et al. (Note 6) pointed to the inappropriateness of linear analytic methods, given the unevenness of developmental change. Sigel, Secrist, and Forman (1972) described problems in longitudinal studies when conducted in intervention programs serving low-income populations. The most serious problem, however, is the fact that longitudinal studies are relatively rare and remain an underdeveloped field both in conceptualization and methodology (McCall, 1977; Wohlhill, 1973).

WHOM SHALL THE EVALUATION SERVE?

Related to the question of the purposes of an evaluation is the issue of whom the evaluation should serve. Sjoberg (1975) charged that evaluators usually align themselves with the powerful or dominant groups in the system and accept these groups' definitions of program goals and desired outcomes. Thus evaluation serves several functions, including reform, manipulation and maintenance of power or structural relations. Sjoberg argues for a countersystem role in which the evaluator works with the less powerful in the system. In a similar vein, House (1976) argues for justice-as-fairness as an important standard for evaluation. "By the second principle (of justice), social and economic inequalities must benefit the least advantaged in the long run. The educationally least advantaged within most settings are the children first and the teachers second. *The evaluator should strive to present their views and perspectives*" (p. 97).

In early childhood programs, staff members and parents have a particular stake in the program and its services, since they are the individuals who are actively involved in implementing the program. If evaluation is to have utility, these individuals must be participants in the process.[8] An example of how evaluation purposes change depending upon the role and perspectives of the groups involved is illustrated in a report on evaluation in Head Start programs written by a group composed largely of staff and parents (Report of the Task Force on Testing and Assessment of Children, 1976). The Task Force advocated

[8]I recognize that young children must also be considered as participants in evaluations, but am not ready to deal with this problem in depth at this time.

procedures "which recognize and support individual rights, facilitate growth and enhance dignity" (p. 17). Its "Statement of Rights" for children, parents, and staff can be found in Appendix I.

It should be clear by now that my bias in arguing for a developmental perspective is that the sole purpose of evaluation is not to judge the effectiveness or efficiency of a program or to meet the perceived needs of public policy makers for quantitative, "hard" data based on large samples of children. In fact, serious challenges have been raised about the evaluator's assumption that evaluations provide information for decision makers (Weiss, 1977; Wise, Note 9). Other writers have pointed to the limitations of large-scale survey research for policy making (Mehan, 1978). Findings from large-scale studies are probabilistic and do not apply to particular programs. They rarely reveal much about the processes which create and maintain programs, and hence are limited in identifying specific actions for change. Finally, since the findings are abstract rather than concrete, motivating staff concern for improvement is understandably difficult.

The purposes of evaluation I would espouse are based on House's (1976) notions of justice in evaluation and are oriented toward program development and serving needs of the staff and children, not primarily the bureaucrats and funding agencies. These purposes also reflect changing conceptions and diversification of evaluation activity in the '70s toward program evaluation and qualitative approaches (Hamilton et al., 1977; Tikunoff & Ward, 1977; Willis, 1978). What I am arguing for, then, is cultivation of alternatives to what presently exists in the evaluation of early childhood programs, recognition of the importance of values in choosing methods, and care in conducting systematic, disciplined inquiry. We have many more options in evaluating early childhood programs than we are currently utilizing (Perrone, Cohen, & Martin, Note 5). Explorations of alternatives will allow us to see new problems, invent new methods, and to understand our programs in ways that better fit our experiences of the complexities of program life and of adult and child development.

CONSTRAINTS ON A DEVELOPMENTAL PERSPECTIVE

An argument for a developmental perspective on evaluation of early childhood programs has been presented. There are, however, a number of constraints on the further development of this perspective. One major constraint is that research in child development has itself neglected a developmental orientation (McCall, 1977; Wohlhill, 1973). Furthermore, there has been an emphasis on concepts of stability, continuity, and equilibrium over those of instability, discontinuity, and change in longitudinal research (Riegel, 1972; 1976; McCall, Eichorn, & Hogarty, 1977; Wohlhill, 1973). Thus, a conceptual and methodological base for a developmental perspective is underdeveloped.

Another critical constraint is that a developmental perspective to evaluation represents assumptions and ideologies which are gaining ascendance,[9] but which are still overshadowed by what have been variously called quantitative or experimental approaches to evaluation. This paper posited earlier that paradigms of evaluation represent views of reality and the selection of one over another is a matter of values. According to Kuhn's notion of the paradigm, a paragidm gains power and dominance because most of the researchers, through socialization into their discipline, agree to believe and trust it.

Levine (1974), among others, observes that science is socially constructed by a community:

> Science is what scientists feel comfortable in recommending to others as principles through which the world may be manipulated, predicted, or understood. Science is what scientists say it is at any given point in time. Science is what scientists feel comfortable in writing about in articles and in textbooks (p. 669).

Developmental perspectives on evaluation which are akin to qualitative, ethnographic, and naturalistic approaches to evaluation are weak in comparison to the dominant model, lack a strong and sizable community of committed workers, and suffer from the lack of legitimation. Strategies for creating parity and tolerance are needed simultaneously with further work on a developmental perspective. Messick (1975) offers Churchman's proposals for the study of systems of inquiry that can aid in the exposure of the implicit value assumptions in research strategies. Levine (1974) suggests an adversary model. Meanwhile, one constraint on the further development of a developmental perspective is the dominance of the experimental and psychometric models.

But there is an even more troublesome constraint related to complex issues in the ethics of evaluation studies. Evaluations that aim at the intensive documentation of program life and at the interpretative understandings of the participants may be *too* revealing. These evaluations may unmask the protective myths surrounding early childhood programs. Quantitative methods, by their very nature, do not have the potential of such illumination. Can we know too much? For what ends will knowledge from these studies be used? Indeed, we are traveling into dangerous uncharted territory. The lack of guidelines for evaluators who engage in qualitative approaches is a central concern of individuals who have used them (MacDonald & Walker, 1975).

Given these very significant and powerful constraints, individuals who are involved in the evaluation of early childhood programs face a major reconsideration of their purposes and methods. Moving toward a developmental perspective

[9]For an excellent, integrative review of declining faith in mainstream social science, see Skinner (1978).

calls for a reorientation in many of the ways evaluation is currently practiced and supported. In this paper, I have aspired to lay the groundwork for an evaluation model that is based on knowledge of the traditions, problems, and practicing realities of early childhood programs and which, in all its considerations, places ideas of *development* as the center of inquiry. In reflecting on the need for a developmental perspective, I am encouraged by John Tukey's observation: "Far better an approximate answer to the right question, which is often vague, than an exact answer to the wrong questions, which can always be made precise" (cited in Rose, 1977, p. 23).

ACKNOWLEDGMENTS

This paper brings together ideas in evaluation, developmental theory and research, and early childhood programs, and reflects my values, training, and experience. The act of pointing to the source of one's ideas is complex, but I would like to acknowledge some especially formative individuals: Lee J. Cronbach, John C. Glidewell, Louis L. Knowles, Beryl Scoles, Louise L. Tyler, and Docia Zavitkovsky. I am grateful to Louise Tyler for her critical comments on an earlier draft of this paper. Lucinda Bernheimer and Arline Dillman provided editorial assistance. Of course, I assume sole responsibility for the constructions and interpretations I have made in this integrative review paper. Work on this paper was supported in part by a Spencer Fellowship from the National Academy of Education.

APPENDIX I*

V. CONCLUSION

This Task Force has considered a range of issues regarding assessment: need, process, use, and impact, in the body of this paper. In reviewing the need for assessment, the Task Force recognizes that assessment of specific developmental processes in young children is an established and necessary practice. The challenge for those who work with children is to *utilize assessment methods which recognize and support individual rights, facilitate growth, and enhance dignity.*

After exploring the process and use of assessment, the Task Force has agreed that there is a wide variation in the quality of assessment methods available for use with young children. Therefore, care must be taken in the selection of instruments and assessors, in order to provide useful information for planning educational opportunities.

Finally, the Task Force recognizes that the effect of the assessment process on a child's family is a critically important factor, and must be taken into consideration at each step in that process. The Task Force members have seriously studied these issues, and as a result of their efforts, have developed a *Statement of Rights* for children, parents, and staff as the blueprint for implementation in any program serving young children and their families. Although parents and staff fulfill the role of advocates for children's rights, they also have rights in this regard.

This Task Force recommends that all programs for young children adopt the following Statement of Rights:

Rights of the Child

A child has the right to be different, and to be accepted as such. Differences in individual children should be approached in a positive, meaningful way so they may function to their fullest capacity in a pluralistic society.

A child has the right to be assessed, and as a result through an assessment, to be provided with a quality developmental program.

A child has the right to be tested under optimal conditions in a nonthreatening environment by a person sensitive to children.

A child has the right to be assessed with a nonbiased instrument by a person who speaks the language in which the child is most fluent.

A child who scores differently from the norm on any given test or assessment has the right not to be labeled.

A child has the right to have his/her observable behavior recorded in functionally descriptive terms rather than in generalized terminology (labeling).

A child has the right to have the results of assessments kept confidential, and the records kept in a locked file. A child's records shall only be made accessible to the child's parents and other authorized persons.

Rights of Parents

Parents have the right that their child receive an overall assessment which includes information obtained from health examinations, classroom observations, parent conferences, and home visits.

Parents have the right to be informed of the purpose of the assessment, and of the instrument(s) to be used in assessing their child.

Parents have the right to give or withhold permission to have their child assessed, and to challenge the content of written records.

Parents have the right to be involved in the total assessment process.

Parents have a right to give input into the overall assessment of their child and provide the person(s) doing the assessment with their views and observations of the behavior, development, and activities of their child.

Parents have the right to be informed about the assessment results, and to have conferences with appropriate staff regarding interpretation of the results and for program planning.

Parents have a right, at their request, to a written summary of a conference following the assessment.

Parents have the right to confidentiality of all information obtained by the assessor.

Parents have rights regarding the releasing of assessment results to other agencies or public schools. Unless they have given permission, the assessment information shall not be forwarded.

Parents have the right to be treated with consideration and sensitivity regarding the psychological and social impact effects that assessment results can have on the family unit.

Parents have the right to receive all supportive services necessary to effectively implement assessment results.

Rights of Staff

The teaching staff has the right to not be overburdened by the assessment process and recordkeeping to the extent that it interferes with their primary teaching function. It should be recognized, however, that making and recording observations of children are an integral part of teaching.

Staff has the right to give input into the selection and appropriateness of assessment instruments (for both group and individual use), and to understand the relevance of the assessment results to the overall program.

Staff has the right to request and receive proper instruction and training in the use of the assessment instrument and consultation in the interpretation of the results.

Staff has the right to receive information, in advance of the time, methods, persons involved, and space to be used when assessment activities will be conducted.

Staff has the right to object to the use of a specific instrument which in their professional opinion, goes contrary to good child development principles.

Staff has the right to receive timely feedback after the assessment has been completed.

*SOURCE: *Report of the Task Force on Testing and Assessment of Children* (Submitted to the Office of Child Development). San Francisco: Development Associates, 1976.

Reference Notes

1. Campbell, D. *Qualitative knowing in action research.* Paper presented at the meeting of the American Psychological Association, New Orleans, September 1974.
2. Haney, W. *Units of analysis issues in the evaluation of Project Follow Through.* Unpublished manuscript, Huron Institute, 1974.

3. Mehan, H., Cazden, C. B., Coles, L., Fisher, S., & Maroules, N. *The social organization of classroom lessons.* (Center for Human Information Processing Report No. 67). University of California, San Diego, 1976.
4. Patton, M. Q. *Alternative evaluation paradigm.* Grand Forks, N.D.: Center for Teaching and Learning, University of North Dakota, 1975.
5. Perrone, V., Cohen, M. D., & Martin, L. P. (Eds.) *Testing and evaluation. New views.* Washington, D.C.: Association of Childhood Education International, 1975.
6. Shipman, V. C., et al. *Notable early characteristics of high and low achieving Black low-SES children.* Princeton, N.J.: Educational Testing Service, 1976.
7. Slaughter, D. T. *Parent education for low income black families.* Presented at the General Mills American Family Forum on "Parenting—The Crucial Years," Washington, D.C.: October 17-18, 1977.
8. Takanishi, R., & Spitzer, S. *Children's perceptions of human resources in team teaching classrooms. A cross-sectional developmental study.* Paper presented at the meeting of the American Educational Research Association, Toronto, Canada, March 1978.
9. Wise, R. I. *What we know about the decision-maker and decision settings.* Paper presented at the American Educational Research Association, Toronto, Canada, March 1978.
10. Zigler, E. *The effectiveness of Head Start: Another look.* Paper presented at the meeting of the American Psychological Association, San Francisco, August 1977.

REFERENCES

Almy, M. *The early educator at work.* New York: McGraw-Hill, 1975.
Ball, S., & Bogatz, G. *The first year of Sesame Street: An evaluation.* Princeton, N.J.: Educational Testing Service, 1970.
Benedek, T. Parenthood as a developmental phase. *Journal of the American Psychoanalytic Association,* 1959, *7*, 389-417.
Bronfenbrenner, U. *Is early intervention effective?* Washington, D.C.: U.S. Office of Child Development, 1973.
Brown, L. K. Familial dialectics in a clinical context. *Human Development,* 1975, *18*, 223-238.
Carini, P. F. *Observation and description.* Grand Forks, N.D.: University of North Dakota Press, 1975.
Cazden, C. The neglected situation in child language research and education. In F. Williams (Ed.), *Language and poverty: Perspectives on a theme.* Chicago: Martham, 1970.
Cicourel, A. V., Jennings, K. H., Jennings, S. H. M., Leiter, K. C. W., MacKay, R., Mehan, H., & Roth, D. R. *Language use and school performance.* New York: Academic Press, 1974.
Cook, T., Appleton, R., Conner, R., Schaffer, G., Tamkin, G., & Weber, S. *Sesame Street revisited.* New York: Russell Sage Foundation, 1975.
Cronbach, L. J. Beyond the two disciplines of scientific psychology. *American Psychologist,* 1975, *30*, 115-127.
Datta, L. The impact of the Westinghouse/Ohio evaluation on the development of Project Head Start: An examination of the immediate and longer-term effects of how they came about. In C. C. Abt (Ed.), *The evaluation of social program.* Beverly Hills, CA.: Sage, 1976.

Davis, H. R., Windle, C., & Sharfstein, S. S. Developing guidelines for program evaluation capability in community mental health centers. *Evaluation*, 1977, *4*, 25-29.

DeVries, R. Relationships among Piagetian, IQ, and achievement assessments. *Child Development*, 1974, *45*, 746-56.

DeVries, R., & Kohlberg, L. Relations between Piagetian and psychometric assessments of intelligence. In L. G. Katz (Ed.), *Current topics in early childhood education* (Vol. I). Norwood, N.J.: ABLEX, 1977.

Eisner, E. W. On the uses of educational connoisseurship and criticism for evaluating classroom life. *Teachers College Record*, 1977, *78*, 345-58.

Falender, C. A., & Heber, R. Mother-child interaction and participation in a longitudinal intervention program. *Developmental Psychology*, 1975, *11*, 830-36.

Frank, L. K. Evaluation of educational programs. *Young Children*, 1968, *24*, 167-74.

Geertz, C. *The interpretation of cultures.* New York: Basic Books, 1973.

Glick, J. Some problems in the evaluation of preschool intervention programs. In R. D. Hess and R. M. Bear (Eds.), *Early education.* Chicago: Aldine, 1968.

Guba, E. G. The failure of educational evaluation. *Educational Technology*, 1969, *9*(5), 29-38.

Guidelines for program evaluation in CMHCs. *Evaluation*, 1977, *4*, 30-34.

Guttentag, M. On quantified sachel: A reply to Apsler. *Evaluation*, 1977, *4*, 18-20.

Hamilton, D., Jenkins, D., King, C., MacDonald, B., & Parlett, M. *Beyond the numbers game: A reader in educational evaluation.* Berkeley: McCutchan, 1977.

Harré, R. The conditions for a social psychology of childhood. In M. P. M. Richards (Ed.), *The integration of a child into a social world.* New York: Cambridge University Press, 1974.

House, E. R. (Ed.) *School evaluation: The politics and process.* Berkeley, Calif.: McCutchan, 1973.

House, E. R. Justice in evaluation. In G. V. Glass (Ed.), *Evaluation studies review annual* (Vol. 1). Beverly Hills, Calif.: Sage, 1976.

House, E. R., Glass, G. V., McLean, L. D., & Walker, D. F. Critiquing a Follow Through evaluation. *Phi Delta Kappan*, 1978, *59*, 473-474.

Jensen, A. How much can we boost IQ and school achievement? *Harvard Educational Review*, 1969, *39*, 1-123.

Jones, M. C., Bayley, N., Macfarlane, J., & Honzik, M. *The course of human development.* Waltham, Mass.: Xerox College Publishing, 1971.

Kamii, C. K. Evaluation of learning in preschool education: Socioemotional, perceptual-motor, cognitive development. In B. S. Bloom, J. T. Hastings, and G. F. Madaus, *Handbook on formative and summative evaluation.* New York: McGraw-Hill, 1971.

Kamii, C. One intelligence indivisible. *Young Children*, 1975, *30*, 228-38.

Kamii, C., & Elliott, D. L. Evaluation of evaluations. *Educational Leadership*, 1971, *28*(8), 827-31.

Katz, L. G. Sentimentality in preschool teachers: Some possible interpretations. *Peabody Journal of Education*, 1971, *48*, 96-105.

Katz, L. G. Developmental stages of preschool teachers. *The Elementary School Journal*, 1972, *23*, 50-54.

Katz, L. G. Where is early childhood education going? *Theory into Practice*, 1973, *12*, 137-42.

Katz, L. G. Early childhood programs and ideological disputes. *Educational Forum*, 1975, *10*, 267-71.

Katz, L. G. Teachers in preschools: Problems and prospects. *International Journal of Early Childhood*, 1977, *9*, 111-23.

Kilmer, S., & Weinberg, R. The nature of young children and the state of early education: Reflections from the Minnesota Roundtable. *Young Children*, 1974, *30*(1), 60-67.

Kohlberg, L., & Mayer, R. Development as the aim of education. *Harvard Educational Review*, 1972, *42*, 449-96.

Koocher, g., & Broskowski, A. Issues in the evaluation of mental health services for children. *Professional Psychology*, 1977, *8*, 583-92.

Kuhn, T. *The structure of scientific revolutions.* Chicago: University of Chicago Press, 1962.

Kvale, S. The technological paradigm of psychological research. *Journal of Phenomenological Psychology*, 1973, *3*, 143-59.

Kvale, S. The psychology of learning as ideology and technology. *Behaviorism*, 1976, *4*, 97-116.

Lazar, I. et al. *The persistence of preschool effects. A long-term follow-up of 14 infant and preschool experiments.* Washington, D.C.: U.S. Government Printing Office, 1977.

Leifer, M. Psychological changes accompanying pregnancy and motherhood. *Genetic Psychology Monographs,* 1977, *95*, 55-96.

Levine, M. Scientific method and the adversary model: Some preliminary thoughts. *American Psychologist*, 1974, *29*, 661-77.

Looft, W. R. Socialization and personality throughout the life span: An examination of contemporary psychological approaches. In P. B. Baltes and K. W. Schaie (Eds.), *Life-span developmental psychology. Personality and socialization.* New York: Academic Press, 1973.

MacDonald, B., & Walker, R. Case study and the social philosophy of educational research. *Cambridge Journal of Education*, 1975, *5.*

Magoon, A. J. Constructivist research. *Review of Education*, 1977, *49*, 651-94.

McCall, R. B. Challenges to a science of developmental psychology. *Child Development*, 1977, *48*, 333-44.

McCall, R. B., Eichorn, D. H., & Hogarty, P. S. Transitions in early mental development with commentary by I. C. Uzgiris and by E. S. Schaefer, with reply by the authors. *Monographs of the Society for Research in Child Development*, 1977, *42* (3, Serial No. 171).

McClelland, D. C. Testing for competence rather than for "intelligence." *American Psychologist*, 1973, *28*, 1-14.

Mehan, H. Structuring school structure. *Harvard Educational Review*, 1978, *48*, 32-64.

Merleau-Ponty, M. *Phenomenology of perception* (trans. C. Smith). London: Routledge and Kegan Paul, 1962.

Messick, S. The standard problem. Meaning and values in measurement and evaluation. *American Psychologist*, 1975, *30*, 955-66.

Murphy, L. B. *The widening world of childhood.* New York: Basic Books, 1962.

Murphy, L. B. The strangehold of norms on the individual child. *Childhood Education*, 1973, *49*, 343-49.

Overton, W. F., & Reese, H. W. Models of development: Methodological implications. In J. R. Nesselroade and H. W. Reese (Eds.), *Life-span developmental psychology: Methodological issues.* New York: Academic Press, 1973.

Partlett, M., & Hamilton, D. Evaluation as illumination: A new approach to the study of innovative programs. In G. V. Glass (Ed.), *Evaluation studies review annual* (Vol. 1). Beverly Hills: Sage, 1976.

Petrie, H. G. Theories are tested by observing the facts: Or are they? In L. G. Thomas (Ed.), *Philosophical redirection of educational research.* Seventy-first yearbook of the National Society for the Study of Education, Part 1. Chicago: University of Chicago Press, 1972.

Pinar, W. F. *Currere:* A case study. In G. Willis (Ed.), *Qualitative evaluation: Concepts and cases in curriculum criticism.* Berkeley, CA.: McCutchan, 1978.

Reese, H. W., & Overton, W. F. Models of development and theories of development. In L. R. Goulet and P. B. Baltes (Eds.), *Life-span developmental psychology. Research and theory.* New York: Academic Press, 1970.

Riegel, K. F. Influence of economic and political ideologies on the development of developmental psychology. *Psychological Bulletin*, 1972, *78*, 129-41.

Riegel, K. F. From traits and equilibrium to developmental dialectics. In W. J. Arnold (Ed.), *Nebraska Symposium on Motivation, 1975*. Lincoln: University of Nebraska Press, 1976.

Rose, R. Disciplined research and undisciplined problems. In C. H. Weiss (Ed.), *Using social research in public policy making*. Lexington, Mass.: Lexington Books, 1977.

Ross, L., & Cronbach, L. *Handbook of evaluation research:* Essay review. *Educational Researcher*, 1976, *5*(10), 9-10.

Sameroff, A. J. Early influences on development: Fact or fancy? *Merrill-Palmer Quarterly*, 1975, *21*, 267-294.

Sarason, S. B. The nature of problem solving in social action. *American Psychologist*, 1978, *33*, 370-380.

Shapiro, E. Educational evaluation: Rethinking the criteria of competence. *School Review*, 1973, *81*, 523-50.

Sigel, I. Developmental theory: Its place and relevance in early intervention programs. *Young Children*, 1972, *27*, 364-72.

Sigel, I. E., Secrist, A., & Forman, G. Psycho-educational intervention beginning at age two: Reflections and outcomes. In J. C. Stanley (Ed.), *Sompensatory education for children ages two to eight: Recent studies of educational intervention*. Baltimore: Johns Hopkins University Press, 1972.

Sjoberg, G. Politics, ethics, and evaluation research. In M. Guttentag and E. L. Struening (Eds.), *Handbook of evaluation research* (Vol. 2). Beverly HILLS: Sage Publications, 1975.

Skinner, Q. The flight from positivism (Review of R. J. Bernstein's *The restructuring of social and political theory*). *New York Review of Books*, 1978, *25*, 26-28.

Stake, R. E. the case study method in social inquiry. *Educational Researcher*, 1978, *7*, 5-8.

Stake, R. E. The countenance of educational evaluation. *Teachers College Record*, 1967, *68*, 523-40.

Strike, K. A. Explaining and understanding: The impact of science on our concept of man. In L. E. Thomas (Ed.), *Philosophical redirection of educational research*. The seventy-first yearbook of the National Society for the Study of Education. Chicago: University of Chicago Press, 1972.

Tikunoff, W. J., & Ward, B. A. (Eds.), Exploring qualitative/quantative research methodologies in education. *Anthropology and Education Quarterly*, 1977, *8*.

Tyler, L. L. Curriculum evaluation and persons. *Educational Leadership*, 1978, *35*, 275-79.

Weikart, D. P. Relationship of curriculum, teaching, and learning in preschool education. In J. C. Stanley (Ed.), *Preschool programs for the disadvantaged*. Baltimore: Johns Hopkins, 1972.

Weiss, C. *Using social research in public policy making*. Lexington, Mass.: D. C. Heath and Co., 1977.

Willis, G. *Qualitative evaluation. Concepts and cases in curriculum criticism*. Berkeley: McCutchan, 1978.

Wilson, S. The use of ethnographic techniques in educational research. *Review of Educational Research*, 1977, *47*, 245-65.

Wohlwill, J. *The study of behavioral development*. New York: Academic Press, 1973.

Wolf, R. L., & Tymitz, B. Ethnography and reading: Matching inquiry mode to process. *Reading Research Quarterly*, 1977, *12*.

Zigler, E., & Butterfield, E. C. Motivational aspects of changes in IQ test performance of culturally deprived nursery school children. *Child Development*, 1968, *39*, 1-14.

Zimiles, H. A radical and regressive solution to the problem of evaluation. In L. G. Katz (Ed.), *Current topics in early childhood education*, (Vol. 1), Norwood, N.J.: ABLEX, 1977.

7

An Inquiry into Inquiry:
Question Asking
as an Instructional Model

Irving E. Sigel

Ruth Saunders

Educational Testing Service, Princeton

> I keep six honest serving men
> (they taught me all I know)
> Their names are What and Why and When
> and How and Where and Who.
>
> Kipling, "The Serving Men"

The purpose of this paper is to present a conceptual base for advocating an inquiry-based (question asking) instruction model. Question asking provides direct confrontation to the child's current points of view, thus leading the child to restructure his thoughts. Piaget argues that this process "constitute[s] the fundamental factor in cognitive development" (Piaget, 1977, p. 17). Thus, question asking instructional strategies provide a critical exogenous set of stimulations which can create the conditions for a shift from one cognitive level to another.

The development of a model for question asking requires the consideration of the following: linguistic structure of particular question, psychological function of questioning process, cognitive processes activated by particular question, teacher strategies in executing the model, and evaluations of children's responses to types of question.

Question asking as an instructional strategy rests mainly on pragmatic grounds—namely, on the efficacy of question asking in promoting thought. Since getting children to think is a "social good" and a desirable educational objective, question asking as a method for teaching seems to be a reasonable choice (Suchman, 1961; Taba, 1962, 1967).

169

Accepting the proposition that question asking is good, a number of investigators have undertaken studies that deal with question asking as an instructional technique and as an information processing model. Studies have focused on types and frequencies of questions used by teachers (Haupt, 1966; Isaacs, 1974), modifications of children's question asking behaviors (Rosenthal & Zimmerman, 1972; Zimmerman & Pike, 1972), determinants of incidence of types of questions children ask (Berlyne & Frommer, 1966), and the strategies children use to ask questions (Denney & Conners, 1974; Mosher & Hornsby, 1966).

All these studies share two assumptions: (1) question asking is a "good" since it is a method for enhancing problem solving, and (2) question asking by children *reflects* thinking, while question asking by teachers *promotes* thinking. More precise work sharing these assumptions has been reported, demonstrating that the type of question helps determine the efficacy of question asking in problem solving (Boller, 1973; Buggey, 1972; Hopper, 1971; Martin, 1970; Mosher & Hornsby, 1966; Smith, 1974; Turner & Durrett, 1975).

These studies, while demonstrating the efficacy of question asking, have not provided a systematic conceptual base for advocating the use of question asking strategies as an instructional model, nor have they explained why use of questions should enhance problem solving skills. It is important to provide a conceptual base, not only for explanatory purposes, but also for guiding research to further our understanding of the role of questions in cognitive development.

We shall first discuss the definition of inquiry, outline the conceptual basis for question asking, and describe briefly teacher strategies for an inquiry-based preschool program. We will conclude our presentation with a discussion of the relation of our model to other conceptual frameworks and to some empirical findings.

WHAT IS A QUESTION: A STRUCTURAL/FUNCTIONAL DESCRIPTION

Kearsley, using syntactic elements, has provided a structural categorization of questions (see Fig. 1). Questions have a characteristic form, with the exception of indirect questions in which the inflection is in the utterance or in the intent. For example, an utterance such as "Tell me about your trip to the zoo" can be used as an indirect question. Such an utterance can be classified as a directive statement, with emphasis on "*tell*," or stated with the inflection on "*zoo*."

While the structure of most direct questions takes the *wh* form (*what, why, where who, when*), each of these *wh*'s sends a different message. Open direct questions can be simple, complex, or embedded: e.g., "What do we need to build a house?" (simple); "If we wish to build a house, what do we need? (complex); "This is a nice house which we have built. What do we need to build

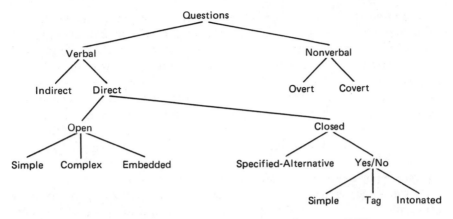

Figure 1 A taxonomy of questions forms (Kearsley, 1976).

it, because if we could figure it out, it will help us next time?" (embedded). These structural components may have different effects depending, of course, on the developmental level of the child.

The particular *wh* term employed sets the direction for the addressee. To be asked "where" orients one in space, whereas "why" asks for causal analysis. As we shall see later when we come to explicate the rules of the question, the particular emphasis here orients the child to aspects of reality. An example from Piaget (1959, pp. 104-105) illustrates the differential responses that occur when the questions use different *wh* forms or structure:

E: What is a brother?
C: A boy.
E: Are all boys brothers?
C: Yes.
E: Is the boy who is the only one in the family a brother?
C: No.
E: Why are you a brother?
C: Because I have sisters.
E: Am I a brother?
C: No.
E: How do you know?
C: Because you are a man.
E: Has your father got brothers?
C: Yes.
E: Is he a brother?
C: Yes.
E: Why?
C: Because he had a brother when he was little.
E: Tell me what a brother is.
C: When there are several children in the family.

The questioning helps the child make his idea explicit. The questioning shifts from direct questions to indirect questions. In addition, *how* questions are used. The illustration demonstrates also how the questions shift targets and messages—from definitions ("What is a brother?") to a request to verify ("How do you know?").

The *complexity* of the question refers to both *syntactic content* and *temporal quality*. A set of elements may be incorporated in any single inquiry, for example: "Where did you go with Mary yesterday while you were visiting New York?" or, "Do you think that if I boiled the water first and then put the egg in, it would take as long for the egg to get hard?" The structure of the question is complicated by a series of clauses, differences in temporal features, etc.

While the temporal feature can be considered structure, in the strict grammatical sense, it seems from our perspective also to define a functional contribution orientation. The particular temporal aspect has considerable potential in influencing the development of representational schema because it can refer to the past, the ongoing present, or the future. A question which requires the child to recount previous experiences in contrast to anticipating what will happen exemplifies the interplay of content and temporal relations. Since recollection is a retrieval of an already experienced event, response to this type of question may be easier than anticipating and dealing with incomplete knowledge. Further, both the temporal and content comprehension will vary with the development of the child. Structural features, temporal quality, and content of questions have to be gauged relative to the child's experiential developmental state. For example, Vygotsky (1962) points out that while the young child finds it easy to remember experiences, the adolescent can not only remember experiences but also apply them to the future. In addition, the temporal orientation of a question will differentially affect the child's response, depending on the child's comprehension of time.

Another critical structural attribute is the message in the inquiry. The message involves a particular content that *demands* a response. Kearsley's *structural* model presupposes a content. Every question is asked about something—known or unknown. This is of particular importance in teaching strategies since it is *via* content that the teacher contributes to the child's substantive learning. In complex questions, the message may not be clear because of the way the question is structured, or because the content is not comprehended. This requires the respondent to decide just *what* the question is.

The primary function of every question, whether direct or indirect, is to elicit a response. (Rhetorical questions are an exception to this claim and are not regarded as "true" questions in our discussion.) There are at least three types of responses to a question: (1) making a relevant response which reveals a direct compliance to the message; (2) making an irrelevant response (by responding to a question such as, "What kinds of animals did we see when we visited the farm?" with an answer like, "My brother has a new bike."); and (3) ignoring the question by simply not attending or by leaving the scene.

The type of response anticipated can vary as a function of the open-closed characteristics of the question. If the question is closed, the appropriate response will be closely tied to the content: "John, what is your brother's name?" or, "What color is this pencil?" In each instance, the type or class of response is clear: in the first instance, a boy's name is expected, in the second, a color. It would certainly be a surprise if the reverse came about, to wit, the child gave a color to the first question and a boy's name to the second question. But it is possible that when Johnny is asked his brother's name he answers, "Red." This would perforce create an unanticipated discrepance; "Red" is ambiguous, since it could be his brother's nickname. Thus, while it is possible for surprises to occur in response to closed inquiries, the probability is that the response fits the expected class.

By contrast, open-ended questions have responses that are not as clearly predictable. For example, asking a child, "What did you do yesterday?" can elicit an answer that can deal with any number of different kinds of events or actions.

An effective feature of the open-ended question is the consequence of the lack of specificity in the demand expectations. For example, if the question, "What can you tell me about your trip to the orchard?" is asked, the demand quality is nonspecific; the particulars required are ambiguous; the amount of information required is unstated, and the correctness of the response is not clear. While the child may believe he/she has produced *all* the necessary information and has answered the question, the teacher may not agree and may well proceed with another question. (Such a sequence of questions and answers need not be unique to a teacher-child interaction; adult-adult communication may function similarly.) Since there are no criteria for what is required, the respondent is not sure when the question is indeed answered relative to the request of the questioner.

The functions described above are related manifestly to content and to structure. However, questions can function on a less explicit level. The tone, the timing, the accompanying gestures can all serve to communicate demands that may not even be intended. A question such as "What is your brother's name?" uttered in a benign manner may be interpreted by the child as just a request for information; but if uttered in an imperious tone or cloaked in suspicion, may be interpreted as a threat (Katz, 1977).

In sum, questions covered may convey two levels of messages: the level of manifest messages which are present in the content and structure; and the level of latent messages which are tacit and expressed in the tone or the ambiguity. These features cannot be isolated from one another since they in part form a unit. The recipient of the question can potentially receive all the messages. The nature of the response is no doubt influenced by how the recipient encodes the units.

The analysis of the question in terms of its structure and function leads us now to our conceptualization of an inquiry strategy as a teaching stragety.

THE CONCEPTUAL BASIS FOR QUESTION ASKING

Cognitive Demands Made by Questions

In responding appropriately to the demands generated by question asking strategies, the respondent has to deal with the nonobservable and with discrepancies. A. R. Luria (1976), who holds a perspective consistent with that of Vygotsky (1962), has cogently described the first ability. He writes:

> Men can deal even with "absent" objects and so duplicate the world through words, which maintain the system of meanings whether or not the person is directly experiencing the objects the words refer to. Hence a new source of productive imagination arises: it can reproduce objects as well as reorder their relationship and thus serve as the basis for highly complex creative process. . . Such codes enable a person to go beyond direct experience and to draw conclusions that have the same objectivity as the data of direct sensory experience. (p. 10)

Human beings are able to deal with "absent" objects because of the ability to transform experience into representations—that is, to represent experience in the form of images, language, and actions. The ability to represent is increased as it is exercised through responses to environmental demands. The opportunities for actively exercising representation abilities are enhanced when one is presented with questions. Thus the use of question asking as a basic teaching strategy is justified because of the important role questions play in enhancing cognitive development.

Let us turn now to the issue of discrepancies and their resolution. Questions can create discrepancies and provide motivation for resolving them.

It is because of the realization that inquiry can create a discrepancy or a mismatch between sets of events that we were led to develop a dialectical model. This in turn provides a framework for the interactions necessary for cognitive development (Sigel & Cocking, 1977).

Posing an open-ended question in contrast to a closed one imposes a demand for an answer but carries no message as to what constitutes a "correct" or "appropriate" answer. Whereas a closed question usually has a clear referent as well as a clear message, an open question forces the respondent to decide what is appropriate and how much to say. For example, "What can you tell me about your trip to the orchard?" is an open-ended question allowing for many options: the child can begin at any point in the history of the trip, relate any number of possible events, feelings, or what not. This is in contrast to closed questions, e.g., "Did you go to the orchard? Who too you? How did you get there?"

Tension is created by the adult's request that the child reconstruct a previous experience with minimal guidelines as to "correctness" of the response, as well as select from an array of options that he/she thinks best meets the adult's demands. Such a question forces the child to distance himself in time and place from the present. The interrogator is using a distancing behavior which requires the child to "create temporal and/or spatial and/or psychological distance between self and object. *Distancing* is proposed as the concept to denote behaviors or events that separate the child cognitively from the immediate behavioral environment" (Sigel, 1970, pp. 111-112). The response to the distancing strategy is a re-presentation of a past experience or a construction of an anticipated experience. In the example of the reconstruction of the trip to the orchard, the child has to separate himself mentally from the ongoing present, re-present the trip, and transform the retrieved information in the same symbolic way—e.g., words, gestures, pictures, etc.

The tension generated by this type of question may well be minimal because the inquirer's demands are relatively straightforward. However, this may be only the beginning of the interaction. Further tension can be generated by following up the child's answer with another question, or beginning an inquiry dialogue. For example, if the child reported that the trip was by car, the teacher might then ask, "Could we have gone to the orchard any other way?" Now the teacher is asking the child to consider alternatives—in effect creating a discrepancy between what *was* (the ride in the car) and what *might be* or *might have been.* Again, the cues are limited and the responsibility for coming up with an adequate solution is left to the child. It is this type of responsibility, in the context of problem solving, that enhances cognitive growth.

Functions of Distancing Behaviors and of Discrepancy

Distancing behaviors vary in the degree to which they activate the separation of the person from the ongoing present. Simple declarative statements, for example, require passive listening and associative responses; open-ended inquiry demands active engagement (Sigel & Cocking, 1977). Because they demand active engagement, open-ended inquiries "function as *instigators, activators,* and *organizers* of mental operations" (Sigel & Cocking, 1977, p. 216).

Discrepancies created by inquiry "propel the organism to change because of the inherent nature of the organism's inability to tolerate discrepancies" (Sigel & Cocking, 1977, p. 216).

We hypothesize that distancing behavior creates discrepancies which contribute in a major way to cognitive development. Our contention is that the inquiry generates tension while creating a discrepancy, thereby increasing the stress level, and that this stress then causes disequilibrium, which the child strives to resolve via some mental action (Sigel & Cocking, 1977). The resolution is perhaps short-lived. Another question can reinstitute the cycle.

Discrepancies may be of any of the following: (1) Discrepancies can occur between an internal perspective and an external demand. For example, in a conservation experiment with clay in which one of the balls is deformed, the child argues that the deformed ball has more clay than the other ball. Even when told that nothing was added or taken away, the child does not believe that the balls have the same amount of clay. (2) Discrepancies can occur between two internal events. For example, in answering the question, "Will you tell me the best way to drive to your house?" the respondent may be in conflict over which of two possible routes to present. (3) Discrepancies can occur between two external events. The child is shown clear water and a set of colorings. He is asked to predict what would happen if two of the colors (red and green) are mixed and put into the water. After the colors are mixed, another question is posed: "Why do you think the water is colored purple and not red or green?" The discrepancy in this case arises in the context of the action and is external to the child.

The child, however, may not be aware of discrepancies or contradictions. When presented with a drawing of a human figure with no neck or six fingers, the child may well not attend to these discrepancies in spite of the fact he knows he has a neck. To be sure, children at virtually every level notice or react to discrepancies—the infant reacts when his comfort state is disturbed and becomes quiescent when the discrepant event is handled, either through his own volition or through the intercession of the caretaker. But, as we shall see, there are many areas in the world of physical and social knowledge in which the child is apparently not aware of discrepancies. In sum, discrepancies differing in kind and content can occur at various stages of life.

Implications of Resolution of Discrepancy for Cognitive Growth

Movement toward discrepancy resolution is a necessary, albeit not sufficient, condition for cognitive growth. The lack of awareness of a discrepancy is interpreted as "nonattending" to that specific event. The awareness of a discrepancy produces a "cognitive conflict" and resultant tension which may or may nor always require resolution. Action toward resolution, however, comes about not only when the child is "aware" that a discrepancy exists, but also when "intuitive awareness" (a feeling that a discrepancy exists) occurs. Arousal to resolve the discrepancy leads to either mental or motor actions. These actions in the service of resolving conflicts lead to evolution of a stable (temporary) solution. Resolution thus "moves" the child from one knowledge level to another. A child building a block structure notices that whenever a Y block is placed on a tower, the tower collapses. Employment of a cube or a rectangular-shaped block, however, does not destroy the tower. Implicitly, the child comes to realize that one type block is more appropriate than another. In this way, the child has extended his practical knowledge vis-à-vis balance. It is doubtful that the child can articulate either the principle or the heuristic rationale for such a state of affairs; but chances are that in subsequent tower building the child will consistently reject a Y block and substitute the appropriate one.

Actions leading to resolution, then, transfer the child's knowledge state from one level to another. The resolution can be temporary, since interaction with the environment is an ongoing dynamic process. The child can resolve a problem at one stage of his development only to have a similar problem recur.

Now, with new knowledge and experience, discrepancies reappear in what may even be the same domain. For example, children's definition of an animal as "something having four legs" shifts to "something that is alive." At the "four leg" period, children may resolve discrepancy in classification of animals by using the legs as a criterion; later, leggedness is no longer the most appropriate criterion and the "living" criterion is used. When the child has mastered a certain body of knowledge, discrepancies may no longer occur.

Role of Inquiry in Resolution of Discrepancy

In the previous discussion, we have focused on knowledge acquisition under conditions in which the child's own action state led to discrepancy resolution. In the context of an educational or group setting, appropriate inquiry on the part of the other person can facilitate discrepancy resolution.

At the outset of an interaction, the child is actively employing his own existing knowledge base to cope with the situation. The teacher also enters that situation with his or her knowledge. We can diagram the development of the interchange as follows:

State 1:   (T)   (C)

Two independent parties are in contact. The teacher notes the child's activity and the child notes the teacher's presence, leading to:

State 2:   (T) → (C)

The teacher observes that the child is trying to build something, continuously piling block upon block. The teacher may begin a dialogue by asking, "What are you building?"

State 3:   (T ↦ C)

The child says, "A car," and the teacher and child are communicating. They have begun a process of sharing a definition of the situation. As the teacher probes further ("Tell me more about your car," or "Tell me about the parts of your car," or, pointing to a section of the car, asks, "What is this?"), there is an increase in shared understanding of the physical features of the production, diagrammed as follows:

(T ● C)

The shaded area depicts the *shared meaning* about the event. Not everything the child knows or feels about his production is shared, nor are the teacher's intentions regarding the interaction necessarily explicit. This is the white space. The nonstated feelings, knowledge, etc., may not be articulated or even be in awareness, but may impinge on the quality of the response. Children anxious in test situations may find the task boring and not say anything, but this feeling will influence what is shared and not shared.

As the child and teacher interact in an inquiry interaction, the direction the dialogue will take and the kinds of ideas generated will vary as a function of the kinds of questions posed.

The type of question may facilitate the resolution of the discrepancy. For example, in the classic conservation task, the type of inquiry employed for assessment yields information as to the child's understanding of the problem. If, however, the experimenter or teacher were to continue to employ inquiry, the nonconserving child may become aware of the discrepancy and come to realize the equality that exists.

Of course, resolution of discrepancy also depends on what level of resolution is sought. For example, let us consider a classification task. A child is presented with an array of objects (such as animals, vehicles, and human dolls). The task for the child is to classify these items into groups. Say that the child includes some human figures in the vehicle class. The reason for such a choice may be functional—the people use vehicles. On one level, this is a nondiscrepant situation, from the point of view that any relationship is reasonable. On the other hand, looking at this array from a logical hierarchical perspective, there is a discrepancy: the human figure does not "belong" in the group so created, but rather to the class "animal." Organization of the animals and humans into one category, "living," would be a logical hierarchical arrangement. If the teacher then decides to "force" the classification to a superordinate level, appropriate questions could perhaps facilitate the child's moving to a superordinate category. The question may well facilitate the child's becoming aware of the discrepancy. In other words, discrepancy not only may be resolved by inquiry but also may be "discovered" by inquiry.

Let it not be construed that discrepancy is always resolved. There may well be occasions when the teacher's questions are not facilitative. The skill of the teacher becomes the critical consideration in discrepancy resolution. The skill depends on the teacher's understanding of children's cognitive development in general and the specific interaction in particular.

Inquiry, Discrepancy Resolution, and Cognitive Growth

We have suggested that resolution of a discrepancy can be accomplished by using inquiry and that discrepancy resolution leads to cognitive growth. But we still have to address the question of *how* resolution of a discrepancy can lead to cognitive growth. We take our lead from the Piagetian perspective that cognitive growth is a function of changes from a static equilibrated state to a dynamic nonequilibrated state. A discrepancy is a dynamic state of tension, whose resolution comes about through a reorganization of an ongoing state. Where no discrepancy exists, the status quo reigns and there is therefore no external or internal need to change. The individual is cognitively organized, in that knowledge states are in harmony. The child believes what he sees; his construction of reality is such that the world appears ordered.

When questions are introduced at any time, they have the potential of disturbing the equilibrium. Cognitive processes and affective states are activated.

Not only does a question disturb the equilibrium, but it also orients the child in time and space. Questions which make demands for prediction ("What will happen to the glass if it is dropped? What will happen to the egg when I put it in the cake?") orient the child toward the future. The child who responds does so in an anticipatory sense, projecting himself in the future. Employment of anticipatory schema in order to articulate an idea is not usual in the daily life of the child. To be sure, the individual probably does employ anticipatory schema in planning his or her daily activities. However, the pressure to articulate the schema is not a necessary condition—in contrast to the inquiry context in which there is pressure for just such articulation.

The child may be encouraged not only to anticipate, but also to re-present the previous experience. This demand to retrieve information forces the individual to reconstruct and consequently to re-present previous experience.

Not only can the past and/or future, be the focus, but also the present. The child can be oriented to attend to the ongoing present, when the child may be asked to attend to the observable or to infer relationships between events or objects. When the time focus is the past or the future, the child is required to create mental images of events of the past and even of the future. The level of symbolization required for the child to attend to the present may not be as high as that required for anticipating or re-presenting experiences.

We have argued here that questions varying in time dimensions play a role in the children's schema development. Now let us turn to a more detailed account of cognitive demands of questions.

Table 1 lists a number of types of descriptors categorizing mental demands that can be made of another through an inquiry.[1] They range from descriptive labeling to inferential types of queries. Each of these implies a demand—but the demand also defines the process for the child. To be asked, "What color are your new shoes?" immediately structures the child's intellectual and possibly perceptual orientation. He will attend to the shoes and provide the color label. This is a much different demand than asking, "What are the shoes made of?" In each case, the child may have to attend to the physical features, *but* to answer the second question, the child has to enlist the aid of his memory, as well as analyze the shoe itself. Thus, a different set of processes is activated.

Other types of questions listed in the table demonstrate the variety of functions that questions can serve.

The sequence of question asking, as well as the skill in knowing how and when to ask what type of question, must be mastered if inquiry is to enhance cognitive growth. Although it can be argued that the frequency of asking questions is what is important, our hypothesis is that *cognitive growth is enhanced through disciplined inquiry and depends on the demand qualities of the ques-*

---

[1]The complete list of inquiry strategies is available from the first author.

Table 1   Exemplars of Distancing Question Strategies

Label (lab)	**Definition:**	*Naming* a *singular* object or event or action; naming a place, appropriate designation of something, *locating;* identify, a single discrimination; no elaboration; ownership, possessives. Labeling is discrete and does not involve inference.
	Examples:	"Do you know the name of this?" "What is the color?" "What do you have on your feet?" "What do you call what she is doing?" "Where is the book?" "Whose book is this?" "Do you remember her name?"
	Comment:	To be distinguished from concept or class labeling which is symmetrical classifying (see symmetrical classifying).
Reproduce (rep)	**Definition:**	*Reconstructing* previous experiences; dynamic interaction of events, interdependence, functional; *open-ended;* child's organization of previous experience.
	Examples:	"What happened?" "How did you make that?" "What did we do yesterday?" "Tell me about your dream."
Propose alternatives (pro alt)	**Definition:**	Different options, different ways of performing the task; no negative aspect. Possible key words are *other, another, different from before.*
	Examples:	"What other way could we mix this?" "What is another way of blowing up the balloon?" "What is a different way we could catch the mice?"
	Comment:	Not additive as in "What else do we need to add?" or "Can you tell me something else?" No articulation of judgment as in a "better way to do it."
Resolve conflict (res con)	**Defintion:**	Presentation of contradictory or conflictful information with a resolution; problem solving; negative condition exists with focus on an alternative solution—one situation which is an impossibility needs to be resolved in another way; does include inferences of cause-effect relationships, but includes an additional element of identifying the central element in one situation that can be transferred to another situation.

Table 1   cont'd

	Examples:	"When there is not electricity, how could we pop corn?" "Since my mike is disconnected, how could you hear me?" "What if we don't have a spoon, what else could we use?"
Compare	Definition:	Describing or inferring characteristics or properties across classes, not within—two separate instances being compared; noting the existence of a similarity or difference, describing or inferring *only how alike* or different.
	Comment:	No explicit statement of what characteristic is common to both is coded here, since that is symmetrical classification.
(a) Describe similarities (des sim)	Definition:	Noting ostensive common characteristics. Perceptual analysis—comparison of sensory materials present in the interaction, (e.g., objects, rhymes, pictures, etc.).
	Examples:	"Are those the same?" "How are Joel's shoes like Dee Dee's?"
(b) Describe differences (des dif)	Definition:	Noting ostensive differences among instances. Perceptual analysis—comparison of sensory materials present in the interaction, (e.g., objects, rhymes, pictures, etc.).
	Examples:	"Are those different?" "How are Joel's shoes different from Dee's?" "Which foot is the big foot, mine or Adam's?"
(c) Infer similarities (inf sim)	Definition:	Identifying nonobservational commonalities. Conceptual analysis—instances not present for sensory comparison (see comment below); analogies, part-whole relationships.
	Examples:	"Are a lion and a tiger alike?" "How are a lion and a tiger alike?" "How is Joel's story like Dee Dee's?" "What part of the chair is like an animal?" "Does this look like flour?" "What part of this picture is like the part you hold on a real hammer?" "What letter does it looke like?"
(d) Infer differences (inf dif)	Definition:	Identifying nonobservable differences. Conceptual analysis—instances not present for sensory comparison (see comment below).
	Examples:	"Are a cat and a dog different?" "How are a cat and a dog different?" "How is Joel's story different from Dee's?"

181

Table 1 cont'd

	Comment:	Inference refers to literal non-presence of all or part of the materials. In inferring "Are a dog and a tiger alike," neither instances may be present which requires an inference about both of them; or one of them may be there, e.g., as a toy, picture, or live, which still requires an inference although only about one of them.
Continued	Definition:	Stating the *reason for combining.*
(a) Symmetrical classifying (sym class)	Definition:	Identifying the commonalities of a class of equivalent instances or labeling the class; stating *why* instances are alike, not how.
	Examples:	equivalence—"Why are those alike?" "Why did you put those two together?" class label—"What do we wear to keep our feet warm?" "What do you call yellow, blue, green, and black?"
(1) Estimating (esti) (esti)	Definition:	Estimating quantity.
	Examples:	"How many drops do we need?" "How much do you think you'll use?" "If you have five balls on your card, you may hold up your hand."
(b) Asymmetrical classifying (asym class)	Definition:	Organizing instances within the same class in some sequential ordering; logical hierarchy; viewing the relationship as a continuum; seriation of any kind; comparative where each instance is related to the previous one and the subsequent one; relative (bigger to smaller, more or less).
	Examples:	"Is this tree bigger than that one?" "Where is the corner nearest to you?" "Which valentine is the prettiest?"
(1) Enumerating (enum)	Definition:	Seriation, enumeration of number of things; ordinal counting (1, 2, 3, 4, 5).
	Examples:	"Count how many there are." "Count the number of drops."
(c) Synthesizing (synth)	Definition:	Organizing components into a unified whole; explicit pulling together; creating new forms; sum of a number of discrete things.
	Examples:	"Do we have a class of children?" "How many things do you see that will spill?" "When you add "c" to "at," what do you have?"

Table 1 cont'd

Evaluate	**Definition:**	Assessing the quality of any givens.
(a) Consequence (eval con)	**Definition:**	Assessing the quality of a product, or outcome, or feasibility, or the aesthetic quality of personal liking. Criteria needed for evaluation, e.g., good—bad, right—wrong, fun—not fun, silly—not silly. Evaluation of teacher's interpretation of what the child means.
	Examples:	"What do you think?" "What's the best way to do that?" "Is that right?" "That's a good clue." "How do you like the way it looks?" "Are you being silly?" "Are you having fun?" "Do you mean . . . ?" "Is it whipped cream yet?"
	Comment:	Conditional competencies or qualified "can you" questions are included under this category, e.g., "If the rule is four children here and there are already four here, can you play here?" or "Can we pour whipped cream?"
(b) Own competence (eval comp)	**Definition:**	Assessing own competence or ability.
	Examples:	"Can you carry that box?" "Do you know how to cut our paper dolls?" "Can you get me a piece of paper?" "Can you tell me what we are going to do?" "Can you tell me who goes next?"
	Comment:	Includes those statements that use the word *can* literally, e.g., physical and/or social feasibility; also must contain a personal reference (not a collective "you" or "we").
(c) Affect (eval aff)	**Definition:**	Assessing the quality of a feeling state.
	Examples:	"Is it fun to feel happy?" "Do you like to feel sad?" "How do you feel about feeling sad?"
(d) Effort and/or performance (eval perf)	**Definition:**	Assessing the quality of the performance and/or the effort expended on a task (ignore confirming, e.g., "That's neat."; "That's good.").
	Examples:	"Did you work hard at that?" "You did that well." "Did you do that efficiently?" "Are you working hard or are you playing?"

Table 1   cont'd

(c) Effects (inf E)	**Definition:**	Predicting what will happen without articulating causality; effects of a cause; prediction of someone else's competence, or feasibility, or location.
	Examples:	"What will she do?" "Do you see anything in the picture that might make a noise?" "Is he able to escape?" "Will the trap work this way?" "Where might it be afterwards?"
Generalize (gen)	**Definition:**	Application or transfer of knowledge to other settings or objects; a new situation going beyond the immediate task or context.
	Examples:	"Now that we've seen the ice and snow melt when the sun shines on them, what will happen to the snowman?"
Transform (tran)	**Definition:**	Changing the nature, function, appearance of instances; focusing on the process of change of state of materials, persons, or events. Inferring is a part of this—the prediction of what will happen relating to a change of state.
	Examples:	"What do we need to do to change it into butter?" "What did it turn into?" "What will happen when we put in a little red and a little blue?" "What happens to the popcorn when you pop it?" "You've been playing the fireman, now be a cowboy." "What will you be when you grow up, a mommy, a daddy, a child, or a baby?"

tions. Questions which create discrepancies, pose contradictions, and require shifting of perspective are believed to have maximal impact on cognitive growth. In effect, questions that create a dialectical interaction are considered as prototypic of those that would have the greatest potential for influence.

BASIC CLASSROOM STRATEGIES

The creation of an optimal environment for cognitive growth leans heavily on the concept of distancing. Basically, this concept refers to aspects of the environment which stimulate the resolution of discrepancies by the child, foster the acquisition of "conservation of meaning," and result in the growth of the child's internal representational system. Distancing can occur in verbal strategies, in activities and materials, and in classroom management (scheduling, rules, etc.).

In defining distancing, the form cannot be distinguished from the content. Thus, one cannot simply give a list of particular verbal strategies which together make up the set of verbal distancing behaviors. Whether or not a particular question has the distancing dimension depends on its effect on the person to whom it is directed—or its potential effect given the appropriate motivational state. A question stimulates discrepancy resolution only when the child perceives the discrepancy. Furthermore, whether or not a discrepancy is perceived depends on the *state of the child* as well as on the particular form and content of the inquiry.

This framework is designed to help determine when and how to use those behaviors and physical materials which have distancing potentials so that these potentials are realized. Distancing potentials are realized when, through luck and/or knowledge, situational demands are appropriately matched to a child's interests and cognitive abilities. If we can decrease the dependence on luck and increase the knowledge base from which to create appropriate situations, we are way ahead of the game. In general, the teacher's knowledge base will consist of two parts: (1) knowledge of each particular child with whom one works, and (2) knowledge of strategies and procedures which increase the probability both of finding out how those children think (and what they know) and of activating their thinking processes. Fortunately, many of the same strategies which help us find out what is in the child's mind also serve to activate the child's thought processes.

For example, when we ask the right question, instead of simply telling, we find out what the child already knows *and* we stimulate the child to think about the issue.[2]

Distancing behaviors can be used in all aspects of the preschool environment to *activate the child's thinking*. In addition, they help the teacher find out what the child thinks, how the child thinks, and what interests him or her. In general, one is using the distancing model when one tries to:

1. Ask questions rather than give statements.
2. Give real choices—the kind in which children make the decision and are helped to follow through on it.
3. Wait, watch, and listen while the children are doing something; let them solve their own problems and discover the consequences of their actions (whenever it is safe to do so).
4. Be responsive when children initiate interactions, and use questions and suggestions in teacher-initiated interactions. (Avoid being a "TV teacher.")

[2]The following discussion on question asking is taken from Sigel, Saunders, and Moore (1977).

5. Arrange the physical environment to stimulate problem solving (e.g., create or rearrange materials, resources, space, routines, etc.)
6. Apply these strategies in socioemotional, ethical, aesthetic, and motor skill domains as well as in areas typically called "cognitive."

These are important considerations, each of which will be discussed in more detail in the sections to follow.

Ask Questions

Questions are essentially two-way communications: a question usually gets an answer. But questions can do more than that—good questions foster genuine dialogue. Good questions are reasonable, rational, and appropriate, rather than mere fillers for silence. Simple "yes-no" questions or "Guess what answer I'm thinking of" are *not* usually the most beneficial. For example, the questions listed under the "minimize" column below are to be used as little as possible since they require very little mental activity. The questions listed under the "maximize" column, however, require more mental activity on the part of the respondent and are likely to be followed up with a genuine exchange of information and opinion.

Maximize the use of questions like these.	*Minimize the use of questions like these.*
Tell me about this (object).	What color is this block?
What might have happened?	What is the first thing that will happen, the second, the third, etc.
What if (state opposite). . .?	Is this a spoon?
Why do you think that?	

Questions can be directed toward the understanding of a concept, but throughout such a process, *any* answer by the child should be accepted as legitimate—not as an accurate account of reality, but as a true reflection of the child's level of thinking and his or her perception of reality. Follow-up questions are used to help the child move closer to more sophisticated understandings. When questions are used to activate thinking, they help children focus their mental energies on the issue at hand, and, in so doing, help them construct *for themselves* the relevant concept.

Give Real Choices

Posing conflicting issues or alternatives is an important strategy. For example, one might ask: "If I want to boil an egg, should I put it in a pan with water or without water?" or "Would you rather build a house with blocks or with wood scraps?" When children have to choose between two or more alternatives, they have strong motivation for carefully examining each possibility. This is only true if two conditions are met:

1. the choices must be mutually exclusive (e.g., you can't eat your cake and have it too); and
2. there is some consequence of having made the choice. Thus, if a child is asked whether she would like the soup hot or cold, and she chooses cold, she should be given it cold. If she asked to make a prediction, (1) she should be helped to examine why she puts faith in her choice of prediction, (2) she should be allowed to test her choice, and (3) she should be helped to relate the results of the test to her prediction.

When these two conditions are met, the child is likely to be *motivated* to consider each option as thoroughly as possible. However, she still needs help in *knowing how* to weigh options. Questions can be used here to help the child consider pertinent details, make inferences, and relate pieces of information in a way which allows her to make a rational choice.

Wait, Watch, Listen

No matter how good the initial question, its value can be lost by not waiting long enough between question and answer, by showing approval only for correct answers, or by accepting answers without posing alternatives. Children need a chance to concentrate—they must understand the question, and they must formulate an answer. This takes time.

When a child has produced an answer, one can ask further questions to determine the conviction with which a child holds the response and to establish the basis for holding that point of view. These aims hold for both correct and incorrect answers. Both teacher and child benefit from such an exchange: the teacher learns more about the child's view, and the child examines his/her own beliefs more carefully. In general, if given a chance to *test their knowledge themselves*, children may even change their beliefs in accordance with the results. When this happens, they have a good reason for holding the new belief—a better reason than one which depends on having been told to believe it by an "authority."

The guiding principle here is that, whenever it is safe, *let children discover the consequences of their actions themselves.* The teacher's role is to help keep conditions safe for testing consequences and to help children notice and analyze the consequences. Nonverbal looks, gestures, or manipulation of materials, as well as verbal questions, may help children attend to the consequences of their actions.

Be Responsive

A teacher's response to child-initiated questions serves as a model for valuing questions, giving serious thought to questions, and turning question-asking into a genuine dialogue. A child's plea for information should not be ignored, but it does not have to end with a simple statement from the teacher. The teacher can help *the child* solve the problem when strategies like this are used: "That's a good question; let's figure it out. Is there anything else we know of that looks like that when it's wet?"

In many cases the teacher can help the child devise a way to find the answer to the question. This might involve bringing a snowball inside, asking another child why he's hiding the book, or looking on a chart to find out whose turn is next. Questions can be used to help the child think of an appropriate way to get the information. The idea is to free the child from dependence on the teacher, not to be unhelpful or to withhold information. For this reason, a good deal of judgment is needed in deciding how much help to give and when and how to give it.

In response to a child's question, the teacher engages the child in finding the answer. This is in contrast to the "TV teacher" who, in an admittedly entertaining and appealing way, takes over the problem and presents its resolution as a completed package.

Arrange the Physical Environment

The preschool classroom can be arranged to enhance children's use of problem solving abilities. Blocks near the dramatic play area, for example, lend themselves to use in improvising stoves, beds, etc. Signs and pictures at children's eye-level enable children to make good use of them for ideas and information. Activities should be arranged so that potentials for integration are obvious *to the child*. A teacher may remember about the clothespins in the top cupboard, but will the child? Keeping materials within children's reach and/or labeling storage spaces with pictures gives children more control over the integration of their play. It also helps them to make full use of the classroom resources in solving their own problems. The key point is to test the effect of the arrangement on children—not on what adults might do in it, nor on adult values and aesthetics.

The materials one provides also influence children's full use of their developing mental abilities. Choose materials which lend themselves to a variety of purposes (e.g., sturdy blocks; construction materials like clay, lego blocks, or pipe cleaners; old cans and plastic containers, etc.) and introduce novel materials to stimulate discussion and exploration. Even stories can be selected for how well they elicit ideas from children. A story such as *Good Luck, Bad Luck*, for example, can generate excited discussions of what kind of rescue or what mishap is coming up next.

Routines can also provide ways to involve children in planning and problem solving. Regularity is crucial if children are going to be able to get a feel for the amount of time with which they have to work. A variety of signs (pictures, musical sounds, etc.) can be used to help children know what is coming next.

Finally, to foster children's comprehension of representational media, teachers should take care to illustrate an object or experience shared by the members of the class in a variety of media. Circle-time activities can use 3-dimensional models, pictures, photographs, music, and pantomime to communicate stories or express feelings. Children can be helped to use a variety of media to express themselves. For instance, teachers can suggest telling the same story in another way, and/or provide a variety of materials to be used for communicating the story.

Apply the Strategies Above

Children's problem-solving capacities need not be artificially limited to the so-called "cognitive" areas. Representational thinking is needed in understanding why certain rules have been set, in resolving disputes with other children, in estimating physical prowess, and in evaluating one's own preferences as well as in learning about numbers or learning about colors. Since the underlying processes are the same, teacher strategies can be expected to be similar. Questions are used to explore with the child why he thinks it is all right to take all the crayons or how he knows he will be able to run all the way across the play yard without stopping. The physical environment will also influence the child's developing ability to think rationally about these areas.

Using the distancing approach in the preschool classroom will encourage children to interact with their environment independently, cooperatively, and thoughtfully. Not only will children tend to use whatever capacities they already have for such interaction, but they will be in an optimal environment for further developing and refining their abilities. It is an exciting and challenging environment for both children and teachers. Otherwise,

> Education with inert ideas is not only useless; it is above all things, harmful—corruptio, optimi, pessimi. (Whitehead, 1949, p. 13)

THE DISTANCING MODEL:
ITS TIE TO OTHER CONCEPTUAL FRAMEWORKS

The framework presented here and the subsequent rules for question asking are consistent with a number of current theories of cognitive growth. First, let us start with the concept of an active organism. Once one is convinced that the child is an "active" organism, reaching out to engage experience, then it becomes crucial to come to terms with how the instructional experiences are to be arrayed. For us, the educational environment must allow children the opportunity to discover and to construct for themselves, since through activity and consequent discovery children transform actions into representations.

We would like to point out that our construction of the significance of "question asking" actually is consistent with the conceptualizations of Whitehead (1949), Bruner (1973), Luria (1976), and Piaget (1951). Essentially, we believe that there is considerable convergence in the fundamental assumptions regarding the role of inquiry in processes of learning and development.

We begin with the primary construct that the child is an active organism. In building on this concept we can accept Whitehead's (1949) orientation:

> In training a child to activity of thought, above all things we must be aware of what I call "inert ideas"—that is to say, ideas that are merely received into mind without being utilized or tested or thrown into fresh combinations. (p. 13)

Bruner's (1973) elaboration of this basic position is also consistent with our view. He writes:

> Emphasis on discovery learning through inquiry has precisely the effect on the learner leading him to be a constructionist to organize what he is encountering in a manner not only designed to discover regularities or relatedness, but also to avoid the kind of information drift that fails to keep account of the uses to which information might have to be put. Emphasis on discovery indeed helps the child to learn the varieties of problem solving, of transforming information for better use, helps him to learn how to go about the very task of learning. So goes the hypothesis; it is still in need of testing. But it is an hypothesis of such important human implications that we cannot afford not to test it—and the testing will have to be in the schools. (p. 87)

Engagement in inquiry is an aid or support for enriching the child's engagement with the social and physical realities. Question asking plays a critical role because it: (1) occurs in an interactional context, (2) employs language, and (3) allows for expanding the range and breadth of the child's approach.

Support for these assertions comes from Vygotsky (1962), Piaget (1962) and Luria (1976). A few quotations from these writers will confirm our assertions.

Luria cogently argues for the role of adult-child verbal interaction:

> Under the influence of adult speech, the child distinguishes or fixes on behavioral goals; he rethinks relationships between things, he thinks up new forms of child-adult relations; he reevaluates the behavior of others and then his own; he develops new emotional responses and affective categories which through language become generalized emotions and character traits. This entire complex process which is closely related to the incorporation of language into the child's mental life results in a radical reorganization of the thinking that provides for the reflection of reality and the very process of human activity. (p. 11)

Adult speech or, in our terms, interaction, requires cooperation. The child must be a participant, exchanging communications with the adult. Unless this occurs, the impact of the adult is reduced, or can even be rendered insignificant.

All logical thought is socialized because it implies the possibility of communication between individuals. But such interpersonal exchange proceeds through correspondence, reunions, intersections and reciprocals, i.e., through operations. Thus there is identity between intra individual operations and the inter individual operations which constitute cooperation in the proper and quasi-etymological sense of the word. (Piaget, 1962, pp. 13-14)

Our argument to this point has focused on the rational and cognitive aspects of question asking. However, we must take into account the affective features involved. The initial affective aspect is the child's comfortable willingness to engage cooperatively in the interaction. As Vygotsky (1962) says:

Behind every thought there is an affective-volitional tendency, which holds the answer to the last "why" in the analysis of thinking. A true and full understanding of another's thought is possible only when we understand its affective-volitional basis. (p. 150)

The attitude and tone of the adult are probably critical features influencing the child's participation. If questions are asked in ways which suggest that the questions are criticisms, "put downs," or attempts to "test" the child, the chances are that such affective features will provoke the child's anxiety and make him or her reluctant to participate. In effect, such features encourage a noncooperative attitude. Unless the affective atmosphere is conducive to legitimate inquiry directed toward solving problems, children will not engage in the interaction with a spirit that would enhance cognitive development. Thus, when engaged in an inquiry encounter, the adult should be concerned with the type of question and quality of follow through in a context that takes account of affective conditions.

SOME EMPIRICAL SUPPORT FOR INQUIRY

Relatively little systematic research has been done on evaluating question asking as a teaching strategy among preschoolers. Results with older groups of elementary and secondary children, for example, have shown that learning is enhanced when questions requiring high level inferences are used (Buggey, 1972).

As for preschool children, we have found that those who are exposed to question asking programs do in fact show greater gains in problem-solving tasks requiring anticipation (Cocking & Sigel, in press), memory for places (Johnson & Sigel, 1977), and kinetic memory (Sigel & Cocking, 1977). While these results are preliminary, the differences already found are consistent with expectation.

Not only do we find differences among children who experience question asking engagements in a school setting, but also among children whose parents show preferences for question asking as an informal teaching strategy. Children of parents who indicate preference for "distancing" strategies perform significantly better cognitive tasks involving employment of anticipatory schema, (McGillicuddy-DeLisi, Sigel, & Johnsn, 1979).

In effect, formal (school) or informal (home) educational experiences weighted in favor of questioning (distancing) strategies seem to enhance cognitive development.

The results of our research are consistent with our conceptualization of the conditions necessary for the development of representational thought.

> The transition [between preschool and older children] depends upon the development of representational systems. And one of the important aspects of such development is the shift to symbolic or linguistically mediated representation. (Olson, 1966, p. 135)

The shift, we maintain, is fostered through question asking strategies providing children with the opportunity to discover, to construct, and to evaluate their social and physical reality.

REFERENCES

Berlyne, D. E., & Frommer, F. D. Some determinants of the incidence and content of children's questions. *Child Development*, 1966, *37*, 177-189.

Boller, D. H. The effects of inquiry activities on the questioning strategies of third and fifth grade students. *Child Study Journal*, 1973, *3*, 201-212.

Bruner, J. S. *On knowing: Essay for the left hand.* New York: Atheneum, 1973.

Buggey, L. J. A study of the relationship of classroom questions and social studies achievement of second-grade children. Paper presented at the meeting of the American Educational Research Association, Chicago, March, 1972.

Cocking, R. R., & Sigel, I. The concept of decalage as it applies to representational thinking. In N. Smith & M. Franklin (Eds.), *Symbolic functioning in young children.* Hillsdale, N.J.: Lawrence Erlbaum Assoc. Publishers, in press.

Denney, N. W., & Connors, G. J. Altering the questioning strategies of preschool children. *Child Development*, 1974, *45*, 1108-1112.

Haupt, D. Relationships between children's questions and nursery school teachers' responses. Detroit, Mich.: Wayne State Univ., 1966. (ERIC Document Reproduction Service No. ED 046 507).

Hopper, R. W. Communicative development and children's responses to questions. *Speech Monographs*, 1971, *38*, 1-9.

Isaacs, N. *Children's ways of knowing.* New York: Teachers College Press, 1974.

Johnson, J. E., & Sigel, I. E. Memory and memory verification capability of young children. Paper presented at the meeting of the Society for Research in Child Development, New Orleans, Louisiana, March, 1977.

Katz, L. G. Teachers in preschools: Problems and prospects. *International Journal of Early Childhood*, 1977, *9*, 111-123.

Kearnsley, G. P. Questions and question asking in verbal discourse: A cross disciplinary review. *Journal of Psycholinguistic Research*, 1976, *5*, 355-375.

Luria, A. R. *Cognitive development: Its cultural and social foundations.* Cambridge, Mass.: Harvard Univ. Press, 1976.

Martin, F. Questioning skills among advantaged and disadvantaged children in first grade. *Psychological Reports*, 1970, *27*, 617-618.

McGilluddy-DeLisi, A. V., Sigel, I. E., & Johnson, J. E. The family as a system of mutual influences: The impact of parental beliefs and distancing behaviors on children's representational thinking. In M. Lewis & L. A. Rosenblum (Eds.), *The social network of the developing infant.* New York: Plenum, 1979.

Mosher, F. A., & Hornsby, J. R. On asking questions. In J. S. Bruner, R. R. Olver, & P. M. Greenfield (Eds.), *Studies in cognitive growth*. New York: Wiley, 1966.

Olson, D. R. On conceptual strategies. In J. S. Bruner, R. R. Olver, & P. M. Greenfield (Eds.), *Studies in cognitive growth*. New York: Wiley, 1966.

Piaget, J. *Play, dreams and imitation in childhood*. New York: Norton, 1951.

Piaget, J. *Judgment and reasoning in the child*. Totowa, N.J.: Littlefield, Adams, 1959.

Piaget, J. *Comments on Vygotsky's thought and language*. Cambridge, Mass.: MIT Press, 1962.

Piaget, J. *The development of thought: Equilibration of cognitive structures*. New York: Viking Press, 1977.

Rosenthal, T. L., & Zimmerman, B. J. Instructional specificity and outcome-expectation in observationally-induced question formulation. *Journal of Educational Psychology*, 1972, *63*, 500-504.

Sigel, I.E. The distancing hypothesis: A causal hypothesis for the acquisition of representational thought. In M. R. Jones (Ed.), *Miami symposium on the prediction of behavior, 1968: Effect of early experiences*. Coral Gables, Fl.: Univ. of Miami Press, 1970.

Sigel, I. E., & Cocking, R. R. Cognition and communication: A dialectic paradigm for development. In M. Lewis & L. A. Rosenblum (Eds.), *Interaction, conversation, and the development of language*. New York: Wiley, 1977.

Sigel, I. E., Saunders, R. A., & Moore, C. E. On becoming a thinker: A preschool program. Unpublished paper, Educational Testing Service, Princeton, N.J., 1977.

Smith, C. T. The relationship between the type of questions, stimuli, and the oral language production of children. Doctoral dissertation, University of California at Berkeley, 1974. (University Microfilms No. 74-16, 538).

Suchman, J. R. Inquiry training: Building skills for autonomous discovery, *Merrill-Palmer Quarterly*, 1961, *7*, 147-169.

Taba, H. *Curriculum development: Theory and practice*. New York: Harcourt Brace & World, 1962.

Taba, H. *Teachers' handbook for elementary social studies: Introductory edition*. Palo Alto, Calif.: Addison-Wesley, 1967.

Turner, P. H., & Durrett, M. E. Teacher level of questioning and problem solving in young children. Paper presented at the meeting of the American Educational Research Association, Washington, D.C., March, 1975.

Vygotsky, L. S. *Thought and language*. Cambridge, Mass.: MIT Press, 1962.

Whitehead, A. N. *The aims of education*. New York: New American Library of World Literature, 1949.

Zimmerman, B. J., & Pike, E. O. Effects of modeling and reinforcement on the acquisition and generalization of question-asking behavior. *Child Development*, 1972, *43*, 892-907.

8

Play
and the Acquisition
of Symbols

Greta G. Fein

The Merrill-Palmer Institute

Between the years of one and three, a profound change occurs in the play of children. Prior to this period, the baby sleeps when tired and eats when hungry; objects are banged, waved, or pushed; a spoon might be put into a cup, a top on a jar, but even these gestures of relatedness are brief and tentative. Then, quite suddenly a new element appears. Piaget's (1945, from the 1962 ed.) classical observation vividly illustrates the nature of this new element:

> In the case of J., the true ludic symbol with every appearance of "make-believe" first appeared at 1;3 (12) in the following circumstances. She saw a cloth whose fringed edges vaguely recalled those of her pillow; she seized it, held a fold of it in her right hand, sucked the thumb of the same hand and lay down on her side laughing hard. She kept her eyes open, but blinked from time to time as if she were alluding to closed eyes. Finally, laughing more and more, she cried "nene" (nono). The same cloth started the same game on the following days. At 1;3 (13) she treated the collar of her mother's coat in the same way. At 1;3 (30) it was the tail of her rubber donkey which represented the pillow! And from 1;5 onwards she made her animals, a bean and a plush dog also do "nono." (pp. 96-97)

Piaget's (1932, from the 1965 ed.) interpretation of this behavior is also worth noting:

> As for symbols, they appear towards the end of the first year . . . For the habit of repeating a given gesture ritually gradually leads to the consciousness of "pretending." The ritual of going to bed. . .is sooner or later utilized "in the void," and the smile of the child as it shuts its eyes in carrying out this rite is enough to show that it is perfectly conscious of "pretending" to go to sleep. (p. 32)

The purpose of the present discussion is to examine children's play, the acquisition of symbols, and the relation between them. Play, of course, is a generic term that designates an awesome array of different behavior patterns: the sports and games of older children, the pretend activities of early childhood, and the sensorimotor manipulations of infancy. There is considerable controversy about the meaning of the term, whether it can be used profitably to label common elements of widely varying behavior, or to mark a distinctive consequential psychological process. The term will be used here in a more restricted sense to refer to activities that have an "as if" element in the judgment of an adult observer. There are a great many unresolved issues regarding the basis of such adult judgments and these will be discussed later. For the time being, let me simply note that observers identify pretend episodes easily and reliably; the "as if" element seems to announce itself, and most adults, regardless of their previous training or experience with young children, have little difficulty reading the message.

The development of pretend play is of interest as an expression of the child's capacity for symbolic functioning, and this capacity in turn is viewed here as a major intellectual accomplishment. A symbol is something which stands for or designates something else by reason of relationship, association, or convention. To most of us, symbols designate things in the real world or properties of these things—particular, physical, touchable things, categories of things, or concepts of the qualities and relationships linking things. A symbol may be a word, a picture, a gesture, an object or combinations of these; the word "lion" designates a kind of animal, both picture and word designate courage, and the sound film of a growling lion designates a motion picture company. The relation between symbols and what they designate is more or less arbitrary and more or less regularized by social convention—the sound pattern of the word "lion" suggests little of the animal, but the lion is more appropriate than the weasel as a symbol of courage, and the lion as logo is chosen deliberately to evoke a cluster of positive associations. A symbol may be intensely personal and have meaning primarily for the person who constructed it; or, a symbol may be public, a socially agreed upon representation of shared information. Whether personal or public, symbols represent information in a condensed, compact form. But underlying the construction and use of symbols is the person's recognition of a surrogate relationship between the symbol and that which it represents. The word "lion" stands for what a person knows about the animal; when used, the word can designate what is known or label a given instance. Piaget and others (cf. Furth, 1969) make a distinction between a symbol and its signification, i.e., the structure of meaning designated by the symbol. Symbols are mental constructions, efficient tools for coding and communicating meaning. The symbolic function (or, more accurately, the semiotic function) refers to the capacity to separate meanings and real world events from coding vehicles such as words, images, sounds, and gestures that represent those meanings and designate those events (Piaget, 1962; Vygotsky, 1967; Werner & Kaplan, 1964). Although language is a striking expression of the capacity to construct and use a symbol system, the capacity appears as well in nonlinguistic—graphic, musical or gestural —media (Wolf & Gardner, in press).

In examining the development of pretend play, we will stress the child's growing understanding of symbols as expressions of what is known, as mental constructions that provide a way of representing and commenting on experiences that is different from the experiences themselves. First, we will review the changing forms of pretend play in early childhood, touching upon the observational and experimental research that illuminates its structure. Then we will examine theoretical issues and controversies concerned with the interpretation of pretend phenomena. Finally, we will examine evidence that pretend play influences development, and consider the possibility that the exercise and use of symbols contributes to the development of adaptive behavior.

THE CHANGING STRUCTURE OF PRETEND PLAY

According to Piaget, the first five stages of sensorimotor development reflect changes in the baby's tendency to repeat and vary activities, to attend to external rather than bodily events, to separate means (actions) from ends (outcomes). During the first year of life, the infant acquires the concept of the permanent object which, according to Piaget, is the realization that there are categories of external events which are independent of the baby's perceptual or motoric acts. Stage 6 in Piaget's model marks the beginning of representational thought, i.e., the capacity to construct mental elements that stand for raw perceptions and actions, and the capacity to manipulate these elements according to coherent and fundamental logical principles. In the Piagetian framework, the onset of pretend play coincides with other milestones of cognitive development and so warrants detailed attention. Although other investigators have noted the early beginnings of pretend activities (Valentine, 1937) and although the implications of these activities have attracted considerable theoretical discussion (cf. Buhler, 1930; Stern, 1924), it was Piaget who first provided a detailed documentation of the developmental sequence of pretend activities.

Precursors of Pretend Play

The precursors of pretend play appear during the fifth stage of sensorimotor development. The child indicates an understanding of object use or object relations by brief gestures of recognition; the child touches a comb to his hair, a spoon to his mouth, puts a spoon in a bowl, a top on a jar, or rubs a pencil along a surface.

In an illuminating study, several of Piaget's colleagues (Sinclair, 1970;

cf. Inhelder, Lezine, Sinclair, & Stambak, 1972, for details) examined changes in the form of spontaneous play behavior between 12 and 26 months of age. The observed behavior was coded into three categories suggested by distinctions which have an important place in Piagetian theory. The first category included activities with a single object used according to its physical characteristics—its softness, smoothness, heaviness, weight, noisiness, or pliability. The second category included activities that organize an array of objects by forming a spatial or functional arrangement (grouping objects together, or next to one another, putting a spoon in a cup, and so forth). The third category included make-believe activities (feeding the doll, putting a toy animal to sleep). The results suggest a sequence of developmental transitions such that simple one-object behaviors decline between 12 and 26 months, and combinatorial arrangements increase eventually to the point where they reflect the child's use of a classificatory principle (cups in one group, spoons in another). Pretend activities first appeared at 16 months and became increasingly elaborated thereafter. A recent study of children between the ages of 7 and 20 months confirmed these age trends (Fenson, Kagan, Kearsley, & Zelazo, 1976). Almost all of the 9-month-olds engaged in simple two-object acts (touching a spoon to the base of a pot) but relatively few 7-month-olds did so. All of the 13-month-olds formed simple accommodative (functional) relations (spoon in cup), but only a third of the 9-month-olds did so. Symbolic acts (pretending to eat or drink) were performed rarely at 9 months, more frequently at 13 months, and by all of the children by 20 months. The data imply a distinct developmental sequence in which the spatial elements of a relationship and perhaps the coordinations necessary to produce it (e.g., spoon in cup) must be well mastered before a symbolic representation of the actual social function of that arrangement (stirring and eating) can be produced.

Early Forms of Pretend Play

Pretend play first appears as fleeting gestures. The child produces the motions of sleeping without intending to sleep or the motions of eating without intending to eat. These activities seem to take place outside their customary context and seem divorced from their customary functions of rest and nourishment.

Then, over the next year and a half, these ephemeral gestures become elaborated and enriched. At first a doll is simply an object to be touched, moved, banged. Somewhat later, the doll (rather than the child) is used as the recipient of food and eventually is made the recipient of a complex array of caregiving activities: it is put to bed, dressed, patted, and spanked (Fein & Apfel, in press; Nicolich, 1977; Piaget, 1962). The child's voice quality might change to sound like a parent; gestures, clothing, and other elements might combine to indicate that a role enactment is occurring (Garvey & Berndt, 1977; Sachs & Devin, 1976).

At first, the objects used in pretense tend to be similar to the things used in the real life situations that pretend activities mimic (babylike dolls, cuplike cups). Gradually, the need for verisimilitude weakens and assorted objects (sticks and shells) can be used as substitutes in pretend enactments (Fein, 1975; Piaget, 1962; Vygotsky, 1967). Eventually, the child can create the semblance of an object (cupped hand; molded clay) or use pantomime gestures in the absence of a physical entity (hand holding absent cup or arms rocking absent doll). Piaget (1962) cast these empirical observations into a sequence of developmental levels recently replicated by Nicolich (1977). As summarized in Table 1, the developmental sequence proposed by Piaget notes the appearance of new components that become coordinated into increasingly elaborate and flexible representational behaviors.

Sociodramatic Play

Initially, pretend play is a solo activity. Adults may participate and organize it, but children under three years of age rarely share pretend sequences with one another except, perhaps, in brief, imitative, parallel exchanges. By 2½ years of age, the beginnings of sociodramatic play appears and, by the age of 5 years, what began as a few simple gestures begins to encompass intricate systems of reciprocal roles, ingenious improvisations of materials, increasingly coherent themes, and weaving plots. Consider the following episode of sociodramatic play:

> Karen began to push the carriage. Harvey said, "Let me be the baby, Karen," and started to talk like a baby. He got into the carriage. Karen pushed him around the room as he squinted his eyes and cried. She stopped the carriage, patted his shoulder, saying, "Don't cry, baby." He squirmed around, put his thumb in his mouth, and swayed his body.
>   Josie came to the carriage and wanted to push Harvey. He jumped out and hit her in the face. She walked away almost crying. He went to her, put his arm around her and said, in a sympathetic manner, "Come, you be the baby, I'll push you in the carriage." She climbed in. He ran and got the dog and gave it to her saying "Here, baby." She smiled and began to play with the dog. He . . .got a cup and held it to her mouth. He smacked his lips, looking at her, smiling. He pushed her around in the carriage. Karen ran to him and said "Harvey, let me push the carriage, I'll be the mamma, you be the daddy." Harvey said "O.K.," and reached his hand in his pocket and gave her money. He said "Bye, baby," waving his hand. He went to the shelf, took a hammer and a bed, then sat on the floor and vigorously nailed spokes in it. Karen. . . said, "What are you doing, Harvey?" He said, "I'm making a bed." He looked at Josie and smiled. (Hartley, Frank, & Goldensen, 1952, pp. 70-72)

The episode contains several characteristics typical of most sociodramatic sequences. Some of these appear in earlier forms—decontextualization, the shift from self-related to other-related activities, object substitutions, role enactments. Others are new. First, the symbolism is collective; the theme, the definitions of

Table 1 Sequence of Symbolic Levels: Piaget (1962) and Nicolich (1977)

Level	Scheme	Examples
Prior to Stage VI	Presymbolic schemes: The child shows understanding of object use or meaning by brief recognitory gestures. No pretending. Properties of present object are the stimulus. Child appears serious rather than playful.	The child picks up a comb, touches it to his hair, drops it. The child picks up the telephone receiver, puts it into ritual conversation position, sets it aside. The child gives the mop a swish on the floor.
Stage VI	Autosymbolic schemes: The child pretends at self-related activities. Pretending. Symbolism is directly involved with the child's body. Child appears playful, seems aware of pretending.	The child stimulates drinking from a toy baby bottle. The child eats from any empty spoon. The child closes his eyes, pretending to sleep.
	Symbolic schemes:	
	I. Symbolic projection	
Type I A: Assimilative	A. Child extends symbolic schemes to new objects, actors or receivers of action.	A. J. said "cry, cry" to her dog and imitated sound of crying (Stabe VI). On following days she made her bear, a duck, her hat, cry.
Type I B: Imitative	B. Child extends imitative schemes to new objects. Pretending at activities of other people or objects such as dogs, trucks, adults, etc.	B. J. pretended to be telephoning, then made her doll telephone; she telephoned with all sorts of things: a leaf instead of a receiver.

Table 1 cont'd

Level	Scheme	Examples
	Symbolic Identification:	
Type II A	A. Identification of one object to another.	A. Child picks up play screwdriver, says "toothbrush," and makes the motions of toothbrushing.
Type II B	B. Identification of the child's body with some other person or object; pretending to be other person or object.	B. She crawled into my room on all fours saying "miaow."
Type III	Symbolic combinations: Combinations with planned elements: These are constructed of activities from other levels, but always include some planned element. They tend toward realistic scenes.	Child puts play foods in a pot, stirs them. Then says "soup" or "Mommy" before feeding the mother. She waits, then says "more?" offering the spoon to the mother.
Type IV	Collective symbolism	Sociodramatic play: Julie finds a dirty popsicle stick and gives it to Teddy "This is your spoon baby." Teddy pretends to eat like a baby.

roles and role relationships, and the meaning of gestures and substituted objects are shared. Second, the children use signals to announce the onset of a pretend sequence and they talk about pretending. By 3 years of age, collective symbolism is deliberately managed through a variety of verbal and nonverbal communications (Garvey & Berndt, 1977).

Components of Pretending

The development of pretend play reveals the phasing in and coordination of several discrete strands of mastery that seem to reflect the growth of the symbolic function. Some strands have attracted more attention than others, but each constitutes an issue in the analysis of symbolic processes. These strands are depicted in Fig 1. In the figure we have attempted to indicate transitions from

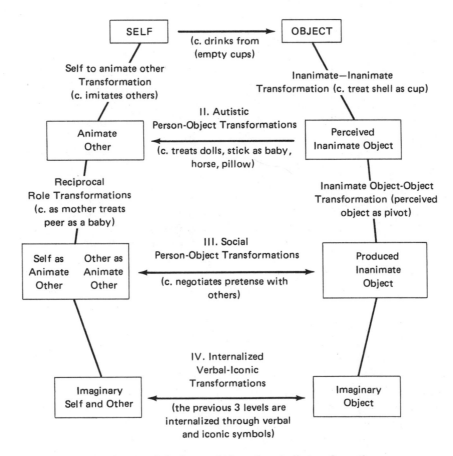

Figure 1   Levels in the acquisition of symbolic transformations

situation transformations to a purely imaginary self, companion and thing (Manosevitz, Prentice, & Wilson, 1973).

1. *Decontextualization: Situation transformations.* In the earliest appearing form of pretend play, the child's behavior becomes detached from the real life situation in which it ordinarily occurs (mealtime, bedtime) and the motivational underpinnings ordinarily associated with it (hunger, fatigue). In a sense, a familiar behavior is reframed and placed under voluntary control free of specific situational and motivational demands. It is curious that this early period of pretending coincides with the ritualization of routines in real life (Gesell, 1925) as if some degree of stable patterning were required either as prerequisite or contrast.

Piaget claims that the child is consciously aware of having decontextualized the behavior, a claim difficult to confirm since the knowing smile does not always occur. And yet, by 3 years of age the intention to pretend is communicated clearly from one child to another with words, gestures, and other communicative acts. Metacommunicative signals that say "this is play" are produced by infrahuman primates as well as children (Blurton-Jones, 1972), and serve to mark a situation with boundaries and rules that others understand (Bateson, 1955; 1956). It was Bateson (1955) who first noted that people bracket life situations into "frames" that may be viewed as definitions of situations "built up in accordance with principles of organization which govern events and our subjective involvement in them" (Goffman, 1974, p. 10). Children seem able to organize a general play frame into subframes so that a play episode might be initiated by a general invitational announcement ("You're going to play with me 'cause I'm your friend. I gave you peanuts.") which is accepted in the response, ("Shall we play house?"). The subframe might be organized by role assignments ("You be the mommy and Teddy and I will be the baby."), whereupon one of the players enters the frame with a first move ("You must have your supper now.") which leads to an appropriate in-frame response ("I don't want any supper now.").

Once begun, the episode might shift from pretend play to nonpretend play as the child, still in a play frame, orchestrates a variation within the subframe, e.g., "You're supposed to call me on the phone now." And if children are uncertain about the play mode of a partner, they check it out (Garvey, 1974, p. 170):

> Child X: I've got to go to the potty (he is sitting on a three-legged stool with a
> magnifying glass in its center).
> Child Y: Really? (He turns to look.)
> Child X: No, pretend. (He grins.)
> Child Y: (Smiles and watches child X.)

The preceding examples illustrate two ways in which the symbolic aspects of play are manipulated by children when a pretend sequence is initiated. One way is ideational: the initiation depends on ideas of things not actually present in the immediate environment ("Shall we play house? you be the mommy. . . ."). Another way is material: the initiation depends on an actually present object (the stool referred to as a potty). In a recent study, Mathews (1977) compared these modes of initiation in 4-year-old children. Approximately half the initiations were ideational.

Clearly, these children act as if they have mastered a definition of pretend play as a rule governed situation distinctly different from real life but yet related in some way to it. By 5 years of age, children can talk about their mastery as well as act it out. Although the results are preliminary, we have been asking children to discuss the differences between work and play, what they play, and how they play. Our informants note without exception that work is what people "have to" do, and play is what people choose to do when they can do what they want to do. Pretend play is the form of play most frequently mentioned by these children, and they have little difficulty describing how they play house, doctor, fireman, or monster.

Of course, exactly when the child becomes aware of the relation between pretense and reality and becomes able to deliberately manipulate the transition is not clear. Piaget makes a distinction between awareness which occurs with the first autosymbolic schemes and planning which appears later. But why familiar activities become decontextualized in the first place is not clear except as an incidental fallout from general changes in the organization of sensorimotor activities, namely, the separation of means from ends (Miller, 1973).

2. *Object substitutions.* During the early stages of pretend play, an object must be present in its familiar form if it is to be used as an object in pretense. Initially, the spoon must be "spoonlike," but eventually an object which does not appear to have any apparent spoonlike features (a leaf) can be used as if it were a spoon provided it can be held, lifted, and brought in some fashion to the child's mouth. As development progresses, the dependency of pretending upon a perceivable object of any sort is reduced and eventually the child is able to produce a purely imaginative object with no apparent reliance upon the immediate stimulus field (Overton & Jackson, 1973).

Piaget (1962) views the substitution phenomenon as a significant component of symbolic development but also as a reflection of the essentially autistic orientation of the child. The symbols created are personal, private, and perhaps even accidental. By contrast, Vygotsky (1967) views the phenomenon as an essential step in the separation of thought from objects and actions. In discussing the example of a child using a stick to ride on as if it were a horse, Vygotsky (1967) argues:

> Play is a transitional stage. . .At that critical moment when a stick—i.e., an object—becomes a pivot for severing the meaning of horse from a real horse, one of the basic psychological structures determining the child's relationship to reality is altered. . .To a certain extent, meaning is emancipated from the object with which it had been directly fused before. (pp. 12-13)

The issue of object substitutions was examined in a study by Fein (1975) and in another by Fein & Robertson (1975). In the former study, it was argued that by 2 years of age, the child who feeds a horselike toy horse with a cuplike cup knows that real animals eat and that a cup is for drinking. Pretense is operating insofar as the child behaves as if he were attributing living functions to an inanimate object, adding liquid to an empty cup and, importantly, establishing the relation between horse and cup. In a sense, neither the horselike horse (a toy) nor the cup (empty) are "real" but when realistic, prototypical objects are used the child pretends to "feed the horse" with little difficulty. The scheme developed to describe these relationships is illustrated in Fig. 1. Three types of transformations are represented: (a) the shift from self to other (the child who is usually fed by another becomes the one who feeds); (b) the transformation of an inanimate object into an animate one (horse-shape into horse); and (c) the transformation of one inanimate object into another (a shell into a cup). In the above example, the relation "feeding/eating" requires more transformations as the "horse" and the "cup" become less horselike or cuplike. Now, suppose pretending in young children depends on the number of transformations necessary to produce a relation (such as "horse eats from cup"). The hypothesis is that pretending in young children will vary as a function of the number of substitutions required of them. Two of the relationships diagrammed in Fig. 1 are open to experimental manipulation: a less prototypical cup (or horse) can be substituted for a highly prototypical one. Substitutions can occur singly or jointly.

When 2-year-olds were asked to "feed the horse" under double, single, or no substitution conditions, the results were in accord with predictions derived from a transformational analysis. Over 90% of the children were able to enact the pretense when no substitutions were involved, 70% could do so when single substitutions were involved, and only 33% could do so when a double substitution was involved. In Vygotsky's terms, the children required a pivot, a more or less realistic anchor, to support a symbolic transformation. The symbolic function is operating, but symbols and symbol making are not completely emancipated from perceivable objects.

Additional evidence comes from a study reported by Fein & Robertson (1975). In a free play situation, children who were 20- and 26-months-old were presented two toy sets: a highly prototypical set with realistic dolls, trucks, and other toys, and a less prototypical set with less realistic toys. Toys in the latter set were scaled according to the degree of realism. Results indicated that within the less prototypical set the pretend use of objects increased as the objects became more realistic and the use of less realistic materials increased with age.

The purpose of the above studies was to examine the type of symbolic competence required of the child if pretend play is to occur. For the young child, nonrealistic materials place cognitive demands the child is unable to meet. For the older preschool child, the child who has reached the golden age of make-believe play, the relationship may be reversed. According to studies reported by

Phillips (1945) and Pulaski (1970), a greater variety of fantasy themes are evoked by nonrealistic than realistic toys. But even at this age there are limits to the child's substitution of one thing for another (Elder & Pederson, 1978). For example, when children were offered a number of substitution alternatives for food to feed the "hungry baby," children tended to reject incongruous alternatives such as a toy animal and a hair brush (Golomb, 1977).

3. *Self-other transformations.* The third strand appearing in the development of pretending concerns how the child as "self" participates in a pretend sequence. Initially, the child's pretend activities are self-related in that the child functions as both agent and recipient (e.g., the child feeds himself). In time, other actors and agents are added to the pretend game and persons as well as things become substitutable (e.g., the child pretends to feed mother or a doll). Eventually, the child becomes a detached generalized "other" who makes the doll feed itself or a parent doll feed a family of dolls.

In one study, Fein and Apfel (in press) examined how the structure of object-action relationships changed between 12 and 30 months. The children were presented a set of realistic play materials, which were either actual eating utensils (cup, spoon, bottle, pot), or toys (doll, doll-bottle, toy tea cup). The question was how pretend feeding changed with respect to who was fed (child or doll) with what utensils. One of the major findings was that the 12-month-olds, all of whom had been bottle-fed, rarely used the bottle to feed themselves but preferred the spoon and the cup. The doll was ignored until 18 months and then it was fed with the bottle rather than the other utensils. The results help to make two points: first, even at 12 months, the child's choices do not seem to be haphazard. Pretense seems to be a selective and deliberate activity. Second, the results pose a question with respect to the function of pretense. At 12 months, the children avoided a familiar object, the bottle. On the other hand, they ignored the doll, as if the equation "doll=baby" has yet to be formed. Rather, they initiated a familiar activity (eating or drinking) with objects they were just beginning to use in real life, objects which pose a serious challenge when filled with real liquid or food. The structure of early pretend behavior thus suggests a possible function. Pretense might provide special opportunities for the partially understood and the dimly grasped to become more firmly mastered. Vygotsky (1967) stated the case quite clearly: "...play creates the zone of proximal development...In play a child is always above his average age, above his daily behavior" (p. 16).

Using a modeling technique to facilitate pretend play, Watson and Fischer (1977) studied the way infants between the ages of 14 and 24 months make objects act as agents. These investigators proposed four steps in the developmental sequence. First, the infant uses self as agent (e.g., puts his head on a pillow to pretend to go to sleep). At the next step, the infant uses a passive "other" as agent (puts a doll to sleep), and at the third step, a substitute object (a block) can be used in place of the doll. Finally, at the fourth step, the infant makes the doll an active agent and puts the doll to sleep as if the doll were actually carrying out the action.

These findings raise another issue in the analysis of symbolic development. Several theorists agree that in early development, actions and objects are psychologically undifferentiated from one another (Vygotsky, 1967; Werner & Kaplan, 1964). But Werner and Kaplan add another element, the person, and characterize the early understanding of the child as consisting of "ego-bound things-of-action." According to these theorists, the development of symbolization involves a progressive distancing of, first, person from referent, and second, symbol from referent. With development, the child comes to understand the world as made up of "ego-distant objects-of contemplation." The third strand in the development of symbolic play traces changes in the role of the child in pretend episodes. As the child comes to symbolize others as agents, he or she becomes able to symbolize himself or herself as a different "other," and finally achieves sufficient psychological distance to permit what Vygotsky (1967) refers to as a "dual affective plan" in which the "child weeps in play as a patient but revels as a player" (p. 14).

4. *Symbol socialization: Collective transformations.* The fourth strand in the development of pretend play represents the socialization of symbols. In the early stages, representations and substitutions may be highly personal and idiosyncratic, though not entirely haphazard (Fein & Apfel, in press; Golomb, 1977). In sociodramatic play, a stick can be food, a child a baby, and a scene represent mealtime only if the players understand the substitutions, roles, and themes and negotiate the arrangements. In spite of the novelty, originality, and inventiveness of sociodramatic play, there is often a high degree of standardization in the way role-appropriate actions and objects are defined—babies drink from bottles, cry, and curl up; adults drink from cups, talk on telephones, make dinner, and wheel baby carriages (Lowe, 1975). The earliest appearing roles are those of child and adult and these roles are designated by a relatively small number of objects and gestures. A baby is invariably bottle-fed and the adult is invariably cup-fed; babies sleep and adults are wakeful; babies are the passive recipients of adult initiated actions. The standardization of seemingly core role characteristics begins to appear by 2 years of age (Fein & Apfel, in press) when primitive feeding routines begin to evolve into more elaborate caregiving sequences. It is as if some stabilization of the way reality is to be construed and represented is a prerequisite of new variations and collective pretend enterprises. In this sense, pretend play becomes "rule-governed" and socialized.

Little is known about the early beginnings of sociodramatic play. Typically, sociodramatic play is studied in preschool children, whereas other forms of play are studied in infants who have few opportunities for sustained group activities. In a currently ongoing study we are beginning to study the development of sociodramatic play in children who enter a group care arrangement during the second year of life.

In the study, we are observing the children in the classroom, and in groups of two in a laboratory playroom where their behavior is videotaped. It is becoming evident that sociodramatic play rarely occurs before 30 months of age, and even when initiated, it falls flat. Consider the following observation of a relatively advanced exchange between two 2-year-olds:

> Amy finds a lady's hat. She puts it on and then goes over to the mirror. Looking in the mirror she adjusts the hat, smiling at herself as she does so. She returns to the shelf of dress-up clothes and selects a purse. She opens it, looks inside, closes it several times. She then picks out a pair of high-heeled shoes and puts them on. She turns to a caregiver, announcing "I'm going to the store," and marches across the room. Halfway across, she notices Judy who is playing a running game with a caregiver, and pauses to watch. She then returns to the dress-up corner, selects another purse, and brings it over to Judy. She offers the purse to Judy, who, glancing at Amy's outfit, accepts the purse. Amy takes Judy's hand and together, holding hands, they walk across the room, smiling at one another. Judy abruptly stops, and looks back to the site of her previous activity. Without comment she lets go of Amy's hand, drops the purse, and returns to the game. Amy watches her depart, and returns to the house corner.

Later in the observation, Amy turns to a doll and begins an elaborate sequence of caregiving, dressing up, going out, and so forth. In other observations, Amy has been observed using dolls and dress-up clothes in pretend sequences although the sequences are less elaborate and sustained. What is it, then, that stands in the way of group play?

One possibility concerns the distance between self and other. It may be that young children can only construct symbolic representations of distinctively different, well-differentiated, familiar, but puzzling "others"—adults who are perceived as "out there," separate, independent, and autonomous objects. The young child may still be too close to herself to represent an "other" that is like the self. At the same time, the child can attribute babyness to a doll and appropriately render an adult role in relation to the doll. If so, sociodramatic play between 2-year-olds cannot get started for lack of suitable role partners able to maintain the reciprocal relation of parent-child. Since the earliest pretend themes revolve around child care and family relations, age associated roles are of central importance.

Another possibility concerns the motivation of pretense. If, as Vygotsky (1967) claims, "Play is invented at the point where unrealizable tendencies appear in development" (p. 7), the difficulty may not be one of self-other differentiation as much as one of challenge or mastery motivation (White, 1959).

Just as the 12-month-old avoids pretending to drink out of a bottle, so the child a year later may refuse to assume a role he or she knows too well. The child can represent and adopt the role of baby but has no interest whatsoever in doing so. A baby is simply too well understood and the symbols are too well formed. Within the framework of mastery motivation, the content of pretense is likely to reflect matters that the child partially understands and wishes to understand better.

Finally, the child's notion of pretend play as a situation "frame," or transformational "set" (Bateson, 1955; Sutton-Smith, 1972) may not have become sufficiently formed. If so, a necessary requirement for a pretend theme to be shared has not been satisfied and the metacommunicative messages about that theme cannot be produced and understood (Garvey & Berndt, 1977). Children may simply have not grasped the notion that pretend play can be a social endeavor with shared rules about the production and communication of symbolic representations.

Some of the possibilities are amenable to more systematic study. Suppose Amy or Judy were to play with a more skilled sociodramatic player? Would either one play the role of baby, and if so would the role be sustained through various thematic variations? Would they be able to reverse roles and would they respond to metacommunicative messages? Or, suppose an effort were made to train 2-year-olds in sociodramatic play. How effective would such training be? What would be acquired and how lasting would the acquisition be?

THEORETICAL PERSPECTIVES

In the previous section, we described the changing forms of pretend play in late infancy and early childhood. Of course, the description was not theoretically neutral. Information about the development of pretense comes largely from the work of investigators concerned with the sequence of changes in the patterning of a form of behavior over relatively long periods of time. These investigators focus their attention on the structure and development of behavior, the nature of the child's achievement from its earliest to most mature expression. Another group of investigators brings a strikingly different perspective to the study of pretend play. These investigators tend to focus on the frequency rather than the form of the behavior and the conditions that govern relatively short-term changes in the frequency of occurrence. The symbolic character of pretense has been a central issue for the first group and an afterthought for the second. By contrast, the motivation of play is of casual interest to the first group and of primary concern to the second. Each perspective independently contributes to an understanding of the phenomenon, but as yet there has been no attempt to conceptualize a common framework within which both might operate.

Structural-Developmental Issues

Structural-developmental theorists see the "as if" characteristic of pretend play as its defining characteristic. Accordingly, the form is defined as the representation of actual or imagined experience through the separate or combined use of objects, motions, or language under circumstances different from those in which the actual experiences are likely to occur (see Wolf & Gardner, in press, for an alternative definition). The central issue for these theorists is the relation between pretense and the child's ability to construct and use symbols. Wolf and Gardner (in press) state two aspects of this issue in linguistic terms:

> The central achievement is 2-fold, requiring both the construction of an adequate vocabulary of signifiers for a wide range of contents, and the invention of a "grammar" which permits the individual signifiers to be combined into more complex statements. . .In symbolic play, the fundamental process of signification (the decision about how aspects of experience. . .shall be rendered) is up to the symbolizer. (p. 3)

Two central variables in the development of symbolic play are changes in the vocabulary and grammar of the signifiers. During the early stages of pretense, the child has a limited vocabulary (a few gestures represent a small number of themes) and pretend episodes represent single elements. The child's pretend vocabulary grows during the second year of life and several elements are combined to produce elaborated themes.

But there are two other aspects of the achievement and these can be stated in sociolinguistic terms. For one thing, the child constructs a self-other system that governs the formulation of statements designating personal and interpersonal positions; in a sense, the child becomes able to speak as either himself or herself, a particular "other," or a generalized other, and so represent a network of roles and identities. In addition, the child acquires a way of socially negotiating decisions about how aspects of experience are to be rendered. As we described earlier, the child comes to understand that pretense can be talked about or in other ways communicated and so acquires a set of metacommunicative strategies for sending and receiving the messages needed for these negotiations.

Awareness and intentionality. The problem of awareness, the ability to distinguish play from nonplay, real from pretense, is an old one. Most symbolic behaviors appear at a given age and tend to change in complexity and function until they reach a level of stabilization. By contrast, pretend play shows an inverted U-shaped function: it appears at 12 months of age, blossoms between 5 and 6 years, and then begins to decline. Although the particular age of the decline is controversial (Eifermann, 1971), the shape of the curve is not. If pretend play is a sign of the child's sophistication, why does it disappear? William Stern (1924) and Karl Buhler (1930) debated this question, and Stern proposed the "ignorance" hypothesis. According to Stern, the 12-month-old who "drinks" from an empty cup knows something about the world, but not very much. The child has only "hazy memories and echoes" and poorly formed notions about things that are cups and things that are not cups. When a 2-year-old treats a wooden stick as if it were a doll, the child believes, at that moment, that the stick *is* a doll. By 6 years of age, when pretend play begins to decline, the child knows a great deal about the fixedness of role relations, objects, and boundaries in the real world. Stern implied that children know enough by then so that their behavior can be governed by a healthy respect for reality. Buhler's succinct response to Stern's argument was in the form of a penetrating question: If the stick cried would the child be surprised?

Later theorists expanded these earlier discussions. Piaget (1962) offered a position similar to Stern's in its reference to the child's ignorance, but different in that it stressed intentionality as well as awareness. Before the age of 12 months the child has not acquired an adequate system for representing objects and object relations. As long as the meaning of objects is governed by sensori-motor knowledge, the child cannot go beyond behaving in accord with the immediate, concrete situation. As the child acquires a mental system to represent objects and object relations, he can ignore things as they are by assimilating the here and now to well-formed mental categories. The child is fully aware of the difference between a full cup and an empty one, between a cup and a noncup. When a pretense happens, the child knows it. During subsequent stages in the development of pretense, the child knows before it happens; of course, intention is a prerequisite for collective pretense. According to Piaget, pretense is a transitory phase in mental development (Piaget, 1966; Sutton-Smith, 1966). Eventually, logical structures dominate earlier prelogical forms, and pretense is supplanted by constructive activities and games with rules. However, the child's prelogical status does not preclude the acquisition of symbolic forms (language, images) to represent the object and action knowledge previously acquired (cf. discussions of the figural and operative aspects of thinking in Furth, 1969; Piaget, 1966; Piaget & Inhelder, 1971). The form reflected in symbolic play is distinct from language in that the symbols are not arbitrary. It is distinct from images in that it is not derived from perceptions. Play symbols have a special status because they are derived from imitation and indicate that the child is coming to grips with the configural properties of situations. In Piaget's view, the child's memories are clear enough, but he is simply not bound by a system of logical operations. Thought and symbols are still embedded in objects and actions. As far as the child is concerned, eating from an empty spoon could produce food, drinking from an empty cup could produce milk, and the stick could cry.

Vygotsky (1967) contributed a middle-of-the-road position to the discussion. At 12 months the child perceives an object and reacts to it. Later, the child generates an idea and acts upon the immediate perceptual field accordingly. The child's use of substitute object (e.g., a stick for a doll) is viewed by Vygotsky as a first step in the child's transition from things perceived as objects of action to things perceived as objects of thought. A substitute object (e.g., a stick) acts as a "pivot" that serves to detach meaning (e.g., a baby) from a real object (e.g., a doll that has already become a substitute for a living baby). For Vygotsky, substitution activities contribute to and reflect cognitive development. The child may initially be hazy about the distinction between real and not real and, in that sense, substitution activities reflect the child's ignorance. In pursuing these activities the child acquires clarity; in fact, the stick does not cry.

Psychoanalytic theorists, and others whose work is based on psychoanalytic thinking, also consider the symbolic aspects of pretend play. During its early stages, play symbols represent that which is not comprehended but is deeply felt. In play, the child expresses wishes associated with the satisfaction and frustration of primary drives and since the child does not have to hide anything, s(he) produces a fairly direct body-analogous interpretation of the environment (Peller, 1954; Waelder, 1933). During later stages, the symbolism becomes less direct and the child's focus shifts from the expression of wishes to more active efforts to cope with overwhelming experiences. Diagnostically, pretend play is viewed as an access route to information about the child's "inner person" (Sears, 1947), his underlying conflicts and anxieties, and from there to information about the life experiences which produced them (Levin & Wardwell, 1962; Sears, 1947). As such, it made sense to suggest, for example, that aggression in fantasy would be associated with frustration and punishment in the home (Chasdi & Lawrence, 1951). Psychoanalytic formulations have been difficult to study systematically. While pretend play might reflect a child's "real" social and emotional experiences, reality becomes distorted in such a way that the literal content of pretense, whether in the expressions of anger, affection, or joy, or in the details of a story and its characters, are neither isomorphic with reality nor, taken in isolation from other sources of information, sufficient to determine the nature of the child's latent anxiety (Gould, 1972; Peller, 1954; Waelder, 1933). Therapeutically, pretend play is held to have a cathartic function insofar as it permits troublesome experiences to be expressed and pent up feelings to be vented. At the present time, there is little evidence that catharsis operates according to psychoanalytic formulations (Biblow, 1973).

Developmental functions. Structural theorists differ with respect to their views of the function served by pretend play. Piaget views symbolic play as an aberrant phenomenon that reflects the child's limitations but does not reduce them. By contrast Vygotsky views pretend play as facilitating the child's construction of a functioning symbol system detached from objects and actions. Other investigators have defined the cognitive benefits of pretend play in somewhat different terms: creativity (Klinger, 1971; Lieberman, 1965); divergent thinking (Sutton-Smith, 1967); or associative fluency (Dansky & Silverman, 1973, 1975).

There is a growing body of evidence that pretend play may have a facilitating influence on several aspects of cognitive development. In one study, increases in spontaneous play behavior were associated with improved performance on a creativity test in which a child was asked to complete unfinished pictures in a way "that no one else will think of" (Feitelson & Ross, 1973). Other investigators have reported a correlational relationship between play and creativity (Bishop & Chace, 1971; Lieberman, 1965; Wallach & Kogan, 1965). In one study, Sutton-Smith (1968) argued that in play the child might increase the range of associations to objects. If in play things are combined with other things for a novel result, then play creates the optimal conditions for the discovery of new relationships. The results indicate that a greater variety of functions was attributed to toys that were more frequently played with. Similar results were reported by Dansky and Silverman (1973, 1975) who investigated the associative fluency of children who were permitted to play freely with a group of objects.

What happens when children are given training and practice in thematic fantasy activities? Saltz and Johnson (1974) report that training in the play enactment of stories such as "The Three Billy Goats," "Gruff," or "Little Red Riding Hood" and in sociodramatic play increases spontaneous sociodramatic play. More important, children who receive such training were better able to reconstruct a story sequence from a series of pictures. In telling a story from a pictured sequence, fantasy trained children were better able to see causal relations and use inference to connect one picture to another. They also used more connectives and their total verbal output was higher. In a second study, Saltz, Dixon, and Johnson (1977) report an increase in intellectual performance as measured by standard IQ tests and an increased ability to distinguish reality from fantasy.

The distinction between reality and fantasy was addressed specifically in a study reported by Golomb and Cornelius (1977). These investigators argued that in play the child transforms objects and roles while maintaining their original identity and function. The child employs a kind of pseudoreversibility by recognizing both the real identity of the play object and its transformem identity in the play situation. The reversibility expressed in pretend play might be analogous to that required in conservation tasks in which the child must mentally transform an object from its altered state to its original one. In the study, the children were encouraged to transform a real object (chair) into a pretend object (truck) and then reverse the transformation. As predicted, the children who participated in these play activities scored higher on conservation tasks than those who did not. A similar effect was reported by Braine and Shanks (1965) who reported improved conservation performance when children were trained to discriminate between two questions: "Which *looks* bigger?" and "Which is *really, really* bigger?"

Training studies show changes in a wide variety of behaviors not customarily associated with strictly cognitive functions. Role enactment training increases the ability of preschool children to understand and identify the affective states of other children (Saltz & Johnson, 1974). When sociodramatic play is enhanced in a preschool setting, children show improved skill in group problem solving on tasks which require cooperation and role-taking ability. Sociodramatic play helps children see things from another's perspective and understand the needs and preferences of others (Rosen, 1974).

The pattern of effects emerging from the research suggests that pretend play is associated with a large number of particular capacities. A wide variety of training techniques lead to increased play, and particular techniques do not seem to be associated with one or another set of outcomes. Clearly, pretend play has implications for development, but these implications span a broad band of skills and understanding. Vygotsky's notion that pretense touches the development of the symbolic function, rather than specific cognitive skills or knowledge places the issue at a level of generality needed to accommodate the emerging evidence.

On the other hand, children may be achieving more than an internal system of representation that frees them from the control of external stimulation and permits them to think about objects and people. It was Bateson (1956) who, in discussing sociodramatic play, suggested that children may be mastering the *concept* of role rather than a particular role, or, at an earlier period, the *concept* of an object category rather than the category of a particular object.

A view similar to the one being suggested here was recently discussed by Fagan (1976), who proposed that the playing organism is building or modifying an internal model of itself or its environment. When the organism performs symbolic "experiments" it is essentially reorganizing information pertaining to such a model. If so, pretend play may touch two aspects of symbolization—the symbols themselves and the meanings that symbols designate. Pretense, then, may serve two general functions: (a) it may serve to separate meaning from action and object, helping the child acquire a system of signifiers to represent meaning, and (b) it may provide an opportunity to use these signifiers to organize higher levels of meaning.

Functional-Process Issues

An analysis of play in terms of the immediate situation and the variables governing behavior in that situation has emerged relatively recently (Berlyne, 1966, 1969; Ellis, 1973; Weisler & McCall, 1976). Those investigators who have adopted this perspective tend to treat play as a generic term and attempt to place different types of play (e.g., physical play, social play, exploration, manipulative behavior, symbolic play) within a common theoretical framework.

Since Berlyne's (1966, 1969) theory of specific and diversive exploration provides the major constructs for this framework, we will present his position in some detail. Berlyne noted that the two forms of activity differed in the degree to which they are tied to events in the external environment. Specific exploration occurs when the organism is disturbed by a "lack of information and thus left a prey to uncertainty and conflict" (Berlyne, 1966, p. 26). A lack of information occurs when the organism encounters stimulation that is novel, surprising, incongruous, complex, or in other ways too difficult to assimilate easily. Berlyne used the term curiosity to describe the condition of discomfort that motivates specific exploration. By contrast, there are other situations when stimulation in the environment is too easy to assimilate. When events are too predictable and unvarying, organisms will seek out stimulation that affords a more desirable level of variation. Diverse exploration is the term Berlyne used to describe this form of behavior. Specific exploration is stimulus dominated, whereas diverse exploration is organism dominated.

Berlyne used the concept of "arousal level" to account for the motivational aspects of this behavior. According to Berlyne, there is an optimal level of arousal at which the organism is comfortable. Specific exploration serves to reduce arousal produced by excessive uncertainty whereas diversive exploration increases arousal when it is below the optimum level. Berlyne also suggested that diversive exploration might have "more affinities with autistic or free associative thinking" and that "directed thinking and reasoning must be more closely related to specific exploration." Several investigators have subsequently proposed that exploration be viewed as a behavior aimed at reducing uncertainty and play as a behavior aimed at inducing it (Hutt, in press; Weisler & McCall, 1976).

In the framework provided by Berlyne's theory, play serves a stimulus-seeking function. As developed by Ellis (1973) and Hutt (in press), play serves to keep neural centers alert and active, a function that is of special importance to those organisms that have a long and protected childhood free from stress and survival demands.

Situational variables. Studies of the conditions under which play occurs are consistent with this analysis. Children tend to play longer with toys that are more novel (Gilmore, 1965; Mendel, 1965), more complex (Moyer & Gilmer, 1955; Gramza & Scholtz, 1974; Gramza, Corush, & Ellis, 1972; McCall, 1974), and more manipulable (Gramza, 1976). In a recent study, Switzky, Haywood, and Isett (1974) distinguished between exploratory behaviors (visual and tactual investigation) and play behaviors (sensorimotor behaviors, such as bouncing or bending an object, and symbolic activities, such as using an object as if it were a gun). In children between 4 and 7 years of age, exploratory behavior increased with the complexity of the vinyl shapes, but play behavior did not. However, in 2-year-olds, both play and exploratory behavior peaked at moderate levels of complexity and then declined. In older children, for whom pretend capacities are well established, it is not surprising to find play unrelated to stimulus configurations. In a fairly dull situation, older children are likely to create fantasies to alleviate boredom in a manner similar to that described by Singer (1961) when children were asked to wait with nothing to do. By contrast, younger children have not yet acquired stable representational schemes separated from sensorimotor activities, and their behaviors are still dominated by the characteristics of objects in the immediate environment. It is likely that moderately complex objects are more likely to "look like" real things, the more complex objects resemble abstract shapes and the most complex objects are weird forms. Unfortunately, the category "play" used in the study contained both manipulative and symbolic behavior, so that a developmental account of the above findings is not possible.

Another recent study examined the influence of complexity in a naturalistic, familiar situation that offered children far more diverse opportunities for doing things. Scholtz and Ellis (1975) observed groups of 4- and 5-year-olds in a situation that permitted contact with materials as well as with one another. Complexity was varied by introducing apparatus (trestles, blocks, ropes) which differed in the number of playable units. Groups of children played with apparatus at a given level of complexity during 15 sessions over a 3-week period. The results were striking. When apparatus contacts were examined, more object contacts occurred when complexity was high rather than low. When peer contacts were examined, more occurred when the complexity of the apparatus was low. Regardless of complexity level, apparatus contacts declined over sessions as the apparatus became less novel. However, for peer contacts, the trend over sessions was vastly different. Regardless of apparatus complexity, peer contacts *increased* over sessions, as if peer play provided a richer and more useful source of interest.

Temporal effects. As every parent knows, children eventually lose interest in a new toy but they do not lose interest in playing. Hutt (1970) investigated children's behavior in a situation which contained a novel, manipulable object surrounded by several other toys. Even when response contingent feedback was available (i.e., when manipulations of the object produced a sound or a visual display), the amount of time children spent manipulating the object decreased over sessions. In contrast, the amount of time children spent in other forms of activity increased. Although Hutt refers to these alternative activities as "play" or "diversive exploration," given the age of the children and descriptions of what they were doing, it is likely that their activities involved many symbolic components as well as sustained manipulations and combinations of the other available toys (cf. Hutt, 1966).

These temporal phases are represented in a model advanced by Nunnally and Lemond (1973) in which heightened attention is followed by specific exploration, uncertainty reduction, play, eventual boredom, and the search for new stimulus encounters (diversive exploration). The evidence reviewed thus far, however, suggests that pretend play may not necessarily terminate in boredom and, to the contrary, might alleviate boredom (Ellis, 1973; Hutt, in press; Weisler & McCall, 1976). The problem arises because play is forced to fit a paradigm associated with exploration. The role of familiar toys (the beloved teddy bear or match box cars) and familiar friends is neglected (Scholtz & Ellis, 1975).

Emotional state. Play is most likely to occur when the organism is free from strong biological drives or emotional stress (White, 1959). Even though the clinical literature suggests that the content of play often expresses anxiety and aggression, play is disrupted when the anxiety becomes too great (Erikson, 1950; Gould, 1972; Peller, 1954). Conditions that frustrate the child (Barker, Dembo, & Lewin, 1941), or in the case of the young child, that separate him from his mother in unfamiliar situations, interfere with exploratory and manipulative play behavior (Ainsworth & Wittig, 1967).

One study examined the interaction between levels of anxiety and the toys that children prefer (Gilmore, 1965). Gilmore hypothesized that children would rather play with state-relevant toys; that is anxious children (children who were hospitalized) would like toys in keeping with what they were anxious about (such as stethescopes and thermometers), but nonanxious children (children who were not hospitalized) would like novel toys. Anxious hospitalized children did indeed prefer toys with a medical theme, but all children preferred novel toys.

These and other findings suggest that factors that place children under stress are likely to disrupt or substantially alter play activity. Stress factors in natural settings have not received nearly enough attention, although many of the variables studied by Prescott and Jones (1967), Johnson (1935), and Jersild and Markey (1935) highlight the importance of stress producing factors such as crowding, inappropriate play equipment and inadequate supervision.

Some Productive Differences

Structural and functional approaches differ in their stand on three central issues: the nature of definitions, the role of antecedent conditions, and the meaning of outcomes. These differences are summarized in Table 2. Although the differences stem from profoundly different world views, matters that are hazy in one approach are clear in another and so the two approaches might complement one another.

Definitions. Recently, investigators in the functional mode have attempted to define play in relation to exploration focusing on characteristics of the organism's

Table 2 Some Differences between Structural and Functional Perspectives

	Structural Theories	Functional Theories
Definition	Form derived	State derived
Antecedents	Life history	Immediate situation
Outcomes	Acquired concepts or skills	Optimum arousal, maintenance, or control

state, such as level of uncertainty, or the relative dominance of stimulus and organism in the production of behavior. In these discussions, pretend play is but one of the varied forms on a continuum fixed firmly by the attributes of specific exploration on one end and diversive exploration on the other.

By contrast, structural theorists define pretend play according to its behavioral characteristics. These characteristics change with age as more mature forms of representational behavior emerge. Implied in the structure analysis is the idea that true organism-dominated behavior involves the capacity to construct and use symbol systems. The study of pretend play can be seen as the study of how the organism achieves this dominance through the acquisition and application of symbolic processes. If in exploration the organism is seeking or receiving new information about the environment, then in pretend play that information is reorganized, interpreted, tagged, and made available for future use. From a general cognitive perspective, exploration and pretend play are complimentary in that they deal with the organism's informational requirements in different ways.

Antecedent conditions. As indicated in Table 2, these perspectives differ also in their view of the circumstances that promote play. Functional theorists are concerned with the relation between environment and organism in the immediate situation. The problem is one of examining when and how this relation changes. In studies of exploratory behavior, attention focuses on the influence of stimulus parameters (complexity, novelty, discrepancy) that depend upon the state or condition of the organism with respect to stimulus variations. As Weisler and McCall (1976) note, stimulus parameters assume strikingly different characteristics with respect to pretend play. Some of these can be derived from the issues posed by structural theorists, e.g., the stimilarity between an object and its referent. In this example, there is a discrepancy between the conventional meaning of an object and the meaning given to it by the child. The discrepancy is produced by the child, not the environment.

However, stimulus parameters are not a central issue for structural theorists, who are more concerned with the influence of experiential factors on play. Studies of socioeconomic differences suggest that children from economically advantaged homes are more likely than those from disadvantaged homes to engage in elaborate sociodramatic games (Feitelson & Ross, 1973; Rosen, 1974). In one study, an experimental procedure was designed to separate two factors that might have contributed to the difference between advantaged and disadvantaged groups. Smilansky (1968) hypothesized that the disadvantaged children might lack either the concepts or knowledge necessary for dramatic reenactment or the techniques for initiating, elaborating, and maintaining "as if" sequences. In one type of training, teachers emphasized concepts involving roles (such as fireman, storekeeper, policeman) in an effort to enrich the ideas available to the children. In a second type of training, they taught play techniques by intervening in ongoing play sequences. In these interventions, the teacher might suggest a role, an elaboration of a theme, an interaction with another child, or an object substitution. A third group received both theme and technique training and a fourth group received no special remedial attention. Technique and theme-and-technique groups improved, but the most dramatic improvement occurred in the theme-and-technique group. In view of structural notions such as "transformational set," "frame," and "meta communication," it may be that the teacher's behaviors were influencing the children's appreciation of play as a distinctive and controllable domain of activity and providing the social strategies needed to negotiate play with others. Parent attentiveness, encouragement, and tolerance of play seems to influence a range of characteristics associated with the quality of imaginativeness or creativity (Bishop & Chace, 1971; Dreyer & Wells, 1966; Freyberg, 1973; Maw & Maw, 1966; Weisberg & Springer, 1961). How these parent characteristics operate is not clear, but one hypothesis is that they help the child to define play as a special situation for the creation of variation, surprise, nonsense, and other forms of stimulation associated with pleasurable arousal (Aldis, 1975). At any rate, there is some evidence that an interacting adult is a crucial ingredient for enhancing the play of preschool children (Singer & Singer, 1974).

Outcomes. Finally, the two perspectives differ in their view of outcomes. Structural theorists are prone to stress the child's acquisition of concepts, skills, or general coping strategies. Almost any kind of benefit can be made to fit the structuralist framework and a large number of particular benefits have been demonstrated.

Suppose pretense is viewed as a way of maintaining an optimum level of arousal. On the one hand, the pretending child produces novel, perhaps incongrous arrangements—the stick that cries, the peer turned baby—and suppose these induce a moderate, pleasurable level of uncertainty. Of course, occasionally the level becomes too high. For example, group fantasies of aggressive animals and monsters lead to more stimulation (more uncertainty) than the children can manage, and play disintegrates (Gould, 1972). On the other hand, these novel arrangements are inherently interesting. They present old information in new forms and so become the target of uncertainty reduction efforts. When children play different roles, they are, in a sense, using what they already know. But when they reverse or change roles, old information is used in an unusual way and a new problem is posed. The new problem may encourage the inference that roles have the characteristic of reversibility and substitutability, but the role-playing person stays the same. From a developmental perspective, the issue may be conservation of self over varied transformations. Pretend roles might provide "pivots" for the separation of self from others and the shift from an egocentric to a sociocentric perspective (Piaget, 1955). Pleasurable arousal may come from the uncertainty associated with control over these relations and the situations that produce them, and arousal reduction from evidence of such control.

Studies of severe environmental deprivation in infancy suggest that infants under 12 months of age, who have limited abilities to produce alternative stimulation, are dependent upon external sources of stimulation but that these abilities expand considerably thereafter. Play cannot be separated from the life circumstances and developmental proficiencies of the organism. The notion that play serves to keep neural and behavior systems active in the absence of immediate stimulation and outcomes that change these systems might be expanded by using two elements: (1) in order to maintain activity, the organism must be able to generate behavior outcomes that are appropriately stimulating; and (b) sources of new information are required over time if the organism is to generate outcomes that continue to be stimulating.

THEMES FOR EARLY EDUCATION

Symbolic processes begin to function during the second year of life. They appear in several areas of child behavior and one of these areas is pretend play. In this discussion, we have described changes in children's pretense during the preschool years. In comparing functional and structural approaches to the study of pretend play, we noted that motivational theorists suffer from an unnecessarily homogenized definition of play. It might be a useful strategy for these theorists to accept pretense as a focal play behavior that fits the construct of organism dominated behavior remarkably well. Not surprisingly, theorists who adopt a structural approach have difficulty specifying the outcomes of play. Current motivational constructs may help to clarify how play "creates the zone of proximal development," and how "in play it is as though the child were trying to jump above the level of his normal behavior" (Vygotsky, 1967, p. 16).

If at one time the benefits of play were speculative, recent research has begun to demonstrate, as well as define, its value. During the thirties and forties early education programs stressed imaginative play activities. In the late sixties, the trend shifted away from play and toward structured activities which if not explicitly academic, were often justified by their presumed contribution to intellectual or verbal growth (cf. Fein & Clarke-Stewart, 1973). The "no nonsense" look in early education emphasized planned activities and materials structured to demonstrate physical attributes (e.g., size, form, color, spatial, and topological relationships) and processes related to the organization of attributes (e.g., matching, discriminating, seriating, classifying, attending), often in the hope of advancing more general features of intellectual competence (e.g., conservation or quantification).

Criticisms of play-oriented early childhood programs reflected specific concerns regarding: (a) the stress on an unobtrusive teacher role which may amount to detached (though benign) neglect in the hands of the unskilled or the untalented; (b) individual differences either in the ability of some children to use play effectively or in the needs of others for well-structured activities; and (c) the pervasive lack of clarity regarding the function of play in development. The results of recent research represent the beginnings of a response to these criticisms in that play promoting adult behaviors and strategies for enhancing play have been identified. More important, the benefits of play are being documented and better ways of conceptualizing the issues are emerging. In a sense, symbol acquisition is a structural issue and play is a motivational issue. Although the two can be separated for analytical purposes, theories can be addressed to a synthesizing framework that enables structural and motivational issues to be joined. Contemporary research may be moving in a direction that will make the construction of such a framework possible.

REFERENCES

Ainsworth, M., D. & Wittig, B. A. Attachment and exploratory behavior of one-year-olds in a strange situation. In B. M. Foss (Ed.), *Determinants of infant behavior*, (Vol. 4). New York: Wiley, 1967.

Aldis, O. *Play fighting*. New York: Academic Press, 1975.

Barker, R. G., Dembo, L., & Lewin, K. Frustration and regression: An experiment with young children. *University of Iowa Studies in Child Welfare*, 1941, *18*, (386).

Bateson, G. A theory of play and fantasy. *Psychiatric Research Reports*, 1955, *2*, 39-51.

Bateson, G. The message "This is play." In B. Schaffner (Ed.), *Group processes: Transactions of the Second Conference*. New York: Josiah Macy Foundation, 1945. Pp. 145-246.

Berlyne, D. E. Curiosity and exploration. *Science*, 1966, *153*, 25-33.

Berlyne, D. E. Laughter, humor and play. In I. Lindzey and E. Aronson (Eds.), *The handbook of social psychology*, Vol. III. Reading, Mass.: Addison-Wesley, 1969.

Bilbow, E. Imaginative play and the control of aggressive behavior. In J. L. Singer (Ed.), *The child's world of make-believe: Experimental studies of imaginative play*. New York: Academic Press, 1973.

Bishop, D. W., & Chace, C. A. Parental conceptual systems, home play environment, and potential creativity in children. *Journal of Experimental Child Psychology*, 1971, *12*, 318-338.

Blurton-Jones, N. G. Categories of child-child interaction. In N. G. Blurton-Jones (Ed.), *Ethological studies of child behavior*. Cambridge, Mass.: Harvard Univ. Press, 1972.

Braine, M., & Shanks, B. The development of the conservation of size. *Journal of Verbal Learning and Verbal Behavior*, 1965, *4*, 227-242.

Buhler, K. *The mental development of the child*. New York: Harcourt, Brace, & Co., 1930.

Casler, L. Maternal deprivation: A critical review of the literature. *Monographs of the Society for Research in Child Development*, 1961, *26*, 2, Serial #80.

Chasdi, E. H., & Lawrence, M. S. Some antecedents of aggression and effect of frustration in doll play. *Personality*, 1951, *1*, 32-43.

Dansky, J. L., & Silverman, W. I. The effects of play on associative fluency in preschool-aged children. *Developmental Psychology*, 1973, *9*, 38-43.

Dansky, J. L., & Silverman, I. W. Play: A general facilitator of associative fluency. *Developmental Psychology*, 1975, *11*, 104.

Dreyer, A. S., & Wells, M. Parental values, parental control and creativity in young children. *Journal of Marriage and the Family*, 1966, *28*, 83-88.

Eifermann, R. R. Social play in childhood. In R. E. Herron, & B. Sutton-Smith (Eds.), *Child's play*. New York: Wiley, 1971.

Elder, J. L. & Pederson, D. R. Preschool children's use of symbolic objects. *Child Development*, 1978, *49*, 500-504.

Ellis, M. *Why people play*. Englewood Cliffs, N.J.: Prentice-Hall, 1973.

El'Konin, D. B. Some results of the study of the psychological development of preschool-age children. In M. Cole & Maltzman, I. (Eds.), *A handbook of contemporary Soviet psychology*. New York: Basic Books, 1969.

Erikson, E. H. *Childhood and society*. New York: Norton, 1950.

Fagan, R. Modelling how and why play works. In J. S. Bruner, A., & Sylva, K. (Eds.), *Play: Its role in development and evaluation*. New York: Penguin, 1976.

Fein, G. A transformational analysis of pretending. *Developmental Psychology*, 1975, *11*, 291-296.

Fein, G. G., & Apfel, N. Some preliminary observations on knowing and pretending. Hillsdale, N.J.: Lawrence Erlbaum Associates, in press.

Fein, G. & Clarke-Stewart, A. *Day care in context*. New York: Wiley, 1973.

Fein, G., & Robertson, A. R. Cognitive and social dimensions or pretending in two-year-olds. Yale University, 1975. ERIC #ED 119806.

Fein, G., & Stork, L. Sociodramatic play in an integrated setting. In preparation.

Feitelson, D., & Ross, G. S. The neglected factor—play. *Human Development*, 1973, *16*, 202-223.

Fenson, L., Kagan, J. Kearsley, R. B., & Zelazo, P. R. The developmental progression of manipulative play in the first two years. *Child Development*, 1976, *47*, 232-235.

Freyberg, J. T. Increasing the imaginative play of urban disadvantaged kindergarten children through systematic training. In J. L. Singer (Ed.), *The child's world of make-believe*. New York: Academic Press, 1973.

Furth, H. G. *Piaget and knowledge*. Englewood Cliffs, N.J.: Prentice-Hall, 1969.

Garvey, C. Some properties of social play. *Merrill-Palmer Quarterly*, 1974, *20*, 163-180.

Garvey, C., & Berndt, R. The organization of pretend play. *Catalogue of Selected Documents in Psychology*, 1977, I, No. 1589, American Psychological Association.

Gesell, A. *The mental growth of the preschool child*. New York: Macmillan, 1925.

Gilmore, J. B. Play: A special behavior. In R. N. Haber (Ed.), *Current research in motivation*. New York: Holt, Reinhart & Winston, 1965.

Goffman, E. *Frame analysis: An essay of the organization of experience*. Cambridge, Mass.: Harvard Univ. Press, 1974.

Golomb, C. Symbolic play: The role of substitutions in pretense and puzzle games. *British Journal of Educational Psychology*, 1977, *47*, 175-186.

Golomb, C., & Cornelius, C. B. Symbolic play and its cognitive significance. *Developmental Psychology*, 1977, *13*, 246-252.

Gould, R. *Child studies through fantasy*. New York: Quadrangle, 1972.

Gramza, A. F. Preferences of preschool children for enterable play boxes. *Perceptual and Motor Skills*, 1970, *31*, 177-178.

Gramza, A. An analysis of dimensions which define children's encapsulating play objects. *Perceptual and Motor Skills*, 1973, *37*, 495-501.

Gramza, A. F. Responses to manipulability of a play object. *Psychological Reports*, 1976, *38*, 1109-1110.

Gramza, A. F., & Scholtz, G. "Children's response to visual complexity in a play setting," *Psychological Reports*, 1974, *35*, 845-899.

Gramza, A. F., Corush, J., & Ellis, M. J. Children's play on trestles differing in complexity: A study of play equipment design. *Journal of Leisure Research*, 1972, *4*, 303-311.

Hartley, R. E. Frank, L. K., & Goldenson, R. M. *Understanding children's play*. New York: Columbia Univ. Press, 1952.

Hutt, C. Exploration and play in children. *Symposium of the Zoological Society of London*, 1966, *18*, 61-81.

Hutt, C. Specific and diverse exploration. In H. W. Reese & L. P. Lipsitt (Eds.), *Advances in child development and behavior*, Vol. 5. New York: Academic Press, 1970. Pp. 120-172.

Hutt, C. Towards a taxonomy and conceptual model of play. In S. J. Hutt, D. A. Rogers, & C. Hutt (Eds.), *Developmental Processes in Early Childhood*, London: Routledge & Kegan Paul, in press.

Inhelder, B., Lezine, I., Sinclair, H., & Stambak, M. Les Debut de la function symbolique. *Archives de Psychologie*, 1972, *41*, 187-243.

Jersild, A. T., & Markey, F. V. Conflicts between preschool children. *Child Development Monographs*, 1935, No. 21.

Johnson, M. W. The effect on behavior of variations in the amount of play equipment. *Child Development*, 1935, *6*, 56-68.

Klinger, E. *Structure and functions of fantasy*. New York: Wiley, 1971.

Levin, H., & Wardell, E. The research uses of doll play. *Psychological Bulletin*, 1962, *59*, 27-56.

Lieberman, J. N. Playfulness and divergent thinking: An investigation of their relationship at the kindergarten level. *Journal of Genetic Psychology*, 1965, *107*, 219-224.

Lowe, M. Trends in the development of representational play in infants from one to three years—An observational study. *Journal of Child Psychology and Psychiatry*, 1975, *16*, 33-47.

Manosevitz, M., Prentice, N. M., & Wilson, F. Individual and family correlates of imaginary companions in preschool children. *Developmental Psychology*, 1973, *8*, 72-79.

Mathews, W. S. Modes of transformation in the initiation of fantasy play. *Developmental Psychology*, 1977, *13*, 212-216.

Maw, W. H., & Maw, E. Children's curiosity and parental attitudes. *Journal of Marriage and the Family*, 1966, *28*, 343-345.

McCall, R. B. Exploratory manipulation and play in the human infant. *Monographs of the Society for Research in Child Development*. 1974, *39*, 2, Serial #155.

Mendel, G. Children's preferences for differing degrees of novelty. *Child Development*, 1965, *36*, 453-465.

Miller, S. Ends, means and galumphing: some leit-motifs of play. *American Anthropologist*, 1973, *75*, 87-98.

Moyer, K. E., & Gilmer, B. von H. Attention spans of children for experimentally designed toys. *Journal of Genetic Psychology*, 1955, *87*, 187-207.

Nicolich, L. Beyond sensorimotor intelligence: Assessment of symbolic maturity through analysis of pretend play. *Merrill-Palmer Quarterly*, 1977, *23* (2), 89-99.

Nunnally, J. C., & Lemond, L. C. Exploratory behavior and human development. In H. Reese (Ed.), *Advances in child development and behavior*, Vol. 8. New York: Academic Press, 1973. Pp. 60-106.

Overton, W. F., & Jackson, J. P. The representation of imagined objects in action sequences: A developmental study. *Child Development*, 1973, *44*, 309-314.

Peller, L. Libidinal phases, ego development, and play. *Psychoanalytic Study of the Child*, 1954, *9*, 178-198.

Phillips, R. Doll play as a function of the realism of the materials and the length of the experimental session. *Child Development*, 1945, *16*, 145-166.

Piaget, J. *The moral judgment of the child*. New York: Free Press, 1932, 1965.

Piaget, J. *The language and thought of the child* (M. Gabain, trans.). New York: World Pub., 1955.

Piaget, J. *Play, dreams and imitation in childhood*. New York: Norton, 1945, 1962.

Piaget, J., Response to Brian Sutton-Smith. *Psychological Review*, 1966, *73*, 111-112.

Piaget, J., & Inhelder, B. *Mental imagery in the child*. New York: Basic Books, 1971.

Pintler, M. H., Phillips, R., & Sears, R. Sex differences in the projective doll play of preschool children. *Journal of Psychology*, 1946, *21*, 73-80.

Prescott, E., & Jones, E. *Group day care as a child-rearing environment: An observational study of day care programs*. Pasadena, Calif.: Pacific Oaks College, 1967.

Pulaski, M. A. Play as a function of toy structure and fantasy predisposition. *Child Development*, 1970, *41*, 531-537.

Rosen, C. E. The effects of sociodramatic play on problem-solving behavior among culturally disadvantaged preschool children. *Child Development*, 1974, *45*, 920-927.

Rubin, K. H., Maioni, T. L., & Hornug, M. Free play behaviors in middle- and lower-class preschoolers: Parten and Piaget revisited. *Child Development*, 1976, *47*, 414-419.

Rubenstein, J. Maternal attentiveness and subsequent exploratory behavior in the infant. *Child Development*, 1967, *38* (4), 1089-1100.

Sachs, J., & Davin, J. Young children's use of age-appropriate speech styles in social interaction and role-playing. *Journal of Child Language*, 1976, *3*, 81-98.

Saltz, E., & Johnson, J. Training for thematic-fantasy play in culturally disadvantaged children: Preliminary results. *Journal of Educational Psychology*, 1974, *66*, 623-630.

Saltz, E., Dixon, D., & Johnson, J. Training disadvantaged preschoolers on various fantasy activities: Effects on cognitive functioning and impulse control. *Child Development*, 1977, *48*, 367-380.

Scholtz, G. J. L., & Ellis, M. J. Repeated exposure to objects and peers in a play setting. *Journal of Experimental Child Psychology*, 1975, *19*, 448-455.

Sears, R. R. Influence of methodological factors on doll play performance. *Child Development*, 1947, *18*, 190-197.

Sigel, I. E., & McBane, B. Cognitive competence and level of symbolization among five-year-old children. Paper presented at the meeting of the American Psychological Association, New York, September, 1966.

Singer, J. L. Imagination and waiting ability in young children. *Journal of Personality*, 1961, *29*, 396-413.

Singer, J. L. *The child's world of make-believe*. New York: Academic Press, 1973.

Singer, J. L. & Singer, D. G. Fostering imaginative play in preschool children: Effects of Television viewing and direct adult modeling. Paper presented at the meeting of the American Psychological Association, New Orleans, 1974.

Sinclair, H. The transition from sensory motor behavior to symbolic activity. *Interchange*, 1970, *1*, 119-129.

Smilansky, S. *The effects of sociodramatic play on disadvantaged pre-school children*. New York: Wiley, 1968.

Stern, W. *Psychology of early childhood*. New York: Henry Holt, 1924.

Sutton-Smith, B. Role replication and reversal in play. *Merrill-Palmer Quarterly*, 1966, *12*, 285-298.

Sutton-Smith, B. The role of play in cognitive development. *Young Children*, 1967, *6*, 364-369.

Sutton-Smith, B. Novel responses to toys. *Merrill-Palmer Quarterly*, 1968, *14*, 151-158.

Sutton-Smith, B. Play as a trans-formational set. *Journal of Health, Physical Education and Recreation*, 1972, *43*, (6), 32-33.

Switzky, H. N., Haywood, C. H., & Isett, R. Exploration, curiosity, and play in young children: Effects of stimulus complexity. *Developmental Psychology*, 1974, *10*, 321-329.

Valentine, C. W. A study of the beginnings and significance of play in infancy. *British Journal of Educational Psychology,* 1937, *7,* 285-306.

Vygotsky, L. S. Play and its role in the mental development of the child. *Soviet Psychology,* 1967, *5,* (3) 6-18.

Waelder, R. The psychoanalytic theory of play. *Psychoanalytic Quarterly,* 1933, *2,* 208-224.

Wallach, M. A., & Kogan, N. *Modes of thinking in young children.* New York: Holt, Rinehart, & Winston, 1965.

Watson, M. W., & Fischer,K. W. A developmental sequence of agent use in late infancy. *Child Development,* 1977, *48,* 828-836.

Weisler, A., & McCall, R. B. Exploration and play: Resume and redirection. *American Psychologist,* 1976, *31,* 492-508.

Weisberg, P. A., & Spring, K. J. Environmental factors in creative function. *Archives of General Psychiatry,* 1961, *5,* 64-74.

Werner, H., & Kaplan, B. *Symbol Formation.* New York: Wiley, 1964.

White, R. W. Motivation reconsidered: The concept of competence. *Psychological Review,* 1959, *66,* 297-333.

Wolf, D., & Gardner, H. Style and sequence in early symbolic play. In B. Sutton-Smith (Ed.), *Pediatrics round table on play and learning.* New Orleans, La.: Johnson & Johnson, in press.

9

Can Education Be Made "Intrinsically Interesting" to Children?

John Condry

Barbara Koslowski

Cornell University

All moral culture springs solely and immediately from the inner life of the soul, and can only be stimulated in human nature, and never produced by external and artificial contrivances.

Whatever does not spring from a man's free choice, or is only the result of instruction and guidance, does not enter into his very being, but still remains alien to his true nature; he does not perform it with truly human energies, but merely with mechanical exactness. — W. von Humboldt

Motivation has been a persistent problem in American education since compulsory education was adopted (Cremin, 1961). While there have always been children ready and eager to learn, there also have been those who were apparently disinterested, recalcitrant, and unwilling to apply themselves to their studies. Because the approach of educators has been to study the organism and to speculate about its character, theories have focused on how to motivate the disinterested child. The assumptions of behaviorist psychology were thought to be well suited to this task. The individual of any age, it was said, is motivated to attain rewards. Scheduled rewards, contingent upon proper performance, were introduced into educational systems, and the result has been the token economy and the current system of offering grades for proper school work.

While it is true that adults often work for rewards (a paycheck, for example) and it is not unreasonable to suggest that children may be motivated in the same way, this system of teaching has certain drawbacks; we might be wise to study them in the hopes of discovering other processes that might be involved, and other means of educating children. A major disadvantage of extrinsic reward systems, for example, is that they motivate the child more to get the reward

than to arrive at a complete understanding of the educational task at hand
(reading, math, science, etc.). In the 1820s, for example, the Society for
Progressive Education in New York introduced a system of redeemable tokens as
rewards for correct school work and a system of fines for various offenses in the
school. This was done in order to discourage corporal punishment, of which the
Society disapproved. This early version of the token economy was abandoned in
the 1830s because the trustees of the Society came to feel that "they were more
often rewarding the cunning than the meritorious," and that the system of
tokens "fostered a mercenary spirit" (Ravitch, 1974).

In this paper, we will attempt to demonstrate that there are different
learning processes which are dependent, in the first instance, on what or who
initiates the process. There is one type of learning that is most common whch we
shall call self-initiated learning; and it is driven, we shall contend, by intrinsic
motivation. A second type of learning, which we shall call other-initiated, is
called into play when rewards are offered in an attempt to motivate a child. A
basic contention of this chapter is that these two forms of learning are different
in their processes and their outcomes, and that one is incompatible with the
other.

We will attempt to show that when rewards are offered, they change the
nature and definition of the task and eventually diminish the subject's control of
the learning situation. A number of recent studies are reviewed, all of which
suggest that when performance on a task "for its own sake" is compared with
performance initiated by the desire for an extrinsic reward, the subjects' show
different patterns of interaction with the task and different motivational effects
after the experience.

We will also attempt to develop a picture of intrinsic motivation in terms
of the child's cognitive abilities or capacities for learning about the world. Much
of the first part of this paper is paraphrased from another article by the senior
author (Condry, 1977; see also Condry, in press; Condry & Chambers, in press).
We begin with a consideration of the background literature that led to the
current round of research on the topic of the effects of reward on motivation.

A LOOK AT THE LITERATURE

Early Research

The fact that "rewards" (grades, surveillance, exams) and other extrinsic incentives have a disruptive effect on some kinds of motivation has been remarked
upon for some time. Albert Einstein is quoted as having commented about
exams: "This coercion had such a deterring effect that, after I had passed the
final examination. I found the consideration of any scientific problem distaste-

ful to me for an entire year" (Bernstein, 1973). A quarter of a century ago Harlow (1950, 1953; Harlow, Harlow, & Meyer, 1950) commented upon the inverse relationship between extrinsic incentives and the learning of complex problems in primates. Briefly, primates deprived of food (in order to "motivate" them) performed poorly on complex problems. Well-fed (and thus presumably "unmotivated") primates solved the same problems with ease. Shortly thereafter, White (1959), Berlyne (1955, 1957, 1958, 1966), Hunt (1965) and Koch (1956) all called attention to the distinction between extrinsic and intrinsic motives, and most (Koch is the exception) offered theories of intrinsic motivation. Basic to most of these theories is the idea that intrinsic motivation is undermined *by certain extrinsic conditions* (see DeCharms, 1968). Thus, White (1959) suggested that anxiety was the "enemy of exploration," while Koch (1956, p. 69) noted that "any factor . . . . that brackets the work on the task as instrumental . . . will disrupt intrinsically motivated activities." These early theories suggested the existence of different motivational patterns which were, to some extent, defined by the circumstances of their initiation. Moreover, several theorists (especially Koch, White, and DeCharms) felt that the different patterns of motivated activity were antagonistic.

The operation of extrinsic incentives was also called into question by Festinger and the dissonance theorists. In 1959, Festinger and Carlsmith published the findings of a study showing that subjects who were paid a small amount of money to lie about their degree of interest in a dull experiment changed their attitude more (in the direction of actually liking the experiment) than did a group of subjects who were paid a great deal *more money.* This negative relationship between incentive magnitude and attitude change has since been confirmed—subject to a variety of qualifications—in a number of studies (cf. Bem & McConnell, 1970; Carlsmith, Collins, & Helmreich, 1966; Cohen, 1962; Helmreich & Collins, 1968; Linder, Cooper & Jones, 1967; and Nel, Hemlreich, & Aronson, 1965). Basically, the greater the extrinsic pressure exerted to "motivate" attitude change, the *less* real change is observed. Essentially, the same effect for the interaction of powerful extrinsic incentives and internalization (this time for a prohibition) was found by Aronson and Carlsmith (1963), Freedman (1965), Pepitone, McCauley, and Hammond (1967); and Zanna, Lepper, and Abelson (1973). Children given a "mild" as opposed to a "severe" threat to motivate avoidance of a toy were *less* likely to play with the toy given a future opportunity to do so. Apparently there was greater internalization when the external pressure for compliance was less. All told, the line of research arising from dissonance theory raised another series of questions about the interaction of extrinsic incentives and subsequent attitudes and behavior, and caused yet another crack in the facade of traditional motivation theory.

These two lines of evidence, then, the one represented by Harlow, White, Hunt, Berlyne, and Koch and the other by the DeCharms, Festinger, and the dissonance theorists, converge in the most recent research on this topic. The earlier theorists questioned the *interaction* of different forms of motivation, but the specification of the exact nature of this interaction and its ramifications has only recently been investigated.

Current Research

Recent studies of the effects of rewards on motivation all have much the same general structure: first, a person's level of motivation for doing some task is either measured or assumed. This is the "base rate" measure of intrinsic motivation, usually defined as the person's willingness to do the task *in the absence* of task extrinsic pressure to do so (Deci, 1975; Lepper, Greene, & Nisbett, 1975). Next, some experimental intervention is attempted, usually involving a reward. And finally, a second attempt is made to assess a person's willingness to engage in the behavior under question. Any change in the level of interest from the first to the second measure is taken as the primary dependent measure of the effect of reward on motivation.

The first of these studies was done by Edward Deci (1971, 1972a) in an attempt to shed some light on these issues. Deci used a game called "SOMA" (trademark, Parker Brothers) composed of a number of blocks which may be arranged to form a variety of patterns. The task in this research involving college students was to reproduce certain patterns presented to the subject. During the middle of each of three experimental sessions, the experimenter left the room, and, without the subject's knowledge, observed the subject's willingness to play with the puzzle in the absence of demands that he do so. In different experimental conditions, subjects were offered nothing, a monetary reward, or a social reward for every configuration produced with the puzzle. Deci's interest was in the amount of time spent playing with the puzzle during the unsupervised session, indicative of continued intrinsic interest in the task. In general, Deci found that (a) when money was used as an external reward, intrinsic motivation tended to decrease; and (b) when verbal reinforcement was used, intrinsic motivation tended to increase.

Although apparently unaware of Deci's work at the time of their study, Kruglanski, Friedman, and Zeevi (1971) sought to clarify the same confusing literature on rewards and motivation. They were particularly interested in examining the negative relations between the magnitude of incentive and subsequent liking for a task described by the dissonance theorists. Kruglanski et al. theorized that the "liking" found in earlier studies (e.g., Bem & McConnell, 1970; Carlsmith, Collins, & Helmreich, 1966, etc.) is only one aspect of a more general syndrome of behavior that was intrinsically, rather than extrinsically, motivated. If so, these authors suggest, intrinsically motivated individuals "might be expected to exhibit superiority on those aspects of performance contingent upon preoccupation with the *task,* as opposed to concentration upon attaining the *goal*" (emphasis mine, Kruglanski et al., 1971, p. 607).

To test this proposition, 32 subjects from a local high school were assigned at random to either a reward (called "extrinsic incentive") or a no reward condition. The rewarded subjects were offered a "guided tour of the Department of Psychology." The no reward subjects were offered nothing, and all subjects were given two measures of creativity, two measures of short-term recall, and a measure of the recall of a series of uncompleted tasks (the Zeigarnick effect).

On each of these dependent variables, subjects in the no reward group received higher scores than subjects in the reward group. Subjects in the no reward group also liked the experiment slightly more and were slightly (but not significantly) more willing to participate in similar projects in the future.

The main finding of this study, then, is the same as Deci's: the offer of a reward prior to understaking a task (or in this case a series of tasks) appears to lower subsequent interest in the task. Furthermore, a reward offer also appears to *lower the quality of performance* on the task itself.

While both the Deci and Kruglanski et al. studies have powerful implications for education, both were done in laboratory settings. The next study to be reported, however, was done in a nursery school with "typical" incentives (for that situation). In this study by Lepper, Greene, and Nisbett (1973), 51 nursery school children were selected on the basis of their demonstrated interest in a drawing task. Only high interest subjects were used, and these were exposed to one of three experimental conditions. In the *expected award* condition, subjects agreed to perform an activity in order to receive a "good player" award, comprised of a certificate and a gold star. In the *unexpected award* condition, the same reward was given to unsuspecting subjects after they completed the task, and in the *no award* group, subjects neither anticipated nor received an award. The critical measure of continued interest was the time spent playing with the drawing task during a subsequent "free play" observational period. Lepper, et al. found that the award undermined interest in the "anticipated" condition only, and that there was no significant difference between the unanticipated and the no award conditions in terms of later free play activity. This study introduces several methodological innovations and also raises some important questions for theoretical consideration. It should be noted, for example, that the reward alone cannot be said to undermine anything, since the effect is obtained only in the anticipated reward condition (in which the behavior is initiated by the offer of a reward).

From the three studies described so far, several findings emerge to challenge the traditional notions of the effect of reward on human motivation, and several issues are raised which require clarification. For example, it appears that rewards do not always have salutory effects on motivation. The suggestion that the offer of a reward may lower quality of performance and lead to loss of interest in an apparently interesting and attractive task merits serious consideration.

AN ANALYSIS OF ISSUES RAISED
IN RECENT RESEARCH

Subsequent studies which support and extend these early findings were initiated in response to the issues raised by the research just reported. These studies will be described in terms of the characteristics of the incentives studied, the nature of the dependent variables, the characteristics of the situations or tasks studied, and the characteristics of the subjects studied.

Characterisitics of the Incentives Studied

Expected vs. Unexpected Rewards. One of the most important facts to arise from this series of studies is that it is not the reward per se that affects subsequent interest, but the timing of the reward. Rewards used to initiate task activity have different effects than do rewards given after the activity is initiated by the subject. In other words, when the subject anticipates a reward, his behavior is substantially different from that of comparable subjects who receive the *same reward* unexpectedly. This effect is clear in the research of Lepper et al. (1973), and Smith (1974). In addition, Lepper and Greene (1975) and Greene and Lepper (1974) have replicated these findings in studies involving different subjects and a different task, and obtained the same results as in their earlier research. The Deci (1971, 1972a, 1972b) and Kruglanski et al. (1971) studies show substantially the same results when comparing rewarded to unrewarded subjects, but these authors do not use the unexpected reward condition, and so their findings are not directly comparable in this respect. The fact that unexpected rewards do not undermine interest focuses our attention on the *context* of the situation and not on the reward per se.

Contingent vs. Non-Contingent Rewards. The contingency between the reward and performance on the task is another issue considered in the current research. Some of the early work made the reward contingent only on "doing the task" (Benware & Deci, 1975; Deci, 1971; Kruglanski et al., 1971; Lepper and Greene, 1975; Lepper et al., 1973; Ross, 197; Upton; 1973), while other studies have drawn a more explicit contingency between the quality of performance and the reward (Deci, 1972a; Deci & Cascio, 1972; Garbarino, 1975; Karniol & Ross, 1977; McGraw & McCullers, 1975; Ross, Karniol, & Rothstein, 1975; Smith, 1974). Early researchers investigating this topic reached apparently opposite conclusions about the effects of contingency on performance. Deci (1972b) found no undermining effect for noncontingent rewards, but rewards contingent upon performance did produce an undermining effect similar to that found in most other research. Greene and Lepper (1974), on the other hand, employed contingent and noncontingent rewards in a replication of the earlier Lepper et al. (1973) study, and found that *both* contingent and noncontingent rewards had the effect of undermining future interest. One difficulty in interpreting findings across a number of different studies is that researchers often use the same word to describe different events. Thus the noncontingency employed by Deci (1972b) refers to rewards which were *unrelated* to the task (e.g., paying subjects at the outset for participating in the experiment), while the noncontingency in the Greene and Lepper (1974) study refers to rewards for "doing the task" but not explicitly tied to a performance criterion.

One interesting possiblity that may account for the inconsistency in the early research on this topic could be that most of the researchers who have used contingent rewards have done so with adults, while msot of the researchers using a noncontingent design have done so with children. It may be difficult for a young child to completely understand contingency instructions ("We do not have enough rewards to give everybody one, so we will only give awards for very good drawings"). First, nursery school children are seldom put in the position of having their work judged and "rewarded" on a contingency basis. A child who has experienced a relatively undifferentiated environment, especially with respect to art work, might not be able to judge his work comparatively and thus be unresponsive to contingency demands. Secondly, many young children have not yet developed the "adult" usage of comparatives. (Witness the child who gets into a hot bathtub and says, "It's too hot, make it warmer.") Yet contingency manipulations depend, for their successful employment, upon an understanding of comparatives. Finally, in addition to being unable to discriminate between "good" and "very good" work, young children may not possess the conscious control over their behavior to be able to produce a "very good drawing" when called upon to do so. When children are told to look at something "in order to remember it," they don't behave differently than when just told to look at it. Neither do they remember it any better. Adults do use different strategies in these same circumstances, and they do remember better when told to do so (Neisser, 1976). Skills and strategies which have not yet been developed, or which are not yet stable, cannot be produced on demand. The most recent studies on this topic have traced the decrement in interest to contingent reward situations (Ross, 1975).

Salience of reward. In two studies, the salience of the reward was manipulated and the effects of this procedure examined. Ross (1975) manipulated the salience of the reward directly by leaving the anticipated reward in front of the subject (albeit under a box) while the task was being done. Undermining effects were observed for the salient reward condition only. Although the same reward was offered and given to the nonsalient group, it was simply not available during the task. In a similar design with a different purpose, McGraw and McCullers (1974) gave children rewards (M & M's) in two conditions: one in which they were given a reward for each correct response (the candy was dropped in a bowl beside the subject), and another one in which candy was given for each correct resonse, but the child was told he would not be allowed to eat the candy (it was simply a token of correctness).

Subjects in these two conditions did more poorly in a discrimination learning task than children in a third (control) group given neither rewards nor tokens. Subsequent interest was not measured in this study, but the demonstration is important for the suggestion that the effect of reward was to undermine *actual performance* on a task, and the more salient the reward, the more undermining of performance was observed.

Type of Reward. Many different kinds of rewards have been used in the research described in this paper, although there have been few attempts to vary the nature of the reward within a given study. Monetary rewards are commonly used with adults (Benward & Deci, 1974; Deci, 1971, 1972a, 1972b, 1974; Smith, 1974; Upton, 1973), while tokens, certificates, and edibles of one sort or another are more commonly used with children (Garbarino, 1975; Greene, 1974; Greene & Lepper, 1974; Kruglanski, et al., 1971; Lepper & Greene, 1975; Lepper et al., 1973; McGraw & McCullers, 1974). We have already seen that more salient rewards produce stronger effects than less salient ones; so it stands to reason that the stronger the incentive, the more powerful the undermining effect, although no manipulations of this sort have been tried using a paradigm that looks at continued interest as the primary dependent variable.

1. *Monetary vs. social rewards.* One interesting conflict to emerge from this research concerns the role of social rewards (or feedback, as Deci calls it) as compared to monetary rewards. In a series of studies (Deci, 1971, 1972a; Deci, Cascio, & Krusell, 1975), Deci has shown that positive feedback (praise) can enhance subsequent interest in males, while it seems to have the opposite effect for females. Smith (1974) was unable to replicate these findings when he used a "Lepper type" (expected, unexpected, & no reward) design for both social and monetary reward. Smith found that both types of anticipated reward undermined future interest for both sexes. It is difficult if not impossible to resolve this issue with the evidence at hand. Deci used unanticipated social reward only, while Smith used both anticipated and unanticipated social reward. In addition, the tasks used were different. The task used by Smith (learning about art) might have been seen as less sex appropriate than the "SOMA" puzzle used by Deci. There is evidence from research that children see both tasks and activities as sex appropriate (Hartley & Hardesty, 1964; Stein & Smithells, 1969), and evidence to indicate that information about the sex appropriateness of activities affects children's responses to them (Liebert, McCall, & Hanratty, 1971; Montimayor, 1974; Stein, Polky, & Muller, 1971).

2. *Surveillance.* Two studies are worth mentioning for the light they shed on other contextual manipulations that appear to have the same undermining effect as the "positive" incentives used in most studies. Lepper and Greene (1975), in a clever variant, used a condition of surveillance and found undermining of interest effects similar to those found with the various reward conditions discussed above. In this study, nursery school children did a task while being "observed" by a TV camera. Those in the surveillance conditions were less interested in the task in a latter free choice period than children in a nonsurveillance condition.

In a study done in the context of a different line of research, Zivin (1974) had adults try to interest distractable children in a boring toy. Contrary to her expectations, the treatment had no such effect. Children told to "think about interesting things you could do with this toy" played no more with the target toy than did children who were given no adult encouragement.

These findings are particularly interesting when one takes into consideration Zajonc's (1965) review of social facilitation. Zajonc reviewed fifty years of research on the effect of the presence of others on learning and performance and came to the conclusion that the simple presence of other people tends to have the effect of *undermining* the development of a poorly learned skill, while it facilitates the performance of well learned skills. Based on this observation, then, we are led to suggest that, as in the expected reward condition, the presence of others in the surveillance conditions changes the *context* of the learning situation in ways that are detrimental to task performance as well as subsequent interest.

3. *Negative incentives.* Finally, while most of the research has focused upon positive incentives, at least two researchers have analyzed negative feedback and threats. Deci and Cascio (1972) looked at changes in intrinsic motivation as a consequence of threats and negative feedback (failure). These researchers found that negative incentives also decrease intrinsic motivation. Weiner and Mander (1977) studied the effects of either a shock or the anticipation of a shock on subsequent interest. Subjects who were shocked at random while performing an anagrams task showed greater willingness to pursue the task (when neither the shock nor the experimenter were present) than subjects who received no shock during the manipulation phase of the experiment.

Earlier research by dissonance theorists (e.g., Aronson & Mills, 1959; Gerard & Mathewson, 1966) on the severity of initiation into a group found that the more sever (unpleasant) the initiation, the greater the subsequent attraction to a group on the part of subjects.

The implication of these studies is that even negative incentives, when used as sanctions against unwanted behavior, have complex effects. If a negative sanction (threat or punishment) is *not* effective in stopping the behavior, it may actually *increase* a subject's interest in, and attraction to, the prohibited behavior.

In sum, a variety of anticipated, salient, positive incentives (the primary independent variable in this research) and some additional task extrinsic conditions (surveillance and negative incentives) have been shown to be associated with lower subsequent interest in a task when compared to conditions where no task extrinsic incentives are available. The fact that the same incentives given after the performance of the task (unanticipated by the subjects) produce no such undermining effects suggests that it is the context created by the offer of rewards and not the rewards themselves which is responsible for these findings.

These facts alone are contrary to theories of motivation which assume extrinsic and intrinsic motivation to be additive, as both Deci (1975) and Calder and Staw (1975) have noted. Consequently, a number of researchers have offered theories to account for the decrement of interest findings (cf. Calder & Staw, 1975; Deci, 1975; Green & Lepper, 1975; Kruglanski, 1975), and some have denied the validity of them (Reiss & Sunshinsky, 1975; Scott, 1976). But before attempting to theorize about these effects (or to deny their existence), it is necessary to outline and describe the entire range of effects. In addition to the undermining of interest described in these studies, there is an additional suggestion from some of this research that rewards may have detrimental effects on both the process of learning and the products of learning. For a consideration of these effects, we now turn to an analysis of dependent variables studied, and the tasks or situations utilized in the current research.

Nature of the Dependent Variables

Subsequent Interest. In most of the foregoing research, the dependent variable of primary importance was the degree of subsequent interest in the task shown by the subjects. Two different measures of subsequent interest have been used: attitudinal measures of liking for the task and/or willingness to return at a later date (e.g., Calder & Staw, 1975; Kruglanski, Alon, & Lewis, 1972; Kruglanski, Riter, Amitai, Margolin, Shabtai, & Zaksh, 1975; Kruglanski, Riter, Arazi, Agassi, Monteqio, Peri, & Peretz, 1975) and behavioral measures of persistence in the activity in the absence of "extrinsic" demands (e.g., Deci, 1971, 1972a; Green & Lepper, 1974, 1975; Lepper et al., 1973). In some cases, both attitude and behavior measures have been used (Greene, Sternberg, & Lepper, 1976; Karniol & Ross, 1976; Ross, 1975; Smith, 1974). In general, these measures show similar effects, and the choice of what type of dependent measure to use is primarily of theoretical interest.

Quality of Performance. In addition to measures of subsequent interest, some measures of quality of performance during the task have been taken, and the results suggest that anticipated rewards lower the quality of activity *during* a task as well as the desire to return to a task at a later time. Kruglanski et al.

(1971), for example, found that the promise of a reward effected "qualitative" differences in task performance, for memory, creativity, and the recall of uncompleted tasks (the Ziegarnic effect), and Lepper et al. (1973) reported lower *quality* drawings for the expected reward group. Greene and Lepper (1974) replicated this result for the quality of drawings in the anticipated reward condition in a second study, and they found, in addition, that the expected reward group produced quantitatively more drawings. These findings suggest that one of the effects of anticipated rewards on task performance is to increase activity but to lower the quality of that activity.

McGraw and McCullers (1975) report a number of studies with children which find that tangible rewards given on a trial-by-trial basis lead to more errors and less learning as shown by the performance of rewarded subjects when compared to that of nonrewarded subjects. These tasks range from perceptual discrimination (Miller & Estes, 1961), concept identification (Masters & Mokros, 1973; McCullers & Martin, 1971; Terrell, Durkin, & Wiesley, 1959), verbal discriminations (Hadded, McCullers, & Moran, noted in McGraw & McCullers, 1975, p. 14; Spence, 1970), picture discriminations (Miller & Estes, 1961), concept identification (Masters & Mokros, 1973; McCullers & Martin, 1971; Terrell, Durkin, & Wiesley, 1959), verbal discriminations (Haddad, McCullers, & Moran, noted in McGraw & McCullers, 1975, p. 14; Spence, 1970), picture discriminations (Schere, 1969; Spence & Dunton, 1967; Spence & Segner, 1967), and a patterned probability task (McGraw & McCullers, 1974), In short, in the words of McGraw and McCullers (1975), "within the confines of children's discrimination learning ... the detrimental effect of reward is a very general one" (p. 3).

In addition to discrimination learning, McGraw and McCullers have been able to extend their analysis of these effects on performance to probability learning (McGraw & McCullers, 1974, 1975) and incidental learning (Staat & McCullers, 1974). Taken together, these studies suggest that task performance is disrupted more for subjects who are given task irrelevant rewards than for comparable subjects performing these same tasks for no reward. Subjects given tangible incentives make more errors, solve the problems more slowly, make more stereotypical responses and do less well in S–R recall (in an incidental learning task) than do subjects who are offered or given no reward.

Characteristics of the Tasks or Situations Studied

Few of the studies reported have discussed the ongoing process of task performance. In part, this is due to the fact that the tasks used by researchers have not been ones in which characteristics of process can be easily assessed. Examples of actual tasks used in the research have ranged from solving a puzzle called "SOMA" (Deci, 1971, 1972a, 1972b; Deci et al., 1975), to drawing with a felt-tipped pen (Greene & Lepper, 1974; Lepper et al., 1973); from solving a simple concept formation problem (Garbarino, 1975; Lepper & Greene, 1975; Maehr & Stallings, 1972) to pro-attitudinal advocacy (Benware & Deci, 1975)[1], and beating a drum (Ross, 1975).

Interesting vs. Dull and Boring Tasks. While much of the recent research has utilized tasks *chosen* to be interesting (and thus "intrinsically motivating"), it will be recalled that earlier research by dissonance theorists tended to use dull and boring tasks in order to make theoretically similar points. Thus, as mentioned earlier, the dissonance theorists were able to show how a dull task could be made "more interesting" by inducing the subjects to lie about it for a small (as opposed to a large) reward. In contrast, the intrinsic motivation researcher has shown how an interesting task may be made boring with the introduction of a reward.

Few of these studies have varied the nature of the task within the experiment. In one study which does so, results appear to be a variance with the earlier dissonance research. Thus, Calder and Staw (1975) find that while rewards decrease interest in "interesting" tasks, they may "enhance interest in dull and boring tasks." More research is needed to clarify the circumstances under which a dull task may be made more interesting.

The Process of Learning. Partly as a consequence of the tasks used, most of the foregoing research is couched in terms of the products of learning, (i.e., the number of problems solved, the number of errors made, the number of items recalled, etc.). But it is also possible to study the *process* of learning in terms of the step-by-step strategies of action that subjects take. When this is done, even more of the picture emerges. Condry and Chambers (in press), for example, using a problem-solving task originally designed to study strategies of thinking (Bruner, Goodnow, & Austin, 1956), found that rewarded subjects attempted easier problems, required more information before they achieved a correct solution (i.e., were inefficient), were more answer-oriented, and were less logical in their problem-solving strategies than comparable nonrewarded subjects. Similarly, Maehr and Stallings (1972) found that children who believed they would be "evaluated" by an "external" source chose easier problems than children who believed they would evaluate their own problems ("internal evaluation"). Thus, there is evidence that extrinsic incentive conditions lead subjects to different *strategic activities* in a learning or problem-solving situation than do conditions which encourage exploration without the offer of a task extrinsic incentive as a reward.

---

[1] Pro-attitudinal advocacy is research on a person's beliefs about some object which the individual *likes,* after the person has advocated usage of the object.

Apparently these same process and strategy effects extend to interpersonal interaction as well. Garbarino (1975) looked at the effects of anticipated rewards on children teaching other children, in a field setting experiment. Based on some of the early research reviewed above, he predicted that if a child were offered a reward to teach another child something, the quality of the interaction would be more "obtrusive, concrete, direct, and impatient in response to frustration" than in a situation in which one child teaches another with no expectation of a reward. In essence, Garbarino argued, like Kruglanski et al. (1971) before his, that the child in the reward condition would adopt an instrumental approach toward the situation and focus more on the goal of receiving the money and less on the task of teaching.

Specifically, Garbarino hypothesized that the tutor in the no reward condition would be more positive in her response to her tutee (all subjects were female), and more efficient and less intrusive in her teaching style. He predicted that the younger child (the tutee was a younger child in all conditions) would learn more when her tutor was in the no reward condition.

The subjects in this experiment were 48 female elementary school children. Twenty-four fifth- and sixth-graders acted as tutors for 24 first- and second-graders. The school in which the experiment was done was one in which cross-age tutoring occurred regularly, so the experimental situation was not an unusual one.

The older children were taught a game (a symbol substitution task) by the experimenter and then asked to teach it to a younger child, under either reward or no reward conditions. While the older child taught the game to the younger child, the interaction was observed and coded by the two experimenters. The results of Garbarino's study supported his predictions and add an important dimension to the work just reviewed. The tutor's behavior toward the young child was more negative in the reward condition and more positive in the no reward conditon. In addition, the tutors in the reward condition made more demands upon the younger child than did the tutors in the no reward condition.

The promise of a reward not only affected the people to whom it was offered, but also had secondary effects on the learning of the younger children (who were offered nothing). The younger children taught by tutors in the reward conditions scored lower for task ability and higher for number of errors than did children taught by tutors in the no reward condition.

Garbarino's research substantially extends the range of the effects we have been observing. His findings suggest that in addition to undermining continued interest, the process of exploration, and the *products* of learning, promise of a reward has an important effect on the *context* of an interdependent, interpersonal situation. Apparently, when the actions of one person may interfere with an extrinsic goal of another, a negative evaluation of the task is translated to a negative evaluation of the person. The instrumental orientation among tutors in the reward condition suggests that they valued the younger child as a function of her utility in obtaining the desired goal and devalued her in proportion to the degree to which she failed and thus frustrated the tutor (Garbarino, 1973).

Reward Endogenous vs. Exogenous Tasks. A further point regarding the nature of tasks used in this research is worth mentioning. Kruglanski has shown in a number of studies (cf. Kruglanski, Riter, Amital, et al., 1975; Kruglanski, Riter, Arazi, et al., 1975) that when money was endogenous to a task (e.g., games such as coin tossing or poker, in which the winner traditionally keeps the money), its presence enhanced intrinsic motivation; but when it was exogenous to a task (e.g., doing a jigsaw puzzle), its presence depressed intrinsic motivation. Essentially, the same conclusion is reached by Staw, Calder, and Hess (1974).

Characteristics of the Subjects

One would think that a consideration of variables associated with the subject might be the first place to look for differences in the effects of rewards and other extrinsic demands, since neither the *rewards* themselves nor the *tasks* exist independently of the value the subject places on them, (in terms of rewards) or the interaction he has with them (in terms of tasks). Yet this important area for research has received relatively little attention.

Personal Characteristics of Subjects: Age, Sex, and Personality. The effect of rewards in undermining interest has been demonstrated throughout a wide range of ages. The studies reviewed have demonstrated the effect on nursery school children (Greene & Lepper, 1974; Lepper et al., 1973; McGraw & McCullers, 1974; Ross, 1975; Zivin, 1974), elementary school children (Garbarino, 1975; Greene, 1974; Kruglanski et al., 1972; Maehr & Stallings, 1972; McGraw & McCullers, 1974; Zivin, 1974), high school students (Kruglanski et al., 1971), college students (Benware & Deci, 1974; Deci, 1971, 1972a, 1972b; Deci et al., 1974; Deci et al., 1975; Smith 1974) and adults beyond college age (Kruglanski & Cohen, 1973; Upton, 1973).

   Aside from demonstrating the effect on a large range of subjects, however, few studies have attempted to explore other subject variables that may interact with the reward context and/or with the task. Subjects of both sexes have been used in many of the studies reported, but few significant differences due to sex are reported, with the exception of Deci's (1972a; Deci et al., 1975) finding that females react differently to positive verbal feedback, and Smith's (1974) findings to the contrary. These results were discussed earlier in terms of the interaction of sex with the reward and task characteristics.

   Two investigators have looked into the effects of personality. Maehr and Stallings (1972) found that subjects high in Need Achievement volunteered more for difficult tasks when the evaluation context was internal, and more for easy tasks when the evaluation context was external. In addition, Haywood and his colleagues (Haywood, 1971; Haywood & Switzky, 1971) have developed a personality test for intrinsically motivated (IM) as opposed to extrinsically motivated (EM) individuals. Switzky and Haywood found that personality interacts with the reinforcement context. In this study, two reward contexts were studied: self-reward, in which performance standards are set and rewards delivered by the subjects themselves, and external reward, in which standards are imposed and reinforcers externally administered. IM children "maintained their performance longer than EM children under self-reinforcement, while EM children showed greater performance maintenance than IM children under external reinforcement" (p.). Clearly, individual differences modify the effect of each of these reward contexts, and these need to be studied.

Initial Interest. One of the most fascinating yet least studied factors concerns the effect of reward upon people who vary in initial interest. Attractiveness of the task was considered earlier; in this section we consider initial interest of the subject, with the task held constant. Most of the researchers to date have selected for study only those subjects who are high on initial interest. This leaves unanswered the question of whether rewards may have different effects on people with low initial interest. Only three of the studies reported have addressed this topic.

Lepper et al. (1973) did a reanalysis of their high initial interest sample by dividing it at the median on interest. They found an increase in subsequent interest among the low interest subjects in the unexpected reward condition only. Greene (1974) also studied subjects who varied in initial interest. Using a between treatment groups analysis, Greene (1974) found an overjustification effect for low interest subjects, but not for high interest subjects, when these groups were compared to a control. Using a within groups analysis, he found a significant post-treatment decrement for high interest subjects, but not for low interest subjects. Thus, even though Greene attempted to study this issue, this particular comparison was ambiguous because the data from the control subjects did not remain stable over time, and the between and within subject analyses did not agree (Greene, et al., 1976).

Finally, Upton (1973) studied the offer of a monetary reward as it affects people's willingness to donate blood to a blood bank. Subjects were divided on interest in terms of the number of pints of blood they had donated in the last year. At this point, half of the subjects in the low interest group and half of those in the high interest group were offered, and later given, a reward of ten dollars to donate a pint of blood. The other half of the sample was asked to donate, but no money was offered. The results indicate that subjects high in initial iterest are significantly more willing to donate blood when they are *not* offered a sizable incentive to do so. Subjects in the low interest group go slightly, but not significantly, in the other direction; that is, they are equally willing to donate whether money is offered or not. So we have some evidence that unexpected rewards may increase interest in low interest subjects; but on the whole, the question of the effects of rewards on low interest subjects is still very much up in the air.

All in all, the evidence described above suggests that task extrinsic rewards, when used to motivate activity, particularly learning, have widespread and possible undesirable effects. These effects extend to the process as well as the products of the task activity, and to the willingness of the subject to undertake the task at a later date. It is difficult to summarize this research adequately, but in general, in comparison with nonrewarded subjects, subjects offered a task extrinsic incentive choose easier tasks, are less efficient in using the information available to solve novel problems, and tend to be answer-oriented and more illogical in their problem-solving strategies. They seem to work harder and produce more of whatever is demanded; but the product is of a lower quality, contains more errors, is more stereotyped, and is less creative than the work of comparable nonrewarded subjects working on the same problems. Finally, after being rewarded to do a task, subjects are less likely to come back to a task they at one time considered interesting. These facts appear to be true for a wide range of subjects doing a wide range of tasks. Attempting to account for them is a formidable challenge.

The studies just reviewed suggest that the *conditions of initiation* are immensely important, both in terms of what the individual puts into a task and what he or she gets out of it. When a person chooses to engage in a task, his behavior during the task is more coherent and his subsequent interest in the task remains higher than that of a comparable individual pressured into doing the same task by the offer of task extrinsic rewards.

It is easier to understand the meaning of all this research if we imagine the ecological circumstance we are trying to understand. Perhaps the entire pattern of these results would be seen more easily if we imagine motivated activity as having at least four discriminable states or phases: (1) initial engagement; (2) activity or manipulation (the process); (3) disengagment; and (4) subsequent engagement. That is, it is possible to ask about the "forces" that act in each of these phases and of the relations between actions in one phase and another. We would want to know why a person engaged in a task in the first place, what is done with, or to, the task while one is actively "manipulating" it, and what leads one to disengage from the task and possibly return to it.

Most of the research reviewed in this paper has focused on the relationship between the conditions of task engagement (Phase 1) and the degree of subsequent interest (Phase 4). Some research has looked at the relationship between Phases 1 and 2, that is, how the conditions of engagement affect the manner of activity and manipulation (including the manipulation of other people, as in Garbarino's study). Few studies of disengagement (Phase 3) are found in the current literature; but in the original research on the Ziegarnik effect, Ovsiankina

(1928) studied what happens when one interrupts activity before it reaches its natural end, and found a strong desire to return to the interrupted behavior (see Ryan, 1970, p. 96ff.). In most of the research described earlier, the extrinsic conditions are ended when the reward is given. In the intrinsic conditions, however, the task activity is also interrupted and ended by the experimenter (i.e., before the individual chooses to leave it). It is not clear from the research presented here whether a *self-generated* disengagement might produce a different pattern of subsequent interest. An analysis by the various phases in the learning process allows us to see gaps in the research as well as to organize much of what has already been done.

Perhaps we need to take a different view of the child in the educational system. The child we hope to educate is complex, coherent, and eager to learn about the world. Therefore, instead of asking how one might manipulate a disinterested child so as to motivate him or her to learn, the question might rather be how we may arrange the environment of education so as to take advantage of the child's natural curiosity and his intrinsic interest in learning about the world. Before children enter school they acquire a vast range of knowledge about the world. They were not trained to acqurie this information in the sense of being supervised, scheduled, rewarded, and punished; they used their own native, intellective capacities. This interest did not have to be "encouraged" for the most part; it was there, within, all along.

THE CHILD'S CAPACITIES FOR LEARNING

What are the elements of this intrinsic motivation? How does it function? In the following section, we will consider these questions in terms of the child's capacities for learning. It is clear that other people who are aware of the variety of conceptual tools the child has for understanding the world can do much to enhance the child's knowledge of the world. This effort could be facilitated by a more detailed analysis of intrinsic interest and motivation.

Intrinsic Interests and Capacities

The argument that extrinsic rewards are of limited utility in educational settings is a useful argument only if it can be shown that a child is intrinsically motivated to learn on his own, and has the basic capacities to carry out what he is intrinsically motivated to do. Without intrinsic motivation accompanied by the appropriate capacities, a reliance on extrinsic rewards may be the only option open to an educational system.

In order to argue that children are intrinsically motivated to learn about important aspects of the world and are equipped with a capacity to do so, we will focus on findings from two areas of research: the first deals with the way in which children make sense out of, or explain, their environments; the second, with the process involved in solving nonroutine problems. We have chosen these two areas primarily because the issues examined in such research are not bound to learning in particular content areas. Rather, they cut across and underlie learning in arithmetic and reading as well as in social studies and history; they occur when the child is engaged in subjects that are part of a formal curriculum as well as when he is engaged in trying to make sense out of the various social rules and conventions that govern his behavior with other people. These areas were chosen for another reason as well. Implicit in the first part of this discussion was the premise that there is more to learning than acquiring the skills necessary to churn out the correct answer. Learning is much deeper (and, in the long run, substantially more useful) when one also understands the underpinnings of the correct answer—the *process* which enables one to understand why the correct answer is correct. One can correctly solve (i.e., correctly apply the mechanical formula for solving) quadratic equations or correctly notice that certain events routinely occur together without having a very thorough understanding of what quadratic equations are all about or of *why* various events frequently cooccur. The research areas we have chosen are concerned with the question of how the child learns about process.

One of the most unequivocal activities children are intrinsically motivated to engage in is the enterprise that consists of organizing and explaining the world. In its most basic form, this enterprise involves the detection of organization and regularity that actually does occur. In a more sophisticated form, it involves imposing organization on, or inferring it in, situations in which it either does not exist or else exists in a less than perfect form. But the child does not limit himself to attempts to organize the world; he asks, in addition, *why* various regularities exist as well as *how* a particular kind of regularity or organization comes to be. In short, he searches for explanations for, as well as instances of, organization in the world. And, although his explanations may be false, they do nevertheless follow certain rules.

The Concern with Environmental Regularity

Evidence of the child's concern with environmental regularity comes from a wide variety of behaviors and situations. Some of the evidence is provided by children's spontaneous behavior, some by behavior that was elicited. For example, researchers such as Watson (1977) and Bower (1974) have found that even young infants will quickly learn to detect the regularity with which one of their own responses (such as sucking, head turning, or limb movement) is followed by a particular effect (such as the movement of a mobile or the appearance of a person who says, "Peek-a-boo"). Infants will also detect regularities between two types of events when neither type consists of one of the child's own actions (i.e., when both events are external to himself). For example, if an object disappears behind a screen and reappears on the other side, the infant will soon come to look at the other side of the screen *before* the object reappears there (Bower, 1974). By anticipating the reappearance, he gives evidence of having detected the regularity. Similarly, if an object appears first in one window and then another, an infant will soon anticipate its appearance in the second window (Anglin & Mundy-Castle, cited in Bower, 1974). The fact that even young infants detect environmental regularity is some evidence of how basic this tendency is.

Findings in studies of older preschool children show an adeptness at dealing with even more subtle instances of regularity. For example, children of this age can easily perform concept attainment tasks that require them to detect the systematic occurrence of a common element in a number of different contexts (Vinacke, 1952). Indeed, children can detect environmental regularity even when the regularity is not perfect. For example, children are able to learn the correct response in probability tasks in which reinforcement follows the correct response only some, rather than all, of the time (Stevenson, 1970).

In addition, there is evidence that, once children do detect some modicum of organization or regularity, they will spontaneously extend what they have detected. In doing so, they often structure aspects of the world in a way that is actually more organized than the existing structure. For example, Ginsburg (1977) describes a child who is in the process of learning to count, and who extends the rule for forming tens of numbers in the following way: "Ten, twenty . . . ninety, tenny." In the same vein, there is the classic example of children who have just learned to form the past tense by adding the suffix *-ed* to verb stems. Such children will frequently also produce such constructions as "runned," in spite of being exposed only to "ran." Finally, in some cases, children will actually invent their own way of organizing the environment. Ginsburg, for example, reports that a not uncommon belief among grade school children is that, in adding columns of two-digit numbers, when the sum of the righthand column is itself a two-digit number, one carries over to the lefthand column the larger number of the two-digit sum (i.e., the 9 in 19), rather than the number that is on the left.

At this point, we cannot resist reporting an anecodote that illustrates an additional way in which the tendency to impose organization on the environment manifests itself in the real world. A fourth-grader came to the conclusion that the names of national leaders reflected the names of the countries which they represented. Her evidence was that Kenyatta was the head of Kenya, deGaulle was the head of France (which, after all, used to be called Gaul), and Franco was the head of Spain. (Having heard that the early inhabitants of Europe were often nomadic, she assumed that Spain had at one time been inhabited by Franks.) Of course, this theory did not hold for the United States, but then she reasoned, maybe that was why they called the United States a melting pot; things got mixed up in it. But there were vestiges of this correlation even here: Witness, for example, George Washington and Washington, D.C. What this theory lacked in accuracy (or even coherence) it made up in the extent to which it imposed organization on what, in the absence of this theory, was nothing more than a collection of facts.

The child's acquisition of knowledge about the social world follows a similar pattern. The child begins to learn about gender identity for example, by first categorizing the world into two clusters (male and female) and then arriving at stereotypical views of the roles occupied by each sex (Condry, in press; Kohlberg, 1976). This device allows the child a form of control, since the child knows—in a broad way—what to expect. Control involves both the ability to *anticipate* the correlational structure of the world, and to *manipulate* the causal structure of the world.

There is fairly extensive evidence, then, that one way in which children try to achieve control over their world is by organizing it. If the organization is built into the world, children will detect it. If the organization is less than perfect, they will improve upon it. If the intended organization is not detected, they will construct their own version. Children come equipped with a tendency to gain control over a large number of discrete (and possibly even unrelated) pieces of information by reducing them to particular instances of rules that are more general, and thus fewer in number, than the individual facts that the rules subsume.

Intrinsic Interest in Causal Explanations

However, the intrinsic motivation to detect regularity in (or impose it on) the world is frequently not enough to satisfy a child. Often, he seeks to know *why* and *how* this regularity is brought about. Detecting regularity provides the child only with the information that various events in, or aspects of, the environment are associated with one another. It provides him with information only about correlation. It does not provide the child with any information about *why* events are associated, about *how* it is, for example, that one event regularly cooccurs with, or follows, another. Answering these sorts of questions requires *causal explanations* for the way the world is organized. The child must move from correlation to cause. Sometimes explanations for why events are associated consist of no more than an identification of exactly which aspect of the environment is functioning as the causal agent in a particular situation. For example, the child may note that the wheels of a bicycle turn because the pedals are pushed, and that lights go on because switches are turned. This information in itself makes the environment more manageable, because it enables the child to learn that particular phenomena are associated with only some aspects of the environment (some causal agents) rather than others. Often, however, the child also becomes involved with the underlying mechanism or causal underpinnings that explain how it is that a particular causal agent (such as a switch) is able to make an event happen. That is, he concerns himself with questions about the *intervening connection* that *mediates* between causal agent and the effect, enabling the causal agent to bring about the effect. For instance, in the example just mentioned, the child may note that moving pedals brings about movement of the wheels, because the pedals and wheels are connected to one another by intervening chains and gears.

Evidence that the child seeks to know about more than mere correlation or association between events comes from two studies in which children spontaneously concerned themselves with going beyond mere correlation by also trying to learn about what *caused* one event to be correlated with another. In one study (Koslowski(a), in preparation), preschool children were shown an apparatus in which the movement of a bolt lock was associated with the ringing of a bell. Not satisfied with simply detecting this correlation, the majority of the children spontaneously suggested that there must be a connection *someplace* between the lock and the clapper, and many of the children spontaneously went on to search for the connection. An even more striking example of the concern for mediating mechanisms as a way of moving from correlation to cause comes from a study (Koslowski & Snipper, in preparation) in which turning a knob attached to a battery was associated with the ringing of an electric bell. There was a visible wire that ran from the battery to the bell. However, even when the wire was disconnected from the bell, some of the children made positive predictions that turning the knob would still cause the bell to ring. They made this prediction because they postulated an intervening connection that, though invisible, must nevertheless have functioned as a mediator between cause and effect. Positive predictions were based on the premise that this intervening mechanism would continue to mediate between cause and effect even with the wire no longer contacting the bell. For example, children would suggest that the "battery stuff" or the "electric stuff" from the battery would go through the wire and "shoot out" or "spray out" and hit the bell. Those children who predicted that the bell would *not* ring with the wire disconnected also based their predictions on considerations involving underlying mechanisms. They would argue, e.g., that the "battery stuff" would "spray out" of the wire and *miss* the bell. In short, even when these children could not actually see the intervening mechanism that mediated between two correlated events, they were not satisfied with merely detecting the correlation. They either tried to find the causal connection, or else they postulated an invisible connection in order to explain the correlation.

The two studies just reported involved simple relationships: only one antecedent event preceded a subsequent event. In the real world, however, there are often many antecedent events that precede an effect. The child searching for an explanation in this sort of situation must first identify which particular antecedent event(s) is the causal agent before he can concern himself with finding out what it is that mediates or connects the antecedent event or cause to the effect. We turn now to the issue of the sorts of cues which children rely on in order to decide that one event (rather than another) is the cause of a phenomenon. We begin by examining how the child deals with unfamiliar situations.

When a child is faced with an unfamiliar situation (as children often are), his or her main task in finding a causal explanation for that situation is somehow to choose a *likely* cause from among a large number of *possible* causes. We know that in making such a choice, children are capable of relying on various rules about the ways in which causes and events tend to be related. Preschool children are most likely to rely on the index of causal relationship that consists of temporal contiguity. That is, in identifying the agent that caused an effect, preschool children will search for the event that was closest in time to the effect. As children grow older, they take into account the additional cue of regularity of cooccurrence, and look for an event that *consistently* precedes or cooccurs with the effect (Shultz & Mendelson, 1975; Siegler, 1975; Seigler & Liebert, 1974).

It must be stressed, however, that the indices of regularity and temporal contiguity are, in some sense, "cues of last resort." They are the cues that children rely on when there are no other cues present. They are cues of last resort because they do not enable one to distinguish relationships that are merely correlational from those that are genuinely causal as well. And, as we have already seen, even young children are not satisfied with simply noticing that two events are correlated: they also seek to learn about the *process* by which one event is able to cause the other. As we have noted previously, an important distinction between correlational and causal relationships concerns the presence of an intervening mechanism that mediates between causally related, but not between merely correlated, events. Thus, we would expect that children who are concerned with finding causal explanations would be concerned as well with information about possible intervening mechanisms that might be operating in a situation. And children oblige us. Indeed, they oblige to such an extent that, often, even in unfamiliar situations, conclusions based on the cues of temporal contiguity and regularity will be overriden by information that suggests possible intervening mechanisms that might have mediated between cause and effect.

For example, in a study by Mendelson & Shultz (1976), two possible causal agents (i.e., antecedent events) preceded an effect. The temporal delay between one event and the effect was longer than the delay between the other event and the effect. When length of delay was the only information available, children chose as the causal agent that event which was associated with the shorter delay. (That is, they relied on the cue of temporal contiguity.) However, children were less likely to do this if a visible connection (in this case, a tube) mediated between the effect and that causal agent which was paired with the longer time interval. Presumably, the intervening tube suggested a rationale or an explanation for the loger delay. The children probably assumed that it took a fairly long time for the result of the causal agent to "travel through" the tube on its way to producing the effect. Thus, children were less likely to rely on temporal contiguity when they could rely instead on information about a possible intervening mechanism that could have mediated between the effect and the temporally distant event.

Just as inferences based on the index of temporal contiguity are often overridden by other considerations, the index of regularity of cooccurrence is also less likely to be used when children can rely instead on information that suggests possible intervening mechanisms. In a study now in progress (Koslowski & Levy), preschool children are shown three instances of a particular event, with each instance depicted in a separate drawing. One such event consists of a boy who has fallen from his bike. Two of the three drawings of the event also portray a particular environmental feature (i.e., a bump on the road) while all three of the drawings depict an additional environmental feature (i.e., a bumblebee flying in the vicinity of the fallen boy). The irregularly occurring feature can be related to the event by means of a possible intervening mechanism (e.g., the bump could have caused the boy to fall by making him lose his balance). In contrast, the other feature, although it occurs regularly in all three instances, cannot be (or, at least, cannot as easily be) related to the event in such a way. In spite of the fact that the presence of the bumblebee regularly occurs with the bicycle accident, children explain the accident by citing the irregularly occurring bump on the road as the cause. Furthermore, even when it is pointed out to them that the bump does not occur in one of the pictures, their judgments remain unshaken ("The bump was on a different part of road that's not in the picture, and the boy was able to keep his balance until he got to *this* part of the road."). Indeed, the main age difference in this study has to do with the number of possible intervening mechanisms that children can generate. When questioned further, many young children were unable to suggest any possible way in which the bumblebee could have brought about the accident. Older children, in contrast, were able to suggest that the bee (or his sting) might have distracted or scared the boy and caused him to lose his balance that way. That is, older children were more likely to have access to collateral or related information about the way in which the proximity of a bumblebee *could* have caused the accident. This collateral information included the information that a bee might function as a distractor, that distraction can result in a loss of balance, etc. The importance of having access to collateral information will be discussed in more detail below.

We have seen that young children are capable of relying on the cues of temporal contiguity and regularity in order to decide which one of a large number of *possible* causes is likely to be the *probable* cause of an event. We have also seen that judgments based on these cues can be overriden by judgments that are based instead on information about possible intervening mechanisms (information about causal *process* rather than outcome). We now turn to evidence that information about the causal process can also be used in order to decide which feature (among many features of a situation) might be related to a causal explanation of an event. Thus, even when the child does not have the option of relying on the cues of temporal contiguity and regularity, he need not choose at random; he can base his choice instead on information about possible intervening mechanisms.

As an example of how this might occur in adult reasoning, consider a situation in which one is trying to explain a patient's death. One situational feature might be that the person was being treated with penicillin. On the face of it, it looks as though *this* feature is not causally relevant to the patient's death. Penicillin cures rather than kills. However, if we find that the patient was allergic to penicillin, then this information provides a possible intervening mechanism according to which the situational feature (treatment with penicillin) *could* have been causally related to the patient's death.

When confronted with simpler situations, grade school children seem to engage in analogous reasoning. For example, in another study (Koslowski, Levy & Diamant, in progress) children are shown a picture of a boy who has fallen from his bike. A bumblebee is shown flying in the vicinity and a small dog is near the side of the road. When children are told that the bee was flying near the boy's face, the children are likely to incorporate the bumblebee into a causal explanation of the event. For example, they might suggest that the bee distracted the boy or that the boy let go of the handlebars in order to swat at the bee. Thus, they use information about the bee's proximity to the boy as suggesting an intervening mechanism by which the bee could have been related to the accident. If, on the other hand, children are told something about the bee that is causally irrelevant (that it is yellow and feels fuzzy) and are told instead the dog was running across the road in front of the boy's bike, then children will incorporate the dog (rather than the bee) into a causal explanation of the event. In this study, as in the one reported above, an important age difference is that older children are more able than younger ones to generate a larger number of possible intervening mechanisms that could have enabled a particular causal agent (a bumblebee or a dog) to bring about an effect. That is, they have access to more collateral information that they can rely on in order to generate a wider range of possible explanations for an event.

In the studies described in this section, we have argued that children are intrinsically motivated to detect regularity, and that they also concern themselves with the process or underlying mechanism by which this regularity occurs. To use the terminology introduced in the first section, children seem predisposed to become *initially engaged* in those tasks that involve either questions about the way the world is organized or questions about how the organization might be explained. In light of children's self-initiated concern with the process by which things happen, it is worth recalling the findings reported earlier that concern for process is not likely to be facilitated by a motivational system that places heavy reliance on external rewards.

Achieving Causal Explanations

Given evidence that children show a spontaneous concern for understanding the processes or underlying mechanisms by which events are brought about, a natural next step is to ask about the process that children themselves go through as they attempt to achieve causal explanations or descriptions of the processes by which things happen. Again, to use the terminology previously introduced, what can we say about the *activity* or *manipulation* that children engage in when they become involved in a task? The studies described thus far do not provide a very complete answer. In some of these studies, information about the possible intervening mechanism was actually suggested to the child by the experimenter. In other studies, although the child initiated a search for the intervening mechanism, the mediating connection was found so quickly that there was no time to study the search process. In order to learn more about what the search process consists of, we turn to research aimed at describing the process by which non-routine problems are solved. The link between searching for causal explanations and solving problems is clear. Arriving at an explanation for a phenomenon is often tantamount to solving a problem. Solving a problem often requires one to learn about the underlying mechanism that connects the various subcomponents of a solution.

We will first focus on that step in the problem solving process that consists of the exploration that precedes achievement of the correct solution. Our information is based on problems that range from the concrete to the abstract and include: learning how to manipulate tools in order to bring a goal object within reach (Harter, 1930; Koslowski & Bruner, 1972; Minskaia, 1970; Richardson, 1932, 1934; Sobel, 1939; Zhukova, 1970); discovering how to compute the area of a parallelogram (Wertheimer, 1959); mastering quadratic equations (Bruner & Kenney, 1961); devising a procedure for eliminating an inoperable tumor (Duncker, 1945); and making scientific discoveries (Wallas, 1926).

There are five aspects of presolution exploration which deserve consideration. First, presolution exploration must be extensive before a correct solution can be obtained (Duncker, 1945; Harter, 1930; Koslowski & Bruner, 1972; Richardson, 1932, 1934; Wallas, 1926; Zhukova, 1970). The problem solver must be thoroughly familiar with various facets of the problem situation; superficial acquaintance will not suffice. Thorough familiarity includes learning about *all* aspects of the problem situation, not just those obviously relevant to the solution. Second, presolution exploration of those aspects of the situation that might constitute the means of solving the problem sometimes actually takes precedence over attainment of the goal (Koslowski & Bruner, 1972; Minskaia, 1970; Richardson, 1932, 1934; Sobel, 1939; Wallas, 1926). Presolution exploration is often so consuming that it becomes an end in itself—often to such an extent that the goal or aim of the problem is actually forgotten. Notice how these first two aspects of the problem-solving process would be hindered by a motivational system that overemphasized the products of learning by making rewards contingent on a number of correct answers. A child in such a system would be taking a risk by exploring facets of the situation not obviously related to the correct answer or by exploring potential strategies that might not lead to goal achievement.

The third aspect of presolution exploration often involves the translation of abstract notions into concrete instances (Bruner & Kenney, 1962; Wertheimer, 1959); a reliance on analogies between the situation at hand and other situations; and, a reduction (when possible) of new problems to other, more familiar situations (Bruner & Kenney, 1962; Wertheimer, 1959). This third aspect again brings to mind an issue that was raised earlier: the importance of the availability of collateral information. Clearly, having access to a large reservoir of collateral information makes it more likely that analogies can be drawn between a current problem and other situations, and also makes it more likely that there will be other familiar situations which can be seen as being similar to the current problems.

An additional aspect of presolution has to do with a possible function of this exploration. Although the evidence is not conclusive, one possibility is that exploration of the means enables the problem solver to discover which properties of the means are potentially useful in achieving a correct solution, and which are largely irrelevant. For example, Sibulkin and Uzgiris (1978) had an adult model the procedure required to make an apparatus work. Some of the model's movements were, in fact, irrelevant to achieving the correct solution. During the early repetitions, children imitated the irrelevant as well as the relevant behaviors. However, as the children came to understand for themselves how the apparatus worked, the irrelevant behaviors were no longer included in their repetitions. Zhukova (cited in Berlyne, 1970) gave preschool children (3 to 6 years of age) the task of bringing a lure within reach by selecting the correct one of a number of different kinds of hooks. One group of children was given hooks of different shapes and colors; the other, hooks of different shapes but the same color. Both groups of children tried out different hooks in turn, but the second group of children achieved correct solutions faster, presumably because they did not have to explore the irrelevant cue of color as being possibly relevant to correct solution.

The final point about presolution exploration is that it facilitates achievement of the correct solution only if the exploring child has already achieved a certain age (a different age for different problems). One can only speculate about why this is so. One possibility is that, for it to be efficacious, exploration of the means must take place in the context of previously acquired background or collateral information, and that young problem solvers have not yet had a chance to acquire this background. For example, to use a rotating lever in order to solve a problem, it may well be that one needs collateral information about rotation (e.g., that direction of rotation does not matter) in order to benefit from exploration of the lever itself.

In short, the second phase of motivated activity, the phase that involves *activity* or *manipulation,* includes a large component of exploration for its own sake as an end in itself; a heavy reliance on collateral information; and a tendency to make use of analogies and experience gained in previously mastered similar situations.

At present, we have little information about the third phase of motivated activity, *disengagement.* One reason for this is that, in most problem-solving studies, the reason for disengagement is unambiguous: The child achieves the goal object, whether it be a toy, the correct answer, or some particular level of mastery. In many real world situations, the goal of an activity is not as clear-cut as this. We have yet to learn what it is that makes children satisfied with their performance of real world tasks and their achievement of real world goals.

Exploring the Explanations

Regarding the last phase of motivated activity, *subsequent engagement,* we have only slightly more information. Again, this information comes from the problem-solving literature and concerns the kind of exploration that sometimes occurs after the correct solution has already been achieved. This activity consists of exploring the solution itself. For example, in a study that required children to rotate a lever in order to bring a toy within reach (Koslowski & Bruner, 1972), children who had learned how to solve the problem often spontaneously began to investigate the solution itself by varying the direction in which the lever was rotated, varying the way in which they positioned their hands while they held the lever; and rotating the lever by pushing as well as by pulling it. In a study that required children to seriate a set of size-graded sticks from smallest to largest (Koslowski, in preparation), children engaged in analogous behavior. After achieving correct seriation, some of the children spontaneously varied the order in which sticks were chosen (largest to smallest as well as smallest to largest), varied the direction of seriation (right to left as well as left to right), and changed from keeping the bottoms of the sticks to keeping the tops arranged on a straight line. These variations were often accompanied by comments such as, "Huh! It works this way, too!"

Finally, there is Piaget's observation of a child who counts, by moving clockwise, a number of elements that have been arranged in a circle. He then counts the same arrangement by moving in a counterclockwise direction. This child also notes that it "works" both ways. We can only guess at what children are accomplishing by such exploration. One reasonable possibility is that it enables them to learn exactly which aspects of the solution are necessary (e.g., to learn that direction of rotation or direction of seriation does not alter the essential outcome). A second possibility, not incompatible with the first, is that children use this exploration in order to fit a newfound solution into a broader context or background. For example, it may enable a child to relate his new-found knowledge of how elements of a set can be seriated against his already acquired information about size, direction, etc. That is, it may enable his to relate new information to background or collateral information, thus making both types of information richer and potentially more useful. Again, a system that provided extrinsic rewards for the attainment of a product would not be likely to encourage *exploration* of the product. Such a system would push the child to achieve, instead, yet an additional product. There would be pressure to achieve yet another correct answer rather than to more fully understand the correct answer already attained.

Intrinsic Interests and Capacities in the Content of Education

We began this section with a question about the sorts of intrinsic motivation and capacities that characterize the young child. In summary, four general points emerge which seem to be of special relevance to issues in education.

First, children are interested in detecting and constructing regularities or patterns in the world. They also concern themselves with explanations for the underlying mechanism, or process, by which events or outcomes are brought about. In practice, this means that the initial phase of engagement of learning something about the way the world is organized or about the processes by which things happen. This also means that problems the child has in understanding an adult's explanation or way of organizing the world may not result solely from a failure to grasp what the adult is saying, but may reflect, as well, an actual conflict between the adult's position and the one the child has constructed. In order to help the child, an adult may first have to understand how the child organizes or explains the world on his own. Furthermore, the tendency of the child to construct explanations also means that explanations or beliefs which are wrong from an adult's view, may nevertheless be reasonable in the sense of being warranted by the information that is actually available to (or remembered by) the child. This brings us to the second point, namely, the important role played by background or collateral information.

False beliefs about the way the world is organized or explained need not be instances of a lack of intellectual capacity or of faulty thinking. They can be, instead, what Kohler has called "good errors"—guesses or hypotheses which, though wrong, are nevertheless reasonable. Thus, they might reflect the child's limited repertoire of (and often limited access to) the kind of factual information that would be required to achieve a correct explanation. This point is important because of its implications for education. If faulty thinking is the problem, then one type of educational remedy is called for. If, on the other hand, limited information is the culprit, then the remedy ought to consist, not of fostering new ways of thinking, but rather of providing or making available a larger body of factual information.

The third point that emerges from the above findings is the importance of allowing children who are attempting to solve nonroutine problems to explore the problem situation as an end in itself without simultaneously requiring them to keep the goal or end product in mind. It seems likely that it is exactly this sort of exploration that is undermined by extrinsic rewards. The studies just described seem to indicate not only how important such exploration is in achieving correct solutions to nonroutine problems but also to show that children are adequately motivated to engage in this sort of exploration and are capable of benefiting from it (assuming access to adequate background information). This suggests that periods of exploration in which the goal seems to be shunted to the side may not only be natural but may also be facilitative.

254

A final point concerns additional ways in which collateral information plays a role: it may well increase the ease with which a child can rely on analogies and relate new problems to other more familiar situations. It may also enable the child to make new information (or solutions) substantially richer and more useful by relating it to previously acquired systems of information.

SUMMARY

In the title of this review, we raised the question of whether education could be made more intrinsically interesting to children. As may be evident from the text, we believe that it is both possible and desirable to do so. In order for this to happen, we must do two things. On the one hand, we need to reexamine the idea that children who appear to be disinterested in learning may be encouraged to learn by the use of task extrinsic rewards. When these incentives are introduced into the learning situation, they carry a heavy baggage. The research reviewed in the first section suggests that, when used to encourage learning, task extrinsic rewards tend to have detrimental effects on both the performance of a task and the individual's subsequent interest in the task. Thus, the attempt to encourage children to learn by offering some kind of a reward is an inefficient use of time.

On the other hand, children may be more sophisticated learners than we have given them credit for being. The research reviewed in the second section suggests precisely this. Children are disposed to try to make sense out of their environments. A happy consequence of this tendency is that children often have a genuine interest in achieving explanations of various phenomena. They are motivated to delve beneath the surface in order to learn about the causal underpinnigs of things. We suggest that this natural tendency might be exploited; that instead of relying on external rewards to motivate children, we might instead try to provide them with the sort of information that would maximize their "intrinsic" interest in learning. In short, we suggest enticing children rather than forcing them to learn.

REFERENCES

Aronson, E., & Carlsmith, J. M. Effect of the severity of threat on the devaluation of forbidden behavior. *Journal of Abnormal Social Psychology*, 1963, *66*, 584-588.

Aronson, E., & Mills, J. The effect of severity of initiation on liking for a group. *Journal of Abnormal and Social Psychology*, 1959, *59*, 177-181.

Bem, D. J., & McConnell, H. K. Testing the self-perception explanation of dissonance phenomena: On the salience of premanipulation attitudes. *Journal of Personality and Social Psychology*, 1970, *14*, 23-32.

Benware, C., & Deci, E. L. Attitude change as a function of the inducement for respousing a pro-attiudinal communication. *Journal of Experimental Social Psychology,* 1975, *11,* 271-278.

Berlyne, D. E. The arousal and satiation of perceptual curiosity in the rat. *Journal of Comparative Physiological Psychology,* 1955, *48,* 238-246.

Berlyne, D. E. Attention to change, conditioned inhibition (S—R) and stimulus satiation. *British Journal of Psychology,* 1957, *48,* 138-140.

Berlyne, D. E. The present status of research on exploratory and related behavior. *Journal of Individual Psychology,* 1958, *14,* 121-126.

Berlyne, D. E. Curiosity and exploration. *Science,* 1966, *153,* 25-33.

Berlyne, D. E. Children's reasoning and thinking. In P. H. Mussen (Ed.), *Carmichael manual of child psychology,* Vol. 1. New York: Wiley, 1946/1970.

Bernstein, J. Profiles: The Secrets of the old One. *The New Yorker.* March 16, 1973, pp. 87-88.

Bower, T. G. R. *Development in infancy.* San Francisco, Calif.: Freeman, 1974.

Bruner, J. S., & Kenney, H. J. *Mathematical learning, cognitive development in children.* Chicago: Univ. of Chicago Press, 1962/1970.

Bruner, J. S., Goodnow, J. J., & Austin, G. A. *A study of thinking.* New York: Wiley, 1956.

Calder, B. J., & Staw, B. M. Self-perception of intrinsic and extrinsic motivation. *Journal of Personality and Social Psychology,* 1975, *31,* 599-605.

Carlsmith, J. M., Collins, B. E., & Helmreich, R. G. Studies in forced compliance I: Pressure for compliance on attitude change produced by face-to-face role playing and anonymous essay writing. *Journal of Personality and Social Psychology,* 1966, *4,* 1-13.

Cohen, A. R. An experiment on small rewards for discrepant compliance and attitude change. In J. W. Brehm & A. R. Cohen (Eds.), *Explorations in cognitive dissonance.* New York: Wiley, 1962.

Condry, J. C. Enemies of exploration: Self-initiated versus other-initiated learning. *Journal of Personality and Social Psychology,* 1977, *35,* 459-477.

Condry, J. C. The role of incentives in socialization. In Greene & Lepper (Eds.), *The hidden costs of rewards.* Hillsdale, N. J.: Lawrence Erlbaum Associates, in press.

Condry, J. C., & Chambers, J. Intrinsic motivation and the process of learning. In Greene & Lepper (Eds.), The *hidden costs of rewards.* Hillsdale, N.J.: Lawrence Erlbaum Associates, in press.

Cremin, L. A. *The transformation of the school,* 1961, New York: Random House.

Deci, E. L. Effects of externally mediated rewards on intrinsic motivation. *Journal of Personality and Social Psychology,* 1971, *18,* 105-115.

Deci, E. L. The effects of contingent and noncontingent rewards and controls on intrinsic motivation. *Organizational Behavior and Human Performance,* 1972, *8,* 217-299. (a)

Deci, E. L. Intrinsic motivation, extrinsic reinforcement, and inequity. *Journal of Personality and Social Psychology,* 1972, *22,* 113-120. (b)

Deci, E. L. *Intrinsic motivation.* New York: Plenum Press, 1975.

Deci, E. L. Benware, C., & Landry, D. Attributions of motivation as a function of output and rewards. *Journal of Personality,* 1974, *42,* 652-667.

Deci, E. L., & Cascio, W. F. Changes in intrinsic motivation as a function of negative feedback and threats. Paper presented at the meeting of the Eastern-Psychological Association, Boston, April, 1972.

Deci, E. L., Cascio, W. F., & Krusell, J. Cognitive evaluation theory and some comments on the Calder—Staw critique. *Journal of Personality and Social Psychology,* 1975, *31,* 81-85.

deCharms, R. *Personal causation.* New York: Academic Press, 1968.

Duncker, K. On problem solving. *Psychological Monographs,* 1945, *58,* Whole No. 270.

Festinger, L., & Carlsmith, J. M. Cognitive consequences of forced compliance. *Journal of Abnormal and Social Psychology,* 1959, *58,* 203-210.

Freedman, J. L. Long-term behavioral effects of cognitive dissonance. *Journal of Experimental Social Psychology*, 1965, *1*, 145-155.

Garbarino, J. *The impact of reward on cross-age tutoring.* Doctoral dissertation, Cornell University, 1973. *Dissertation Abstracts International*, 1973, *34*, 7327A. (University Microfilms No. 74-10878).

Garbarino, J. The impact of anticipated rewards on cross-age tutoring. *Journal of Personality and Social Psychology*, 1975, *32*, 421-428.

Gerard, H. B., & Mathewson, G. C. The effects of severity of initiation on liking for a group: A replication. *Journal of Experimental Social Psychology*, 1966, *2*, 278-287.

Ginsburg, H. *Children's arithmetic: The learning process.* New York: Van Nostrand, 1977.

Greene, D. Immediate and subsequent effects of differential reward systems on intrinsic motivation in public school classrooms. Doctoral dissertation, Stanford University, 1974.

Greene, D., & Lepper, M. R. Effects of extrinsic rewards on children's subsequent intrinsic interest. *Child Development*, 1974, *45*, 1141-1145.

Greene, D., & Lepper, M. R. An information-processing approach to intrinsic and extrinsic motivation. In J. C. McCullers (Chair), The hidden costs of rewards. Symposium presented at the meeting of the American Psychological Association, Chicago, August 31, 1975.

Greene, D., Sternberg, B., & Lepper, M. R. Overjustification in a token economy. *Journal of Personality and Social Psychology*, 1976, *34*, 1219-1234.

Harlow, H. F. Learning and satiation of response in intrinsically motivated complex puzzle performance by monkeys. *Journal of Comparative Physiological Psychology*, 1950, *43*, 289-294.

Harlow, H. F. Mice, monkeys, men, and motives. *Psychological Review*, 1953, *60*, 23–32.

Harlow, H. F., Harlow, M. K., & Meyer, D. R. Learning motivated by a manipulation drive. *Journal of Experimental Psychology*, 1950, *40*, 228-234.

Harter, G. L. Overt trial and error in the problem-solving of preschool children. *Journal of Genetic Psychology*, 1930, *38*, 361-372.

Hartley, R. E., & Hardesty, F. P. Children's perceptions of sex-role in childhood. *Journal of Genetic Psychology*, 1964, *105*, 43-51.

Haywood, H. C. Individual differences in motivational orientations: A trait approach. In H. Day, D. E. Berlyne, & D. E. Hunt (Eds.), *Intrinsic motivation: A new direction in education.* Toronto: Holt, Rinehart, & Winston, 1971.

Haywood, H. C., & Switzky, H. N. Changes in the verbal behavior of children and adolescents as a function of motivational orientation. Paper presented at the meeting of the Psychonomic Society, St. Louis, November, 1971.

Helmreich, R., & Collins, B. E. Studies in forced compliance: Commitment and magnitude of inducement to comply as determinants of opinion change. *Journal of Social Psychology*, 1968, *10*, 75-81.

Hunt, J. McV. Intrinsic motivation and its role in psychological development. In D. Levine (Ed.), *Nebraska symposium on motivation*, Vol. 13. Lincoln: Univ. of Nebraska Press, 1965.

Karniol, R., & Ross, M. The effect of performance relevant and performance irrelevant rewards on intrinsic motivation. *Child Development*, 1977, *48*, 482-488.

Karniol, R., & Ross, M. The development of causal attributions in social perception. *Journal of Personality and Social Psychology*, 1976, *34*, 455-464.

Koch, S. Behavior as "intrinsically" regulated: Worknotes towards a pre-theory of phenomena called "motivational." In M. R. Jones (Ed.), *Nebraska symposium on motivation*, Vol. 4. Lincoln: Univ. of Nebraska Press, 1956.

Kohlberg, L. Moral stages and moralization. The Cognitive-developmental approach. In T. Lickoma (Ed.) *Moral Development and Behavior*, 1976, New York, Holt, Rinehart & Amston, p. 31-54.

Koslowski, B. Acquiring the concept of causation. In preparation: (a)

Koslowski, B. Learning to Seriate: Some skills that accompany stage changes. In preparation. (b)

Koslowski, B., & Bruner, J. S. Learning to use a lever. *Child Development,* 1972, *43,* 790-799.

Koslowski, B., & Levy, A. Reasoning about causal explanations: Coping with imperfect covariation. In progress.

Koslowski, B., Levy, A., & Diamant, I. Reasoning about explanations: Deciding which features of the situation are causally relevant. In progress.

Koslowski, B., & Snipper, A. Learning about an instance of non-mechanical causation. In progress.

Kruglanski, A. W. An endogenous-attribution theory of intrinsic motivation. In J. C. McCullers (Chair), The hidden costs of rewards. Symposium presented at the meeting of the American Psychological Association, Chicago, August 31, 1975.

Kruglanski, A. W., Alon, S., & Lewis, T. Retrospective misattribution and task enjoyment. *Journal of Experimental Social Psychology,* 1972, *8,* 493-501.

Kruglanski, A. W., & Cohen, M. Attributed freedom and personal causation. *Journal of Personality and Social Psychology,* 1973, *26,* 245-250.

Kruglanski, A. W., Friedman, I., & Zeevi, G. The effects of extrinsic incentives on some qualitative aspects of task performance. *Journal of Personality,* 1971, *39,* 606-617.

Kruglanski, A. W., Riter, A., Amitai, A., Margolin, B. S., Shabtai, L., & Zaksh, D. Can money enhance intrinsic motivation: A test of the content−consequence hypothesis. *Journal of Personality and Social Psychology,* 1975, *31,* 744-750.

Kruglanski, A. W., Riter, A., Arazi, D., Agassi, R., Monteqio, J., Peri, I., & Peretz, M. Effects of task-intrinsic rewards upon extrinsic and intrinsic motivation. *Journal of Personality and Social Psychology,* 1975, *31,* 699-705.

Lependorf, S. The effects of incentive value and expectancy on dissonance resulting from attitude-discrepant behavior and disconformation of expectancy. Doctoral dissertation, State University of New York at Buffalo, 1964. *Dissertation Abstracts,* 1966, *26,* 6159-6160.

Lepper, M. R., & Greene, D. Turning play into work: Effects of adult surveillance and extrinsic rewards on children's intrinsic motivation. *Journal of Personality and Social Psychology,* 1975, *31,* 479-486.

Lepper, M. R., Greene, D., & Nisbett, R. E. Undermining children's intrinsic interest with extrinsic rewards: A test of the overjustification hypothesis. *Journal of Personality and Social Psychology,* 1973, *28,* 129-137.

Liebert, R. M., McCall, R. B., & Hanratty, M. A. Effects of sex-typed information on children's toy perferences. *Journal of Genetic Psychology,* 1971, *119,* 133-136.

Linder, D. E., Cooper, J., & Jones, E. E. Decision freedom as a determinant of role of incentive in attitude change. *Journal of Personality and Social Psychology,* 1967, *6,* 245-254.

Maehr, M. L., & Stallings, W. M. Freedom from external evaluation. *Child Development,* 1972, *43,* 117-185.

Masters, J. C., & Mokros, J. R. Effects of incentive magnitude on discrimination learning and choice preference in young children. *Child Development,* 1973, *44,* 225-231.

McCullers, J. C., & Martin, J. A. G. A re-examination of the role of incentive in children's discrimination learning. *Child Development,* 1971, *42,* 827-837.

McGraw, J., & McCullers, J. The distracting effect of material reward: An alternative explanation for the superior performance of reward groups in probability learning. *Journal of Experimental Child Psychology,* 1974, *18,* 149-158.

McGraw, J., & McCullers, J. Some detrimental effects of reward on laboratory task performance. Paper presented at the meeting of the American Psychological Association, Chicago, September, 1975.

Mendelson, R., & Shultz, T. Covariation and temporal continuity as principles of causal inference in young children. *Journal of Experimental Child Psychology,* 1976, *22,* 408-412.

Miller, L. B., & Estes, B. W. Monetary reward and motivation in discrimination learning. *Journal of Experimental Psychology,* 1961, *61,* 501-504.

Minskaia, G. I. The transition from vuscio-active to rational thought. Unpublished candidate's thesis, Moscow State University, 1954. Cited in Berlyne, D. (1970) *op. cit.*

Montimayor, R. Children's performance in a game and their attraction to it as a function of sex-typed labels. *Child Development,* 1974, *45,* 152-156.

Neisser, U. *Cognition and reality.* San Francisco: Freedman, 1976.

Nel, E., Helmreich, R., & Aronson, E. Opinion change in the advocate as a function of the persuasibility of his audience: A clarification of the meaning of dissonance. *Journal of Personality and Social Psychology,* 1965, *1,* 28-42.

Ovsiankina, M. Die Wiederaufname unterbrochener Handlungen. *Psychologische Forschung,* 1928, *11,* 302-379.

Peiptone, A., McCauley, C., & Hammond, P. Change in attractiveness of forbidden toys as a function of severity of threat. *Journal of Experimental Social Psychology,* 1967, *3,* 221-229.

Ravitch, D. *The great school wars.* New York: Basic Books, 1974.

Reiss, S., & Sushinsky, L. W. Overjustification, competing responses, and the acquisition of intrinsic interest. *Journal of Personality and Social Psychology,* 1975, *31,* 1116-1125.

Richardson, H. M. The adaptive behavior of infants in the utilization of the lever as a tool: A developmental and experimental study. *Journal of Genetic Psychology,* 1934, *44,* 352-372.

Richardson, H. M. The growth of adaptive behavior in infants: An experimental study at seven age levels. *Genetic Psychological Monographs,* 1932, *12,* 195-359.

Ross, M. Salience of reward and intrinsic motivation. *Journal of Personality and Social Psychology,* 1975, *33,* 245-254.

Ross, M., Karniol, R., & Rothstein, M. Reward contingency and intrinsic motivation in children: A test of the delay of gratification hypothesis. *Unpublished manuscript, University of Waterloo, Canada, 1975.*

Ryan, T. A. *Intentional behavior.* New York: Ronald Press, 1970.

Schere, R. A. Differential reinforcement with exceptional children. Doctoral dissertation, New York University, 1969. *Dissertation Abstracts International,* 1970, *31,* 1088A. (University Microfilms No. 70-15,981).

Scott, W. E. The effects of extrinsic rewards on "intrinsic motivation": A critique. *Organizational Behavior and Human Performance,* 1976, *15,* 117-129.

Shultz, T., & Mendelson, R. The use of covariation as a principle of causal analysis. *Child Development,* 1975, *6,* 394-399.

Sibulkin, A. E., & Uzgiris, I. C. Imitation by preschoolers in a problem-solving situation. *J. Genetic Psychol.,* 1978, *132,* 267-275.

Siegler, R. S. Defining the locus of developmental differences in children's causal reasoning. *Journal of Experimental Child Psychology,* 1975, *20,* 512-525.

Siegler, R. S., & Liebert, R. M. Effects of contiguity, regularity, and age on children's causal inferences. *Developmental Psychology,* 1974, *10,* 574-579.

Smith, W. E. The effects of social and monetary rewards on intrinsic motivation. Doctoral dissertation, Cornell University, 1974.

Sobel, B. A study of the development of insight in pre-school children. *Journal of Genetic Psychology,* 1939, *55,* 381-388.

Spence, J. T. The distracting effect of material reinforcers in the discrimination learning of middle- and lower-class children. *Child Development,* 1967, *38,* 29-38.

Staat, J., & McCullers, J. C. *The distracting effect of material reward on the recall of incidentally acquired R—S associations.* Paper presented at the meeting of the American Psychological Association, New Orleans, August, 1974.

Staw, B. M. Calder, B. J., & Hess, R. *Situational norms and the effect of extrinsic rewards on intrinsic motivation.* unpublished manuscript, University of Illinois, Urbana, Champaign, 1974.

Stein, A., Polky, S. R., & Mueller, E. The influence of masculine, feminine, and neutral tasks on children's achievement behavior, expectancies o success, and attainment value. *Child Development,* 1971, *42,* 195-207.

Stein, A., & Smithells, J. Age and sex differences in children's sex-role standards about achievement. *Developmental Psychology,* 1969, *1,* 252-259.

Stevenson, H. W. Learning in children. In Paul H. Mussen (Ed.), *Carmichael's manual of child psychology.* Vol. 1. New York: Wiley, 1946/1970. Pp. 849-938.

Terrell, G., Jr., Durkin, K., & Wiesley, M. Social class and the nature of incentives in discrimination learning. *Journal of Abnormal Social Psychology,* 1959, *59,* 270-272.

Upton, W. E. Altruism, attribution, and intrinsic motivation in the recruitment of blood donors. (Doctoral dissertation, Cornell University, 1973). *Dissertation Abstracts International,* 1973, *34,* 6260B. (University Microfilms No. 74-12652).

Vinacke, W. E. *The psychology of thinking.* New York: McGraw-Hill, 1952.

Van Humboldt, W. The Limits of Action. In J. W. Burrow (Ed.), *Cambridge Studies in the history and theory of politics.* Cambridge, England: Cambridge Univ. Press, 1969. Pp. 76, 63, 27-28.

Wallas, G. *The art of thought.* New York: Harcourt, Brace, 1926.

Weiner, M. J., & Mander, A. The effect upon intrinsic motivation of the withdrawal of an aversize consequence. Unpublished manuscript, Eisenhower College, Seneca Falls, New York, 1977.

Wertheimer, M. *Productive thinking.* New York: Harper & Row, 1959.

White, R. W. Motivation reconsidered: The concept of competence. *Psychological Review,* 1959, *66,* 297-330.

Zajonc, R. Social facilitation. *Science,* 1965, *149,* 269-274.

Zanna, M. P., Lepper, M. R., & Abelson, R. P. Attentional mechanisms in children's devaluation of a forbidden activity in a forced compliance situation. *Journal of Personality and Social Psychology,* 1973, *3,* 355-359.

Zhukova, I. M. The role of analysis and generalization in cognitive activity. In S. L. Rubenstein (Ed.), *Protsess myshleniia i zakonsmernosti analiza, senteza i obobshcheniia* [The thought process and the lanws governing analysis, synthesis, and generalization]. Moscow, USSR: *Acad. Sci.,* 1960. Cited in Berylne, D. (1970), *op. cit.*

Zivin, G. How to make a boring thing more boring. *Child Development,* 1974, *45,* 232-236.

How Children Understand Stories: A Developmental Analysis

Nancy L. Stein

University of Illinois, Urbana-Champaign

INTRODUCTION

In the past few years, a productive area of investigation has concerned the process by which children comprehend complex linguistic information, such as a story. Because stories are an integral part of the school curriculum and are told frequently in everyday social interactions, teachers and psychologists have raised questions about those procedures which would ensure a high rate of comprehension for all children. Other important questions to be answered concern methods for evaluating whether comprehension has occurred and training techniques to be used when children fail to understand stories. The goals of this paper are: to discuss these issues, to provide a review of previous research on children's comprehension of stories, and to give an overview of the field.

A close examinination of the linguistic and anthropological literature (Colby & Cole, 1973; Greimas, 1971; Levi-Strauss, 1955; Prince, 1973; Propp, 1958) indicates that the study of stories has been a major concern for some time. Because stories often contain information relating to the moral codes, values, and social customs of a society (Levi-Strauss, 1955), they serve as an excellent source for an examination of the similarities and differences among cultures with respect to these dimensions. In an attempt to investigate the commonalities across different stories, several complex analyses of both story content and structure have been done (Bremond, 1973; Greimas, 1971; Levi-Strauss, 1955; Prince, 1973; Propp, 1958). Although different in many respects, all lead to similar conclusions regarding the structure of a story. Despite the variation in the semantic content of stories, these analyses document the existence of stable organizational patterns regarding the types of information included in stories and the logical relations among the parts of a story. Some analyses (Bremond, 1969; Levi-Strauss, 1955) also illustrate how the specific content of stories can be classified into stable, consistent patterns.

In order to substantiate further the claim that a structural prototype for a story exists, Todorov (1969) provided anecdotal evidence that children and adults could easily identify the types of prose which conform to and violate the structure of a story. Todorov also argued that when presented with narratives that do not conform to the specific requirements of a story, listeners will transform, add, or delete information so that the resulting story does conform more to the prototypical structure of a story. Thus, a major implication derived from this study is that a listener has some prior knowledge about the structure of a story, and that this knowledge plays a critical role in determining how a story will be retold, as well as determining what types of prose will be classified as stories.

There are two components, however, that are absent from these analyses of story structures. First, none of the descriptions states exactly how preexisting knowledge of stories influences the comprehension process, and second, none of the studies clearly specifies whether the structure of a story lies in the head of a listener or in the text of a story.

In contrast to the linguistic and anthropological studies, a review of the early psychological literature on stories has shown a primary concern with how prior knowledge of stories interacts with memory and comprehension, but only a general interest in the structural characteristics of a story. Until recently, the sole investigator of the cognitive processes and structures involved in story understanding was Bartlett (1932).

In describing how subjects remembered stories, he came to certain conclusions. Bartlett found that people rarely recalled stories exactly as they heard them. Instead, he observed that transformations of the information often occurred, with new information being added, and some of the original story information being deleted. From these results, he concluded that story memory was not only a function of the organization of incoming information, but was dependent upon the mental operations and cognitive structures already acquired by the listener. He called these structures "schemata," and, his elaboration of the concept of schemata, originally used by Kant and Binet (Anderson, in press; Rumelhart & Ortony, 1976), became one of Bartlett's lasting contributions to the study of psychology. His notion of a schema has strongly and directly influenced recent psychological investigations of story comprehension as well as studies in other areas of cognition.

To Bartlett, a mental schema represented "an active organization of past reactions and experiences which are always operating in any well-developed organism" (Bartlett, 1932). He emphasized the reciprocal interaction between incoming new information and existing mental structures by stating that incoming information is actively integrated into a subject's mental structure, but at the same time, the presence of new information modifies the old structures. If the same type of information occurs repeatedly, new structures will emerge from the old and will enable the listener to encode the "new" information more quickly. Bartlett recognized the variability in the process of recalling stories. Although he believed schemata to be stable and shared by individuals within a given culture, he argued that differences in attitudes, interests, and affective and cognitive states could also produce differences, and therefore variability, in these structures.

Bartlett made several predictions regarding the interaction between incoming information and prior knowledge structures during comprehension. For example, he stated that when the text structure of a story violated or did not conform to the underlying cognitive structures, story recall would conform more to the prototypical or expected structure than to the actual text structure. However, one cannot predict the type of transformations that would occur in story recall, since Bartlett did not describe further the specific nature of a story schema.

If the process of story comprehension is to be studied systematically, a detailed description of a story schema appears to be necessary. Although several linguistic studies provide detailed analyses of story structures, these descriptions were constructed by analyzing the text structure of many stories. In spite of the commonalities that may exist between the text and underlying cognitive structures used to guide the representation of story material, there is no guarantee that an isomorphic relationship exists between the two. The demands on working memory and the types of strategies used during story encoding and retrieval may limit the types of text structures which can be comprehended with a high degree of accuracy. It is necessary to formulate a description of the underlying representation of stories, and then to analyze the comprehension of different types of text.

THE DEVELOPMENT OF STORY GRAMMARS

Based upon Bartlett's (1932) initial work on story memory and Propp's (1958) morphology of the folktale, Rumelhart (1975) developed a story grammar which describes the underlying cognitive structures used to encode, represent, and retrieve story information. Because Rumelhart's grammar was difficult to use in the analysis of many different stories, several investigators (Glenn & Stein, 1978; Mandler & Johnson, 1977; Stein & Glenn, 1979; Thorndyke, 1977) modified his grammar so that the underlying representation of a wider variety of stories could be described. These grammars differ from the linguistic study of stories, not only because they emphasize the psychological structures guiding the comprehension process, but also because a set of specific predictions concerning the quality of comprehension can be derived from them.

In order to facilitate an understanding of a story grammar approach, this section will outline the basic assumptions underlying the construction of a grammar, and then illustrate how a listener attempts to break down a simple story into its component parts. The Stein and Glenn (1979) grammar will be used for illustrative purposes. However, in discussing studies completed on story comprehension in children, an attempt will be made to integrate the findings from all grammatical approaches, especially those of Mandler and Johnson (1977).

The Stein and Glenn (1979) grammar assumes that some type of schematic representation of stories is used to guide encoding and retrieval of incoming story information. These schemata may be acquired in two ways: through hearing or reading a variety of different stories, and by the acquisition of knowledge regarding human social interactions. The latter source of information is important for story comprehension, since stories are similar to the content and structure of social perceptions and human action sequences.

One of the assumed functions of story schemata is to guide a listener or reader in breaking down story information into its components. This occurs because the schema specifies the types of information which should occur in a story and the types of logical relations which should link the components of a story. Thus, a story schema guides the listener in determining what parts of the story have not been included and in determining when a story has deviated from the normal temporal sequence of events. One implication is that when the text structure violates the expected story sequence, the resulting representation will tend to correspond more to the expected story sequence than to the original text sequence.

A story schema may be defined as a set of rewrite rules containing knowledge about the generic structure of stories. It is assumed that although there are individual differences in acquired story knowledge, some common type of schematic representation is acquired by all who listen to and tell stories. The development of story grammars illustrates an attempt to describe the general structural characteristics of stories.

Story Analysis: The Single Episode Story

The *primary unit* of analysis in a story is a category, and several categories occur within a story structure. Each category refers to a specific type of information, and serves a different function in the story. Normally, each sentence in a story can be classified into a particular category. However, the sentence is not the critical variable defining how information is classified into categories. There are instances in which the initial part of a sentence belongs to one category, and the latter part belongs to a second category, depending upon the functional role each portion plays in the story.

A story structure can be described in terms of a tree diagram which is an hierarchical network of story categories and the logical relationships which connect them. (For a detailed description of these structures, see Glenn & Stein, 1978; Mandler & Johnson, 1977; or Stein & Glenn, 1979). In order to illustrate how stories are represented, a brief example of the story analysis process is presented. Table 1 lists a description of each of the categories included in a simple story structure and provides an example of how statements in a specific story, "Albert Gets Caught," are broken down into different categories.

The initial division of a simple story consists of two parts: a setting plus an episode structure. The setting begins the story with the introduction of a protagonist and normally includes information about the social, physical, or temporal context pertaining to the remainder of the story. The setting is not part of the episode, as it is not directly related to the subsequent behavioral sequence described in the episode. However, information in the setting category may constrain the possible types of behavioral sequences which then occur.

Table 1   Categories Included in a Simple Story

Category	Definition
Setting	Introduction of the protagonist; can contain information about physical, social, or temporal context in which the remainder of the story occurs.
Initiating event	An action, an internal event, or a natural occurrence which serves to *initiate* or to cause a response in the protagonist.
Internal response	An emotion, cognition, or goal of the protagonist.
Attempt	An overt action to obtain the protagonist's goal.
Consequence	An event, action, or endstate which marks the attainment or nonattainment of the protagonist's goal.
Reaction	An emotion, cognition, action or endstate expressing the protagonist's feelings about his goal attainment or relating the broader consequential realm of the protagonist's goal attainment.

	Example of a Well-formed Story
Setting	1. Once there was a big gray fish named Albert. 2. He lived in a big icy pond near the edge of a forest.
Initiating event	3. One day, Albert was swimming around the pond. 4. Then he spotted a big juicy worm on top of the water.
Internal response	5. Albert knew how delicious worms tasted. 6. He wanted to eat that one for his dinner.
Attempt	7. So he swam very close to the worm. 8. Then he bit into him.
Consequence	9. Suddenly, Albert was pulled through the water into a boat. 10. He had been caught by a fisherman.
Reaction	11. Albert felt sad. 12. He wished he had been more careful.

The remainder of the story consists of an episode, the primary *higher order unit* of analysis. A sequence of five categories is included in the episode: initiating event, internal response, attempt, consequence, and reaction. The initiating event category contains some type of event or action which marks a change in the story environment. Its major function is to evoke the formation of a goal. The goal is included in the internal response category. Internal responses not only include goals, but also include affective states and cognitions, and serve to motivate a character's subsequent overt behavior. Actions referring to overt, goal-directed behavior are defined as attempts. A character's attempts then result in the consequence which marks the attainment or nonattainment of the goal. The final category is the reaction, which includes a character's response to the consequence or broader consequences caused by the goal attainment. It is apparent that each category in the episode logically follows the preceding one. Furthermore, according to the grammar, these categories always occur in a specific temporal sequence.

Several factors signal the ending of one category and the beginning of the next. Temporal markers such as *One day, Suddenly, Finally*, etc., facilitate the analysis of a story into its components. However, the semantic content of a statement and the logical relationships among story statements are equally important in determing the classification of story statements into different categories in an episode.

In describing the structural characteristics of an episode, the distinction between the text structure versus the underlying cognitive structure of an episode is critical. There are many stories that have one or two categories in an episode deleted from the text structure. For example, internal responses and reactions are frequently omitted. At times the text structure of an episode begins with the character's internal response and does not include an initiating event. However, it is assumed that although these categories are omitted from the text structure, they are *inferred* during the encoding process, and are represented in the underlying cognitive structure.

Some episodes in the text omit more than one or two of these categories. In these cases, an episode is considered to be incomplete, since there are three basic requirements which must be met in order for a category sequence to be considered a complete episode. The sequence must contain: (1) some reference to the motivation or purpose of the character's behavior; (2) an overt goal-directed action; and (3) the attainment or nonattainment of the goal. Therefore, the categories which must be included in an episode are: (1) the initiating event which signals the reason for the formation of a goal *or* an internal response which normally includes the goal; (2) an overt action, signified by the attempt category; and (3) a direct consequence, marking the attainment or nonattainment of the goal.

Multiple Episode Stories

If one examines many different folktales and fables, it is evident that few stories are represented as simply as the structure just described. Most stories contain several episodes, and the individual story can vary, not only in the number of episodes contained in a story structure, but also in regard to the types of logical relations which connect the various episodes. Both the Stein and Glenn (1979) and the Mandler and Johnson (1977) grammars describe the different type of interepisodic complexities that occur in stories and provide several analyses of more complex stories. However, only the types of relations which connect episodes in these multiple episode stories will be discussed.

Any two episodes in a story structure can be connected by one of three relationships: AND, THEN, and CAUSE. The most common relations connecting episodes are THEN and CAUSE. The THEN relation is used when one episode follows a second, where the first episode sets up the necessary preconditions for the second episode to occur; however, the occurrence of the first episode does not directly cause the second to occur. An example of the THEN relation is found in the classic folktale, "Goldilocks and the Three Bears." When Goldilocks enters the bears' home, two episodes occur in succession. The first episode recounts Goldilocks' discovery of the porridge, her desire to eat it, and the act of finishing the baby bear's portion. The second episode describes her becoming fatigued, the discovery of the chairs, and her action sequence of trying out all of the chairs so that she might rest. In this story, the first episode does not directly cause her behavior in the second sequence, as she might have chosen another course of action after eating. However, the events in the first episode do set up the necessary preconditions for her goal and attempts in the second episode.

The second type of connection, the CAUSE relation, implies a direct connection between two episodes such that the first episode directly ensures the occurrence of the second episode. Certain problems arise in deciding whether episodes are connected by the THEN or CAUSE relation, because the perception of a direct causal link is dependent upon the prior knowledge acquired about the events in a story. If more than one alternative episode can be generated after the occurrence of the first episode, the most accurate connection between the two episodes would be a THEN relation. However, if the subject perceives that only one type of episode could result as a function of a previous episode, then the connection between the two episodes is a CAUSE relation. Therefore, the types of relations connecting two episodes are strictly dependent upon the inferences made by a subject during the process of organizing story information, either at the time of encoding the information or during the process of reorganizing story information once encoding has occurred.

The third type of relation connecting two episodes is the AND relation. This type of relation describes a story sequence where two episodes occur in a temporal sequence according to the story time but where the episodes may have occurred in any order, or may have occurred simultaneously in real time. For example, many stories relate how two characters desire to pursue the same goal, e.g., two knights who want the hand of a beautiful princess. In the beginning of the story, a description containing two episodes may be given explaining why each knight desired the hand of the princess, or how each knight formulated his current goal. These episodes occur in a sequence in the story line, but there is no a priori reason to believe that one episode occurred before another. In fact, many of the rhetorical markers in the story (e.g., meanwhile, at the same time, etc.), directly cause the reader to infer that the two episodes were occurring simultaneously. After the two episodes occur, each of them is usually related to a third episode by a THEN or CAUSE relation.

RESEARCH ON STORY COMPREHENSION

The following section is devoted to the discussion of several studies which have attempted to validate a story grammar approach to comprehension.

Temporal Organization of Stories

From the previous discussion of story grammars, it is apparent that the temporal sequence of category information and the logical relations connecting categories are essential to the definition of an episode. In order to validate the rewrite rules defining a story schema, predictions can be made about those story texts which either correspond to or violate the expected sequence in a story. Specific hypotheses and the results from several studies are presented in the following section.

If a story sequence corresponds to the expected sequence, there should be little or no difficulty recalling the temporal order of events given in the text of a story. Data from two recent studies (Mandler & Johnson, 1977; Stein & Glenn, 1979) support this prediction by showing that children as young as 6 years make very few errors in recalling the correct temporal order of stories corresponding to the expected sequence. Recall data collected from 4- and 5-year-old children (Stein & Garfin, 1977) show that even preschool children experienced little difficulty ordering the events in a story, provided the story corresponded to the expected sequence. These results are important because they contradict Piaget's (1960) findings of poorly organized story recall in 6- to 8-year-old children. The differences between these two sets of results appear to be a function of story complexity, characterized by both the syntactic structure of sentences and the type of logical relations connecting sentences.

Brown (1975) has also completed a series of studies on children's memory for logically organized sequences. She found that when preschool children were asked to reconstruct a series of logically related pictures, very few errors occurred. However, like Piaget, she found that many preschool children had difficulty *recalling* the exact order of picture sequences.

The fact that Brown's recall data conform more to Piaget's data than to the results found in the studies by Mandler and Johnson (1977), Stein and Garfin (1977), and Stein and Glenn (1979) shows the importance of the type of stories used as stimulus materials. In the Stein and Garfin (1977) study, the content of the stories used as stimuli was taken from a group of stories told by 4- and 5-year-old children. The stimuli were also constructed to correspond, in every way, to the expected story sequence. Although Brown's picture sequences had an underlying logical coherence, it may be that the picture sequences did *not* correspond identically to the structure of an expected sequence. Certain categories might also have been missing, and 4- and 5-year-olds may not have been able to make the appropriate inferences to fill in the "gaps," leading to a semantically cohesive representation in memory. The high accuracy of reconstruction memory in Brown's study, however, appears to contradict this argument. At present, it is unclear why young children have difficulty with some story sequences and not others. However, the results from the story grammar studies strongly suggest that children as young as age 4 have little difficulty with "well-formed" stories (i.e., those corresponding to the expected story sequence), suggesting that by this age, a story schema similar to the one proposed in the story grammars is used to guide story processing. A more direct test of young children's internal representation of stories may shed light on these issues.

If children have acquired story schemata as described by the grammars, then their spontaneous organization of story material should correspond to the expected story sequence. Furthermore, if children are presented with stories that contain any deviation from the expected sequence, then some type of reorganization of the incoming information should occur so that story recall conforms more to the expected sequence than to the structure in a given text.

In a study conducted by Stein and Glenn (1978) 7- and 11-year-old children were given twelve sentences from a well-formed story, similar to the one presented in Table 1. All children were asked to make a "good" story, similar to stories they would either tell a friend or find in a storybook. Each child constructed three separate stories. The results from both age groups showed a significant positive correlation when the constructed orders were compared to the order proposed in the Stein and Glenn (1979) grammar. However, the results also showed that many of the constructed stories did not identically correspond to the expected sequences. This was particularly true for the younger children. The mean correlations between the constructed and expected story sequences were .44 for 7-year-olds and .77 for 11-year-olds.

Two types of errors accounted for the majority of variance found in this task: (1) children constructed stories in which statements in the internal response category were placed in positions other than the ones specified in the expected sequence; and (2) children placed consequence and reaction statements in positions other than the predicted order. In most cases, the repositioning of the internal response statements did *not* disrupt the logical sequence of story events. If the story in Table 1 is used as an example, it can be seen that repositioning statements 5 and 6 so that they occur after statement 7 results in a logical story. Statements 6 and 7 may also be inverted and a semantically coherent story remains. Similarly, the types of errors made in reordering consequence and reaction statements resulted in semantically cohesive stories.

Rather than indicating that young children have not acquired a consistent prototypical story schema, some of the errors indicate the problems associated with defining category membership. The semantic content of a statement is not sufficient for classifying a statement into particular categories. For example, action statements are included in more than one category. Therefore, it is not surprising that children reordered some of the story statements.

The more striking finding is that children often inverted affective statements or cognitions with preceding action statements, as if they were inferring that a "because" relation connected the two statements. For example, in Table 1 many children ordered statements 9, 10, 11, and 12, by placing statement 10 after statement 12 so that the constructed order read:

Suddenly Albert was pulled through the water into a boat.
Albert felt sad.
He wished he had been more careful.
He had been caught by a fisherman.

The inversion of internal response or reaction statements with action statements may indicate that children can spontaneously infer a "because" relation between two statements so that inverted statements can be remembered accurately. In the studies to be presented later in this chapter, it will be seen that during recall of story material containing this type of inversion, many children do spontaneously insert a "because" relation in order to recall the inverted sequence in the presented order.

Adults' conceptions of "good" stories also have been examined. Stein and Nezworski (1978) completed a study in which adults were instructed to recall a "good, coherent" story from texts that did not correspond to the expected sequence. The two types of stories presented were slightly disordered stories, in which one category of story information was moved to a new position within the story, and randomly-ordered stories. Recall of these stories corresponded almost identically to the expected sequence rather than to the text order presented to subjects.

Mandler (1977) also conducted a study in which adults were asked to recall specific story violations in such a fashion that the stories would be considered "good" stories. The stimulus materials were constructed by taking a story with two episodes and interweaving statements from each episode so that the resulting story contained a text structure which continually violated the expected sequence of events. She found, like Stein and Nezworski, that adults recalled the stories by separating the statements into two coherent episodes that were identical to the expected story sequence.

The evidence from these studies shows a substantial basis for inferring that the expected story sequence described in the grammar directly corresponds to an adult's conception of a "good" story. The results from the Stein and Glenn (1978) study indicate positive support for this conclusion, especially for older children. However, the variation in reconstruction in the second grade data remains unexplained. Although many of the second-grade children constructed semantically coherent stories, some of the constructed stories, if recalled by children and adults, should undergo a greater reorganization than stories matching the description of an expected sequence. Memory demands and the complexity involved in reconstructing a sequence of twelve lines may have accounted for the variability in some of the orders produced during reconstruction. Young children may not be able to keep track of a logical sequence of this length. Thus, their strategy may be to break down the sequence into smaller units, adhering to a strict logic within each unit.

Two studies (Stein & Glenn, 1978; Stein & Nezworski, 1978) then examined second- and sixth-graders' skill at recalling stories which contained inverted sequences of information, thereby deviating from the rules specified by a story schema. Stories containing inversions can be constructed in two ways. The first method involves simply moving information in one part of the story, for instance, the consequence in an episode, to another position in the episode, without changing or adding any new semantic information to the content of the story. A second method of creating inversions is to change the position of one category, as in the first method, and then add rhetorical markers, signaling the occurrence of an inversion in the episode. For example, the consequence category in Table 1 could be moved to a position occurring immediately after the initiating event. When the first method of creating inversions is used, no rhetorical markers are added. In the second type of inverted sequence, rhetorical markers would appear after the consequence category so that the story would read:

> One day, Albert was swimming around the pond
> when he spotted a big juicy worm on top of the water.
> Suddenly, Albert was pulled through the water into a boat.
> He had been caught by a fisherman.
> *This happened because . . .*

And so the story continues by relaying the remainder of the information in the episode, omitting the consequence from its normal position.

The Stein and Glenn (1978) study examined recall of unmarked inverted stories (not containing rhetorical markers). If the grammar is valid, any deviation from the expected sequence of events in a story should cause a reorganization in recall which conforms more to the expected sequence than to the presented text sequence. Furthermore, the recovery of accurate story information may be quite difficult when inversions occur in a text, with recall decreasing significantly when compared to recall of expected story sequences. This implies that if subjects do expect certain types of logical sequences in stories, they may become confused when sequences contrary to expectations occur. As a result of the confusion, they may spend more time on the confusions and not attend to other parts of the story as well. The Stein and Glenn (1978) study showed strong support for the reorganizational prediction and partial support for the prediction concerning the amount of accurate information retrieved during recall.

In their study, Stein and Glenn (1978) constructed nine deviations of an expected story sequence by manipulating the location of three different categories. Each category was placed in three different positions other than its normal location within an episode. For example, the initiating event was placed either one, two, or three locations away from its normal position in the episode. The resulting stories contained sequences with the initiating event occurring after: (1) the internal response, (2) the attempt, or (3) the consequence. Similar types of story deviations were constructed by moving the internal response and consequence categories to new positions in a story.

The data were analyzed by comparing recall from stories conforming to the expected sequence to recall from story deviations containing temporal inversions. The results showed that reorganization of the text sequence occurred in almost all conditions in which stories deviated from the expected sequence. The type of reorganization was specific to both the category moved and the distance each category was moved from its normal location. Independent of the type of reorganization occurring during retrieval, however, recall of the stories conformed more to the expected story sequence than to the presented text sequence.

The amount of accurate information recalled decreased significantly, in comparison to groups receiving the expected story sequence, when either the initiating event or consequence category was placed in a new location. Figure 1 summarizes the mean proportion of accurate recall found in both the control and experimental conditions in this study.

The surprising result from this study was that the internal response category could be placed anywhere in the episode without decreasing the amount of accurate recall. Thus, there may be more variability in positioning this type of information than a strict reading of the grammar would allow. Another explanation for this finding is that rules for comprehending inverted internal response information may be acquired at a fairly early age.

Marked temporal inversions occur so frequently in stories used in school textbooks that it becomes imperative to examine the effects of these inversions

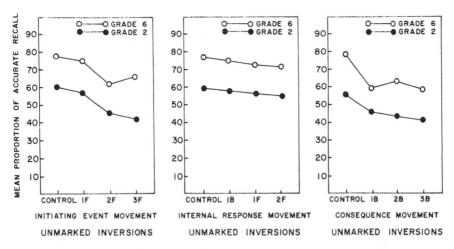

Figure 1 Mean proportion of statements accurately recalled in the control and experimental conditions when unmarked story deviations were presented to 2nd and 6th graders. From the Stein and Glenn (1978) study.

on story memory and comprehension. Marked inversions, in contrast to unmarked inversions, provide a signal that a deviation is occurring in the normal sequence of events. The inclusion of rhetorical markers in a text may also inhibit the initiation of certain processing strategies and direct the listener's attention to the more relevant types of transformations that should be made during the encoding process. For example, if the consequence is placed in a position at the beginning of an episode, followed by a rhetorical marker such as: "This happened because," the listener immediately becomes aware that the beginning events occurred later in the story sequence. The presence of markers, then, may facilitate the encoding of a cohesive representation of the text sequence so that recall does not decrease when compared to recall of expected sequences.

On the other hand, stories containing inversions, even though well marked, should place greater demands on working memory. The inverted information must be "tagged" in some fashion so that it can be held in memory and retrieved at the appropriate time in order to construct a cohesive logical sequence. The ability to remember these marked inversions may depend upon children's familiarity with deviate structures.

In order to investigate the effects of marked temporal inversions on recall, Stein and Nezworski (1978) conducted an experiment in which the position of each of three categories (the internal response, consequence, and reaction) was systematically varied by placing each category in different locations throughout the story. Six- and 10-year-old children participated in this study. The results, appearing in Fig. 2, were provocative regarding both developmental differences in recall and effects of different category movements on recall.

For fifth-grade children, all stories containing marked inversions were re-

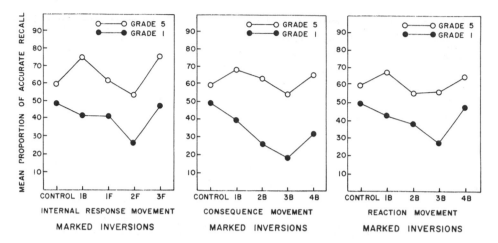

Figure 2 Mean proportion of statements accurately recalled in the control and experimental conditions when marked story deviations were presented to 1st and 5th graders. From the Stein and Nezworski (1978) study.

called as well as stories containing the expected sequence of events. Furthermore, three deviations containing marked inversions were recalled significantly better than the expected story sequence. All of these inversions included some movement of the internal response or reaction category. The two movements most effective in increasing recall were those in which the internal response occurred *before* the initiating event or *after* a character's reaction at the end of the episode. Recall also increased significantly when the reaction, the last episodic category, occurred before the character's consequence.

The first-grade results, however, indicated a different pattern of recall. Although some of the story deviations with marked inversions were recalled as well as stories containing expected sequences, none were recalled better than the expected sequence. In fact, the majority of inversions significantly decreased recall when compared to the recall of expected sequences. Thus, a significant developmental difference emerged when the effects of marked inversions on story recall were examined. Younger children could not remember deviations from the expected sequence as well as older children.

Younger children may not have acquired a specific set of strategies or rules necessary to guide them in recovering as much of the original story content as older children. These children may be more dependent upon the story following the expected sequence than older children. This explanation for developmental differences in recall has also been given in a study completed by Mandler and DeForrest (1977). They argue that younger children are less familiar with deviant structures and that their memory is more apt to decline when they are presented with any type of deviation from the expected sequence.

If this assertion is true, then the next question to be raised concerns *how* children acquire strategies or rules which allow them to maintain a high level of recall when inversions do occur. A second question concerns the order in which these rules are acquired. It is clear that younger children remember some temporal inversions more easily than others. This finding suggests that some inversions may be more easily represented or may require fewer transformations during encoding than other inversions. Piaget (1960) has argued that a definite hierarchy does exist in the acquisition of rules used to comprehend "because" relationships. His data, similar to Stein and Nezworski's (1978), showed that the first type of "because" relationship remembered was an action-affective inversion. He then illustrated that rules regarding inversions of personal causation events were acquired before rules for inverting sequences relating to physical causality.

At the present time, there is no conclusive evidence that illustrates a definite hierarchy of acquisition rules, primarily because there is a lack of knowledge about children's comprehension and usage of "because." Furthermore, not enough data have been collected to determine what children's conceptions of personal and physical causation are. The first necessary step in investigating this issue is to determine just what events children perceive as being *directly* related to one another. The types of *semantic* knowledge structures guiding the perception of causal sequences must be described in detail. Chilren may comprehend sequences of physical events as well as personal events, depending upon whether the sequence matches the prior knowledge structures they have acquired.

The second step in understanding the acquisition of rules for comprehending "because" relations involves the description of children's knowledge concerning the functional usage of this relation. It may be necessary to determine when young children spontaneously use the "because" relation and what types of information are connected when "because" occurs. If these issues are investigated systematically, then methods for constructing training techniques to ensure comprehension can be developed.

Probability of Accurately Recalling Story Events

Besides regulating the order in which events are expected to occur, a story schema also specifies the type of information which is expected in a story sequence. Both of these factors are important in determining the accuracy of recall. This section will discuss the probability of story statements occurring in recall. The next section will present studies which illustrate how structural variation in stories affects recall.

In the Stein and Glenn (1979) study, when children heard stories in the normally expected sequence, certain categories of information were always recalled more frequently than other categories. These findings were consistent across the four stories presented and across grade conditions. The most frequently recalled categories were: setting statements introducing the protagonist, initiating events, and consequence statements. The least frequently recalled statements were: setting statements describing contextual information, internal responses, and reaction statements. Attempts were recalled with some frequency but never as often as were the most salient categories.

The one exception to the low probability of recalling internal response statements was the salience of the protagonist's major goal. Children in both the first and fifth grades frequently included this information; however, all other statements in this category were seldomly recalled, especially by first-grade children. A summary of the salience of category recall in the Stein and Glenn (1979) study is presented in Fig. 3. The pattern of recall found by Stein and Glenn (1979) was similar to that demonstrated by Mandler and Johnson (1977). Additionally, Mandler and Johnson showed that although adult recall was better and somewhat different from children's recall, consistent patterns were found across all age groups.

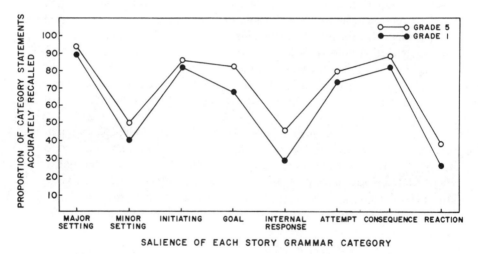

Figure 3   Mean proportion of statements recalled from each category when stories constructed according to the expected sequence were presented to 1st and 5th graders. From the Stein and Glenn (1979) study.

There are several reasons which might account for the saliency of individual statements within an episode. Stories are basically concerned with goal oriented behavior and ideally consist of a sequence of statements directly related to the attainment of the goal. However, statements within each story category can be connected to other statements by relations other than the CAUSE relation, i.e., AND, THEN. It is the type of relation connecting individual category statements and episodes that should determine the probability of statement recall within an episode. If the relations among statements are connected by the CAUSE relation and directly related to the attainment of the protagonist's goal, then story statements have a high probability of being recalled. Statements connected to one another by a THEN relationship should decrease in saliency, and statements connected by an AND relation should be infrequently recalled. Similar predictions can be made about the relative salience of whole episodes in a story.

At the present time, there are no studies which have systematically investigated the effects of varying the types of logical relations connecting statements within an episode. However, Glenn (1977) has manipulated the types of relations connecting episodes, and has shown that stories containing episodes connected by the CAUSE relationship are recalled significantly better than stories containing episodes connected by the THEN relation.

Two other factors may regulate the salience of certain category information. The first factor concerns the type of integration or summarization of story information that sometimes occurs. Two or three statements can be causally related to one another, but the listener will recall only one statement which is either an integration of the three or a higher order summary statement from which the three statements could easily be inferred.

The second factor concerns the semantic redundancy that can occur between story statements. Although two statements may be causally related to one another, the information in one statement or one category may be directly inferred from the information in other story statements. In this situation, certain story statements become redundant and to recall all of them would create an unnecessary load on working memory.

One method that increases the salience of specific category information is the manipulation of the temporal position of statements not frequently recalled. The Stein and Nezworski (1978) study showed that certain marked temporal inversions not only increased general story recall above that of expected sequences, but also increased the salience of certain category statements such as the internal response. These types of inversions, while increasing the probability of recalling certain statements, also have important implications for the type of inferences made about the content of a story. An excellent example of this can be seen in a recent study by Austin, Ruble, and Trabasso (1977).

Austin et al. have shown that in stories in which a positive intent (a protagonist wants to do something good) is stated before a negative outcome (the consequence of the protagonist's actions is seen as being bad), young children will infer that the character's original intentions were negative. However, when the intentions are moved to the end of the episode, children will maintain that the character's intentions were good despite the negative outcome. Austin et al. attribute the change in moral judgments to the fact that by stating the intention at the end of a story, a recency effect occurs. They argue that this change in the temporal location of the intention causes children to integrate and weight the story information differently than when the intention is placed before the consequence.

The results from the Stein and Nezworski (1978) study also suggest that this effect may occur. However, an additional hypothesis can be made concerning this type of temporal inversion. It can be argued that this inversion may prevent the listener or reader from making an incorrect inference about a possible change in the protagonist's original intention.

Although stories often explicitly state the intent of a character, actions which occur after the protagonist's goal statement can often cause children to make additional inferences about the protagonist's intent in the story. These inferences may become more salient in determining the types of moral judgments made about a character. The inclusion of temporal inversions, especially in connection with intentions, should limit the type of inferences made, ensuring that very specific inferences about intentions will be made. The inversion tells the listener that there was no change in the protagonist's intentions throughout the story episode. Thus, it is clearly evident from the Austin et al. study and from our results that certain temporal inversions can increase recall and salience of specific statements, in addition to constraining the types of inferences made about story characters.

A second example of the facilitative function of inverting story information may be related to many of the flashback sequences occurring in stories. In some stories, specific obstacles, many of which are life-threatening to the protagonist, must be avoided or overcome. Often children are put in a state of suspense too great to tolerate until the end of the story. Because of children's awareness that the protagonist could suffer real harm, they may not be able to attend to the remainder of the story events. However, if the uncertainty is reduced by placing the consequence near the beginning of the story, the listener is assured of a positive outcome. This inversion may then enable the child to attend more efficiently to subsequent story events.

Effects of Deleted Category Information

As stated in the previous section, a story schema also specifies the types of information which should occur in the expected story sequence. The implication derived from this assumption is that stories not containing all necessary category information will be transformed so that recall, again, corresponds more to the expected sequence than to the text structure of a story.

In order to test this hypothesis, Stein and Glenn (1977a) carried out an experiment which involved the systematic deletion of each episodic category from a story. By deleting each category from the text structure of a story, the importance of that category could be examined in two ways. When deletions occur, a gap is created in the logical sequence of events. If a schema is activated to guide listeners or readers in organizing the incoming story sequence, then they should attempt to fill in the gap during recall by generating new information which perpetuates the logical sequence of events. If the grammar is valid, the majority of new information should replace deleted information. In situations in which the listeners have difficulty discerning the exact nature of the missing information or are unable to make inferences about the types of events which could have appeared in that category, the encoding of the story events should be disrupted, thereby decreasing recall of the remaining story information.

There are certain exceptions to the above predictions. Again, most of these exceptions concern the internal response and the reaction categories. As shown by several of the previously cited studies, these two categories are often deleted from the structure of an episode. Because the internal response and reaction categories are among the least recalled information in an episode, it appears that subjects may have rules which allow them to delete these two categories from recall without disrupting recall of the remaining story information or without adding new information to the episode. Again, the information contained in these categories is often so apparent from the other events in a story sequence that it becomes redundant to recall them.

The results from the Stein and Glenn (1977a) experiment showed that when initiating events, attempts, and consequences were deleted from a story, the number of new statements included in recall significantly increased in comparison to the control group. Also, a clear majority of the new information added to recall matched the type of information deleted from the story. Figure 4 shows the number of new statements added to recall as a function of the category deleted. Figure 5 shows the type of inferences occurring when each category was deleted from the story. Thus, the tendency to create a coherent logical sequence is quite strong when specific types of information are deleted.

A second finding of importance is that in both grades recall decreased significantly in comparison to a control group when the initiating event was deleted from the story. Recall also decreased in the first grade when the consequence was deleted. The information loss in these conditions may indicate that children had difficulty generating new information that was congruent with the entire sequence of events in the story. Often children generated new information that could be connected to specific parts of the original story, but not to other parts. In order to make the story more coherent, some children would then transform more of the original story to make it conform with the new information they had generated to fit the deleted category.

It can be seen that when certain classes of information are deleted from a story, children will attempt to fill in the missing information, but often at the cost of not recalling other story information. Although this study is only a first attempt to investigate the effects of structural variation of stories on children's memory, the results are important in relation to the development of inferential thinking in children.

One of the major functions of inferences is to disambiguate certain types of story information or to resolve apparent contradictions in the story. Trabasso and his colleagues (Trabasso, Nicholas, Omanson, & Johnson, 1977) have also

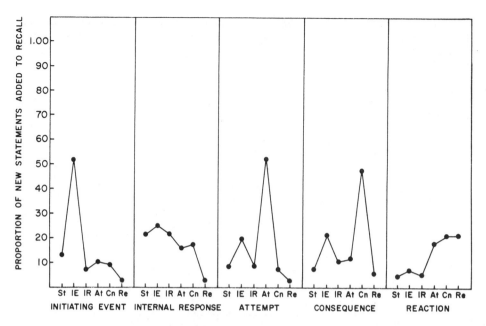

Figure 4 Proportion and category classification of new statements added to recall when each one of five categories (initiating event, internal response, attempt, consequence, reaction) was deleted from the text structure of a story. These data are combined across 1st and 5th graders. From Stein and Glenn (1977a).

made a similar argument. After making an initial set of inferences about incoming information, listeners often can integrate this information into prior world knowledge about stories. In the process of this integration, listeners may have a feeling of understanding a problem in a new frame of reference because of the addition of new knowledge to prior structures.

The presence of ambiguity or contradictions in a text, however, raises an important question concerning recall and comprehension of stories. While these factors might increase the number of inferences made about story events, the amount of accurate information remembered may decrease. Additionally, there may be important developmental differences in the types of strategies and prior knowledge structures used during the comprehension process.

Adults may not initially encode the maximum amount of story detail possible when ambiguities or contradictions occur. However, they are frequently aware that information loss occurs under these conditions, and may have strategies to overcome this problem. Many adults read a story twice: once to understand the plot structure and locate the ambiguities; the second time to locate details that aid in the reduction of ambiguity. At the present time, the exact process by which ambiguity is comprehended is not known. Furthermore, it is not known whether young children can perceive ambiguity in a text and whether

280

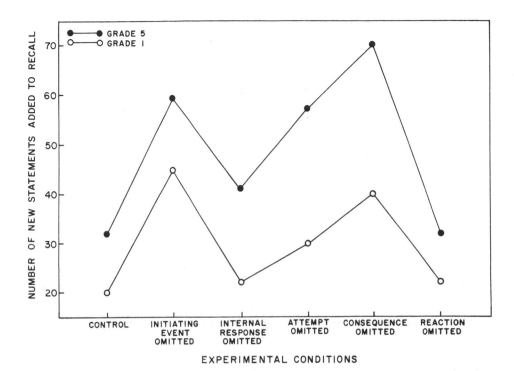

Figure 5 Number of new statements added to recall when each one of five categories was deleted from the text structure of stories presented to 1st and 5th graders. From Stein and Glenn (1977a).

they attempt to make inferences about ambiguous or contradictory information.

In an initial study investigating children's ability to understand contradiction, Stein (1977) constructed stories containing extremely discrepant information. Discrepancies were created by describing the personality characteristics of the protagonist in either a very positive or very negative light and then varying the attempts and outcomes of the story. The attempt and outcome were always at odds with the initial character description. For example, one of the stories described a fox who was very mean and who would never think of helping anyone. However, later in the story, the fox sees a bear who is very weak and looks half starved. The bear is trying to catch a fish for dinner and is having absolutely no luck in getting his supper. The fox walks over to the bear and catches the fish for him and helps him cook it for dinner. The bear is grateful to the fox for doing so. The explicit plans of the fox and the reason for the change in his behavior were never included in the story. Therefore, the story contains incongruent elements.

Children in the first and fifth grade were tested on these stories in two different ways. In the first task, they were asked to recall the story exactly as they heard it. In the second task, children were told that there may have been information which was missing in the story they heard, and they were to retell the story, adding anything they thought was missing from the original version.

In the first recall task, a significant number of first-grade children simply deleted the initial description of the fox and recalled only the actions and the outcome of the story. Even in recalling the story the second time, there was very little mention of the fox's meanness or lack of desire to help others. These children simply deleted the parts of the story that were incongruous. In the fifth grade, however, most children included the initial description of the fox plus all of the fox's subsequent behavior. In an effort to maintain logical consistency, some of the fifth graders included inferences about the fox's reasons for changing his usual pattern of behavior toward other animals.

During the second recall, even more of the fifth-grade children included inferences describing the reasons why the fox had changed his mind about helping the bear. Thus, we can see that children at different age levels respond differently to the conception of contradiction. First graders almost always deleted material to remove the contradiction between the description of the fox's previous behavior and his behavior in the story episode. Even when these children were asked about the initial description of the fox in relation to his behavior in the story, many of the first graders did not see the necessity of giving an explanation for change in the fox's behavior pattern.

Several possible explanations could account for these findings. First-grade children may not have understood that there was any real discrepancy between the initial personality description of the fox and his later behavior. The child's conception of a fox not helping anyone may be limited to specific situations and may not apply to the acquisition of food under starvation conditions. Even though our statement about the fox *never* helping anyone was unambiguous, we do not know exactly what conception children have of helping. Moreover, even if these younger children understood the contradiction between the earlier and later behavior of the fox, they may not have been able to generate a reason for the change in his behavior. Therefore, the most efficient method of constructing the sequence of events would be to delete that information which is not directly related to the remainder of the story content. From the results of this study, it is apparent that the child's concept of contradiction must be defined first so that a more rigorous study of inferential thinking can be completed.

CONCLUSIONS

The studies discussed illustrate the usefulness of a story grammar approach to comprehension and provide support for many of the predictions derived from the development of a grammar. Children, like adults, do expect certain types of information to occur in stories. When stories do not include certain types of information, new information will frequently be added so that story recall corresponds more to the sequence expected in a story than to the presented sequence. Furthermore, in specific instances, recall decreases when stories do not contain all of the expected information. This decrease may occur either because of attentional difficulties during the encoding process, or possibly because of the inability to generate new information for the purpose of constructing a semantically cohesive representation of the incoming material.

Similarly, specific types of temporal sequences are expected to occur in stories. When stories do not correspond to the expected sequence, as in the case of unmarked story inversions, reorganization of the story sequence occurs so that recall conforms more to the expected sequence than to the presented sequence. The inclusion of specific unmarked inversions in a story also causes recall to decrease in comparison to recall of stories containing the expected sequence. Thus, a story schema can be seen to exert a powerful influence on story recall.

Some of the results from the various studies, however, did not support the predictions derived from the story grammar. Not all five episodic categories need be included in a text for story information to be recalled in a form comparable to stories with all of the expected categories. The internal response and reaction categories could be omitted from the text sequence without causing significant decreases in recall when compared to recall of expected story sequences. Furthermore, children did not attempt to include new information in recall that would fill in the gap created by these deleted categories. It was concluded that a set of deletion rules may be used when information in these categories is highly redundant with other story events.

The semantic content of a story was then shown to play an important role in determining whether subjects might add new information to fill in gaps left by deleted category information. If children perceived discrepancies to exist in a story sequence, categories such as the internal response would frequently be added to recall to resolve the discrepancies and to disambiguate the story sequence. The ability to recognize discrepancies and the child's knowledge of discrepant events were also hypothesized to play an important role in predicting whether new information would be added to recall.

Some of the results from the temporal ordering studies did not support the original hypotheses derived from the story grammar. When children were asked to construct "good" stories from a scrambled set of stimulus materials, their stories corresponded positively to the proposed sequence of story events. However, both the internal response and reaction categories were frequently put in positions other than their normal location in an episode. When the internal response category was systematically moved throughout the episode without marking or signaling its new position, recall did not decrease in comparison to recall of expected story sequences.

Several reasons were given to explain why this category movement did not cause a decrease in recall or why, in a spontaneous story construction task, this type of information was placed in locations other than its normal position. As indicated in several of the cited studies, the internal response category is less frequently recalled in comparison to other categories, even when story texts correspond to the expected sequence. Because of the redundancy of its content with other story events, placing the internal response in a new location may not cause any confusion to the listener or reader. The occurrence of this category in new locations may simply serve to reconfirm inferences that have already been made from other statements in a story.

Another explanation for the relative ease of recalling this type of category inversion may be related to children's ability to spontaneously infer the appropriate "because" relations between internal responses and other types of category information. Results from a spontaneous story construction task showed that when children constructed their own conception of a "good" story, they often inverted this type of information and appeared to infer that a "because" relation connected the two statements. These data indicate that children may begin to acquire rules to encode specific temporal inversions at a relatively young age.

Marked inverted story sequences had a different effect on story recall when compared to recall of most unmarked inverted story sequences. This was especially true for older children. Fifth-grade children recalled as much information from stories containing marked inversions as they did from stories corresponding to the expected sequence. Furthermore, many of the marked inverted sequences increased the amount of story information accurately recalled. In contrast, first graders had difficulty with many of the story deviations containing marked inversions. The difference found between the two age groups was attributed to older children's greater familiarity with the occurrence of deviate story structures.

A child's ability to retain information from stories containing deviant structures may be due to knowledge about the function of specific linguistic devices used to indicate the occurrence of a deviant structure, as well as the acquisition of specific metamemorial strategies that facilitate the encoding of information from deviant structures. For example, when a flashback occurs in a story, the listener or reader must first recognize that information is being presented in a deviant sequence. In order to do this, the function of linguistic devices, such as rhetorical markers, must be understood. The information which has been inverted must then be identified, "tagged" so that it can be kept in working memory, and retrieved.

One major issue that has not been discussed here concerns the order in which marked story deviations are recalled. Even though fifth-grade children recalled information from marked inverted sequences as well as children receiving expected story sequences, the grammar would predict that recall of inverted sequences should be transformed to conform more to the expected sequence than to the text sequence. In the analysis of these data, transformations did occur so that recall often corresponded more to the expected sequence than to the text sequence. However, certain marked inversions were recalled in the presented order. Most of these inversions involved the internal response and reaction categories.

Thus, it is clear from many of the studies that children learn to comprehend stories with deviant structures and eventually learn to represent some of these more complex structures with a high degree of accuracy. It is evident, however, that a clear and consistent explanation of the process of acquiring rules for representing more complex stories is still lacking.

In reviewing studies concerned with children's spontaneous generation of stories (Glenn & Stein, 1978; Stein & Glenn, 1977b), one of the most consistent findings was that the structural complexity of children's stories increased dramatically with age. Young children, around 5 years of age, often produce stories that are simple reactions to ongoing events. They frequently fail to include evidence of a planned sequence of behavior and simply describe "script"-like sequences that are representative of everyday habitual patterns. However, as children develop, they begin to include complex goal structures, social interactions among characters, and dialogues between characters in their stories.

The grammars, as they are now formulated, cannot account for all of the variation in structures spontaneously generated by children. Specifically, the current grammars do not describe the types of structures that must be used to comprehend and produce multiple protagonist stories, nor do the grammars contain rules for representing dialogue between two characters. The grammars also fail to indicate the types of changes which occur in story schemata, as a function of age. Clearly, more developmental research is needed to specify the changes which do occur. However, studies which describe the *process* of change must also be initiated. Although many studies have described the various stages of development, especially in Piagetian terminology, few have attempted a detailed study of the process of developmental change. Only when a description and explanation of the process of change is offered can adequate instructional methods be developed.

Another important issue which must be studied concerns the definition and measurement of comprehension. The majority of the studies previously described used only recall procedures. While recall is important in terms of understanding retrieval processes, this procedure cannot adequately describe all of the story information which may have been encoded by a child. As an example, the results from the Stein and Glenn (1979) study showed that much of the story information not recalled was, in fact, remembered. Both first- and fifth-grade children responded with a high degree of accuracy when probed about the protagonist's internal responses, and yet few recalled this information. Stein and Nezworski (1978) have also shown that adults retain some degree of a surface representation of stories violating the expected sequence and that recall undergoes greater reorganization than performance on other tasks, such as recognition or reconstruction.

These findings indicate that the underlying representations of stories are richer in the amount of information and complexity of structure than those produced at recall. Furthermore, they indicate that there are important differences between the use of a story schema during encoding and retrieval. To date, only a few studies have investigated the difference between encoding and retrieval processes (Anderson, 1977). However, if an accurate description of comprehension is to be developed, more studies must be completed.

A more general problem in the study of story comprehension is that the current grammars lack a detailed description of the specific semantic knowledge structure used during comprehension. From analyzing recall data and from listening to children tell stories (Glenn & Stein, 1978; Stein & Glenn, 1977b), it is evident that certain themes occur in older children's stories and are never included in stories by younger children. Although all children might tell stories containing threats to a protagonist's survival, older children include different types of information. The obstacles foreseen, the types of plans generated to overcome the obstacles, and whether or not the protagonist succeeds may be a direct function of the age of a child. The comprehension and production of stories depends upon a child's conception of personal causation (De Charms, 1968; Loevinger, 1976) and knowledge about objects, actions, and social situations in general. In order to understand the process of comprehension in more detail, studies which investigate children's knowledge about all of these variables must be initiated.

IMPLICATIONS FOR EDUCATION

Despite the necessity for more research in the area of story comprehension, there are several findings from the present set of studies which should be helpful to teachers of preschool and young elementary school children. First, it is evident that even young children have acquired skills necessary for the comprehension of story material. For example, the studies earlier reviewed have shown that preschool children can remember the correct temporal order of events in a given story, provided that the order matches their expectations about how the events *should* unfold and that the story content is familiar to them. Furthermore, our studies now in progress indicate that even preschool children have little difficulty answering questions about the *causes* and *consequences* of certain types of actions which occur in stories.

The difficulty that teachers observe when young children attempt to remember and understand stories is often due to the content of the story. If the content is unfamiliar, young children do not make, or cannot make, the same set of causal inferences linking story events that older children make. When questioned about the particular reason for an action or what would happen as a result of a particular action, younger subjects often produce information that corresponds more with what they "know" about the occurrence of particular actions than with information that occurs in the text. Unless causes and consequences occurring in the text are familiar to the young child or the relationship between an action and a cause is made explicit, comprehension of specific stories will be difficult for young children, especially when the standard set is more appropriate for a child with additional knowledge about the story situation.

One method that teachers can use to assess whether a particular story will be well comprehended, is to assess what the child already knows about the story before the actual story is told. By having children tell stories about situations similar to those in the text, an observant teacher can readily assess how the child's spontaneous production differs from the information in a story book. Often children lack very specific knowledge about a character's actions that can be provided by a teacher. At times, a great deal of prerequisite information may have to be provided before a story can be comprehended with a fair amount of accuracy.

As many of the results from the present story studies indicate, the method of ensuring a high rate of comprehension (provided that the story situation is fairly familiar to the young child) is to ensure that the story text contains the expected type of information and temporal sequence described in the several story grammar analyses. If the story proceeds in a forward-going fashion, with a fairly well-established causal sequence, young children have relatively little difficulty performing a variety of comprehension tasks. However, when the text structure deviates from the expected sequence, either in terms of deleted category information or in terms of the expected temporal sequence, comprehension difficulties occur, especially where young children are involved.

To complicate matters, examination of several beginning reading texts and "stories" frequently told to young children has shown that many deletions of critical category information *plus* numerous temporal inversions are often present in one story. Furthermore, in many of these texts, it is difficult to discern exactly what the primary goal of the protagonist is. That is, it is not clear *why* the central character is performing a series of actions. Although some types of internal responses (e.g., feelings and thoughts) of story characters are often deleted from the recall produced by young children, the major goal is recalled very frequently and is also assumed to be critical to the organization of the remainder of story information. Again, when stories do not contain information which enables the child to unambiguously determine the goal, comprehension of entire episodes in a story may be misunderstood. Thus, analyzing the structure of story material in terms of what a child already knows and expects to occur in stories is seen as a necessary prerequisite to successful comprehension.

An issue which must be considered by both educators and researchers interested in the comprehension process is the type of task used to measure comprehension. As indicated previously, using only one type of task (e.g., recall procedures) provides a great deal of information about the information which was encoded during the presentation of a story. However, no one task will provide a teacher with all of the information which was comprehended during story processing. In order to ensure that the teacher attain a deeper understanding of children's skills at text comprehension, a variety of tasks should be used for each story under consideration. Most curriculum texts use a very limited number of tasks, and in prescribing the tasks, give very little rationale as to what should be expected from the child. Furthermore, these guides provide little information as to why certain responses from children are more *valid* than other responses. From the studies reviewed in this paper using different types of tasks on the same story should eliminate some of the ambiguity concerning children's knowledge of a story text. This procedure also emphasized how the child is acquiring information rather than whether the right or wrong answer was given.

A final point should be made. As all of the recent studies on stories indicate, the interaction between the incoming story information and the child's prior knowledge is a critical factor in predicting what types of information will be remembered. This should also hold when other types of discourse structures are considered. For example, much of the material used in classrooms can be classified as expository texts. Although there are few studies which document children's understanding of other discourse structures, many of the same principles highlighted in this review should generalize to the study of text processing where "stories" are not the concern of the teacher. A comparison between the child's already existing knowledge and that information presented in the text provides a powerful source for constructing materials to aid children in acquiring additional information about a topic. This technique often provides information about the order in which new information should be introduced.

Similar types of results should be apparent in the analysis of the text structure of expository texts. There may be several types of higher order schema that children gradually acquire to aid in the comprehension of expositions. As work in this area advances, the number of recommendations that can be given to teachers of young children should also increase.

REFERENCES

Anderson, R. C. Schema-directed processes in language comprehension. In A. Lesgold, J. Pelligreno, S. Fokkema, R., R. Glaser (Eds.), *Cognitive psychology and instruction.* New York: Plenum, 1978.

Austin, V., Ruble, D. N., & Trabasso, T. Recall and order effects in children's moral judgments. *Child Development, 1977, 48,* 470-474.

Bartlett, F. C. *Remembering: A study in experimental and social psychology.* Cambridge, England: Cambridge Univ. Press, 1932.

Bremond, C. *Logique du recit.* Paris: Sevil, 1973.

Bower, G. Comprehending and recalling stories. APA Division 3 Presidential Address, Meeting of the American Psychological Association, Washington, D.C., 1976.

Brown, A. L. The construction of temporal succession by preoperational children. In A. D. Pick (Ed.), *Minnesota symposium on child psychology*, Vol. 10. Minneapolis: Univ. of Minnesota, 1976.

Brown, A. L. The development of memory: Knowing, knowing about knowing, and knowing how to know. In H. W. Reese (Ed.), *Advances in child development and behavior*, Vol. 10. New York: Academic Press, 1975.

Colby, B., & Cole, M. Culture, memory and narrative. In R. Horton & R. Finnegan (Eds.), *Modes of thought: Essays on thinking in western and non-western societies.* London: Faber & Faber, 1973.

Corrigan, R. A scalogram analysis of the development of the use and comprehension of "because" in children. *Child Development*, 1975, *46*, 195-201.

De Charms, R. *Personal causation: The internal affective determinants of behavior.* New York: Academic Press, 1968.

Fillmore, C. The case for case. In E. Back & R. Harms (Eds.), *Universals in linguistic theory.* New York: Holt, Rinehart, & Winston, 1968.

Flappan, D. *Children's understanding of social interaction.* New York: Teacher's College Press, 1968.

Gardner, H. *The arts and human development.* New York: Wiley, 1973.

Glenn, C. G. Memory for multiple-episodic stories: A developmental study. Paper presented at the meeting of the Psychonomic Society, Washington, D.C., 1977.

Glenn C. G., & Stein, N. L. *Syntactic structures and real world themes in stories generated by children* (Tech. Rep. No. 70). Urbana, Ill.: Univ. of Illinois, Center for the Study of Reading, March, 1978.

Greimas, A. J. Narrative grammar: Units and levels. *Modern Language Notes*, 1971, *86*.

Levi-Strauss, C. The structural study of myth. In T. A. Sebeok (Ed.), *Myth: A symposium.* Bloomington, Ind.: Indiana Univ. Press, 1955.

Loevinger, I. *Ego development.* San Francisco: Josey-Bass, 1976.

Lord, A. B. *The singer of tales.* New York: Athenum, 1965.

Mandler, J. M. The use of a story schema. Paper presented at the meeting of the Psychonomic Society, Washington, D.C., 1977.

Mandler, J. M., & DeForrest, M. A code in the node: Developmental differences in the use of a story schema. Paper presented at the meeting of the Society for Research in Child Development, New Orleans, 1977.

Mandler, J. M., & Johnson, N. S. Remembrance of things parsed: Story structure and recall. *Cognitive Psychology*, 1977, *9*, 111-151.

Piaget, J. *The language and thought of the child.* London: Routledge & Kegan Paul, 1960.

Piaget, J. *The child's conception of time.* London: Routledge & Kegan Paul, 1969.

Piaget, J. *Structuralism.* New York: Basic Books, 1970.

Piaget, J., & Inhilder, B. *Memory and intelligence.* New York: Basic Books, 1973.

Prince, G. *A grammar of stories.* The Hague: Mouton, 1973.

Propp, V. *Morphology of the folktale*, Vol. 10. Bloomington, Ind.: Indiana Univ. Research Center in Anthropology, Folklore and Linguistics, 1958.

Rumelhart, D. E. Notes on a schema for stories. In D. G. Bobrow & A. Collins (Eds.), *Representation and understanding: Studies in cognitive science.* New York: Academic Press, 1975.

Rumelhart, D. E., & Ortony, A. *The representation of knowledge in memory* (CHIP Rep. No. 55). La Jolla, Calif.: Univ. of California, San Diego, Center for Human Information Processing, January, 1976.

Stein, N. L. The effects of discrepant information in the comprehension of simple stories. Unpublished manuscript, University of Illinois, Urbana-Champaign, 1977.

Stein, N. L., & Garfin, D. Preschool children's understanding of stories. Unpublished manuscript, University of Illinois, Urbana-Champaign, 1977.

Stein, N. L., & Glenn, C. G. A developmental study of children's recall of story material. Paper presented at the meeting of the Society for Research in Child Development, Denver, 1975.

Stein, N. L., & Glenn, C. G. The effects of increasing temporal disorganization on children's recall of stories. Paper presented at the meeting of the Psychonomic Society, St. Louis, 1976.

Stein, N. L., & Glenn, C. G. An analysis of story comprehension in elementary school children in R. Freedle (Ed.), *Advances in discourse processes, Vol. 2; New directions in discourse processing*. Norwood, N.J.: Ablex, 1979.

Stein, N. L., & Glenn, C. G. The role of structural variation in children's recall of simple stories. Paper presented at the meeting of the Society for Research in Child Development, New Orleans, 1977. (a)

Stein, N. L., & Glenn, C. G. A developmental study of children's construction of stories. Paper presented at the meeting of the Society for Research in Child Development, New Orleans, 1977. (b)

Stein, N. L. & Glenn, C. G. *The role of temporal organization in story comprehension* (Tech. Rep. No. 71). Urbana, Ill.: Univ. of Illinois, Center for the Study of Reading, March, 1978.

Stein, N. L., & Nezworski, M. T. *The effects of linguistic markers on children's recall of stories: A developmental study* (Tech. Rep. No. 72). Urbana, Ill.: Univ. of Illinois, Center for the Study of Reading, March, 1978.

Stein, N. L., & Nezworski, M. T. The effect of organization and instructional set on story memory. *Discourse Processes*, 1978, *1*, 177-193.

Thorndyke, P. W. Cognitive structures in comprehension and memory of narrative discourses. *Cognitive Psychology*, 1977, *9*, 77-110.

Todorov, T. *Grammaire du decameron*. The Hague: Mouton, 1969.

Trabasso, T., Nicholas, D. A., Omanson, R., & Johnson, L. Inferences and story comprehension. Paper presented at the meeting of the Society for Research in Child Development, New Orleans, 1977.